Saint Catherine of Siena

SAINT CATHERINE OF SIENA

From a contemporary fresco by her disciple Andrea di Vanni in the Cappella delle Volte in San Domenico.

Johannes Jorgensen

SAINT CATHERINE OF SIENA

Translated from the Danish by
INGEBORG LUND

WIPF & STOCK · Eugene, Oregon

Nihil obstat: ARTHUR J. SCANLAN, S.T.D.
Censor Librorum

Imprimatur: ✠ PATRICK CARDINAL HAYES
Archbishop, New York

New York, March 4, 1938

Wipf and Stock Publishers
199 W 8th Ave, Suite 3
Eugene, OR 97401

Saint Catherine of Siena
By Jørgensen, Johannes and Lund, Ingeborg
Copyright©1938 by Jerk, Flemming
ISBN 13: 978-1-62032-142-3
Publication date 3/1/2012
Previously published by Longmans, Green and Co., 1938

PREFACE

The book which I here present to the readers of the English edition is a companion to my *Life of Saint Francis of Assisi* published in 1910. Like its predecessor it is based on a study of original documents, but I have endeavoured to render this less noticeable, and for that reason I have collected in an appendix at the end of the volume all the notes and references in which only a restricted number of readers can be interested.

To be sincere, I must confess that at first I felt less in sympathy with Catherine of Siena than with Francis of Assisi. In the energetic nature of the Sienese saint there is somewhat of a domineering spirit, an element of tyranny that was repugnant to me. Her perpetual and very feminine *Io voglio,* "I will," is in absolute contrast to the gentle Umbrian who preferred to see his life-work fail rather than make use of power and authority "like the Podestà of this world." This Catherine was never afraid to do, but that is why, I imagine, her last hour was less peaceful than that of Francis of Assisi. At the supreme moment doubts assailed her: conscience, which becomes a devil's advocate when the light of the world of truth begins to shine in the soul and eternity appears in all its overwhelming reality, whispered to her that the work of her whole life had been inspired only by obstinacy and vanity. He whom the hymn calls "Franciscus pauper et humilis" had no need to defend himself against such accusations.

My relations with Catherine therefore began, to tell the truth, under somewhat annoying conditions; at certain times I was almost afraid of her. But gradually, as I began to know her more intimately, the same thing befell me that befell so many others during her earthly life — I was subjugated by her and had to acknowledge myself beaten. Like the Franciscan who had at first criticised her so violently, I, too, became a zealous "Caterinato," and, like the woman in the fresco of Andrea di Vanni, in the Cappella delle Volte, I, too, fell upon my knees, and with my lips humbly touched the pale hands which, though not outwardly showing any stigmata, were yet pierced by the pain of the Wounds of Christ.

The present book has one advantage over that which I wrote on Saint Francis of Assisi — it has come into being in the city of the Saint herself. It was written in Siena, two hundred paces from Saint Catherine's home, within sound of the bells ringing from her beloved San Domenico. When I looked up from the black lines on the white page I saw afar, beyond the olive orchards, Belcaro, the convent which she caused to be built on a hill in the midst of pine woods, below the blue line of La Montagnuola. Many chapters have been thought out, many phrases formed, while walking along the roads once trodden by Catherine, or while listening (as a young Sienese poet has said) "all' aqua che scorre e parla in Fontebranda."

In now finishing my labours my first thanks, then, go to Siena herself — Sena Vetus, Civitas Virginis. As the inscription above the Porta Camullia says: "The city opens her heart wider than her gates to thee," *cor magis tibi Sena pandit*. And how shall I thank you enough, you open hearts of Siena? I will make no mention of names that the world does not know — at least, does not yet know. But you, who were the youth of Siena, welcomed among you a man who was growing grey; you, the sons and daughters of Tuscany of gentle speech, listened patiently to the barbarian who maltreated your tongue. I will not mention names, but when April comes round again I shall think, "now the grass is green again at Corposanto al Pecorile, and near the old Romanesque church of Marciano, *"alla soglia erbosa,"* between laurel bushes, stands the white hermitage dedicated to the two divinities *"Alma Poësis, Beata Solitudo!"*

* * *

Next, I owe equally sincere and cordial thanks to all those who by their counsel and their share in my work have helped me. First of all I mention my devoted friend, Monsignor Simon Deploige, late President of the Higher Institute of Philosophy of the University of Louvain. Next, Professor Armand Thierry, of the same University; Madame Dugniolle of Brussels; Mademoiselle M. E. Belpaire of Antwerp; Madame la Comtesse Ursel de Boissieu and M. Gabriel Thomas, both of Paris. I also thank Professor Pietro Rossi, of the University of Siena; Professor Alessandro Bonnucci, of the same

… university; Dr. Fabio Jacometti, attached to the Municipal Library of Siena; Professor Vigo of Leghorn; Signor Rugenio Lazzareschi, Keeper of the Archives at Lucca; Signora Matilda Fiorilli of Florence; the Rev. Father Innocenzo Taurisano, O.P. of Rome, and the Rev. Father Remi Coulon, O.P. Finally I render my thanks to the Prior of Stone Convent in England for his kindness in lending me copies of several manuscripts.

With these words I conclude a book which has for so long absorbed me. Amid the trials and turmoil of the present world it has often been difficult for me to concentrate my thoughts on the fourteenth century and confine my feelings within its compass, and I have looked forward impatiently to the last chapters of this book, as to a door opening from a library into reality. I am now at the door and I pause. A book finished, a chapter of your life closed (and how many are still left?). One pauses on the threshhold and one looks for the last time at the study that one is about to leave. One gives a last look at the table beneath the electric lamp that has illumined so many hours of work, at the armchair from which dear friends have so often laughed and talked; from the windows one has looked out over the plain to the distant mountains and seen beyond their blue outlines the sun setting so often in blood-red and gold. All this is past — past for ever, like the words spoken in this room, like the joy or the sorrow that has been lived through here — and one puts the last stroke of the pen on the last page of the manuscript as when one closes a door that one will never open again — *e quello ch'era, non sarà mai più*, "that which once was, will never return."

* * *

Saint Catherine, too, knew this sadness of leave-taking, this tender melancholy of farewell, this *piccola dolce tenerezza*, as she calls it. She knows only too well that everything passes — *come il vento*. She suffered because of it, as we other poor mortals suffer and will suffer. But her strong soul does not linger in tears; she who knows so well how to distinguish the good tears from the hurtful ones, and who devoted a whole treatise in her book to their study.

Everything passes — yes, but not quite everything. There

are tears without hope; they bring death. And there are tears leaving behind them the radiance of a deathless sun; they bring life. Caffarini tells us that in Siena there lived a woman who, after the death of the Saint, told him that she could never look at Catherine without shedding tears of tenderness and devotion.

Those are the good tears that give new birth to the heart. It is for us to imitate this poor woman, of whom we do not know even the name, but who had the immense privilege of contemplating the Saint during her life upon earth. From very far off, alas! let us look at Catherine, and let us weep the tears from which saints are born.

JOHANNES JORGENSEN

N.B: Numbered references in text refer to notes which will be found in the Supplement.

CONTENTS

Book I. Solitude . . . . Page 1
Book II. The Imitation of Christ . . . 63
Book III. The Crown of Thorns 197

Supplement 401
Index 439

BOOK I

SOLITUDE

> Entbildet werden von der Creatur. — *Suso*.
> Serrati nella casa del cognoscimento di te. —
> *Santa Caterina: Lettera a monna Alexa (Ed. Aldus, ep.* 188).

I

One evening in the year 1352 two children came walking through Siena, a little girl of six and a boy who might be a year or two older: Catherine Benincasa and her brother Stefano, who were on their way home to the Via dei Tintori after a visit to their married sister, Bonaventura, at the other end of the town near the tower of Sant' Ansano.

And one evening in the year 1912 a stranger, myself, comes walking through Siena, trying as far as possible to trace the footsteps of those two children, even though the traffic of more than five centuries and a half has since passed over them. For this walk, starting from the old tower in which the apostle of Siena, the martyr Sant' Ansano, is said to have been imprisoned, down to her home near the well of Fontebranda, became for little Caterina Benincasa an event which decided the whole course of her life, from the time when she wore out her little shoes in the streets of Siena, until the day when she sank down in death, at the age of thirty-three, crushed beneath the burden of the ship of the Church upon her shoulders.

I imagine then, the brother and sister walking through the streets where the dusk is falling. Perhaps they are not saying anything to each other; children often walk together without saying a word. But they are thinking and I try to follow their thoughts.

They would hardly know anything about Duccio, the great painter of Siena, whose house they passed close by, that house in which he worked for three years at the altar picture for the Cathedral, and which when it was finished was carried in a great procession through the town, while all the bells rang *a gloria*. "All that day," says the old chronicle, "many prayers were said in the churches and much alms given to the poor, to the end that God and His holy Mother might preserve us from all evil and defend Siena from all traitors and all enemies." [1]

Catherine and Stefano, however, could hardly have heard of that day, then dating forty years back. In their home, in the dyer's workshop of Fontebranda, there was little talk of art or artists. On the other hand, the prison of Sant' Ansano must have made a great impression upon them: tall, gloomy, forbidding, it is still standing up in the Castel Vecchio, the oldest quarter of Siena; it was there that the Roman *praetorium* once stood; it was there that Sant' Ansano made confession of his faith before the governor and was tortured to death. All the children in Siena knew his story:

Sant' Ansano lived a thousand years ago: at that time the emperor was a pagan and the Pope did not live in the Lateran but in the catacombs. The father of Ansano worshipped idols, but his mother being a Christian, he was baptised but not until he was twelve years old, and immediately after he began to preach the faith, at first in Rome, then at Acquapendente and finally in Siena. There were no Christians in Siena yet; the people were all pagans. On the very site of the Cathedral there was a temple dedicated to Minerva. At the foot of the mountain on which the hospital of La Scala was afterwards built, in the direction of Vallepiatta, lie the caverns and grottoes in which the dyers and tanners of later times established their workshops. It was in one of these grottoes that Sant' Ansano assembled the first Christians, said Holy Mass and preached.

At the present day there are still, beneath the hospital, some caves in which the "Confraternity of the Virgin" holds its meettings; this was the earliest church in Siena.

But at that time Lysias was the Roman governor, and when he heard about Sant' Ansano he commanded him to be seized and put in prison, for the emperor had ordered all the Christians to be put to death. Sant' Ansano then, was condemned to be thrown into a cauldron of boiling pitch. The soldiers carried out this order but he came safe and sound out of the seething bath. The governor, in a violent rage, then ordered him to be beheaded at some distance from the town on the banks of the river Arbia — he was only twenty years old! But the Christians came secretly during the night to look for his body which they carefully hid, and later, when the people were all converted, these holy relics were borne with great ceremony to Siena. The gate through which the procession passed is still at the present day called Porta San Viene (the saint comes), and Sant' Ansano was proclaimed patron of Siena and protector of the city.[2]

In our own times, when you walk from the old tower to the Via dei Tintori or the Via Benincasa, as it is now called in honour of Catherine, you must go by a road called Fossa di Sant' Ansano. Notwithstanding this name there is nothing gloomy or funereal about it; on the contrary it is one of the most beautiful roads in Siena. In passing above the big hospital of La Scala you have on one side the high walls of this gigantic building, steep like a rock, and up there you see the Sisters of Saint Vincent of Paul in their blue habits and their great white winged caps, pausing for a moment on the balconies high up under the irregularly placed windows and doors, before going back to the sick wards. The view is indeed worth admiring.

Behind a low parapet of masonry Vallepiatta is hollowed out like a great green bowl, filled to the brim with vines and olives, with large-leafed figs and the golden foliage of walnut-trees and with green maize gleaming in the red soil among the gnarled trunks of the olives. At the bottom of the valley some faded houses; above them the fertile slopes of ripe wheat, the green of young maize and the silver of olives; still higher up dark cypresses enclosing a monastery are outlined against the blue background of the distant heights of Chianti.

It was here, with this view before him, that Sant' Ansano was plunged into the terrible bath of boiling pitch. A marble tablet inserted in the wall bears witness to the fact. The marble and the Latin inscription were not there on the evening when Catherine and Stefano passed by, but the memory was: the tradition, the thought that on this spot a man had suffered himself to be thrown into a boiling cauldron rather than deny Jesus. How lovable this Jesus must be, since for love of Him one would suffer so terrible a death!

The road continues by the peaceful Via de Vallepiatta, passing close by the red walls of Saint Sebastian, the old monastery of the Gésuati. The monastery is old, yet younger than Catherine; it was built in 1363 or 1364, on the site of one of the gates of the town, Porta Sant' Ansano.[3] At the present day it affords houseroom for a Catholic society of young people; through an open door can be seen a garden with rows of lemon trees in large pots of red terra cotta, and huge oleanders crowned with crimson blossoms, dripping like a thousand wounds.

Here the road turns down *il costone,* a broad, steep stairway with brick steps, and at the exact point at which you turn for the second time to go down to Fontebranda, you discover an old fresco framed in stone, and beneath the fresco this inscription: "When Saint Catherine Benincasa, aged only six years, was returning home with her brother, Christ appeared to her above the church of the Dominicans on the other side of the valley, under the appearance of his earthly vice-gerent, surrounded by the holy apostles, Peter, Paul and John, and He gave her His benediction."

If you look very carefully you can still distinguish two figures on the fresco: one kneeling, the hands extended in the attitude of prayer: Catherine; the other a young boy standing: her brother Stefano.[4]

Here Catherine paused that evening; here I too will pause.

The road continues further down towards the right, beside a garden wall with overhanging leaves of vines and figs, and with green and yellow flowers growing between the stones. Beyond, in the same direction, one sees all that part of Siena which is called the Goose Quarter, *Contrada dell' Oca,* with its old, faded roofs, its green shutters on façades of pale rose, with the open lofts of the dyers and tanners, where big yellow and brown hides are stretched out to dry. At the bottom of the valley are Fontebranda and the public washhouse, from which can be heard shouts, laughter and the beating of clothes; the linen is spread on the grass to dry. On the opposite side rises the green hill of Camporeggi, on which stands the church of San Domenico, big and bare, with its pointed windows in the flat walls of the choir and with its massive tower which in the fourteenth century was surmounted by a soaring spire.

Here Catherine stopped, as I stop today, and here she saw that which the inscription and the fresco would recall. In the words of the old legend [5] we are told:

"When she lifted up her eyes she beheld on the other side of the valley, above the roof of the church of the Friars Preachers, an exceeding fair throne, decked as for a king, and on the throne Jesus Christ, the Saviour of the world, in papal raiment and with the Pontiff's crown upon His head. With Him were the princes of the apostles, Peter and Paul, and Saint John the Evangelist

Seeing this vision Catherine stood still, struck with wonder and gazing upon her Saviour who did so miraculously appear to her that He might win her love. Fastening His eyes upon her and smiling upon her with love He stretched forth His right hand and made the holy sign of the cross over her, even as bishops do when they give benediction. So mighty was that benediction from the hand of the Eternal that Catherine was rapt beyond herself, and though by nature timid, she remained standing in the open street, in the midst of the traffic of men and beasts, immovable and with uplifted eyes.

"Meanwhile her brother had walked on, thinking that she was following him, until at length he perceived that she was no longer at his side. He then turned back and saw his sister far off, immovable and gazing up into the sky. At first he called to her but she paid no heed, and he therefore went back, still calling. When he saw that it was of no use" (those who have heard Italian children shout with the full force of their brass lungs will understand that Catherine must have been rapt very far away!) "he pulled her by the sleeve and said, 'What are you doing here? Why don't you come?' Then it was as though Catherine awoke from a deep sleep; for a moment she looked down, then she said, 'Oh, if you had seen what I see now, you would not have disturbed me!' She looked up again but the vision was gone. Then Catherine began to weep bitterly and to reproach herself for having looked away."

The two children walked home together, more silent than ever, we may imagine. Slow-moving wagons drawn by big white oxen came up towards them from the Via Fontebranda, almost barring the road with their wide-spreading horns. At the well, where the water splashes unceasingly into the deep basin under the gloomy vaults, women were going to and fro and filling their copper conchas. An odour of burning juniper twigs and pine cones came from the kitchens, where the kettle was hanging over the fire for supper. Children were playing with kittens on the doorsteps — everything was just as usual, as it still is on a summer evening in these streets. Only for Catherine everything had become different. The highest power in the world had overshadowed her, Eternity had spoken to her child's heart. She had beheld the heavens open, and the Son of

Man sitting on the throne of His glory. He had lifted up His hand and blessed her — with three great and solemn signs of the cross — like the Bishop in the *Duomo* — *in nomine Patris* — *et Filii* — *et Spiritus Sancti.*

II

Caterina Benincasa was born at Fontebranda in Siena on March 25th, 1347, in the house of the dyer, Giacomo Benincasa and his wife, Lapa di Piagenti di Puccio. The 25th of March is the feast of the Annunciation of the Blessed Virgin, and in that year it fell on Palm Sunday. In the cathedral of Siena the Bishop consecrated the branches of olive and the priest carried them from the altar down to the congregation, all the people standing with the silvery-grey twigs in their hands, while the clear boys' voices of the choir sang a jubilant Hosannah: "Blessed be He that cometh in the name of the Lord!" That was the greeting of the Church to the most illustrious daughter of Siena and the most devoted bride of Christ.

Caterina was the twenty-third child of her parents. She came into the world together with a twin sister, Giovanna, who, however, died soon after. Monna Lapa nursed Caterina herself — she had not had time to do this for very many of her other children — "and there was an end of Lapa's childbirths," says the Legend.[1]

Only a few of all these children grew up to maturity. The most prominent among them are: the eldest Benincasa, Bartolommeo, married to Lisa, a niece of Saint Giovanni Colombini; Niccola, married to Palmiero di Nese della Fonte, a brother of Tommaso della Fonte, the Dominican, who was later to have so much influence on Caterina; Maddalena, married to Bartolo di Vannino; Bonaventura, married to Niccolò di Giovanni Tegliacci; Lisa, who died unmarried in 1374, the year of the plague, and finally, Stefano.

Through Bartolommeo's marriage the family had become connected with one of the most religious families in Siena. Giovanni Colombini did not die until 1367; his niece Caterina lived up till so late as 1388. Giacomo Benincasa's sister Agnes, who was married to Chele di Duccio, entered, after the death of her husband, the tertiary order of the Dominicans (le Mantellate) and died in the fame of sanctity. Lapa's father, Nuccio di Piagente, made mattresses and in his leisure hours wrote poetry; he was moreover a pious man, intent on obtaining by almsgiving a share in all the prayers and good works of the Dominican order.[2]

Thus religious influences were at work on various sides, and in particular, as already indicated, it was among the Dominicans that the family found friends. The Grey Friars, one of the two great mendicant orders which the fourteenth century inherited from the thirteenth, do not seem to have played any great part in Siena. Their church was outside the town, and not until the fifteenth century, with the mighty mission preacher, San Bernardino, were they able to draw the mass of the people thither. San Domenico, however, stood just opposite Fontebranda, and it was easy for the Benincasas to slip up there in the morning and hear one of the numerous Masses of the Friars Preachers.

In the dyer's house at Fontebranda Giacomo was the most religious of the family. Lapa, his wife, says Raymond of Capua, was a capable mistress of her house, "as far as any one from the malice of modern people," and even had she wished to do so, she was incapable of telling a lie. In the Legend she is more than once called "the very simple" — "*semplicissima Lapa.*" "She had a great longing, though, for the everlasting blessings," and once, when she was dangerously ill, she was seized with a terrible fear of death, so that Catherine, who was then grown up, had great difficulty in soothing her mother. Lapa recovered, grew very old (over eighty), saw her children and grandchildren die around her, and at last complained that her soul must have been set crosswise in her body, since it could not get out.

From Lapa, Catherine inherited her energy, but her piety and never-failing gentleness was a legacy from her father. Raymond has recorded from Lapa's own lips many a story of her husband's wonderful patience — which was perhaps more admired after his death than really valued while he lived. Energetic wives seldom care for mild-mannered husbands, and if Lapa was as quick with her tongue as with her hands, the dyer must often have gone about among his dye-vats with his heart sore from the thrusts of Monna Lapa's sharp words. But after his death and when talking to the openly admiring Dominican, who was, moreover, of very good family (delle Vigne! a delle

Vigne had been chancellor to Frederick II), when talking to Raymond, Lapa was fond of dwelling on her dear departed husband's unexampled patience! Never would he allow so much as a single sharp word or harsh judgment against anyone. Not even when a man, whom they had long ago paid what they owed him, sued Giacomo and obtained an unjust sentence against him — not even then did the gentle dyer exclaim in anger! Lapa raged with all her might, as only an Italian woman can; it is said that more than once she would scare whole streets with her vocal powers. Giacomo only said quietly: "Just you wait, Mother. God will at last make that man think better of it, so that he will see how he has wronged us" — "which really did happen," as Lapa generally finished the story.

On one matter the dyer was very strict: in his house he would not allow godless or ribald talk. The air was to be pure in the home, and so indeed it was. When Saint Catherine's older sister, Bonaventura, was married, she was therefore surprised and shocked to hear the language used by her husband and his young friends; it was so loathsome to her that it made her ill. "In my father's house I was never used to hearing such talk," she replied to the anxious questions of her husband, "and if you do not want to see me dead soon, I beg of you to cease this filthy chatter."

The name of the family was *Ben(e) in casa*, and they were indeed well housed.[3] The older sons helped Giacomo in the business, which was fairly prosperous. A year or two before the birth of Catherine, in October, 1346, they had been able to lease from Giovanni di Ghezzo, business manager of *Arte della Lana* in Siena, the large house in which they now lived in Fontebranda.[3] About a mile and a half south of Siena, at San Rocco a Pilli, the family also owned a farm, *la Cononica*, which later passed on to Bartolommeo's widow Lisa.[4]

Catherine, then, grew up in the dyer's house in the Via dei Tintori. Like so many others in Siena the house was built on the slope of a hill. That which was the ground floor on the side facing the Via dei Tintori was therefore the basement out to the lane at the back (Vicolo del Tiratoio). The dye-rooms were in the lowest story, a stairway led up to the first floor (or the ground floor, if you entered the house from the back) — and here were the bedrooms. On the top, that is, on the second floor, there was a terrace laid out like a garden, and the large kitchen, which also served as a living-room. Here the family took their meals, here the women worked at their spinning, sewing and darning; here they all gathered about the fire in the evening, keeping *veglia*, as it is still called in the country in Italy, warming themselves before going to bed, talking or telling stories.

Here too, in Giacomo Benincasa's house, in the family circle about the crackling fire, there was one who was to have a decisive influence on Catherine's life. This was the adopted son, the foster-brother Tommaso della Fonte. Nicoluccia Benincasa was married to Palmiero della Fonte, and when the plague of 1349 (Boccaccio's plague) had made little Tommaso an orphan, he found a home with the Benincasas. At that time he was ten years old; he had now grown up into a young man who wished to enter a monastery. He wanted to join the Dominicans at Camporeggi, just above the house. At present he was spending the long winter evenings with the Benincasas and telling them all he had read in Jacopo di Vareggio's book of the Golden Legend, about the apostles and martyrs, about Saint Mary Magdalene and Saint Lazarus who fled from the Jews and came to Massilia in Provence — about Saint Agnes, Saint Agatha and Saint Lucy, whose eyes were put out by the cruel Romans who tore off their virginal breasts with red-hot tongs — about the holy hermits in caves and deserts, about Saint Anthony, to whom the church at the corner was dedicated — but first and last Tommaso told them about Saint Dominic, about the great, pious and learned Saint Thomas Aquinas and about Saint Peter Martyr, who at last could no longer confess his faith in words, but stooped down and wrote with his blood in the sand: *Credo*. . .

Tommaso told them all this, and Catherine listened. She knew the Dominicans of the monastery at Camporeggio very well. They often came through the street in their white habits with the black mantles over them — the colours of Siena, the colours in *la balzana** and the colours of the *Campanile*. The white meant purity, the black humility; Catherine would stand at the casement and watch them pass by, beautiful like the

* The old name of the flag of Siena.

angels of God, with pure, pale profiles, their eyes gazing heavenwards, never glancing to right or left, never looking at the women standing in the doorways and sighing: *Com'è bello! troppo bello per essere frate! che peccato!* No, indeed they were *not* too handsome for God! Why should Jesus always have only the hunchbacked and bandy-legged ones! From her hiding-place Catherine took note where the monks had set their feet, and when they had gone and the black-haired, rosy-cheeked women's heads had disappeared from the windows, she would run down to kiss the stones on which the pious brothers had stepped.

Otherwise Catherine was a merry and lively child and so fleet of foot that it often looked as if she flew up and down the stairs. Everybody in the neighbourhood loved her; she was so sweet that she was constantly being lent to friends and acquaintances who wanted her to spend a day or so with them, and because of her loveliness she was called Euphrosyne, the name of one of the Graces. (Raymond, who does not credit the inhabitants of the Fontebranda quarter with so much classical knowledge, remarks on this, however: "I am more inclined to think that it was a name she invented for herself, as little children often do." There is, though, also a *Sancta* Euphrosyne, and later in her life Catherine saw an omen in this name having been applied to her. For it is related of Saint Euphrosyne that she wished to enter a religious order, but not amongst nuns. She therefore cut her hair short and put on man's clothes, and Catherine was greatly inclined to follow her example.

Meanwhile, in order to enter a religious house, whether amongst men or women, one had to be very pious. And Catherine was, in fact, found praying here and there in lonely corners of the house, or she might be heard walking slowly up the stairs, and at each step she would say, in her little childish voice, a Hail Mary. I can easily imagine it, as I have had a little daughter of six, myself, who would make small private devotions on a stair landing where there was a picture of Our Lady.

Then came the day when the Vision appeared to her above the roof of San Domenico and she beheld Our Lord Himself. "But from that moment Catherine was no longer a child." [5]

III

From the very beginning Christianity has been a religion of visions and revelations. The oldest Christian literature, the Epistles and Gospels, leave no room for doubt about it. The crucifixion of Jesus is followed by His resurrection and after the resurrection the disciples meet their risen Lord and Master again and again. In the garden of Joseph of Arimathea Magdalene falls at the feet of the Gardener when He utters her name, "Mary!" One word is enough to make her exclaim her jubilant *Rabboni!* It is *His* voice, that was what He always called her. At Emmaus, where the two disciples were sitting at table with the Pilgrim Whom they had met on the road, scales, as it were, fell from their eyes — thus did *He* always break the bread, bless it and give it to them. And in Jerusalem the Risen One had appeared to Simon and again in the midst of the disciples, greeting them, as was His wont: *Schalom aleikum*.

Even after the Ascension this communion between here and beyond continues. At the moment of his death Stephen sees heaven open and Jesus standing at the right hand of God. Saul is surrounded by a blinding light outside Damascus and hears a voice like thunder: "I am Jesus whom thou persecutest!" Behind the thin veil of phenomena Jesus is ever present, and in visions and revelations the veil is rent apart.[1] With Stephen and Paul, a Francis of Assisi, a Catherine of Siena, a Birgitta and a Jeanne d'Arc see heaven open and hear "unutterable words." But "whether they are in the body or out of the body they cannot tell. God knoweth." [2]

Like Italian Catherine our northern Birgitta was also a seer. The widow of Ulf Gudmarsson died in Rome on the 23d July 1373, but the saint of Siena had not become acquainted with her. Otherwise they could have greeted each other as kindred spirits. In Birgitta we find a series of attempts to describe what the visionary state really is. Thus it is said in the introduction to her rule: "In the kingdom of Norway it happened to Saint Birgitta, as she was rapt in prayer, that her body became powerless, its strength as it were taken away, but her soul became lively and strong, and able to see and hear and feel the things that are of the spirit. And often was she seized on this wise." Or, in the preface to the fifth book of her revelations: "Once, when she was journeying to Vadstena, she began, as she was riding along the road, to lift up her heart in prayer to God, and she was caught up in spirit, so that she was away from the senses of her body and rapt in ecstasy." During this "ecstasy" she saw and heard the whole content of the fifth book of the "Revelations," just as Catherine in ecstasy dictated her book, The Dialogue. Bishop Alphonso of Jaen relates that he often saw Birgitta when praying suddenly become bereft of the use of her senses, so that she felt and saw nothing of what was going on around her. Of this state Birgitta says herself: "Oh, sweetest God, strange it is what thou dost to me! For Thou dost put my body to sleep, and my soul Thou awakenest to see and hear and feel the things of the spirit. When it pleaseth Thee, Thou dost send my body to sleep, not with bodily sleep, but with the rest of the spirit, and my soul Thou dost awaken as though from a trance to see and hear and feel with the powers of the spirit." [8] This was exactly the case with Catherine.

Everything that in a modern term can be called inspiration can be distinguished by some of these features. The poet or artist who is working intensely feels himself raised above the demands of the body, quite absorbed in his work, and the work is done with ease, without hindrance or constraint, as if a power outside himself, another personality, were really doing the work. "I am but an instrument, the Master plays upon me," a Danish poet has said. Nietzsche says, of the state in which he wrote "Also sprach Zarathustra": "Has anyone at the close of the nineteenth century any clear perception of what the poets of strong ages called inspiration? If not, I will describe it. Possessing only the smallest remnant of superstition one would hardly be able to reject the idea that one is nothing but a medium for super-mighty influences. That which happens can only be termed revelation, that is to say, that suddenly, with unutterable certainty and delicacy, something becomes visible and audible and shakes and rends one to the depths of one's being. One hears, one does not seek; one takes, one does not ask who it is that gives; like lightning a thought flashes out, of necessity, complete in form — I have never needed to choose. It is a rapture, the enormous excitement of which sometimes finds relief in a storm of tears; a state of being entirely outside oneself with the clearest consciousness of fine shiverings and a rustling through one's being right down to the tips of one's toes; a depth of joy in which all that is most painful and gloomy does not act as a contrast but as a condition for it, as though demanded, as a necessary colour in such a flood of light . . . Everything happens in the highest degree involuntarily, as in a storm of a feeling of freedom, of power, of divinity." In the same way Strindberg has described poetical ecstasy as "a state which bestows indescribable happiness," "a state of pure bliss while the writing continued." [4]

The ecstasy in which a Saint Birgitta, a Saint Catherine have their revelations, is a further development of that poetic inspiration. Nowhere perhaps is this more evident than in the great Dominican, Henry Suso, of whose revelations a German Catholic theologian justly says: "It seems to be Suso's own, but his higher nature that breaks out in this way, seeking and finding consolation and enlightenment. The purity of the heavenly visions, the sweetness of the songs, everything that seizes him so profoundly, what is it all but the hidden poet and singer in himself?" [5]

In Catherine as in Birgitta we find a poetic mind matured early. But in the Italian saint there are also certain physical peculiarities which do not occur in her Swedish contemporary. During these ecstasies Catherine was plunged in a state of bodily insensibility and tetanic rigidity, making it possible to thrust a needle through her foot without her feeling it. And often Lapa — "very simple-minded Lapa" — who did not understand ecstasies at all, and was often enough in despair about the cygnet she had hatched in her goose-nest, nearly broke her daughter to pieces in her well-meant attempts to bend Catherine's rigid neck or limbs.[6]

Catherine was a religious genius in a body quite overwhelmed by the spirit. The first time she gave evidence of this awakening was, as in the case of Birgitta, at an early age. On that evening in the Via del Costone six-year-old Catherine had seen Jesus, and out of this vision a slow transformation of her whole spiritual life now began. The essence of merely poetical genius is communion with the human soul, with mankind. The core of religious genius is communion with God, communion with the Highest, who is also the Innermost. "He that heareth my commandments and keepeth them, he it is that loveth me. And I will love him and manifest myself to him." These words of Jesus are the key to all psychology of saints — Catherine's included.[7] She had "seen the Lord," and as the Voice had once sounded on the shores of the lake of Genesareth, so now it kept on ringing in her soul, softly and persuasively, like the ringing of bells far away, which do not leave you in peace until you go and find out where the ringing comes from. "Come follow Me! Follow Me away from father and mother, from sisters and brothers, from house and home, from your town and your country. Follow Me out into the desert to the forty days of fasting and to the temptation by the devil. Follow Me when I go up to Jerusalem. Follow Me to the martyr's stake, to the scourging, to the crown of thorns, to the Cross! Follow Me, not like Peter, but follow Me like John and like Mary — stand beneath My cross and feel My blood dripping down upon you in burning drops. Follow Me as the holy martyrs followed. Follow Me like San Sano to the cauldron of boiling pitch, like Peter Martyr to shed your blood as a witness to the faith. Follow Me like Magdalene to the cave in the rock, like Anthony out into the desert." "That vision and that blessing were so mighty," says Caffarini, "that she could not think of anything but the holy hermits and of imitating them."[8]

Yet this was, so far, half child's play, half real devotion. Here and there in the large house at Fontebranda there were dark hiding-places enough, which could serve Catherine just as well as hermits' caves. Into them she would retire and play at being a hermit as well as she could; there she prayed, fasted while the others were at supper and scourged herself with a discipline of her own making. After a while other little girls found that it was quite an amusing game and Catherine showed them what they had to do, composed their prayers for them, here already showing her dominant nature. In the long run, however, this mummery did not satisfy her, her mind was set on realities and not on imitations. And one day she left home with the firm resolve to go out into the wide world and become a hermit. When she came to Porta San Sano she passed out through it.

It was the first time Catherine went beyond the walls of Siena. The road went down into Vallepiatta, soon the town disappeared behind her and she was alone among the trees. The sides of Vallepiatta consist of rocks of tufa stone, in which there are caves; the desert must be there, Catherine thought, and went into one of them. She had brought a loaf with her from home, and thus provided she began her hermit's life. She knelt down and began to pray, and again she was plunged into that strange state in which everything vanished around her and in which she seemed to float in a world of utter light. She felt as though she were being gently lifted up from the ground; she was borne higher and higher; at last her head knocked against the roof of the cave and this awoke her. She wondered at discovering that she must have spent a long time in the cave. The sun was near setting, the cicada were singing in the fig trees and she could hear the bells of the cathedral ringing for vespers. All her plans of a hermit's life had suddenly vanished; Catherine felt only that she was alone and a long way from home and that very soon the gates of Siena would be closed. Then too, she felt so strangely weak in her legs, they could not carry her the long way up to the gate, up hill all the way . . . she felt giddy and as if a cloud were passing before her eyes, again she had the feeling of floating in the air, and without knowing how, she found herself suddenly standing inside Porta San Sano. With a beating heart she hurried home, but no one had noticed her absence, it was thought that — as so often before — she had gone over to her sister's.[9] Catherine did not repeat this attempt to become a hermit.

One thing, though, had become clear to her while she was praying out there in the cave: that her life was to be entirely dedicated to God. The teaching of the Bible was plain: "the unmarried woman and virgin thinks of what is the Lord's, that she must be holy in her life and soul. But the married woman thinks of what is of the world and how she may please her husband." [10] *The Lord* on one side, *the world* on the other — Catherine's young soul was in no doubt which she would choose. At the age of seven she promised herself to Jesus before an image of Our Lady. "Most blessed and most holy Virgin," it is said that she prayed, "look not upon my weakness, but grant me the grace that I may have for my bridegroom Him whom I love with all my soul, thy most holy Son, our only Lord, Jesus Christ! I promise Him and thee that never will I have any other bridegroom." [11]

With this the decisive step was taken. Catherine was the child-bride of Christ, she had betrothed herself to Him like her namesake, Saint Catherine of Alexandria, who is represented in pictures as giving Mary her hand: Mary places the hand of the Child Jesus in that of Catherine and Jesus places a ring upon her finger. As an obedient bride she would henceforth seek to do the will of her Bridegroom in all things, but the will of Jesus was that above all one should chastise oneself and keep one's nature in subjection. This little Catherine Benincasa had already begun to do, with her disciplinary exercises, half in play, and her prayers in the solitudes of cellar and garret. She now imposed upon herself a diet of bread and herbs alone, either putting her meat on her brother Stefano's plate, or letting it fall under the table to feed the cats, inseparable from all Italian kitchens.

At this time a little incident showed Monna Lapa in how high a degree Catherine was her father's daughter. One morning she had been sent by her mother to the neighbouring church of Sant' Antonio to offer a candle and ask the priest to say a Mass for some intention or other. Catherine performed her errand, but instead of going home at once she stayed and heard the Mass which she had asked to be said for her intention. When she did at last come home, her mother was voluble in her complaints at her absence. Catherine listened to her raging and then said: "*Monna madre,* when I do something that is wrong, then punish me for it, that I may learn to do better. But I beg of you not to use such words, and in particular not to wish anyone ill, no matter whom, for it is not becoming to your dignity as a mother and it grieves my heart."

At that time Catherine was not yet ten years old. When Giacomo came up from the dye-room that evening, his wife exclaimed: "Just listen to what your daughter said to me today." Later on the dyer's daughter of Fontebranda was to utter the truth to the mighty ones of this world.[12]

IV

Catherine was now twelve years old. She was no longer allowed to walk in the streets alone, and the family began to think of a husband for her. Two of Catherine's sisters were already married, and after all that is the purpose of a woman's existence. Monna Lapa began to attend to her daughter's looks and urged upon her — so thoroughly Italian! — to wash herself a little oftener, arrange her hair becomingly and try to please the men-folk.

Catherine, though, would hear nothing about men. She never stood in the doorway or leaned out of the window like other young girls, and at her work she never, like them, sang about love. And if one of her father's journeymen only so much as came into the room she would run away. "Good heavens, they are not poisonous!" her mother scolded. Her daughter, though, fled from them as if they had been snakes.

With the help of Catherine's favourite sister, Bonaventura, however, they succeeded in making her waver a little. At any rate a day came when Catherine consented to go to a festival like other girls, in fine clothes, with her cheeks rouged and her hair dyed fair, in obedience to her mother's wish. "And at that time Siena was so rich in worldly goods that there was feasting almost every day for all the new brides," says Catherine's contemporary, the Augustinian monk, Filippo Agazzari, in his "Moral Tales."[1] If this stern preacher is to be believed, the young Sienese women of the fourteenth century were not less vain than are those of the twentieth; at any rate he tells of a young girl who fell down dead at a feast because she had laced herself too tightly, and of another whose face was eaten up by the paint that she used. There was even one whom the devil himself attended at her toilet as her tiring-woman, her fate was still worse! From the tales of other writers it would seem that the ladies would stand for hours on the roof, exposing their hair to the sun in order to make it fair.[2]

This period of worldliness in Catherine's life seems to have been but brief; at any rate it came to an end with the sudden death of Bonaventura in August, 1362.[3] Beside the dead body

Saint Benedict, Saint Romuald, Saint Bernardo Tolomei, Saint Francis and many others. But she looked only for one: Saint Dominic. He too, looked at her, and coming forward he approached her and handed her a black and white habit. Then he spoke to her and said: "Be of good heart, my daughter, and fear not! Assuredly thou shalt wear this habit." Then Catherine was so happy that she awoke. But the habit which she had seen was that which in Siena is worn by the sisters called the Mantellate.[5]

This dream undoubtedly indicates a new stage in Catherine's soul. She gives up the remote, fantastic dream of going into a monastery and fixes upon that which is near and attainable. For there, in the streets of Siena, and here and there in the houses there were women wearing the colours of Saint Dominic and belonging to the order which he, like Saint Francis, had founded, the so-called Mantellate or cloak-wearing Sisters. Her own aunt, the widow of Michele di Duccio, was a Mantellata.

Everyone knows those moments in which a great thought strikes the mind and now demands to be realised. All doubt, all hesitation is over, it seems that one cannot get the new plan put into action quickly enough. It was as a result of such a firm resolve that Catherine acted, when in the morning after that dream she called the family together and declared to them that "it would be easier for them to melt a stone," than to shake her in her resolve. "I therefore advise you to break off all arrangements about my marriage, for in that matter I do not intend to do your will, inasmuch as one must obey God rather than man. If you will keep me here in the house as your handmaid, then I am willing to serve you with a good heart. If you mean to drive me away then you must know that I will never give up my resolve and that I have a Bridegroom, so rich and so mighty that He can give me all I need, and who will never let me want for anything."

A century and a half earlier Francis of Assisi had spoken similar words to his kinsfolk, and it caused a breach which was never healed between him and his home. But Giacomo Benincasa was no Pietro di Bernardone, and the spirit which had gone forth from the son of Pietro di Bernardone had already for five generations overshadowed the world. "The angel bearing the seal of the living God," as Saint Bonaventura called Francis, had sealed thousands upon thousands, and Giacomo was of their number.

There was silence in the room when Catherine ceased speaking. Then Giacomo summoned up all his courage and spoke from the depths of his heart:

"May God preserve us, dearest daughter, from trying in any way to set up ourselves against the will of God. We have long seen that it was no childish whim of thine, and now we know clearly that it is the spirit of God that constrains thee. Keep thy vow therefore, and live as the spirit tells thee, we will no longer hinder thee. We ask thee only for one thing, always to intercede for us in prayer, so that we may be worthy of the promises of thy Bridegroom."

Turning to Lapa and his sons, Giacomo then added: "Let no one dare in any way to torment or hinder my dear daughter. She is to be left free and in peace to serve her Bridegroom and continually to pray for us. We could never get a bridegroom of mightier kindred." [6]

V

During the period of domestic trial Catherine "had built in her soul an oratory which she resolved never to leave, whatever her occupation. No one could take that interior oratory from her and she never left it." That was the oratory used also by Francis of Assisi and of which he once said: "Our brother the body is like a cell, and the soul is the hermit dwelling therein." [1]

Catherine, then, was now to have a real exterior cell. Below the kitchen in Giacomo Benincasa's house there was a small room with a window overlooking Vicolo del Tiratoio.* This room was given to Catherine and in it she arranged her hermitage.

Catherine's cell can still be seen in the house in Via Benincasa. The floor is on a level with the lane outside the house. The window is walled up, but a stone marked with a cross in the outer wall indicates to those who pass by that this is a holy place.

The cell was very small, fifteen feet long and nine feet wide, and the floor was of large red bricks. There was not room for much furniture — a chest in which she kept her belongings, and a couch, that was all. During the day the couch served as a table, and at night she slept upon it, fully dressed, with a log of wood for a pillow, or resting her head upon the steps leading up to the window, which was placed high up in the wall. Both the door and the hatch before the window were usually closed, the only light in the little room coming from the lamp hanging before the crucifix on the wall. [2]

Here, in solitude and darkness, Catherine could seriously imitate the penitential exercises of the old anchorites of the desert. She had long since given up eating meat; she now denied herself all sweet food and at length reached a point when she could live only on bread and raw vegetables. From her twentieth year she did not eat bread any more, only let-

---

* Tiratoio: a place where cloth merchants displayed their wares for sale. In Florence Arnolfo di Campo built a magnificent Tiratoio for *Arte della Lana* on the site now occupied by the Exchange.

tuce, and at times she would deprive herself of even that slight nourishment. Her constitution changed entirely under the influence of this rigorous fasting, and at last she simply *could* not any longer take nourishment.

In other ways too, she mortified herself, for some time wearing a hair shirt, but for reasons of cleanliness she exchanged it for a thin iron chain which she tied tightly round her waist. Caffarini saw one of the scourges with which Catherine chastised herself; it was furnished with iron hooks and was, when he saw it, quite dark with coagulated blood. He also saw the chain which she wore round her waist, it was furnished with small crosses.[3]

As with her food, so with her sleep, of which she allowed herself less and less; at last she slept scarcely half-an-hour out of forty-eight. "That was the most difficult of all the ways of overcoming self," she confided later to Raymond of Capua.[4]

By nature Catherine was endowed with robust health, and she was vigorous, like all Italian women. Lapa would often relate how her daughter had, when quite young, carried a sack of corn from the street right up to the loft — "and it was all the mule could do, to drag it along. But at that time she was twice as stout as she is now."[5]

The Dominicans have always been fond of corporal penitential exercises. Saint Francis had forbidden his brethren that kind of exterior self-chastisement, and at the "Mat Chapter" at Portiuncula he had all their hair shirts and penitential belts collected and burnt. The life of, for instance, a Henry Suso, though, was nothing but a series of self-torments from his eighteenth until his fortieth year "until his whole nature had been laid waste, and there was no choice but to cease or to die. It was signified to him by God that it had all been only a very good beginning and a breaking-down of his unconverted humanity."[6]

In the solitude of her room Catherine walked in the same path of self-conquest and self-annihilation as the black friar in his monastery in Constance. If she had written the story of her life she, too, could have told of beautiful and terrible things, "of the maceration of the flesh," and of the "painful destruction of self."

Meanwhile, with all this Catherine had not reached the goal of her desires at all, that of wearing the white and black habit. Her parents had given her permission to lead a life of prayer and penance within the four walls of her home, but they did not intend to go further in their indulgence. Besides, Monna Lapa had by no means given up her hope of curing her daughter of her strange ideas. Now why, for instance, would Catherine sleep in there on that hard bench instead of in a good soft bed? Sometimes Lapa would get up and fetch her daughter, making her sleep beside herself as when she was little. But when Lapa awoke in the morning the place by her side was empty — Catherine had quietly stolen away. Or, if she did remain there, it was because she had managed to smuggle a board or a couple of logs under the sheet; then she would lie on them and pray instead of sleeping. So with a sigh Lapa gave up trying to alter her wayward child, but it was with more than a sigh that she made a protest when she came upon Catherine one day while the latter was scourging herself until the blood flowed. Then Lapa wept so that all the neighbours could hear it and screamed aloud: "Daughter, daughter, do you mean to kill yourself? Alas, what power is it that has taken my daughter from me?" "And moreover [Raymond remarks with cool superciliousness], Lapa performed all sorts of strange acts, such as scratching her face and tearing out her hair." It was easy enough for Raymond, that chilly monk; *he* did not know what it was to have a mother's heart! *Semplicissima Lapa* — you loved your little Catherine so much, the darling of your heart, your last born, whom you had nursed yourself, the sunbeam in your house, your lovely Euphrosyne, and now you could not understand why she should so ill-treat herself, and you wept and tore your hair when you saw her blood flow; your blood and Giacomo's blood flowing in Catherine's veins, and each of the precious drops was a drop of youth, a drop of life, a drop of happiness which, once spilt, could never be regained. You very simple Lapa, we feel with you, we understand you, we love you for the sake of your great warm heart, the heart which you bequeathed to your daughter, and which made her so brave and so strong!

Neither with sternness nor kindness could Lapa manage Catherine; she now tried a third way — distraction. She took her to Vignone, a much frequented watering-place in the mountains south of Siena, on the river Orcia. According to Simone di Giacomo Tondi's description of the year 1334, the hot springs in Vignone contained "iron, alum, copper, a little gold and a little silver," and were used particularly in the treatment of liver complaints, catarrh of the stomach and all kinds of nervous diseases. The baths, which are now used only by the peasants in the neighbourhood, were at that time very fashionable, with numerous hotels and a church in the middle of the promenade square.[7] Here then, under Lapa's supervision, Catherine was to give her ill-treated body care, recover and become more reasonable.

Catherine seemed to be willing enough. She only asked to be allowed to take her bath alone, unaccompanied by her mother. This permission being granted, she went — instead of bathing in the temperate water in the baths — straight under the hot spring and nearly scalded herself to death. On being called to account she answered: "I thought of the punishments in hell and in purgatory, and I prayed to my Creator in His mercy to spare me the everlasting torments and accept the pain I felt here instead."

Then Lapa returned home, her object unachieved, and Catherine now began to disclose her real plans in speaking to her mother about becoming a Mantellata. She prevailed upon Lapa to the extent of obtaining her promise to go to the Prioress of the Mantellate and place the matter before her. Lapa, however, returned well pleased from this visit; the Prioress had answered that they only received widows, and that a young girl like Catherine could not become a Sister at all.[8]

Then Catherine was taken ill; she had chicken-pox, which attacked this girl of sixteen in a violent form. Lapa was inconsolable and sat day and night by her daughter's bed. When Catherine refused all the good things her mother brought her, the latter exclaimed in despair: "But is there nothing at all that I can do for you?" Her daughter answered slyly: "If you want me to get well, see to it that I become a Mantellata. Otherwise I really believe that Saint Dominic will see to it that you shall not keep me either in this nor in any other habit!"

Lapa, then, went once more to the Prioress and pleaded her daughter's cause in the dire distress of her heart. "Provided she is not too pretty," the Prioress ventured. "Come and see for yourself," answered Lapa, who could also be diplomatic. The Prioress came and did not find that Catherine, whose skin was peeling, was a very disturbing beauty. On the other hand she was pleased with the girl's manner and her unquestionable piety. The other Mantellate were now consulted, perhaps Anna Benincasa put in a word or two on behalf of her niece; at any rate Catherine at last received the long desired and joyful intimation that she could be received as a Sister. Her happiness over it had such an effect upon her that she recovered very quickly and the day for her reception was fixed.

It was shortly before this day, to which Catherine had looked forward with so much longing, that she had to face a sudden and severe conflict. She was out of bed by this time and after Lapa's nursing she had gone back to her austere room. She was kneeling there one day before her crucifix. It was at the hour of dusk, at that hour when the soul is filled with longings — at which it is itself perplexed — longings that dare not venture forth into the sunshine, longings that flee when the lamp is lit, but that fly about in the borderland between night and day like nocturnal insects, birds of gloom, sad memories, dangerous dreams. . .

In that hour of dusk in the little darkening cell Catherine was visited by these disquieting guests. Was that the voice of her dead sister, Bonaventura? Was she reminded of her joy as a young mother among her children at play? Or was it a memory of a festival — did she see the banners of the *Contrada,* ingeniously waved by the slender young Alfieri — did she see the sunshine upon the festively attired crowd at *il Campo* and the stands covered with red cloth and filled with ladies in beautiful clothes? "You might have been there too, Catherine," a voice whispered to her. "Why did you cut off your beautiful golden hair? Why do you wear a hair shirt next your white body, and now in a few days the coarse habit of the Sisters? Look, is not this raiment much fairer?"

In the falling dusk it seemed to Catherine that a young man was standing before her, handsome and slender like one of the pages of *Contrada dell' Oca,* and that he was holding out to her a garment more beautiful than any she had ever seen, of lustrous silk, glittering with gold, heavy with pearls and precious stones. As though spell-bound Catherine gazed at the glittering garment, and the handsome youth, taking her silence for consent, was already about to throw the dress over her head . . .

Then Catherine awoke, as if from a dream. Suddenly she saw what she was about to do. With a violent movement she drove away the tempter and his delusions. The exterior vision vanished, but the interior temptation remained.

It was as though she had hitherto lived without perceiving the reality of life. She had wandered along in her own thoughts and according to her own liking, and had been quite absorbed in getting her own way. She had now got her own way — and what had she gained by it? What had she gained and what had she given up? When she vowed herself to Jesus as a child, she did not know yet what she was doing; she was only yielding naïvely to a desire to do what the priests said was so pleasing to God, and what so many holy women had done before her. It was now as though veil after veil fell away; she saw human life and human happiness, woman's life and woman's happiness as it was, and understood that she was now renouncing it for ever. . . Never would she place her hand in a man's hand before the altar, never after making the marriage vows turn and go down the altar steps, led by him, and with a little grave and happy nod to her parents. The bridal candles were never to be lit for her, and never would she, white-haired and full of days, show wondering grandchildren her old-fashioned bridal veil interwoven with silver flowers.

Summoning up all her strength Catherine tore herself away from the dreams rushing in upon her woman's heart. "Thou, my only, my dearest Bridegroom," she cried, prostrate before the crucifix, "Thou knowest that I have never desired any but Thee! Come to my aid now, my Saviour, strengthen and support me in this hour of trial!"

The Crucified did not stir, He hung there silent and with lifeless eyes. But there was a rustling of woman's garments in the narrow cell, a crackling as of gold and silk against the cold walls, and before Catherine stood the Blessed among women Herself, the great Lady of Siena, the Blessed Virgin and Mother of God, Madonna Maria. Like the Tempter only a few moments before she, too, was carrying a glittering garment upon her arm, gold-broidered, studded with pearls, sparkling with precious stones. "This garment, my daughter," said the Mother of Jesus in her soft and gentle voice (it makes one weep when one hears it), "I have drawn from the heart of my Son, it lay hidden in the wound in His side, as in a golden casket, and I have wrought it myself with my own holy hands."

Then Catherine bent her head in ardent longing and trembling humility, and Our Blessed Lady clothed her in the heavenly raiment.[9]

VI

When you step into the church of San Domenico in Siena, you see at once on the right side a door to a closed chapel, on a slightly higher level than the rest of the church. In former times this chapel was open, only some arches, traces of which can still be seen, separating it from the main nave. Steps lead up to it; when the arches were walled up, a couple of steps were left standing — they can be seen in a square opening in the wall, and an old inscription says: "Catherine mounted these steps to pray to Christ, her Bridegroom." [1]

This chapel is the Capella delle Volte, mentioned again and again in the story of Catherine. Here the Mantellate held their meetings and here Catherine was clothed by Father Bartolommeo Montucci in the white habit, the belt, the black mantle and the white coif in the presence of all the Sisters, one Sunday morning in 1363. We are told by Raymond of Capua that when she came home from church that day she said to herself: "Look, now you have entered into religion and it is not fitting that you should go on living as you have done hitherto. Your life in the world is over, a new life is beginning. The white robe you are wearing signifies that you must be girded with sheerest purity. The black cloak means that you must be wholly dead to the world. And henceforth you must walk in the narrow path, trodden only by very few."

When at length she was alone in her cell she had a beautiful and significant vision. It seemed to her that she beheld a large tree, full of beautiful fruits. Round the foot of the tree there was a high and thick hedge of thorns, so that it was difficult to get inside to the tree and gather the fruit.

A short way off there was, as it were, a little hill, quite covered with corn already whitening to harvest. The corn looked very beautiful but the ears were barren, and on being touched they crumbled away into dust.

Further, it seemed to her that many people came and passed by. They stopped opposite the tree, and desiring the fair fruit, they tried to get inside to it, but the thorns pricked them and they soon gave up trying to break through the hedge. Then they caught sight of the corn-covered hill near by and ran up to it and ate of the unwholesome corn, which turned to dust between their fingers, making them ill and depriving them of their strength.

Then others came and had more courage than the first. They broke through the hedge, but when they reached the tree they saw that the fruit hung high up, and that the trunk of the tree was smooth and difficult to climb. They too, therefore, turned away and ate of the corn, which only made them more hungry than they were before.

At last some came who both broke through the hedge and climbed the tree. They plucked the fruits and ate them, and were thereby strengthened in spirit, so that from that moment they had a loathing of all other food.

"But Catherine [Caffarini relates] wondered that so many men and women could be so foolish and so blind, that they would follow and love the false and deceitful world, rather than surrender themselves to Jesus Christ, who calls us and invites us and who is faithful in all that He promises, even in this world consoling His servants and bestowing joy upon them. For that tree, she well understood, signifies the eternal incarnate Word, and the ineffable fruits of the tree are all the virtues. The little hill, on the other hand, which does not yield good corn, but only husks, is the barren field of the world, which men till with great and fruitless toil. But they who give up trying to get in to the tree as soon as they feel the thorns, are all those who think they cannot endure a God-fearing life, and give it up before they have tried it. The others, who lose courage when they see how tall the tree is, are those who begin with a good will and a good heart, but who weary after a while and do not persevere in their first resolve. The last kind are those who really believe and who remain steadfast in the truth." [2]

In this vision Catherine's fundamental view of life, which was to grow fuller and deeper with the coming years, was already given. Man is placed, so she feels, between two powers, both of which appeal to his love. One of these two powers is truth, life, peace, happiness and everlasting life; the other is delusion, the world, the ever enchanting and ever disappointing mirage of Satan. There are some who would maintain that this doctrine is Buddhistic or ancient Greek, that it has come down from Sakkhyamuni or from Plato or Plotinus. It comes from the Gospels, it is to be found in the New Testament. It is the entirely firm conviction of primitive Christianity that there is an undying enmity between God and "the world," between the children of God and the children of the world. The disciples of Jesus are "not of the world," therefore the world hates them. Jesus, who prays for sinners, "does not pray for the world." Antichrist is "the prince of this world," the Christian faith "overcomes the world"; it is the duty of a Christian not to love the world, or the things that are in the world. Love of the world is the exact opposite of the love of God: "If anyone love the world, the love of God is not in him." [3]

This evangelical and apostolic teaching has been faithfully preserved by the Catholic Church down through the ages (as the Catholic Church altogether is the unadulterated representative of genuine primitive Christian thought). It is Augustine's doctrine of "the two cities," it is the teaching of the Dominican mystic of "the two kinds of love," it is Ignatius of Loyola's teaching of "the two standards." "The soul that is endowed with reason becomes impure," writes Saint Thomas Aquinas, "when it gives its love to temporal things and gives itself up to them." [4] In wandering unweariedly through land after land, Henry Suso, the other Dominican and the spiritual kinsman of Aquinas, did so, as he said himself, that he might "draw loving hearts from temporal to eternal love," and "make them loathe mortal love and cherish that which is everlasting." [5]

In man everything issues from the heart and the heart is never inactive. "Neither the Creator nor the creature was ever without love," says Dante.[6] We do not know whether Catherine had read Dante (he was read and treasured [7] among her disciples) but she says in almost similar words: "The soul cannot live without loving." Everything then, depends on what we love, "for we must love either God or the world. And the soul always unites itself with that which it loves, and is transformed by it. But if the soul love the world it only gains suffering, for there it finds only tribulations and bitter thorns. . . And the soul is always sorrowful and cannot endure itself . . . but God is the highest and eternal sweetness, and the soul which receives God by grace is satisfied and content, for the hunger of the soul cannot be appeased by anything but God, because He is greater than it, but the soul is greater than all created things. Therefore all that this world contains cannot satisfy man, for it is all poorer than man." "And we were not created to eat dust." [8]

This was what Saint Augustine meant by the famous words: "Our heart is restless till it finds rest in Thee, O God." For Catherine this became the sustaining mood of life which filled her already, even now, but which had to be maintained and secured through conflict and through overcoming and sacrifice of self. Three years of her youth did she devote to training herself in this state of mind, to detaching her heart entirely from the world and fastening it wholly on God. Three years did she live in her childhood's home as if in a desert; spoke only when strictly necessary with those about her and with her confessor, still Tommaso della Fonte; otherwise keeping the "great silence" of the Cistercians, that silence which together with solitude has always been a favourable climate to spiritual growth. Talk distracts and splits up, words stain and wound, but silence collects and strengthens, cleanses and refreshes. It is possible through silence to become sound and whole down to the deepest depths.

Catherine kept silence and lived in solitude. Every morning she walked the short way up to San Domenico to hear Mass, otherwise she was alone in her room. The little she wanted for food was brought to her and she ate it sitting on her couch or "moistening her bread with the tears of repentance." If anything remained the poor were waiting for it outside the hatch.

It was one evening in those three years of silence and solitude. Catherine stepped into her cell, closed and fastened the door and window. The only light now came from the faint glow of the lamp above the images of the Crucified and the Blessed Virgin, Mary Magdalene and Saint Dominic. Too tired to pray Catherine sat down on her bench.

She had been up to San Domenico which was closed now after the Angelus. She had been the last in the church and she had only gone because the sacristan, who was waiting to lock up and go home to his supper, had long and meaningly rattled his keys.

They were beginning to get rather tired of her up there at San Domenico. They found that she was getting troublesome, she did not go home after Mass like the other Mantellate, but stayed in Capella delle Volte saying endless prayers. When she came up to receive Holy Communion with the other Sisters, and among all the wrinkled faces turned her fresh young countenance up to the priest, then — well, piety and devotion are good, of course, but it was almost indecent how Catherine's face glowed a deep, rosy red, and her brow and cheeks were covered with beads as though with fine dewdrops. It would happen, too, that after having received the sacred Host she would burst into a storm of tears. Father Tommaso had asked her to restrain this weeping in church, but Catherine had begged his pardon very humbly and said that she could not help it. Often she would be quite unconscious of herself, kneeling and leaning against one of the stone pillars, motionless like a stone statue and her face as white as snow, seeing nothing, hearing and feeling nothing. One day when she could not come to herself at all, and all shouting into her ears and pinching of her arms were of no avail, two of the lay brothers resolutely took her up and carried her outside the church. There she awoke at last because the people passing by kicked her and she found herself lying in the burning midday sun outside the closed church door.[9]

And yet she particularly wanted to be in the church, just at this time — and to be there as long as she could. For the cell, in which she had hitherto found peace and consolation, was no longer what it had been. Paradise was closed to her, and the abyss had opened to let loose swarming crowds of demons.

Catherine was about sixteen years old when she became a Mantellata, and her life of solitude continued until she was between eighteen and nineteen. At that age an Italian girl is a full-grown woman and Catherine could not but feel it.

A new great conflict, the last, entirely decisive conquest of self was approaching. She had gained the victory over her heart, she was now also to master her senses.

At once when Catherine went into the cell she had heard a buzzing and humming noise, as when all the flies swarm up when you go into the kitchen at night. But she knew that this sound was not caused by flies; it was the demons who had been waiting for her return and that were now stirring their wings. Day and night they swarmed around her, never did they leave her in peace; persistent, impudent, aggressive, they would not be shaken off — just like flies. . .

They approached her in many ways, they had so many voices. Hark, that buzzing at her ear — a thin, metallic sound like that of a mandolin string — and it was ingratiating: "Poor Catherine, why will you torment yourself? What is the use of all the pain you inflict upon yourself, your fasting, your iron chain round your waist and the discipline with which you make the weals on your white shoulders? Why don't you sleep like other people? Why don't you eat and drink — in moderation, of course! — still, having a good, decent meal! Do you really believe you can go on like that? And what is your intention with it? Do you mean to be better than others? In that case you are guilty of pride! And have you considered, by the way, that you are doing nothing but slowly killing yourself — you are simply committing suicide, which is a mortal sin — and an irreparable one. Then you will have gained nothing from this life, and in the life beyond only everlasting damnation awaits you!

"No, you had much better take my advice, Catherine. Stop while there is still time. You are young, somewhat weakened, of course, after these penitential exercises, but not beyond recovery. You can become as healthy and strong again as when you were a quite young girl, when you could carry a sack of corn from the front door right up to the loft. Live like other women, get a good and nice-looking husband, have children, become a happy wife and mother! You can still be good and pious — think of Sarah and Rebecca and

Rachel and so many other holy women in both the old and the new covenant."

Thus spoke the kind, admonishing voice in Catherine's ear, and again the old visions rose up before her: the home, the fireside, the children . . .

Catherine looked around her in the little room and she saw that it was narrow and dark — and lonely — and not many paces away, down at the foot of the hill at Fontebranda, the women were now standing at the well, resting a moment while the conchas were filling, talking to each other about shopping and market prices, about supper and the boys' breeches. And outside the gate lay Vallepiatta, full of love songs; Vallepiatta as it lies to this day, in the warm summer nights when the fireflies dance in the dark bushes and over the maize fields in the falling dusk; when the clear weddingsong of the bull-frogs rises in quavering treble from the meadows; when the mothers stand in the doorways of the houses and chubby little babies sit on their naked little behinds in the warm white dust of the road; and young girls walk arm-in-arm down through the valley, and young men meet them and sing in strong, vibrating voices; the girls answer, and both choirs meet and join in a jubilant and exultantly swelling *Amore, amore!*

The young Italian girl may well have had such visions as these in the bare and gloomy cell overlooking the narrow ill-smelling lane behind Giacomo Benincasa's house. Catherine, however, was not a sentimentalist; her father's will was stronger in her than her mother's passion. That promise which she had given her heavenly Bridegroom she faithfully intended to keep, even though, as the evil spirit said, it were to lead her to hell. Her Saviour had chosen a life of suffering, and she wished to be conformed to Him, to be like Him on the Cross so that she might be with Him in His glory. Had she not but lately heard a voice from heaven speak to her heart, saying: "If thou wouldst be strong in the fight, then let all that is sweet be bitter to you, and all that is bitter will become sweetness to you."

The Tempter paused a moment. But soon he advanced

again to the attack. And now he struck deeper chords, down to the deepest depths of human nature, where it rises from the animal. . . There was a great silence around Catherine; the air seemed all at once so heavy and hot; no voice spoke any longer; she only saw — *saw*. . . In whichever direction she turned, in all the corners of the little room, human beings appeared to her, men and women, half naked — naked — and united. Catherine closed her eyes, but the apparitions moved about in the darkness of her closed eyelids. In despair she fastened her gaze upon the image of the Crucified; the ethereal figures danced like elves before the Redeemer, hid Him from her, beckoned to her, whispered to her: "Do as we do!"

Despairingly Catherine tried to protect herself from them, but the persistent visitors were still there. Now she heard the demon's voice again, softly and derisively it hissed in her ear: "Well, Catherine, what are you going to do now? Do you think you can endure *that* very long? We will go on tormenting you like that till the day and hour of your death — or until you give up and become one of us!" Like Mephistopheles on the Brocken, the Tempter jumped out in the midst of his young witches and whirled them round in a naked dance.

Never had the young woman felt nearer to the abyss, perhaps she was already feeling giddy. With a last immense effort of will she once more thrust the enemy back. "Your threats do not frighten me," she cried, "for I have chosen suffering as my joy. And even if my Creator condemn me in the end, I will not for one instant cease from serving Him. For I am one who is altogether worthy of hell, in that I have sorely offended my Lord, and if He therefore condemn me to everlasting perdition He does me no injustice. In all things I am His and will serve Him alone. Of myself I can do nothing, but I trust in Our Lord Jesus Christ. *Confido in Domino Nostro Jesu Christo!*" [10]

When that Name above all other names had been uttered, Catherine felt the ground beneath her feet growing firmer, and the yawning abyss receding. Then she repeated again and again the saving Name, before which every knee must bend, including those under the earth — said it again and again, like a warrior swinging a bright and blood-dripping sword and fighting his way through a superior hostile force. There was a whirling rout of invisible beings, the air in the room became fresh and pure; a great light broke out, and in the midst of the light Jesus Christ was hanging upon His cross and all His wounds were bleeding.

"My daughter Catherine," said His voice. In ardent love, with streaming tears, she lay at His feet. "Oh good and sweet Jesus, where wert Thou, while my soul was being so sorely tormented?" "I was in thy heart, Catherine," came the gentle answer, "for I will not leave anyone who does not first leave Me." "In my heart, Lord, in the midst of all the temptations, in the midst of all the unclean visions?" asked the young woman in wonder. "If Thou wert with me, why then, did I not see Thee? How could I stand by the fire and not feel the warmth of its flame? For I felt nothing but ice, sadness and bitterness, and it seemed to me that I was full of mortal sin." "Tell me, Catherine," spoke the Lord, "did those visions cause thee happiness or sorrow?" "Oh, I hated them, I was in despair over them and over myself." "And why, thinkest thou, didst thou feel thus, but because I was present in thy soul and kept all its gates closed, so that those evil visions could not enter in. I was in thy heart, as I was on the cross, suffering and yet in glory! Thou didst not feel Me, but I was there with My grace, and when at last thou offeredest of thy own free will to bear all the temptations and the torments and even eternal loss, rather than cease from serving Me, it was all taken from thee, for I delight not in tormenting anyone, but I rejoice when anyone will suffer and endure for My sake. Therefore I will from henceforth show thee greater confidence and be more with thee."

Jesus Christ vanished and Catherine was alone with her beating heart. It was near daybreak and at San Domenico the bells were ringing for Matins. It was the usual sign for Catherine to seek rest. Since she had become a Mantellata it seemed to her that it was her duty to watch and pray while her "big brothers," the Dominicans, slept. So when the bells rang in the church up yonder, so solemnly and so consolingly in the dark night, she knew that now they were standing in the choir beneath the lighted candles, fully robed and in battle array, an army of light, setting out to fight against darkness, and then she could safely lie down to rest.

Soon then, she was lying on her hard bench, her head resting on the brick step, and feeling sleep approaching. One thing she kept on turning over in her thoughts, and which had above all made her happy: it was that the Saviour had called her His daughter. Even in her sleep her lips still moved softly, and with a happy smile she murmured: *"Filia mia, Catharina! Filia mia!"* [11]

VII

Entriamo nella cella del cognoscimento di noi. "Let us enter into the cell of self-knowledge."

This expression occurs again and again in Catherine's letters and it states as if in a short formula all that life in the cell meant to her. "Many live in the cell, and yet in their thoughts they are outside it," she once heard the Saviour's voice saying to her. "I will therefore, that thy cell shall be knowledge of thyself and of thy sins."

The knowledge of self — and the knowledge of God. That was the other secret of Catherine's life in the cell; in it she learned "to know herself and to know her God." Both in the most emphatically literal sense. She asserted plainly to Raymond of Capua: "No one has ever taught me what was needed in the path of salvation, but my most beloved Bridegroom, Our Lord and Master, Jesus Christ, has taught me Himself, either by interior impulses, or in appearing to me and *speaking to me, as I am now speaking with you.*" The last expression leaves nothing to be desired in distinctness, and Raymond does indeed add: "Hardly had she closed the door behind her, when the Lord appeared to her and deigned to teach her all that was good for her soul." [1]

This was the fulfilment of the promise which the Lord had given her of more frequent and intimate communion, after that great conflict and victory. "Every evening, when it began to grow dusk," Caffarini relates, "Catherine felt drawn by an irresistible power to God. Her will and heart drew near to the Will and Heart of God, and the exterior world vanished."

But the interior world, the world of the spirit, heaven, Paradise, opened its gates to her. Again and again did the Saviour visit her in her cell, and often He brought good friends with Him: Mary Magdalene, Saint John the Evangelist, the Apostles James and Paul. Sometimes she would meet the heavenly guests in the garden on the flat roof of the house, when she walked to and fro in the dusk in the lavender-bordered paths, between the roses and lilies. One evening

Catherine was so deeply absorbed in her conversation with the Lord and Mary Magdalene that it was night before she was aware of it. "Master," she exclaimed, "it is not fitting that I should be out so long, permit me to retire." "Do as it seemeth good to thee, My daughter," was the answer. Then, when Catherine arose to go down to her cell, Jesus and Mary Magdalene went with her, even staying with her for some time. They all sat together like good friends on the couch and talked with each other — Jesus on the right, Magdalene on the left and their hostess in the middle between her guests.[2]

On another evening while she was praying she suddenly became conscious that Jesus was by her side, and Saint Dominic was with Him. This made Catherine so happy that she began to sing aloud, and her two heavenly guests joining in, they all three sang together, like the heavenly choirs before the throne of God. Until the vision disappeared and Catherine was alone, with a heart near to breaking with longing for the heavenly home and the countless thousands of angels.

Since that evening of singing Catherine would often stand gazing out of the little window in her cell, or walk in the garden on starlit winter evenings. Standing thus gazing and listening out in the boundless space of the heavens, it seemed to her as if at length she could hear far, far away the singing of the heavenly hosts, and then she would feel the sadness of having to live among the shadows of earth. One evening in January Father Tommaso della Fonte found her in the roof garden and she said to him: "Father, can you not hear them singing in heaven? They do not all sing alike, those who have loved God most here on earth have the clearest and most beautiful voices — ah, Father, can you not hear Mary Magdalene singing — it is so sweet and beautiful — her voice rises above all the others!" Father Tommaso della Fonte heard nothing, only saw the glittering effulgence of red Rigel or blue Vega and the white face of his young penitent, radiant, turned towards the sky. Until she suddenly bent her head and burst into bitter tears of longing for Paradise.[3]

At first these visions filled Catherine with terror. She was afraid that they might be delusions of the devil, and one evening she placed this fear before the Saviour Himself. He then taught her how to "discern spirits."

"The visions that come from Me," said the Saviour, "begin by inspiring fear, but end in a feeling of safety, they begin by calling forth bitterness, but end in sweetness. But in the visions that come from the enemy, it is the opposite. They begin with joy, safety, sweetness, they end in bitterness and terror.

But I will give you another and still safer sign," added the Saviour. "I am the Truth and therefore the visions that come from Me, bring forth an ever growing knowledge of the truth. The soul *knows Me and knows itself;* and from this follows that it honours Me but despises itself, which is humility. *My* visions and revelations thus make the soul more humble, as it gains a deeper and deeper knowledge of its own nothingness. The opposite is the case with the visions that come from the enemy. He is the father of lies and the prince of the proud, and his revelations are followed by a certain self-complacency and over-valuation of self, and the soul becomes puffed up and boastful. Thus thou canst always discern, whence the visions come, whether they are from the truth or from lies. For truth makes the soul humble, but falsehood makes it proud." [4]

After this teaching Catherine gave up herself without fear to communion with the supernatural. Tommaso della Fonte, who paid her frequent visits, always found her radiant and happy like a young bride, sometimes singing, sometimes praying. "On her tongue she had nothing but Jesus, in the street she walked with Jesus, her glance sought only Jesus, she had no thought for anything but that which could lead her to Jesus." [5] In the evening she could be heard weeping over her own sins and the sins of the world. Or she would have long conversations with her guests from the world beyond; she could then be heard talking in the cell, aloud, eagerly and long; then she would be silent, as though listening to an answer; after which she would talk again.

"Lord," she would then exclaim, "I do not wonder at all that human beings are what they are. Thou hast made an exception with me. Thou hast wounded me with Thy love and placed a guard about my purity. Ah, if only all the poor blinded and sensual human beings could but once taste of Thy love, I believe that they would be filled with loathing of their carnal joys and hasten to drink from the well of Thy sweetness! Lord, why dost Thou not draw them to Thyself?"

A few moments of silence, then Catherine spoke again.

"Eternal Truth, I understand Thee," she said. "If men rightly considered and meditated upon the vast benefits Thou dost bestow upon them daily, they could not but love Thee."

Yet Catherine's unrest and doubt do not yet seem to be satisfied, for again she asked:

"But why, Lord, *are* those souls so foolish, that they do not consider Thy benefits towards them?"

A short silence, and again the lonely voice:

"It is only too true, oh Eternal Truth! Their reason is dark and laid waste, and they *can not* feel Thy benefits and have no wish to know their benefactor."

That was the great question, which none of the great thinkers of Christendom has solved, the question of the relation between God's omnipotence and man's free will, God's love and man's everlasting perdition, the riddle of election by grace, on which Catherine pondered that night. *Why* are there vessels of honour and vessels of dishonour?

As though by a roundabout path Catherine tried to find a solution of the problem. "How can it be," she asked again, "that a man can not, even with the best will in the world, save himself, but that only, Thou, Lord, canst save him?"

But it was as though she was troubled at her own boldness and felt thrown to the ground by her own insignificance. "Thou needest not answer me, Lord!" she exclaimed directly after, "I know full well that I am worthy of hell, nay, that one hell is not enough to punish my infinite unworthiness. Everything in me of my own deserves in strictest justice everlasting hell!"

Yet there was salvation for all, there had been salvation for the great sinner of Magdala, for her, who was for Catherine the symbol of hope, the rainbow of the covenant in the sky of the wrath of God — *Qui Mariam absolvisti* — Thou didst forgive Mary, whom, then, wilt Thou not forgive?"

Yes, but — but then Mary Magdalene did love the Lord with a perfect love, never swerved from His footsteps, followed Him on the road of the Cross to Calvary and to the dark tomb. *Dic nobis Maria* — was it not so, Mary? You never turned round to look at Sodom burning behind you; you did not let the plough rest and look back at your sins. Ah, to be like Magdalene, to follow the Master in poverty, in contempt, in the cold, in storms, in need and at last on the thorny road to the death of a felon on the Cross! Overwhelmed by the waves of her feelings, almost swooning in her passion for the Crucified, Catherine exclaimed: "Oh, Eternal Love, oh Love that loved us first, oh abyss of God's love! Oh Heavenly Father, oh dearest Son of God, oh Thou Eternal Word, obedient unto death! Eternal Truth, Thou art Life; Thou art the door by which we must enter to become one with Thee!"

Then she returned to the question of a moment before.

"But as Thou, Lord, art the Way and the open Door, standing ready for all, why, then, do not all Thy children come in to Thee? Their will is wrong, but whence have they this wrong will?"

Again the problem is set. And now, at length, comes the answer from the lips of Jesus:

"I will reveal it to thee. I lead men by the good way. But when they have come half way they grow weary and disheartened, and sit down to rest in the soft bed of self-love, and will not hate themselves with a perfect hate. They perceive that if they keep hold of their first resolve, they must still for many years drag an intolerable burden, and they do not think they can persevere in exercising all the Christian virtues. This is cowardice and meanness, and if thou wouldst know the cause, it is that My love has grown cold in them, and it is that alone which makes My burden light and My yoke easy to bear."

Here Catherine might again have asked why, then, did not God give these tired wanderers and discouraged Christians new grace and new love, as after all it is God who works in us, both to will and to make perfect, and that "without Him we cannot do anything." One gladly yields to him whom one loves, and is content to accept his explanations, and Catherine loved Jesus. Suddenly she attacked the whole question from another angle.

"Yes, Lord," she said, "what Thou sayest is right. Thou art right, again and again Thou art right. When so many perish everlastingly it is altogether their own fault, and no one else's — no one's — it is because they blindly follow their own will and their weak inclinations. But I know now what I will do. I will take all our sins and transgressions, I will gather all our human wretchedness together and bind it in a great bundle, and I will carry all this terrible burden up before the foot of the throne of Thy infinite mercy!"

It was mercy for all, unconditional salvation for all, that Catherine was asking for. After a few moments of breathless listening she continued:

"But it is Thyself, Lord, who hast given me these requests and desires. Thou sayest that Thou canst not at present hear my prayer and not fulfil my importunate demands. And yet it is the goad of Thy grace that drives me on and compels me to cry to Thee!"

Catherine now received no answer any longer. As though dreading that she had gone too far she suddenly exclaimed: "Oh, rash soul, what art thou, that thou darest to lift up thy face against God! Miserable soul, what art thou, that God deigns to speak with thee, face to face? Tell me, Lord, who am I, what am I? Lord, tell me also, who and what art Thou?"

There was a burning silence in the little room, in which a human soul was wrestling with God. Then came the answer, slowly and solemnly repeated by Catherine: "Daughter, thou art she who *is not*. I am He who is." [6]

Night after night Catherine kept vigil thus in this Jacob's wrestling with God, in this prayer of Abraham for Sodom. The thought of the perdition of so many tormented her without ceasing. "I will, Lord, that Thou shouldst have *everything* and Thy enemy nothing!" she cried. . The mere existence of hell seemed to her a failure of God's cause, she wanted to "lay herself like a lid upon the entrance down to it," so that no one could get there — nay, she offered God to be for ever lost, if all others could thereby be saved! [7]

Her offer was not accepted, and again and again she had to be content with the old wisdom, that God's thoughts are not like our thoughts. We cannot see the work of the Eternal as a whole, we cannot penetrate His intentions and motives, therefore we cannot criticise Him. He is, Who is; and we are those who are not. He is Being, we are nothing. And can nothingness comprehend Being?

Henceforth this thought became the foundation of Catherine's conviction and guided her mode of life. She states it hundreds of times in her letters; we must "remain in the cell of self-knowledge and understand that we are not, but that all being is of God." [8]

"I am, Who am," those were the words of Jehovah to Moses. And "I am that which is not" — that was, according to the interpretation of the mediæval mystics the answer of John the Baptist, when the Jews asked him whether he was the Messiah. The simple "I am not He, whom you seek," was understood as a definition of the essence of humanity itself.[9] In the same way Raymond of Capua says: "Every creature has come into being from nothing, therefore it is always seeking to return to nothing. Of itself it can do nothing, and when it sins, it acts in accordance with its essence, for sin is a nothingness. All creatures have thus arisen from nothing, move towards nothing and in sin become nothing. For that which they work of their own power is nothing, as the Incarnate Truth says: 'Without Me ye can do *nothing.*' From which it can be clearly seen that in reality the creature does not exist at all." [10]

This profound consciousness of being nothing is the foundation of Catherine's spiritual life. All the *passive* virtues: humility, selflessness, frugality, abstemiousness, spring from this knowledge of self. How can pride find room in a soul which knows that it is nothing? How can it be proud of what it has achieved, when it knows in its inmost heart, that it does not exist at all? How can it despise others or envy others anything, when it finds itself of no value? How can it wish to own anything, when it knows that it does not even belong to itself but to the Creator? How can it seek pleasures of the senses, when its own nothingness is always present to it?

The *active* virtues, on the other hand, are born from the knowledge of God. "Who is so thoughtless and foolish [thus Raymond, interpreting Catherine's thought], that he does not willingly and gladly submit to Him from whom he has received everything? Who can do aught but love so great a benefactor, who gives us all things in abundance, and who has loved us before we came into being? Who must not fear to offend such a friend and to lose His favour? Who does not eagerly seek to obey Him, to listen reverently to His words, to obey gladly and willingly His commandments which are for our own good?"

Raymond writes somewhat rhetorically, yet he expresses Catherine's intention well enough. We know this from one of her own letters and from her book, *Dialogo*. We know it too, from a little book about Catherine written in 1376 by William Flete, the English Augustinian monk in Lecceto. "Our holy mother," says the English scholar, who was a disciple of the Sienese saint, "once told me that at the beginning of the conversion she made the knowledge of self the foundation stone of her whole life. This foundation stone she again distinguished in three lesser stones.

"The *first* stone was the contemplation of the Creator; that is, that she had nothing of herself, but depended wholly on God who had created her and still sustained her, and that He did this out of pure mercy and goodness. The *second* stone was the contemplation of the redemption: how the Saviour had regained for us with His blood the grace we had lost, and that He did this out of pure love which we had not deserved. The *third* stone was the contemplation of the sins which she had committed after her baptism, and of the goodness of God in not letting the earth open under her feet and hell swallow her up, as she had deserved.

"These three contemplations aroused in her so great a hatred of herself, that she desired nothing of her own will, but everything according to the will of God, for she understood that God willed nothing but her own good. Hence it followed that she welcomed all trials and temptations, both because it was God who sent her them, and because in this way she was punished and chastened as she deserved. She began to find great displeasure in the things which before had pleased her, and great pleasure in those which she had hitherto disliked, so that she fled from her mother's love, which until then had been a joy to her, but rejoiced in reproaches and abuse; and as a conclusion to all of it she said that self-love is a root of all evil and the ruin of all that is good." [11]

Catherine, however, included in self-love not only that which is commonly called egoism, but every natural feeling or inclination which was not subject to the will of God. In the gospel Jesus declares that "he who loves father or mother, wife and children *more* than Me is not worthy of Me." "Catherine," Raymond writes, "often spoke with me of what must be the mind of that soul which loves its Creator, and she said that such a soul neither sees nor loves nor remembers itself or any other creature. When I asked her to explain this to me she answered: 'The soul which sees its own nothingness, and that all good comes from the Creator and is in the Creator, gives up itself and all creatures and becomes wholly immersed in its Creator, and in all its actions it is directed by Him, and in no wise will it go outside Him in whom it has found every good and every happiness and joy. That love of God grows from day to day, so that the soul is conformed to God and cannot think or will or remember anything but God, and it does not remember itself or others except in God. Like one who dives into the sea and swims under the water, neither seeing nor feeling ought but the water of the sea and the things that are in the water, and outside the water seeing and feeling nothing and touching nothing, he can only see through the water the things which are outside it and not otherwise. This is the well-ordered and right love of self and of all creatures, which never goes nor leads astray because it desires nothing but God.'" [12] Or, as Catherine expresses it herself in one of her letters: "The fire of love alone consumes all self-love, the spiritual as well as the love of the senses, and *everything else that it finds in the soul, except the dear will of God.*" [13]

God was regarded by Catherine not only as the highest good, but also as the only good, and she expected to obtain all other good, either conditional or derived, from an uncompromising surrender to the will of God. First the kingdom of God and His justice, then all the rest would follow as a matter of course. "Do not forget Me, My daughter, then I will not forget thee," the Saviour said to her one day. "Do not be troubled, either for the salvation of thy soul, or for the needs of the body, for I know what thou needest and think of it all, and I will care for thee."

All other anxieties were, for Catherine, absorbed in the single one: the anxiety to please God. If only that was achieved, everything else would follow; if that one condition was fulfilled, everything would be fulfilled. "What does it concern you what is to happen to you?" she used, later on, to ask her disciples. "Do you not believe that Providence is always watching over you and caring for you?" This was not only something she said in the security of her cell, it was something she practised during the plague in Siena, during the rebellion in Florence, and on the voyage home from Avignon with her friends, when they were in danger at sea off Genoa. The disciples were in despair and thought they were going to perish, but Catherine remained calm and bade them go on saying their office, as if nothing were wrong. "We obeyed her," Raymond relates, "and the storm abated, and as we drew near to land we had reached the end of Matins and were running into harbour singing the *Te Deum*."

For Catherine, then, it was no mere figure of speech that not a sparrow falls to the ground without the will of the heavenly Father, nay, that even the very hairs of our heads are numbered. She saw traces of a father's hand in all exterior happenings, perceived in them a father's heart. "Whatever happens to you," she taught her disciples later, "never think that it comes from men, think that it comes from God and is for your good. And then see how you may profit by it." [14]

Attempts have been made to make Catherine of Siena, like Joan of Arc, a tool in the hands of ecclesiastics. Neither of them were that. Spiritually Catherine was not only far above her first confessor, the worthy and naïve Tommaso della Fonte, but also above her later spiritual guide, the highly cultivated Raymond of Capua. He, indeed, honestly admits Catherine's superiority. Another of her confessors, Bartolommeo de' Dominici, bears the same testimony. "There were some who thought that we friars had taught her. The opposite was the case." [15]

There is really no other possible explanation, then, that Catherine's wisdom was a fruit of spiritual introversion and of communion with God. For it is impossible to avoid God as a real and active influence in Catherine's life. The modern Immanentist will talk of "sub-consciousness" or of "the transcendental ego." In a Bull of Canonization, Pius II declared that Catherine's teaching "was not acquired, but infused from above." Master William Flete in Lecceto found the best expression, perhaps, when he said, in simple and beautiful words, that she was the instrument of the Holy Spirit — *Organum Spiritus Sancti.*

VIII

Towards the end of the three years Catherine entered upon a new stage of her life. A new world opened out before her: she learned to read. She had already long wished to acquire this art, not very common in her time. At church she constantly saw the missals and large breviaries from which the Dominicans read their prayers; probably there were also among the Mantellate more than one who possessed a prayer book and used it at the service in the Capella delle Volte. One of these Sisters, perhaps it was Alessia Saracini, of noble and therefore cultivated family, and the first to be mentioned as a friend of Catherine, procured for her an *A B C*, and in the solitude of her cell the young girl, now nearly twenty years old, began to teach herself the letters of the alphabet. She made but slow progress, and after fruitless efforts lasting many weeks it seemed to Catherine that she was no further. Then she turned in prayer to Jesus. "If it be Thy will, Lord, that I am to be able to read the Holy Office and sing Thy praise in church, then do Thou help me to do so. If it be not Thy will, I am ready to remain in the simplicity and ignorance in which I have lived hitherto." From that moment she made rapid progress and at length Catherine was able to read fluently. Yet often it was as though she rather guessed at what she was reading, "for," says Raymond, "when she was asked to spell what she had just read, she could not do so, nay, she hardly even recognised the letters." [1] This remark throws a light upon the whole character of Catherine's mental powers, which are wholly intuitive: she knew without being able to give a reason for her knowledge. All poetry, all psychological art, depends on this keen intuition, this deep insight into and perception of the truth, which nevertheless may be entirely lacking in the power to form or follow an argument. A great poet is rarely a keen thinker, which does not prevent the poet from perceiving that which is hidden from the thinker. Intuitive genius is also found among great inventors and discoverers and is very often allied to feeble powers of logic. Moreover, there are many who know how a foreign language, with which one has only an imperfect acquaintance, can at a critical moment become perfectly clear and familiar, even to such an extent that afterwards one has the impression of having been spoken to in one's own language.

In whatever way it happened, Catherine was now able to read and henceforth she spent many hours over books. Her letters show great knowledge of the Gospels and of the Epistles of Saint Paul. The ecstatic and mystic fourteenth Apostle was a man after Catherine's own heart; she generally mentions him as *il glorioso Pavolo* or *questo inamorato Pavolo*. Her favourite and constant reading, though, was above all the breviary. In its psalms and hymns and in its legends of saints her heart and spirit found constant new nourishment. There were certain prayers for which she had a predilection — thus the words with which each of the offices begin: "God, come to my aid, Lord, make haste to help me." "Often [says Caffarini] she would insert into her prayers the ejaculation: 'Lord, I have sinned, have mercy upon me.'" She was to repeat those words again and again upon her death-bed. At the head of her couch she had a little tablet with the text: "Give light unto my eyes, that I may not fall asleep in death, and that my enemy may not say: I won the victory." She knew what it was to fight against "the enemy." [2]

In the breviary she made acquaintance with the inhabitants of heaven, all the great departed Christians, the holy virgins and martyrs who were already standing in white robes before the throne of the Lamb on the further side of the river of death: Saint Margaret, Saint Agnes, Saint Agatha, Saint Lucy . . . "I have found a new and very beautiful light," says Catherine in one of her letters, playing upon the likeness between *luce* (light) and Lucia, "and that is the dear Roman maiden Lucia, who gives us light. And we will pray to the most lovable and loving Magdalene for the deep hatred of ourselves that she felt. Agnes, who is a lamb [*agnello* — again a play upon words] in meekness and gentleness will grant us humility. Thus Lucia will give us light, Magdalene hatred of self and love of God, and Agnes the oil of humility for our lamps." [3]

This reading reappears in her visions, for the visions continued. The heavenly visitants did not only come to her now in the solitude of her cell and in the falling dusk in the garden on the roof, but also in the street and in the church. One day when she was sad Saint Dominic walked by her side on her return from church, comforting and encouraging her, "and it made me so happy," Catherine afterwards confided to her confessor, "that I would gladly have died at the same moment so that I might have gone at once with Saint Dominic into everlasting blessedness." On another day she was praying a long while in the church of San Domenico "and was thinking of Jesus Christ and the mysteries of His holy manhood." Then, suddenly, her soul was filled with a great brightness and it became so clearly obvious to her, that in Jesus there was something other and more than mere humanity. She saw that the essence of His being was a fulness of love, of goodness, of gentleness, of sweetness, of bliss, and it made her sad that she could not find words to tell what she had seen, and that it was impossible for her to express "the beauty and majesty of the countenance of God," but that she had to be content with the short, meagre words: "He is everything good, He is the true and highest good." It is no wonder that Catherine said one day to Father Tommaso: "It is not possible for me to speak with mortal men, for I feel all the time that my Saviour is drawing me to Himself." When with others her manner would be absent-minded, nay, she could be like one intoxicated. Often she had the feeling of hovering in the air, as in her childhood, in the cave outside the town; often she wandered with closed eyes as if walking in her sleep, and yet she never struck her foot against a stone for the Lord walked by her side, aways invisible, yet many times also visible, as on that happy day, when she walked to and fro in the church saying her office, and felt that someone was walking by her side — and·it was Jesus! Like two young ecclesiastics saying their office together, the Saviour and Catherine walked up and down the brick floor of the chapel, and with great diligence and unspeakable awe the young woman spoke the Latin words (hardly hearing them, because of the loud beating of her heart), and when, at the end of each psalm, she had to say the doxology: "Glory be to the Father and to the Son," etc., she altered the words and making a deep reverence towards the Lord, said in a trembling voice: "Glory be to the Father and to *Thee* and to the Holy Ghost. As it was in the beginning, is now and ever shall be, world without end. Amen." [4]

Catherine loved Jesus with all a woman's need of complete surrender. A man can love Jesus as a dear friend — the best friend of all — as an elder brother, as a loved father whom he would not for all the world displease. But a woman loves Jesus as her Bridegroom, as one to whom she would belong altogether: "Here I am, take me, do with me what Thou wilt!" "Thou knowest that thou art a bride," Catherine once wrote to a nun in Pisa, "and that He has betrothed Himself to thee, not with a ring of silver, but with a ring of His holy flesh, for when He was circumcised, just so much as a ring was taken from His holy body." [5]

Catherine knew what earthly love was, and she speaks of it with the most perfect simplicity and the most perfect purity. "Man can not live without love," she says in one of her letters, "for it is through love that man has come into being. Love made the father and mother give the child being and life." [6]

This love between man and woman is for Catherine, as for Saint Paul, the symbol of the highest love, of "the great sacrament," the marriage between Christ and the Church, between Jesus and the soul.[7] The object of this union is, as in ideal marriage, a harmony of souls, a unity of wills, which at last transforms the one who loves into the likeness of the beloved, gives the Church more and more of the mind of Jesus and conforms the Christian more and more to Christ.

This love, too, has its beginning and its consummation, its kisses, its embraces, its betrothal, its wedding. Therefore the Canticle, the Song of Solomon, is included among the holy books of the Church, and therefore Lacordaire could say: "There are not two kinds of love, there is only one. The heavenly love is the same feeling as the earthly one; only its object is infinite." If for that reason anyone wants to speak of "suppressed sensuality," we answer that those who are scandalised at the "suppressed" sensuality are generally those who have no objection to the unbridled one.

Catherine read the Song of Songs with all her deep and rich woman's heart and again and again she repeated the sigh of Sulamith: "May he kiss me with the kiss of his mouth." As yet she did not dare to ask for more, did not dare to repeat the ardent desires: "His left hand is under my head, his right hand doth embrace me." But she dared to long for the kiss which the bridegroom gives his betrothed bride.

"One day when Catherine," Caffarini relates, "was praying in her cell and could not grow weary of repeating the bride's sigh of love in the Canticle, Jesus appeared to her and bestowed upon her a kiss which filled her with unutterable sweetness. Then she dared to ask Him to teach her what to do that she might never, not for one moment, become unfaithful to Him, but always to be His own in heart and soul and mind."

The purely ethical essence of mystic love is here clearly expressed. We are told further: "At times it was as though she rested in the arm of Jesus, or that He pressed her close to His heart. And she was found worthy of this because she desired nothing but the riches of the grace of God and despised altogether the mean joys of this world. . . But above all she prayed to God to grant her true and sincere love of her neighbour — a love so perfect that henceforth she would rejoice more over the good estate of her neighbour than over her own and grieve more over the sufferings and sorrows of her neighbour than over her own griefs." [8] At such moments she would beseech the Lord to betroth her to himself in the faith.

It came then, that day of supersensual betrothal for which Catherine Benincasa had waited so long. It was on Shrove Tuesday in the year 1367, the last day of the Carnival, *mardi gras* . . . Siena was at the height of the Carnival uproar, the streets were crowded with masqueraders, everywhere there were shouts and laughter, singing and lute-playing, sparkling eyes and bold kisses. The Sienese knew how to enjoy themselves — in the Via Garibaldi, opposite Via Magenta, la Consuma can still be seen, the house in which the gilded youth of the city, the "spendthrift brigade," were wont to hold their feasts, and where these devotees of the "gay science" wasted two hundred thousand gold florins in the course of only twenty months. "Were there ever more extravagant people than the Sienese?" asks Dante, scandalised. And he knew them — he had been present at their *palio*, the great summer festival; he had sat at their gorgeous festival banquets and tasted their numerous dainty dishes: game stuffed with cloves and much other ungodly gluttony.[9]

The tumult of the Carnival, however, did not reach the dark and lonely room in the Vicolo del Tiratoio. Catherine was alone in the house, all the others were out enjoying themselves.[10] Perhaps the young girl felt in her solitude something of what less steadfast Christians are so familiar with: the sudden perception that all the world of faith seems to fade, grows pale, like the flames of candles in the light of the sun, shrinks up, grows unreal and unreasonable, when compared with the warm and strong realities of palpable life. "May He kiss me with His lips!" Yes, but out there in the street, twenty paces away, in the midst of the carnival rioting, there is one who puts his arm round your waist without any further fuss, with whom you can dance all night, who will offer you sweet Orvieto wine or foaming Asti and who kisses you at once and eagerly and as often as you like, and at daybreak you will bid him goodbye, with tear-filled eyes and your arm round his neck, and a last kiss as thanks and in farewell — and never to meet again. . .

Perhaps this was, once more and for the last time, Catherine's temptation. We do not know, we only know that on that day of Carnival she prayed without ceasing: "Lord, increase my faith!"

All Christian life, all self-denial, all work of charity and love depends on faith, hangs from it as the globe of the earth and all the gods of Olympus hung in the chain which Zeus held in his almighty hand. For what does it avail me that it is *beautiful* to be a Christian, that it is good to be a Christian, if Christianity is not *true?* Here neither æstheticism nor pragmatism is of any use. If the Word has not become flesh, if the Virgin has not borne the Child, then let the ringing of the Angelus bells be never so lovely when the sky is golden behind the black cypresses of Italy — those bells must be silent, or they must become a mere sound of Nature — like the singing of birds or the soughing of the wind among the leaves of the olive trees! Truth is the most precious possession of humankind, and no one has the right to betray it for the sake of a poetical mood. We dare not imitate those pagan orators and poets who, during the last centuries of antiquity, raved poetically about the deserted temples. Nor do we dare to think like those kings and emperors who thought that religion was useful for the people and ought to be maintained. Nothing but the truth is of any use either to you or me or the people! Christ has therefore asserted most emphatically that He is the Truth. If He were not, how, then, could He save us? No perfect Christian life is possible without a perfect conviction of this. At all decisive moments, at the parting of the ways, at the turning points, doubt will otherwise arise: "Is it true after all, what I believe, so that I do not risk anything by acting upon it?" If you take your stand on a half-belief you cannot act with conviction.

"But the Lord," says Caffarini, "had resolved to use Catherine as an instrument for the salvation of many erring souls." She had therefore to be firmly and unshakably fixed in the faith, like the house on the rock. And therefore Catherine prayed without ceasing on that Shrove Tuesday: "Lord, grant me a perfect faith!"

Catherine prayed and her prayer was heard. It came in this wise:

"Because thou hast out of love of Me renounced all worldly joys and desirest to rejoice in Me alone," said the Lord, "I have now resolved, solemnly to keep My betrothal with thee and to take thee for My bride in the faith."

And behold, while the Lord was speaking, there were with Him His most Holy Mother Mary, the holy evangelist John, Saint Paul, Saint Dominic and the prophet David with his harp. And Mary joined the hands of her Son and of Catherine, while David made music thereto with his harp. And Jesus took a golden ring and put it on the finger of His bride. "I, thy Creator and thy Saviour," He said, "betroth Myself to thee. I grant thee a faith which shall never fail, but thou shalt preserve it whole and intact until our espousals shall one day be solemnised in heaven. Fear nothing; thou art shielded with the armour of faith and shalt prevail over all thy enemies."

Then the heavenly light was extinguished, the glorious visitants vanished with the last dying echo from the harp of David. But in the gloom of the cell the betrothal ring gleamed on Catherine's finger; she pressed it to her lips and gazed intently upon it. It was a gold ring and it was set with a large diamond among four small pearls — "the hard diamond of truth, which nothing can scratch," she understood it to mean, "and pearly clear purity in mind and thought, in word and deed."

Catherine always wore her betrothal ring, but no one but herself could see it. Nay, even she did not always see it; often it seemed to become indistinct or disappear altogether. That was when she had in some way offended her Lord and heavenly Betrothed, by a hasty word, an unkind thought, a thoughtless glance at something that was of the world. Then she would weep at her disloyalty and confess her sin, and when she came out again from the confessional the gold and the diamond and pearls shone plainly again on her hand." [11]

BOOK II

THE IMITATION OF CHRIST

> Gebildet werden mit Christo. — *Suso.*
> Io sono il fuoco, voi le faville. — *Christ to Catherine.*

I

"The city that is set upon a hill cannot be hid." If there is any place in which one is constantly reminded of these words of Jesus, it is in the country around Siena. Among the fertile hills north of the town, from the parapet of Belcaro above the wood of sessile oaks, in the barren, cracked desert land, which stretches its yellowish-red waves southwards to the blue heights of Mont' Oliveto, Santa Fiore and Mont' Amiata — everywhere near and far, Siena can be seen on the top of her three hills; Siena with the faintly blue dome of the cathedral, and the black-and-white striped marble campanile; Siena with the towers on Servi and San Francesco, on Carmine and San Domenico; Siena with the Torre del Mangia rising like a reddish stalk with a white stone flower at a dizzying height in the blue sky.

"A city that is set upon a hill cannot be hid."

As it is with the town so it was with its greatest daughter, Catherine of Fontebranda. In old legends we are often told how light pierces through all the cracks in the door of such and such a saint's cell; it is not the light of lamps or candles, but bright rays of a supernatural light, issuing from the heart of the saint and wanting to spread across the world and put darkness to flight. That light had shone from Giovanni Colombini's room in Via di Città, and now it was lit in Catherine's cell in Via dei Tintori.

At first the light was diffused in the house of Giacomo Benincasa. Raymond says with some wit that the Saviour, who before had appeared to Catherine in the cell, was now standing outside the door and asking her to open it, not so that *He* might come in, but that *she* might go out. And when Catherine, like the bride in the Canticle, answered: "I have put off all worldly cares, must I now put them on again? I have washed the dust of the earth from off my feet, must I now defile them?" then the Saviour taught her that there are *two* commandments in the Law — love of God and love of one's neighbour. "I will therefore, that thou fulfil both these commandments, that thou walk in the way with both thy feet, that thou fly to heaven on two wings. Hast thou forgotten quite thy zeal for the salvation of souls? Dost thou not remember that thou wouldst clothe thyself in a man's garments and become a friar preacher in strange lands? Thou hast now obtained the habit thou didst once desire. Why, then, dost thou shrink, why dost thou complain? I do but desire to lead thee to the calling that thou hast laboured to attain to since thy childhood."

Yet Catherine still made resistance. "I am but a woman," she pleaded, "and I am ignorant. What can I do?"

"In my sight," said the Saviour, "there is not man nor woman, not learned nor unlearned. But know that in these last times the pride of the so-called learned and wise has risen to such heights that I have resolved to humble them. I will therefore send unlearned men, full of divine wisdom, and women who will put to shame the learning that men think they have. And I have resolved to send thee also out into the world, and wheresoever thou shalt go I will be with thee and never leave thee, and I will guide thee in all that thou must do."

Then Catherine bent her head and her heart was filled with obedience: "Behold, I am the handmaid of the Lord." Then Jesus, as was His wont, said the office with her, but when the bell rang for the midday meal, He said: "Thy father and mother are now sitting down to their meal. Go up to them and come back to Me afterwards."

Henceforth Catherine spent her time among her relatives and took her share of the work of the house. "Now when that gentle maiden," says Caffarini, "saw that it was the will of her Bridegroom that she should live among her fellows, she resolved to live in such manner that she might serve them as an example."

Above all she began to serve the others. Not as before, under compulsion, but of her own free will, did she perform a servant's work in the house. When all the family had gone to bed she made a round of the house, collected all the soiled linen and spent the whole night at the wash tub. Once the maidservant fell ill and Catherine did all the work alone. She kneaded dough and baked bread and she carried out her work with such ease that there were some who thought they saw the Blessed Virgin standing beside her and helping her.[1]

As time went on the Benincasa household had grown very

large. The children grew up, grandchildren ran up and down the stairs, as Stefano and Catherine in bygone days had done. Catherine was a kind aunt, like all Italian women she loved children. "If it were seemly," she would say, "I should do nothing but kiss them!" [2]

She conceived a particular affection for her sister-in-law, Lisa Colombini, the wife of Bartolommeo, "my sister-in-law according to the flesh, but my sister in Christ," she used to call her.[3] Lisa had become a Mantellata as early as 1352 and two of her daughters became nuns in the Dominican convent of Santa Agnese in Montepulciano. Later on Lisa accompanied Catherine on her journeys and told Raymond of Capua many things about her. She it was, for instance, who first discovered that her sister-in-law was gifted with second sight, Lisa having one morning been to confession and made a general confession, of which no one knew anything and the confession taking place in a remote corner of a distant church. But when she came back Catherine met her with a smile, saying: "Now Lisa, you have indeed become a good girl!" When the sister-in-law questioned Catherine, the latter gave her to understand that she knew everything and ended by saying: "For what you have done this morning I love you with all my soul, and I shall always love you."

On another occasion Catherine had less cause for joy in what she saw in this way. It was in the evening and she had just said night prayers, when suddenly she became aware of an intolerably rotten stench about her. It was that peculiar unpleasant smell by which sin usually made its presence known to her, and by which she later was nearly suffocated at the papal court in Avignon. And now, in the distance, she saw one of her younger brothers in the act of committing a great sin. Catherine awaited his return home and went to meet the youth with the words: "I know where you have been and how you have defiled your soul."

Was it this brother, or was it another one, who later on left home to try his fortune as a soldier? In any case he fared but miserably, at last he lay, wounded, ill and alone, in a foreign country and thinking he was going to die. Catherine's farsight, though, was watching over him, her intercession was heard, and one day he stood like the prodigal son at the door of his home. Perhaps it was at that homecoming, when they were all gathered about the fatted calf, that Catherine saw Jesus sitting at the head of the table and giving them His blessing? [4]

Catherine's confessor, too, Tommaso della Fonte, the friend of her childhood, had experience of her gifts as a seer. Once when she was lying ill, he came up one morning to see her. "Father," she said suddenly, "what were you doing at three o'clock * last night?" "Why, what should I be doing?" exclaimed the Dominican. "Ah, you won't tell me, but I know, you were writing!" "No," was the answer, "I was not writing!" "That is true," exclaimed Catherine, "you were not writing, but you were dictating to someone else." The Dominican had to admit this. "But *what* was I dictating?" he asked. Catherine was silent a while, then she said slowly: "You were writing down the marks of His grace, which God in His mercy has seen good to bestow upon this His unprofitable handmaid." [5]

Slowly the circle around Catherine began to widen. The monk who had that evening served Tommaso della Fonte as secretary, was called Bartolommeo de' Dominici, and soon Father Tommaso took him with him on one of his visits to his childhood's friend. He became a frequent guest in Catherine's little cell, "and when I first began to visit her," he relates himself, "she was young and her countenance was gentle and gay. I was young too, yet in her presence I never felt the embarrassment that I should have felt in the company of another young woman of her age. Nay, the more I talked with her, the more completely was all earthly passion quenched in my breast." [6]

Bartolommeo de' Dominici seems to have had certain doubts as to Catherine's ability to see distant things and put her to the the test, but she passed it. She told him, among other things, that on the preceding evening he had sat with three other friars in the sub-prior's cell, mentioned the names of those present and gave him the subject of their talk. Then she added: "I always watch and pray for you until the bell in your monastery rings for matins. And if you had good eyes, you would be

* *Tre ore di notte*, according to old Italian reckoning of time, is our 8 o'clock in the evening.

THE IMITATION OF CHRIST

able to see me, just as I see you, each one, where you are and what you are doing!" [7]

In common with all Tuscans, Catherine had a great love of flowers. Even at the present day the great church festivals in Tuscany are also flower festivals. In the smallest village the roads by which the procession on the feast of Corpus Christi is to pass, are, as it were, paved with flowers and the brick floor of the church is completely hidden under a brilliant floral mosaic: the gold of gorse, the blood red of poppies on a green ground of box and with a dainty border of laurel leaves laid in layers like tiles. When the *contradas* of Siena keep the feast of their patron saint, posies of flowers are blessed and distributed during Mass. And in Florence on the feast of San Zenobio the peasants stand, on the dewy May morning, on the steps of the cathedral with large baskets full of red roses, and everyone who goes in, buys a bunch. There are roses on all the altars and their pure and cool fragrance fills the whole of the lofty Duomo — *Santa Maria dei Fiori, Santa Maria delle Rose*. . .

Catherine had the same flower-loving spirit. In her day-dreams she beheld angels descending with wreaths of lilies of Paradise and placing them upon her head. And when she walked alone in her garden on the roof of the house, she would, while singing softly, bind little posies, mostly in the form of a cross, and send them by Father Tommaso to pious men and women as a greeting from a sister in Christ.[8]

Among those who received Catherine's floral greetings there was one who was to become one of her most zealous disciples and tireless apostles — Tommaso d'Antonio Nacci Caffarini. He was two years younger than Catherine and like Tommaso della Fonte and Bartolommeo de' Dominici a Dominican in the monastery at Camporeggio. He made her personal acquaintance about 1366, sat at table with her in the dyer's home, ate of the bread which she had baked herself (and kept a piece of it as if it had been a relic), listened to her when in the ardour of her enthusiasm she quite forgot to eat and talked of God instead. Often he too visited her in her cell, saw her in ecstasy behold the supernatural and heard her pray "as though with the tongue of Saint Augustine." But during the ecstasy Catherine would sometimes laugh softly and happily, sometimes the tears would well up and fill her long black eyelashes, at last she wept and laughed at the same time. When she came to herself again it was with a gentle and smiling face.[9]

For Catherine's ecstasies continued, in spite of the demands of practical life. They were no fruit of her secluded existence, they throve very well too in the kitchen and larder. Too well even: one day Lisa was shocked to find that her sister-in-law had fallen on to the glowing embers on the hearth; she had been rapt in ecstasy while turning the spit. Fortunately Catherine had not taken any harm — as little as she had felt anything one day in church when a lighted candle fell down from its candlestick and lay burning upon her head.[10]

Naturally the rumour of these extraordinary happenings got abroad and Catherine became the object of a growing curiosity. Greater and greater was the number of those who at the intervention of Father Tommaso tried to get a sight of her, and if possible in ecstasy of course. The Dominican Niccolò di Bindo da Cascina came all the way from Pisa and had the good fortune to see Catherine not only in a state of ecstasy but even (we are assured by Caffarini) hovering several inches above the floor in the cell. Father Niccolò made bold to touch one of the saint's hands with only the tip of his finger, and more than a day and a night after, his hand still smelt wondrously sweet, and the fragrance refreshed not only his senses but also his soul.[11]

Meanwhile it was not only the monks who gathered in admiration about Catherine, women also approached her, and chief among them the Mantellata. Her kinswoman Lisa has already been mentioned; next to her come Alessia Saracini and Francesca Gori as Catherine's earliest friends. Alessia in particular became Catherine's confidante, and many are the letters written by the hand of the noble lady for the dyer's daughter, who in her childhood had not learned to write any more than to read. Both Alessia and Francesca (*Cecca*, as she was generally called) were widows, the latter being elderly and having three sons in the Dominican order. Other friends of about this time are Caterina di Ghetto, Giovanna di Capo, Caterina della Spedaluccio.

From the very first the relations between Catherine and these

THE IMITATION OF CHRIST

younger and older friends were such that they involuntarily bowed before her. Although she was no doubt the youngest of them all they honoured her with the name of *madre,* or soon with the more intimate and affectionate *mamma.*

To these friends Catherine often confided her visions and experiences. One day two of them were having a meal with her, the low bench on which she slept at night serving as a table. "This is indeed a holy table," said one of the friends in jest. "Yes," Catherine replied, "if you knew Who has sat here!" And she told them about the visit of Jesus and Mary Magdalene.

Now and then the friends would make an excursion beyond the walls of the town, and the goal of their walk would then be the old Benedictine abbey of Sant' Abbondio e Sant' Abbondanzio, commonly called *Santa Bonda.*

Only a few years before Giovanni Colombini (d. 1367) had been a frequent visitor there. The abbess, Monna Paola di Ser Gino Foresi, had been his close friend; his only daughter Angiolina was a nun there; he was himself buried in the convent church. His letters to Monna Paola were the greatest treasure of the abbey, and were read and meditated upon, after his death too. His kinswoman, Catherine's namesake, Lisa Benincasa's cousin, was abbess in the new convent for sisters of Colombini's order at Porta San Sano.

Catherine never made the personal acquaintance of her great predecessor. His period of activity was so short (only twelve years), his sphere of action mostly outside Siena (Arezzo, Città di Castello, Lucca, Pisa, Montichiello, etc.), and his death occurred before Catherine had yet emerged from her obscurity. It is certain, though, that she had heard the story of his life, heard his letters read and joined in singing his Laudae. In Santa Bonda she would be overshadowed by his spirit. And indeed it is as though one already heard Catherine, when reading lines like these in one of Colombini's letters to Monna Paola:

"A true and holy love is the only thing our sweetest Lord Jesus Christ asks of us. And who will refuse it to Him? He is so good that for the sake of His goodness we must love Him ardently and earnestly. Oh, dearest Mother in Jesus Christ, I leave you my last will, my most earnest wish, I make my testament, I write down my heart,* which is love of Jesus Christ . . . Love did that Holy Father bequeath to us, love was His testament. Whoso would take up the inheritance must keep the testament. If anyone seek love, then seek Christ, if anyone would love, then love Christ. Be wise and loose yourselves from all bonds, let not yourselves be ensnared in any ties, not even under the appearance of obtaining something good. Woe to us if we drive away Christ and his holiest gift! But he who does not loose himself from everything, binds himself and drives away Christ." [12]

* *Scrivovi il cuor mio.*

II

In the book which Catherine wrote towards the end of her youth (which was also the end of her life), and in which, like Colombini, she "wrote down her heart," the Lord, in reply to the question of His bride, said: "The soul that loves Me in truth, also loves her neighbour, and when she does not love her neighbour, her love is not true. For love of Me and love of one's neighbour is one and the same thing, and so much as a soul loves Me, so much more will she love her neighbour. . . This is the means I have given you to work and prove your love for Me. You can not do anything for Me, but you can serve and help your neighbour. . . And the soul that loves Me in truth will never weary of working for the whole world, for all and for each." [1]

Long before Catherine, however, Siena had understood this evangelical teaching: "Whatsoever ye have done unto the least of My brethren ye have done unto Me." As early as in 1186 mention is made in a papal bull of the large hospital Santa Maria della Scala, which the republic had built opposite the cathedral and which comprised an infirmary, a home for foundlings as well as a hostel for pilgrims. Besides this the hospital distributed food to the poor of the town. And the means for all this, like the service within these walls of charity, were not contributed by the State or the municipality, and was not performed by paid male nurses, but by a voluntary brotherhood, the members of which simply *gave themselves and all that they possessed to serve the sick and the poor.*[2]

This is genuinely mediæval. And it is well worth while to dwell a little on the rules of this great old hospital, dating from the year 1305, which have been preserved for us.

"In the name of God, Amen. Glory be to God and praise to the honour of His Mother, Our Lady the Blessed Virgin with all the saints, men and women, to the honour and exaltation of the Holy Roman Church, likewise for the good and peaceful estate and prosperity of the hospital of Our Lady of Siena, which is over against the chief church of the said city, and for the Rector and Brethren and the chapter in the said hospital, and for the refreshment of the sick and poor and the foundlings in this hospital:

"These ordinances, resolutions, rules and regulations, are composed, ordered and ratified by the Rector and Brethren in the said hospital, according to which the Brethren as well as the Sisters shall live their lives."

As the first and foremost duty stress is laid on "loving and honouring Siena," on "serving Siena with all their strength and in no wise to defraud the town of Siena for the sake of the said Hospital." The love of country, of the great common cause, is placed before and above all other interests, even those of the sick and poor.[3]

Then come the other ordinances, which together form a complete monastic rule. One chapter deals with the hour at which the brethren are to rise, and ordains that they are all to come to Mass in the chapel of the hospital and be there at latest "before the Body of Our Lord Jesus Christ is lifted up at the Mass." "And if any brother fails to do this and has no valid excuse, he shall on that day have naught to eat but bread and wine, and that he shall eat in the refectory with the other brethren, and he shall not be suffered to eat by himself elsewhere." The brethren are likewise under obligation to take part in evensong and compline.

Besides the bell for prayers there is another bell in the hospital and when it rings "all the brethren shall wait upon the sick and bring them food," and "each brother shall carry upon him a knife without a point wherewith to cut bread and other food for the sick."

When the sick people have eaten the Brethren shall eat, the Rector presiding at their meals, and no one shall speak but a book shall be read aloud, and without a valid reason no one may eat elsewhere in the hospital, "neither in the dormitory, nor in any cell nor in the kitchen . . . and the cook and his helpers are bound to make known to the Rector all those who eat and drink in the kitchen, albeit they are themselves excepted."

No brother may receive gifts without the leave of the Rector, for there must be no distinction and in the refectory "all shall eat and drink the same."

A series of chapters deal with the officials of the hospital: besides the Rector there are two stewards, among whose duties is that of laying the table and keeping the dining-rooms in order; there is the Vice-Rector who has to settle all urgent matters during his absence; there is an infirmarian, whose task it is to procure and maintain all that is necessary "to remove disease and regain health," and a *"pelegriniero,"* who receives the sick on their admission and supervises the good conduct of the servants "so that the poor folk and the sick are well served." Finally there is the *camerlengo,* the treasurer, and his secretary, the clerk, upon whom rests the duty of "writing all amounts of income by themselves in one book, and all expenses separately in another book." Once a month the *camerlengo* places the accounts before the *Chapter,* which is composed of all the Brethren under the presidency of the Rector, and they settle all matters of doubt by vote. There are of course several other minor offices under these greater and more essential ones, e.g. "the Brother who is elected and appointed to receive all the grass and corn, and all the green stuff used in the hospital and keep it well in the barns of the hospital. . . And he shall write down whence that corn or grass or that green stuff has come, and the names of those who have brought it . . ."[4]

"Every year on the feast of All Saints shall be read aloud in the Chapter from that book, so that the Rector and the Brethren may know who have brought the grass and green stuff during that year. . . The said barn shall be locked with two locks and two keys, the one not like to the other, so that the one lock cannot be opened with the key to the other, neither can it be locked, and two of the hospital brethren shall be chosen, and each of them shall carry one of the two keys. And one of the said two brethren cannot without the other take out or measure of the said corn or hay or green stuff, but they shall both together measure and take out the corn or hay according to the needs of the hospital. And all that they take out or cause to be taken out that they shall cause to be written in the book which is kept by the *camerlengo* in his room as hath been said above."

The same touching attention to detail is found in the rules for the use of the hospital flour, for the baking of bread, the care of the animals belonging to the hospital, viz., the horses and mules and asses and the servants who attend to them and drive them, that there is no lack of "saddles or reins or bridles or shoes." The reading of these numerous and thorough regulations gives one an insight into a simple and substantial world in which everything is thorough and genuine, and which is so far removed from the advertisement and imitation of the present day, and from its hollowness and superficiality.

Meanwhile the spiritual needs are not forgotten in the bodily ones. "All the priests who are housed in the said hospital are requested in charity by the Rector and the Brethren to attend to the confession of the sick and to give them absolution and penance. . . And the said priests shall be bound to give the sick the Body of Our Lord Jesus Christ and all the sacraments of Holy Church when asked to do so and it seemeth right to them. And in all these things the priests must use care and watchfulness. Likewise the nurses attending to the sick and the servants must have a care to tell the sick to confess their sins and receive the sacraments of the Church."

It can be said that in the sixty-one chapters of which the statutes consist everything has been thought of, from "bestowing shelter and well-being on the aged poor in the town and country round Siena," right on to forbidding the Brethren to eat or drink outside the hospital, nay, they may not even sit down when they are "in a layman's house," but must perform their errand standing. Nor may they leave the hospital without the permission of the Rector, "though they may walk as far as to Viviano d'Arrigo's house and to Chele del Travale's house and to the Cathedral." The brethren and sisters had separate dwellings and no brother could enter the house of the Sisters without permission from the Rector, the priest Ugo excepted. Nor was any brother allowed to enter the women's ward of the hospital, "except that Brother Lupo can be permitted to visit his daughter." [5]

The hospital of La Scala is still standing in Siena. Its Gothic façade, half brick, half hewn stone, forms one side of that wonderful cathedral square, which in its peace and quiet is like the large courtyard of a monastery. Here and there too, in the streets of the town, you will find houses with the emblem of the hospital above the door: a ladder (*scala*) surmounted by a cross. Still untouched stands the old vaulted hall where the pilgrims had their quarters at night, and where the frescoes of Domenico Bartoli, painted in 1440, take us straight into life as it was lived five centuries ago.

Here then, you see the hospital brethren distributing bread to the poor and to pilgrims, the latter recognisable by the mussel shell fastened to their cloaks; cripples limping away after receiving their share; an entirely naked man is clothed; a woman carrying a child on her arm and holding another by the hand, receives provisions; a brother returns home with foundling children in a basket on his back. In another place orphan girls are being given in marriage, their outfit being provided by the hospital. One of the frescoes shows a ward in which the sick are tended. In the middle of the picture sits a man almost naked on a cushion-covered bench; on his right leg there is a deep ugly-looking wound. His attendants are busy washing his feet, an elderly man with a clear-cut, refined face is kneeling before the sick man and drying his left foot. Other learned gentlemen, no less then half-a-dozen, are eagerly and anxiously questioning the patient or consulting each other about the case. A little to the right there is another patient, lying in bed. His head is bandaged, his face sallow and partly covered with a stubbly growth of beard; the coverlet, striped red and yellow, is drawn right up to the ears. The patient seems to have just received the last sacraments; at any rate an Augustinian Father, standing with one foot resting on a bench by the bed, is putting a book back into its case. Above the head of the bed there is a shelf with little boxes of medicine and clear bottles, in the foreground can be seen a metal washstand with clean towels, white with black ornaments. Two servants, the first with keys hanging from his belt, are carrying a tray on which is something that is covered, probably food for the sick.

On the left of the fresco, behind the bench on which the wounded man is sitting, can be seen one half of a bed. A hospital nurse dressed in white and wearing a square cap on her head, is slowly and carefully laying a patient down. Two physicians are standing beside the bed, one is handing the other a glass containing urine for his inspection.

The walls of the room seem to be covered with grey fur.

Through a handsome grille of wrought iron can be seen another room in which the white profiles of physicians are bent over sick-beds or gathered in consultation. The whole picture gives a rich and almost festive impression; one sees that no effort has been spared to make everything as comfortable and pleasant as possible for the patients. In 1840 few towns in all the civilised world had a municipal hospital which could compare with that of Siena in 1440.

Moreover La Scala was not the only hospital in the city. In the story of Giovanni Colombini we are told how his wife and his friend, Francesco Vincenti, seek him, first at "the large hospital," then at several others, finding him at last in "a poor and out-of-the-way hospital, where the patients (not very hygienically) are being served with polenta." [6] The Mantellata worked as nurses in the hospital at Camporeggi; outside the town stood the leper hospital of San Lazzaro. Caring for the sick and poor was an old-established Christian custom in Siena.

Catherine followed the traditions of her native town. Caffarini relates that one day she saw from the window of her room a poor, miserable man lying asleep half naked at the street corner. The piteous sight touched her, but as it was just at the time for her prayers she withdrew from the window and began to say her office. But between the black lines of the psalms and the little pictures of saints on the golden ground of the initial letters she still saw the poor man lying so miserably outside on the bare stones, and at last she could not bear it any longer. She closed the book, went up to the kitchen for a loaf and stole out at the back door to lay it unnoticed beside the sleeping man's head, so that he might find it there when he awoke, as if it had been brought by angels. The man had awakened meanwhile, however, when Catherine came out, and he asked her whether she had any cast-off clothes he could have. At first Catherine was at a loss, but as she expressed it later on a similar occasion, she would "rather be without a cloak than without love for her neighbour," and then she gave the poor man her *"mantello,"* the black cloak of her order, which she was so proud and pleased to possess. But at night Jesus appeared to her and said: "Daughter, thou hast clothed and covered My nakedness, I will therefore now clothe thee with the fulness of

My grace." From that hour Catherine never felt the cold any more, even in the most severe winter she could be quite lightly clad.[7] And the winter can be severe in Siena; I write these lines on a day in January and it is freezing five or six degrees; people are going about in furs or with big woollen scarves about their throats and heads.

Quite a number of incidents like these are told of Catherine. Once a beggar came to her in church, and as she had nothing else she gave him the little silver cross hanging from her rosary. Again Jesus appeared to her in a nocturnal vision, holding the cross in His hand, but now it was much more beautiful and shining with jewels. "These jewels," said the Lord, "signify the love wherewith thou didst bestow thy cross upon Me, and I promise thee, that on the Last Day, when the sign of the Son of Man shall appear in the clouds of heaven, thou shalt see *this* cross, and not for judgment but for salvation." [8]

Catherine, however, did not rest content with giving when she was asked and not turning a deaf ear to those who begged; she went out to seek those in need. When everyone was asleep she would come, as in the days of old Saint Nicholas of Bari (he who is still known as Father Christmas or Santa Claus), and place a loaf of bread against the door, a bottle of wine, a sack of flour or a bag of eggs and would be gone before anyone had noticed her presence. Once she was nearly caught; she had an attack of pain in her side which often troubled her and it was so severe that she could not move. Soon people in the house would be awake and catch her in the act of exercising charity. Then she cried to her heavenly Bridegroom: "Dost Thou intend me to be put to shame before everyone? Help me, then, to get home without being seen!" To her body she said: "Home you go, even if you are to die in the attempt!" Crawling rather than walking she reached the dyer's house in Fontebranda.

Catherine's father had given her full permission to take whatever she wanted in the house for her poor people. The other members of the household, however, were not of the some opinion and once, when Catherine had appropriated a shift belonging to the servant, they all carefully locked their cupboards against these pious depredations. Catherine's charity, though, was visibly rewarded with blessings, the wine which she tapped for her poor people tasted better than other wine and it lasted longer. Once there was even a hogshead which they could hardly empty, though Lapa and Catherine both drew freely from it, so that when the vintage time came they were actually needing it for the new wine.[9] To this day that almost inexhaustible cask of wine is still remembered in Siena — *la botta di Santa Caterina*...

Catherine, then, clothed the naked and gave the hungry to eat and the thirsty to drink. She also remembered the words: "I was sick and ye visited me." She was a regular visitor at the hospital at Camporeggi near San Domenico, where the Via del Paradiso is now, and she tended the sick at La Scala. Often she stayed away so late at the large hospital that she could not get home in the evening, and then she would spend the night in a tiny room deep down in the wilderness of rooms, stairs, passages, cellars and crypts of the vast building — not far from the caves where San Sano had said Mass for the first Christians. Here she had her place of rest; visitors are still shown a little narrow room containing a recumbent statue of her. A sanctuary lamp burns before the statue, silver hearts gleam faintly in the niche above the image of the sleeping saint, artless words express Catherine's mind and thoughts: "Father, in Thee I am, in Thee I move and live, whether I am awake or asleep, whether I speak or write." [10]

When spending the night at the hospital Catherine did so in order to be at hand in case of need. She often took the dog-watch, "during the most unpleasant hours of the night," says Caffarini. She had a predilection for the most trying patients, most of all for those whose characters were difficult. For instance, there was a woman who for many years had led a gay and lawless life, and who was now an inmate of the hospital. Of course nothing there was good enough for her; she would rage and complain by turns, weep out of pity for herself and her lot, or in a temper throw the food at the nurses' heads. It was not advisable to mention religion to her, she foamed with the infidelity of a sensual woman and with personal hatred of Jesus Christ.

Catherine approached this soul, sunk in the depths of its

nature. She began by cooking for this woman of the streets and succeeded in pleasing her. Then she tried, slowly and cautiously, to turn her mind. We do not know what the bride of Christ may have said to her unhappy sister in Eve in the hospital of Siena, but there is a letter, dating from a little later in Catherine's life, written to "a public sinner in Perugia," and the tone in it would no doubt be the same.

She uses strong expressions in it. "It seems to me that you are doing like the sow, that wallows in filth," she writes, and she preaches earnestly of death, of judgment, of the terrible everlasting life with the devil. "Nothing awaits you but fire, the stench of brimstone, the gnashing of teeth, icy cold, scorching heat and the endless gnawing of a bad conscience."

And this is only the beginning of the letter. After the deep notes of the bassoons the great artist in words pulls out other stops — *vox humana, vox angelica* — pure, silvery notes, soaring to dizzying heights of radiant light and making the darkest soul listen and the hardest heart tremble with weeping. Gently Catherine reminds her of the sinner of Magdala, of the ointment poured over the feet of Jesus in the house of the Pharisee, and of the blood of Jesus which was shed in return upon her when she knelt the next time at His feet, at Calvary, during those three awful hours. . . Gently she leads her to the throne of Our Lady, where God Himself drinks at the heart of the Virgin: "Mary will show her Son the breast from which He sucked and beg for mercy for thee. . . Hide thyself, then in the wounds of the Son of God, plunge deep down in the fire of love which consumes all thy misery and all thy sin. . . There is a bath prepared in His blood to cleanse thee from the leprosy of mortal sin and wash away all thy uncleanness. Be no longer a limb on the body of the devil and a snare to catch souls, but love the Crucified, remember that thou shalt die and knowest not when; remain in the love of God. I will say no more, only this last word: Sweet Jesus, Jesus love. Mary our sweet Mother!" [11]

Perhaps Catherine did not achieve anything with either the one or the other of these two unhappy souls, perhaps she only reaped abuse as her reward. It often happens that the sick are seized with downright hatred of the person who tends them —

Catherine had that experience more than once. There was, for instance, in the leper hospital outside Porta Romana, an elderly woman named Tecca who had no one to look after her. Catherine heard of it and with her wonted courage began to go out and visit her. That which had been the great conquest of self for the delicate, poetical mind of Francis of Assisi, and the victory leading to the new life in him, was an ordinary matter of course for the brave young girl of Fontebranda. "She saw her Bridegroom in that leper," Raymond writes, "and therefore she served her diligently and with reverence. But in the sick person this aroused pride and ingratitude, which often happens to those who have not a humble mind, as they are often seized with pride when they ought to humble themselves, and instead of being grateful they become unreasonable. It happened so with that sick woman, and when she saw that Catherine was so eager to serve her she began to demand as a right that which had been given out of charity, abusing her nurse like a menial and scolding her when everything was not to her liking."

It might happen, for instance, that Catherine would arrive at the hospital a little later than usual, she was then received with sarcasms such as these: "Welcome, noble queen of Fontebranda! Where has the queen been so long this morning? In the church of the friars, hasn't she? The queen has spent all the morning with the friars! It seems that the queen can never have enough of her friars!" etc. etc. Patiently, without a word, Catherine went to and fro in the narrow, stuffy and ill-smelling sickroom, and prepared a bath, under a continual shower of mockeries from the repulsive, hateful and contemptuous face in the bed yonder.

Probably Lapa was told how little thanks her daughter got for her labour of love, for she tried to intervene. "Besides, you run the risk of infection," Lapa complained, "and *that* I could not bear, that you should go and get leprosy." Lapa's complaints were unavailing, Catherine persevered to the end, even when a suspicious-looking eruption appeared on her hands. And when old, spiteful Tecca died at last, Catherine washed the terrible body herself and buried it with her own hands. But when she stood up, after having patted down the soil over the poor, dead woman — behold, all the eruptions had vanished from her hands, and they were whiter and more beautiful than ever! [12]

Where San Lazzaro once stood there is now a peasant farm; a marble tablet in the wall recalls that here stood once *Domus Sancti Lazari*. It is twenty minutes' walk from the town gate, but from Fontebranda, across Siena, it takes over half-an-hour, and Catherine walked that distance, there and back, twice daily. The walk takes one past houses, villas, old churches; Santa Maria degli Angeli with a fine *chiostro,* San Mamiliano with frescoes and an altar-piece by Sano di Pietro, Santa Maria in Bethleëmme. . . Not until you are right out at San Lazzaro does the view open — behind the green vineclad valleys rises Santa Bonda, with the olive tree growing on the roof of the church, like a plume upon a helmet; *il Monistero* with its round tower and castellated walls, and furthest out Belcaro on its wooded height like a stranded ark. You look out upon the country of Saint Catherine; she walked along these roads, wandered through these valleys and over these mountains so often, alone or followed by the admiring and adoring crowd of friends and disciples. At last it seems as though, at a bend in the road, you might expect to meet her, a frail little figure in a habit of black and white, walking quickly in the service of her Lord and Bridegroom, and as she hurries past gazing at you with two black, intense eyes in the pale, luminous face.

The morning wind or evening breeze sweeps through the olive trees along the side of her path, and they all quietly and solemnly bend their silvery branches, and you seem to hear a quiet whisper: "Blessed be she who cometh in the name of the Lord!" *Benedicta qui venit.* . .

III

On Friday, September 3d, 1260, the republic of Siena gained the victory over the republic of Florence in the battle at Monteaperti. The traitor, Bocca degli Abati, with the flat of his sword struck the arm of Jacopo Pazzi, the standard bearer of the Florentines, who was carrying the banner with the lilies, so that he dropped it, and in the confusion that followed the Sienese rushed upon the enemy and murdered right and left — "like butchers killing cattle before Easter," says the old chronicle. The number of the fallen is given at ten thousand, the waters of the river Arbia ran red, sings Dante. Most fiercely did the fight rage round the Florentine war chariot, *il Carroccio*, where the banners of the guilds and townships stood planted in the ground, and whence *la Martinella*, the tocsin, clanged unceasingly. The best men of Florence closed up round the chariot, fought to the last man and pressed their dying lips to its blood-stained wheels. The chariot was carried off in triumph to Siena, where its gigantic shafts can still be seen, fastened with iron bands to two of the columns supporting the dome of the cathedral.

It was the first and last victory of Ghibelline Siena over Guelphic Florence. After the battle of Benevent (1266), the Guelphs raised their heads everywhere in Italy and in 1268 the saga of the Hohenstaufen had come to an end. In Siena the powerful noble family of the Tolomei had always been on the side of the Guelphs, and in June 1269, the Sienese arms suffered a decisive defeat at Colle di Val d'Elsa. Siena's great statesman and military leader, Provenzano Salvani, was taken prisoner and shamefully murdered by his exiled fellow-countryman, Carolino Tolomei, who placed his head on a pole and rode through the Florentine camp with it. From the castle of Castiglioncello at Monteriggioni the Sienese noblewoman, Sapia Saracini, also exiled, saw the rout of her fellow-countrymen and in exulting, sated thirst for revenge she screamed to heaven: "I fear thee no longer now, thou up yonder!" [1]

The fall of the Ghibellines brought about the fall in Siena of the government of the twenty-four, a magistracy of three groups of eight councillors, elected by the three wards in Siena: Camullia, Città, San Martino. The twenty-four were succeeded by thirty-six, a mixed government, in which both the nobility and men of the people had seats. In 1280, however, the restless nobility, always fond of and prepared for feuds, were entirely excluded from the government, and this was placed in the hands of a democratic welfare committee: *the fifteen rulers and guardians of the town and people of Siena.* Five years later the number of these state guardians was reduced to nine. These nine — *i Signori Nove* — were elected from the wealthy citizen class and (as in Florence) for only two months at a time; during their term of office they lived in the Town Hall at the expense of the State. The adherents of the Nine were called *Noveschi* and formed *il monte dei Nove,* while the party of the nobles was *il monte dei Gentiluomini.*

Under the rule of the Nine Siena reached the height of her prosperity and all that we admire to this day came into being. It was at this time that Dante visited the town, though it is true that he became so absorbed in a book which he found at a bookseller's, and which he read while lying on a bench outside, that he forgot to look at *il palio,* the great summer festival of Siena, which was taking place directly in front of him, and which was celebrated in those days not only with "games of many youths," but also "with dancing of fair women." The stern poet, however, had seen enough to stamp the Sienese as still more profligate than the French and to mock at the she-wolf, in the Sienese coat-of-arms, as having now become a bitch.[2] Like a Sienese Villon, Cecco degli Angiolieri sang of "women, wine and dice-throwing" as the only things of value, and in his poems he praised the shoemaker's daughter Becchina, the exceeding earthly counterpart of Dante's Bice. The spendthrift brigade met in *la Consuma* and set out in the morning for jousts and in the evening for singing and Provençal dances.[3] Fonte Gaja, the chief well in Siena, was adorned with a classic Venus, the work of Lysippos, which was found in 1345 at an excavation on the site of the present Piazza Umberto I, and carried in triumph through the town, exactly like Duccio di Buoninsegna's altar piece in 1311. A new and larger cathedral, which was to surpass that of Florence, was planned and begun; the ruin of the nave, never finished, is still standing as a memorial of the great dreams and ambitious plans of Siena. At *il Campo*, the place among the three hills on which Siena is built, and from which the town still has its Latin plural name (*Senae*) and its three quarters or *Terzi*, the Gothic town hall arose between 1288 and 1308 and between 1338 and 1348 the campanile beside it: La Torre del Mangia, which is so beautiful that Leonardo came to Siena to see that alone. The halls and chapels of the town hall were decorated with beautiful frescoes by Simone di Martino and Ambrogio Lorenzetti. In the hall in which the Nine assembled the latter of these two artists painted two great frescoes, illustrating by imagery good and bad government and the virtues by which the good government of a country should be inspired. There is not much left of the old lime paintings, but one figure still faces us luminously, that of a stately woman clad entirely in white and having an olive branch like a crown about her abundant fair hair — a picture of Peace crowned. Above her head is the word *Pax*, and peace was much talked of in the days when Messer Ambrogio wielded his brush in the town hall of Siena, as men are wont to talk of that for which they are longing and least of all possess.

For peace was exactly what old Siena never knew — altogether those centuries did not know at all what peace meant. In the year 1314, on the sixteenth day of April (the old chronicle reports), "there was a great rising and much fighting in Siena between the house of Tolomei and the house of Salimbeni and the whole city was put under arms." The great families were in a constant state of bitter feud, Tolomei against Salimbeni and Maconi against Tolomei, Saracini against Scotti, Piccolomini against Malavolti. Soon the lower class rose too, *il popolo minuto*, against the ruling upper class and life in Siena was a constant and sudden change from festive music to the din of battle, from wedding bells to funeral dirges, bells clanging *a stormo* and bells chiming *a gloria*. It was in order to escape from such an existence (black and white like *la balzana* and like the campanile of Siena) that three young knights — Giovanni Tolomei, Patrizio Patrizi and Ambrogio Piccolomini — one day in 1313 bade their native town farewell and set out for Accona in the *creta* desert south of Siena. Above their hermitage they wrote the words *Christus pax nostra,* having built it themselves out there among the wild desert heights, and a twig of olive became the crest of that order of monks which they gathered about them, and which was given the name of *Olivetans.*

Then came the year 1348 and with it the Black Death. From May till October the pestilence raged in Siena and over three-fourths of the inhabitants died. "No bells rang, at last there were none left any more to weep over the death of the others, for all looked for the same fate; the father did not wait to see his son die, brother fled from brother, the wife left her husband, for it was said that the infection was caught at a mere breath. . . The dead bodies were buried as best one could, without solemnity of any kind; many were dug up again by the dogs, which devoured them in the midst of the streets of the town . . . And I, Agnolo di Tura, called the Fat, with my own hands buried five of my sons in one grave." [4]

This year of plague is a turning-point in the history of Siena. The Nine fall in 1355 and are succeeded by the Twelve, who were not inspired by the same spirit of humanism and renaissance. Giovanni Colombini and his Gésuati went through the town preaching penitence, and the statue of Venus above Fonte Gaja was thrown down and broken to pieces — nay, the pieces (according to Lorenzo Ghiberti) were carried out of Siena and buried in Florentine soil. [5]

Meanwhile the interior conflict went on unchanged. The adherents of the Twelve had divided into two parties: *Canischi* and *Grasselli.* The former sought the support of the Tolomei, Piccolomini, Saracini and Cerretani; the latter were aided by the Salimbeni. During this period the most powerful man of this powerful family, the mighty Giovanni di Agnolino dei Salimbeni, plays the same part as Provenzano Salvani, the hero who fell at Colle di Val d'Elsa, a hundred years earlier. When the Emperor Charles IV came to Italy in 1368 to be crowned, it was Giovanni Salimbeni who went right up into Lombardy to meet him on behalf of Siena. To the great misfortune of the town, however, Giovanni fell with his horse and died soon after as a result of the fall. The nobles now formed a rising and together with the Nine they compel the Twelve to hand over the government to them. A new government is set up, consisting of thirteen consuls, one for each of the five great houses, five for the lesser nobility, three of the party of the Nine. These new men of the government send word to the Emperor about what has happened, but meanwhile the Salimbeni have made common cause with the adherents of the Twelve and have sent their own ambassadors to the Emperor. On September 24th the Salimbeni sallied forth fully armed from their palace, joined with the party of the Twelve and opened the town to the Emperor's representative, Malatesta de' Malatesta, who was encamped outside with eight hundred horsemen. Street by street, house by house, the imperial forces had to conquer Siena, until at last the Town Hall was taken by storm. The nobles fled and Malatesta fortified himself at Poggio Malavolti (now Piazza Umberto I). In the Town Hall sat the so-called *Reformatori*, one hundred and twenty-four men of the people, who elected a new supreme council, consisting of five representatives of the lower class (*il popolo minuto*), four of the Twelve, three of the Nine, the so-called "twelve defenders of the people of Siena." As a reward for the services which they had rendered democracy the family of the Salimbeni were made commoners, *i.e.*, eligible for the government and were given Massa and five castles in the environs of Siena.

These matters were hardly settled when the Emperor came to Siena on October 12th, accompanied by the Empress. Outside Porta Tufi the Twelve, together with the Salimbeni, stood ready to receive him, wearing wreaths of flowers on their heads and holding branches of olive in their hands. He took up his quarters at the Palazzo Salimbeni and on the following day, in the Cathedral, he bestowed the accolade of knighthood upon Reame and Niccolò Salimbeni. After a short sojourn — three days — he leaves the town but promises to return towards Christmas. On December 22nd he comes back, but in his absence the government of the republic has changed — "the ordinances decided upon by Siena in October do not hold good any longer in November," said Dante, scffiong, not without reason. A rising of the people had led to a new government, which now consisted of fifteen *Difensori*. As before, the Emperor took up his quarters with the Salimbeni. At about the same time a papal legate, the Cardinal of Bologna, arrived and the rumour began to spread that the Emperor wished to sell the town to the Pope.

This suspicion gained ground when Charles demanded the surrender of the fortresses of Massa, Montalcino, Grosseto, Talamone and Casole. Then, on January 18th (in the next year, 1369) Niccolò Salimbeni rides in full armour, through the streets shouting: "Live the people! Down with the traitors who want the nobles back!" At the same time Malatesta took possession of the town hall square with the imperial horsemen and demanded that the three representatives of the Nine should give up their seats in the government. Instantly the tocsin rang out; from the Mangia tower *il Campanone* boomed its judgment day clamour out across town and country (it sounds as if it were clanging against the very vault of heaven). The people rushed to arms and hurried in crowds to the town hall square, where "the Captain of the People," Matteino di Ventura, unfurled the banner of the people with the lion rampant. The Emperor now came forth himself from Palazzo Salimbeni, but at *Croce del Travaglio* (where the three main streets of Siena converge, outside *Loggia dei Uniti*) he encountered Malatesta's horsemen, fleeing from the furious people. The horses stumbled in the chains that were stretched across the streets, while stones and other missiles, thrown from roofs and towers and windows, hurtled down into the narrow streets upon the helpless horsemen. The Emperor himself barely escaped back to the Palazzo Salimbeni with a loss of four hundred men, besides many wounded.

Il Capitano del Popolo then issued, in the name of the victorious people, a proclamation forbidding anyone to provide the Emperor with any kind of food and this put him in a paroxysm of fear. Forsaken by everyone he wept before the envoys of the people, declared that Malatesta and the Salimbeni and the Twelve had deceived him, re-instated the fifteen *Difensori* as his vice-gerents, asked for money for travelling expenses and hastened to depart.

After the flight of the Emperor general anarchy broke out; not until July was a peace arrived at, by which the banished families (Piccolomini, Malavolti, Saracini, Tolomei, Forteguerri,

Cerretani) were allowed to return, and until 1385 the government was in the hands of fifteen *Riformatori*.

Meanwhile the Salimbeni and the Twelve on one side and the adherents of the Nine on the other carried on a relentless civil war. The Benincasa belonged to the party of the Twelve, Bartolommeo having had a seat in the government in September and October 1367. Their lives were often in danger and, with others of the same party, they wanted to seek sanctuary one day in the parish church of Sant' Antonio. Catherine, however, did not consider this refuge safe enough, and in her Mantellata habit she conducted her two brothers unscathed through the middle of the town to La Scala. There they stayed until the danger was over, but all those who had sought refuge in Sant' Antonio were killed or thrown into prison.[6] Catherine's brothers, on the other hand, escaped with a fine of one hundred guilders, nay, Bartolommeo seems even to have sat in the new government in May and June of the following year.

Nevertheless the family had received a shock from which it did not recover. In October 1370, the three brothers, Bartolommeo, Benincasa and Stefano set out for Florence to seek their fortunes there. They had but little success; Catherine had to ask her Florentine benefactor, Niccolò Soderini, to help them with a loan, and after his death they got deeply into debt (a writ against them for a sum of 875 florins has been preserved). Matters were not much better, either, in Siena; the house at Fontebranda had to be given up, and old Lapa spent her last years in a house in Via Romana. Raymond relates that Catherine had always prayed that her family might become poor, "for worldly possessions are blended with much evil, and that is not the kind of wealth that I desire for those nearest to me."[7] Her prayer was heard.

The relations between the brothers in Florence do not seem always to have been very happy. Catherine admonishes them in a letter to mutual love and reminds them of the words: "He who exalts himself shall be abased." "You, Benincasa, who are the eldest, should be the least of all. And you, Stefano, I pray to be subject to God and your brothers." Another letter throws a light upon Benincasa's domestic relations, his sister putting before him the example of patient Job, "who had a wife that tormented him continually." In a third letter she explains to the same brother that it is really a matter of enduring at the moment. "For the suffering which is past we have not any longer, and that which is to come has not yet appeared, it is only the present instant," "and that," she adds elsewhere, "is not more than the prick of a needle."

Benincasa seems to have thought that he ought to have more help from home; Catherine rebukes him and urges him instead to be more grateful to his parents. "Your mother has given you of her body and has nourished you at her breast, and has had much trouble with you and with all of us." [8] A daughter of Benincasa entered a convent and Catherine wrote a beautiful letter to her, "with the desire to see thee as a true bride of Christ, so that thou mayest flee from all that might hinder thee in having the Crucified for Bridegroom . . . And beware above all, daughter, of human praise, and desire not to be praised for aught that thou doest, for then the gate of eternal life will not be opened to thee." [9]

But ere all these upheavals of state and home had come to pass, Giacomo the Gentle had closed his eyes. "He was bound no longer by any earthly longings, but desired only to pass over to the other shore," says Raymond of the good and pious Tuscan craftsman. Catherine knelt by his deathbed and wrestled with God in prayer, that her father might go straight into heaven without any pains in Purgatory. "And Lord, if it cannot be otherwise, then give me the pains my father should have suffered, I will bear them for him!"

Then Giacomo died under the glance and smile of his darling daughter, and at the very moment that he breathed his last, Catherine felt a sharp pain in her side, which was at once stinging and sweet — *un pici dolce fianco,* which never afterwards left her.[10] She understood then that her prayer had been heard, and while the others wept, she laughed in her exceeding joy. Then she laid his body in the coffin herself, and bending over his thin cold cheek with its stiff cold beard she whispered: "Would to God I were where thou art now!" On August 22d, 1368, the Dominicans sang the requiem over Giacomo Benincasa and Catherine "beheld his soul depart from the darkness of the body and enter into everlasting light." [11]

IV

There are two kinds of love in man, the love of God and of his fellow man, and the love of the world. There are two wills, the will of God and self-will. One of these two forces, love of the world, self-will, leads to interior unrest, sin, unhappiness, everything evil and everlasting loss. The other, love of God and one's neighbour, leads to interior peace, health of the soul, every virtue and everlasting life.

The understanding of this great truth is the basis of Catherine's whole life and thought. Sheer egoism compels us to divest ourselves of our self-will and to assume the will of God, for the world, which we would fain possess, will pass away; life is fragile like glass, it is like running water which disappears under a bridge — *tutto passa*. We must put off the old, earthly man, and put on the new, heavenly one — put off Adam and put on Christ — put off the flesh and *put on the Crucified* (an expression stronger still than the Pauline one from which it is derived).

With thoughts such as these Catherine went out from her ruined paternal home, and these thoughts return in every hour of her life later. Her whole life is governed by them and this is her message to humanity.

"The servant should not walk in another path than his master," she declares, "and the path of pleasure is not the path of Christ the Crucified." "We should rejoice in nothing but in bearing reproaches and sufferings." "Crucify thyself with Christ the Crucified," she writes in a letter, "follow Him on the Way of the Cross, conform thyself to Him, rejoice in reproaches, sufferings, contempt, mockery and evil words, persevere to the end and do not fortify thyself with anything but the blood flowing down from the Cross." "When suffering comes, do not shrink from it, but accept it with a joyful face, go out to meet it with joy and desire and say: Be very welcome! . . . Then bitterness will become sweet and consoling and thou shalt end thy life, resting softly on the Cross with Christ the Crucified." "Like the child feeding at its mother's breast, so feeds the soul that loves God, on Christ, the Crucified, and walks always in His steps, following Him on the path of reproaches and suffering and mockery, and not rejoicing in aught else — the soul clings closely to the most sacred wood of the Cross and looks up with a countenance of holy desire, and beholds that burning, consuming Love, whose blood streams from all its wounds. Such a soul is patient in all tribulations, for of its own free will it has renounced all consolation of the world, and pain and affliction and persecution have become its good friends. For it has seen that thus was the Son of God clothed, and without doubt He chose the fairest raiment that could be found." "Put on, therefore, put on Christ, sweet Jesus. He is a garment so strong that no devil and no man can take it from you, when you will it not yourselves. He is the highest and eternal sweetness, which melts away all bitterness. In Him the soul is fed and strengthened, so that it counts all that is outside God as but refuse, and it rejoices in persecutions and reproaches and calumnies, and desires nought but to be conformed to Christ the Crucified." [1]

Here Catherine preaches the core of Christian doctrine, literally and in deadly earnest. She would drink the blood of Christ, like the child drinking milk from its mother's breast. She would live the life of Christ; she would carry the Cross of Christ. This is the bridge over the roaring torrent of the world, the *only* bridge. This is the gate, the narrow gate. There is no choice; one must walk either to Golgotha or to Gehenna.

The year 1370, Catherine's twenty-fourth year, is the year in which this ideal burns through in all its relentless force to full dominion in her soul. Like the betrothal four years earlier, like the stigmatisation five years later, this year marks a stage in her life. "Do you not think that I have become quite another?" she asked her confessor, Padre Tommaso, one day.[2] Everyone who is conscious of spiritual growth knows that feeling of strangeness with which one looks back at one's earlier self, and which sometimes makes one not recognise oneself as one was only a few months, nay, a few weeks, even a few days back. . .

"Would you be at peace in your souls?" Catherine cried later in a letter to her disciples. "Then cast off your own will, from which arises all suffering, and put on the sweet, everlasting will of God, and ye shall taste eternal life." [8] When she wrote down such words as these (and that was often) her thoughts would assuredly revert to the great summer of 1370, which she spent entirely in putting on the will of God, clothing herself as a new being, assuming Christ.

July 17th is the feast of the martyr Saint Alexis, and on that day Catherine wished to receive Holy Communion. Meanwhile she felt unworthy of it and prayed to God for purification. It then seemed to her that a rain of fire and blood descended upon her and burned her clean to the innermost depths. Early in the morning then, she went to San Domenico, but there was no sign of her confessor coming to say Mass. The Cappella della Volte was empty; no candles lit on the altar, no Missal, no cruets with wine and water or any of the other little signs, from which the faithful one concludes that the priest will soon make his appearance. Catherine meanwhile knelt in her usual place — and behold! ere long Padre Tommaso appeared, offered the sacred oblation and gave his penitent the sacrament of the altar. On the following day they spoke to each other and the Dominican declared that he had suddenly had a feeling that she was in the chapel and expecting him. "But thy face was flushed, Catherine, and was all beaded with dew as if with jewels — what was the reason?" asked the monk. "What the colour of my face, Father, I do not know, but this I know, that when I received that ineffable Sacrament from your hand, I saw nothing with the eyes of the body, but with the sight of the spirit I beheld a beauty and I perceived a sweetness that no words can tell. And That which I saw drew me to Itself with such strength, that all other things here below seemed to me but as worthless refuse. . . And I besought the Lord that He would take away my will from me and give me His, and in His great mercy He did so, for He answered and said: 'Behold, My dearest daughter! I here bestow My will upon thee, and thou shalt be conformed to it to such a degree that whatsoever shall befall thee, it shall not touch thee.' " ("And this," added Padre Tommaso, when recounting the story, "was indeed true, for since that year Catherine was always content, whatever befell.") But the next day Catherine confided still further to her confessor that in that vision Jesus had showed her for a long while the wound in His side, "as a mother shows an infant the breast," and not until Catherine had begun to weep for longing had He taken her soul into His arms and pressed her lips to the sacred wound — "and all my soul entered into that most holy wound, and I learned there so much of the nature of God, that I cannot understand how I can continue to live without my heart breaking for love!" Like the Shulamite of the Canticle, the young woman sighed: "Lord, thou hast wounded my heart! Lord, thou hast wounded my heart!"

On the same day, that is, July 18th, Catherine was meditating in prayer on the words of the Psalmist: *Cor mundum crea in me, Domine,* "Create a new heart in me, and renew a right spirit within me," and she prayed fervently to her Saviour to take her heart from her and give her His heart instead. Then she plainly saw how Jesus revealed Himself to her, took her heart out of her breast and departed with it. And for several days, she told her confessor, she lived thus without a heart, and although Padre Tommaso said that it was impossible, she insisted that it was so. Until some days later (Padre Tommaso says on the feast of Saint Margaret, that is, on July 20th) after Mass in the Cappella delle Volte, she suddenly saw the Lord before her, and in His hand He was holding a purple-red and flaming heart, which He inserted in Catherine's side. "My dearest daughter," He said, "newly I took thy heart from thee — today I give thee Mine instead." From that day Catherine always said in her prayers: "Lord, I commend to Thee Thy heart," and no longer, "Lord, I commend my heart to Thee." Below her left breast several of her women friends saw the wound in the place where her heart had been taken out. Often, when she received Holy Communion, this new heart of Catherine's beat so loudly, that one could well understand that it was not a human heart, and with amazement the Sisters and Padre Tommaso heard the strange sound of exultation of the Heart of Jesus in the bosom of the maiden. . .

It was after that exchange of hearts with the Lord that Catherine said to her confessor: "Do ye not feel that I have become quite another?" adding, "Ah, if ye knew what I feel! I do not believe that there can be a heart so hard that it would not melt at it, and no heart so proud, that it would not humble itself at it. My soul is filled with so great a joy that I marvel how I can remain in my body! So glowing am I within that outer flames seem to me refreshing. And that fire burns me so pure and so humble that I feel as if I had again become a little child, and I love my neighbour so dearly that I would gladly suffer death for every single soul."

In words such as these Catherine tried to describe what was passing in her soul — "but it is impossible, unspeakable," she exclaimed, "it seems to me like dipping pearls in mire."

Shortly after, probably on the 22nd, on the feast of St. Mary Magdalene, the Lord again appeared to Catherine together with His Mother and the great, repentant sinner. And Jesus said to her: "What wilt thou have? Wilt thou have Me or thyself?" To which she answered like Simon Peter: "Lord, Thou knowest all things, Thou knowest also that I have no other will than Thine, and no other heart than Thine!" And Catherine looked at Mary Magdalene and thought of how she had anointed the feet of the Master in the house of the Pharisee and was filled with ardent love of her. Jesus saw it and said: "From henceforth I give thee Mary Magdalene for thy mother, and she shall watch carefully over thee." From that hour Catherine always called Mary Magdalene her mother, and from that time she began to imitate her exercises of penitence, in particular in a fasting so severe that at last it became an entire abstaining from all nourishment.[4]

Revelations and ecstasies also continued all through the month of August. On August 3d, the day before the feast of Saint Dominic, Catherine went up as usual to San Domenico. Fra Bartolommeo de' Dominici, who was in the church, beckoned to her and sat down on a bench, while Catherine knelt down by his side. As the Dominican now contemplated the young girl's face, which was radiant with joy, as always (but especially on great feast days), he said: "Of a surety thou bringest good news, thou seemest so happy!" Quickly and with many gestures, like the young girls to this day at Fontebranda, Catherine began to tell him in her pure Tuscan: "Father, do you not see our Father, Saint Dominic? He is there, just there, I see him more plainly than I see you now. He is like Our Lord, an oval face, beautiful features — and fair hair and beard — *tanto bello!*" Just at that moment someone was walking through the church, Catherine's brother Stefano. For one instant she looked after him, again turned to the Dominican and burst into tears. "But what is it, Catherine?" asked the monk, wondering and anxious. The young girl looked up but could not answer for sobbing and Padre Tommaso went away. At the time for Compline, about three hours later, he came back — Catherine was still in the church. He was now told the reason of her sorrow: because of her curiosity the vision had vanished and Saint Paul had appeared instead and severely rebuked her. "But it was only for an instant that thou didst look away!" said the Dominican. Catherine, though, would not be consoled, "I am a great sinner," she exclaimed. Her only comfort had been that while the Apostle had preached so sternly to her, she had seen all the time a dear and gentle little lamb, and then she had thought of Jesus. Shaking his head Padre Bartolommeo went away. "It is a distinctive mark of good people," he murmured, with a quotation from Saint Gregory, "to see sin where there is none." [5]

On August 11th Catherine again had a vision. Her confessor had (as so often before) begged her to restrain her weeping in church, and in any case bidden her to keep at a distance from the altar, as she disturbed the priest with her exclamations. Catherine therefore knelt quite away at the other end of the chapel, did not dare to come up for Holy Communion, but said quite softly, like a child half hoping and half fearing to be heard by stern parents — "I want to have the Body of Our Lord Jesus Christ, I want to have the Body of Our Lord Jesus Christ." Again the Saviour had compassion on her, gave her Communion Himself and let her drink of His blood.[6]

In consequence of all these emotions Catherine fell ill; when the feast of the Assumption came, on August 15th, she was ill in bed in the house of her friend Alessia. The Via del Casato lies deep down and the Cathedral cannot be seen from there, but its bells rang out sonorously over the roofs, in honour of the feast — the Cathedral of Siena being dedicated to *Maria Assunta,* to the Mother of God assumed into heaven. "If only

I could see the pinnacle of the campanile," thought Catherine. And in a vision the whole black-and-white striped marble Duomo suddenly arose before her; she stood in the Cathedral Square; she walked up the yellow marble steps, past the beggar women at the door and into the forest of columns, beneath the cool arches. The Bishop himself was standing before the high altar, a starry sky of golden candles was lit, and the incense was rising in soft spirals from the motionless censers. Out across the weather-beaten, rough peasants and the women with the big, nodding straw hats and the children playing on the altar steps, and the soldiers in their armour, and the merchants in their silken cloaks, the choir in loud and ringing voices was singing the Preface: *Et te in assumptione Beatae Mariae*. Then came the great silence: *Sanctus, Sanctus, Sanctus* — and a silent and adoring people knelt in the dust before the wonder of the Holy Supper. . .[7]

Catherine lay ill in her friend's house for several days. During most of the time she was in deep ecstasy, but from the disconnected words which escaped her now and then her friends could understand that she was holding a colloquy with her heavenly Bridegroom. *O sposo,* she exclaimed, *o giovane amabilissimo, amatissimo giovane!* "Oh, Bridegroom, oh, most beloved youth, whom I love above all things!" "For two hours," writes Caffarini of one of these ecstasies, "she continued to speak thus with God, addressing herself now to the Eternal Father, now to the only-begotten Son become Man. During the whole colloquy, while she was entirely rapt out of herself, she frequently changed colour, so that her face was sometimes as white as snow, sometimes flaming like fire." Sometimes she could be heard laughing, deeply and softly and happily like a young bride being embraced by her bridegroom, and then she murmured softly and blissfully: "Oh Love, Love, Thou art the sweetest of all there is! Oh, eternal beauty, for how many centuries hast Thou been unknown to the world and hidden from it! With all my heart I desire to love Thee, really and always, but grant me also the consolation of seeing the hearts of all those who are here present broken with the passion of holy love of Thee! Lord, I confess that I am wicked and unworthy to beg for things so great, but break down, Lord, the wall that is between Thee and them, that they may love Thee without hindrance. Lord, I will leave Thee no rest or peace either by night or by day, until Thou bestow upon us the true virtues, until Thou bestow Thyself upon us." Often these ecstasies ended in bitter weeping and with the complaining words: "Oh, Spouse, Spouse, when, when? Why not now, at once?" Those standing around her then understood that Catherine ardently desired to go hence and be with Christ.[8]

She told Raymond afterwards what had taken place during those hours of ecstasy. Christ had appeared to her and had reproached her with her egoism. "With great desire I desired to eat the Paschal lamb with My disciples," said the Saviour, "and yet I waited until the hour when it should please my Father. Thou must therefore wait patiently for the hour when thou canst be altogether united to me. "Shall this poor little body really continue to part us," Catherine exclaimed, "then suffer me at least, during the time that I must still live here upon earth, to take part in Thy sufferings and in that manner be united to Thee."

Jesus promised this and vanished, but from that moment Catherine began to feel continual pains, now in her heart, now in other parts of the body, and owing to this experience she believed that she might draw the conclusion that the Saviour had suffered, not only on Good Friday itself, but that all His life had been one long suffering. This, she explained later to Raymond, was the Cup which Jesus had prayed in Gethsemane might be taken from Him; that Cup was emptied and He now prayed that the new Cup of still more bitter suffering might be poured out to Him. In vain did the Dominican, with his theological training, protest that this interpretation was not correct, Jesus had really as true Man felt dread of the terrible things that awaited Him and prayed that the suffering might pass Him by, if it were possible. But Catherine did not understand her Bridegroom thus: she, who in her thirst for pain once exclaimed: "Would that I could gather all the suffering in the world in a sheaf and take it upon myself!" She could not bear the thought that the Master, for even one instant, should have recoiled. "This interpretation may be good for consoling the weak, it does not satisfy the strong and the perfect," she answered.[9] It is not to be wondered at that some of those who had hitherto been her disciples found that in being super-human she was inhuman. They were men and they could not follow Catherine in her woman's passionate desire for entire sacrifice of herself, that passionate love of which the Canticle says that it is "strong as death."

Catherine continued on the path by which her love urged her to go. On the feast of Saint Agapitus, August 18th, she was able to get up again, and in the morning she walked to church to hear Mass and go to Communion. Kneeling at the altar rail she repeated to herself the words with which Communion begins in the Catholic Church: "Lord, I am not worthy that Thou shouldst enter under my roof; say but the word, and my soul shall be healed." "No, I am not worthy," Catherine sighed, with her eyes fastened on the little white Host above the golden chalice in the priest's hand. "But I am altogether worthy, that thou shouldst enter into Me," answered a voice, which she knew, the voice of the Master coming to her in the stainless white pilgrim's robe of the consecrated Bread. And it seemed to her, when the Host was laid upon her tongue, as though she were plunged down in an infinite sea, and she felt like a fish, which lives and moves freely in the water, but must die as soon as it is taken up from it.

This feeling remained with her all the way home and overwhelmed her so much that she had to seek rest a short while on her hard couch. She had that sensation of hovering in the air, which she knew so well as a child, and soon all the outer world around her vanished and the world beyond opened its gates to her. She began to pray, first for herself, then for her kinsfolk, her confessor, Fra Tommaso, her friends, all those whose salvation she had at heart. "Lord," she exclaimed, "I will have Thy promise of everlasting life for them all!" "Lord," she added, "give me Thy hand as a pledge! Give me a sure pledge that my prayer is heard!" Then she felt a sharp pain in her right hand, and saw a golden nail pierced through it, and involuntarily she exclaimed, as was usual with her when suffering from physical pain: "Praised be my sweet, most adorable and beloved Bridegroom and Lord Jesus Christ!" "Thus do I bear" (she declared later to Raymond of Capua), "the wound of the Lord Jesus Christ in my right hand; no one else can see it, but it causes me pain that never ceases." [10]

"But after this holy virgin," continues Raymond, "had felt the suffering of Christ in her body and had thus perceived how much the Saviour had loved her and all mankind, in suffering so great pains for our sakes, she was filled with a love so fervent that her heart could not contain it, but must break . . . And thus it happened that Catherine's heart broke from top to bottom. The veins of life were torn apart and she expired."

This was Catherine's mystical death. "One Sunday morning at about nine o'clock, if I remember aright," Fra Bartolommeo de' Dominici relates, "I was standing in the pulpit in San Domenico, when there was a rumour in Siena that Catherine was dying. Immediately after the sermon I hastened thither and had much trouble in making my way, so many people were already in the house. Those who had been there for some time assured me that she had already yielded up her spirit several hours ago."

Accompanied by another friar, Giovanni da Siena, Fra Bartolommeo pushed his way through to the death chamber. There Fra Tommaso della Fonte, Fra Bartolommeo Montucci and Fra Tommaso d'Antonio Caffarini, besides the faithful friends Alessia, Caterina di Ghetto and the sister-in-law Lisa were already kneeling. They were all weeping and the consumptive young friar, Giovanni, was so overwhelmed by his feelings that he had a hemorrhage. Then Fra Tommaso, confident in Catherine's holiness, seized her hand which had not yet become rigid and laid it upon the breast of the sick friar. And behold! the hemorrhage ceased, and at the same time life began to return to Catherine's cheeks. Her heart beat again, and before long she opened her eyes, looked around her in despair and with an unutterable expression of disappointment she turned to the wall and wept. . .

This weeping continued for two days and no one could wring a word from her except this: "Oh, how unhappy I am!" At length she explained a little more. *Vidi arcana Dei!* she exclaimed — "I have beheld the hidden things of God!" She then confided to her confessor how she, like Dante, had passed through the three kingdoms in the other world, seen all the horror of hell and the pain of Purgatory, and at last had a glimpse of the gates of Paradise, heard the singing of the saints and for a moment had a perception of everlasting bliss. "I was set free from this gloomy prison cage, I saw the blessed light and now I am again confined in the wonted darkness! How can I do aught but groan and weep over my misery?"

"Were you really dead?" asked her confessor, who was still sceptical. "My soul was loosed from the body during those four hours," Catherine assured him, "but Jesus came towards me and bade me return to the world and proclaim what I had seen. For if poor mankind only suspected what purgatory and hell mean, they would rather suffer death ten times, if it were possible, than endure that pain for even one day. But above all I saw the severe punishment of all those who have sinned in holy matrimony by not keeping the laws of marriage, but only seeking their pleasures of the flesh. That sin is very perilous, even though it be little . . .

"And my soul was seized with mortal fear of returning to the world. Then the Lord said: 'The souls of many depend on thy returning. And thou shalt not live any more as hitherto, or keep to thy cell, but thou shalt leave thy home and thy country for the salvation of souls. Thou shalt go from place to place and from city to city, and I will be always with thee and lead thee forth and back again, and I will give thee a tongue and wisdom which no man will be able to withstand. And I will send thee to high priests and to the rulers of the people, and with that which is weak in the eyes of the world I will put to shame the pride of the strong.' And while God was speaking all these things to my soul, I felt in a manner that I cannot tell, that of a sudden I had again returned to my body." [11]

V

"Oh, most dear daughter, seest thou not that our soul is a tree of love, for it is love that has created us? This tree is so well made that no one can hinder it from growing, nor seize its fruits, unless the tree itself permit it. God has given this tree a husbandman to tend it, that is, free will . . . This husbandman sees with the eye of understanding (if it be not darkened by the cloud of self-love) where the tree should be planted . . . to wit, in the soil of true humility (not on the mountain of pride, but in the valley of humility). It then brings forth the fragrant flowers of virtues and above all the fair flower of glorifying and praising the name of God. . . God keeps this flower for Himself, but He wills that the fruits should be for us, for He lacks nothing and has no need of our fruits. He is Who is, whilst we are those who are not, and we are in need of everything. We do not exist for ourselves but for Him, for He has given us our being and every other grace that is added thereto and we cannot be of any service to Him. He, the Highest and Eternal Goodness, sees that man does not live on flowers, but only on fruits (for we should die of the flowers but we live on the fruit) and therefore He takes the flower for Himself and gives to us the fruit. And if, in our pride, we were to begin to nourish ourselves on flowers, that is, to take for ourselves the glory and the praise that we ought to give to God, we should lose the life of grace and die the everlasting death. But if we are content with the fruit and leave the flower to God, then our tree grows in good soil and will grow so tall that no creature can see the top, for the soul is then united to God by infinite love." [1]

Man does not live on flowers but on fruits. These words from Catherine's lips express a thought which from that moment permeated her whole life. In a less poetic form, but quite as forcibly, she already expresses it in one of her first letters to her mother: "Let us give glory to God, and work for our neighbour." Later she adds a third clause: "Let us glorify God, love our neighbour, hate and despise ourselves." [2] In "The Dialogue," the spiritual testament which she dictated two years before her death, she causes the Saviour to say:

"Ye can not render Me any service, but ye can help your neighbour, and if ye seek My glory and the salvation of souls, that will prove that I live in your hearts by grace.

"The soul that loves My truth never leaves herself any rest, but ever seeks to serve others. It is impossible for you to give Me the love that I ask, but I have given you a neighbour that ye may do for him that which ye cannot do for Me: love him without any worldly thought, without looking for any gain or return. That which ye do for him, then, I look upon as done for Me." [3]

After her mystical death Catherine proved clearly that she was in this world only to save souls. If until then she had sought above all to succour the bodily needs of her neighbour by works of charity, she understood now that it was to the care of the soul that she must devote her life. "What can a man give in exchange for his soul?" "It is no wonder," she said one day to Raymond, "that I have so great a love for those whom the Lord has sent me, to warn them and turn them from evil to good, for I have bought them at no small price, in that for their sakes I have chosen to be exiled from the Lord. Nor can they wonder that I speak so freely to all men." [4] "Deeply didst Thou love me, Jesus, my most dear love," she exclaims in a letter, "and teach me how much I must love myself and my neighbour, and that it is fitting that we should always hunger and thirst after the souls of others." [5]

It was in her native town that Catherine's ardent love of souls began to fall "like refreshing dew and rain." [6]

Caffarini relates that there lived in Siena a rich and distinguished man called Andréa di Naddino de' Bellanti, whose poverty in the true riches of the Christian virtues was as great as his wealth in worldly goods.* He was enslaved by the vices of drinking and gaming, he never entered a church, even on holy-days, and it was many years since he had made his last confession. His talk was full of blasphemy (and one must have heard a Tuscan blaspheme to know what that means), and one day, having lost a large sum of money, he fell into such a rage that, seizing a crucifix that was hanging on the wall,

* Among other activities the Bellanti carried on the large banking business, *Compagnia de' Buonsignori*, at Vignone, a fashionable watering-place south of Siena.

he threw it on the ground and stamped upon it, like the Neapolitan *lazzarone* to this day, who, when anything happens to annoy him, repeats the names of all the saints he can think of into his hat, throws it on the ground and stamps upon it! [7]

This young man, who was only twenty years old, had fallen dangerously ill, and death appeared to be imminent. His relatives called in one of the parish priests to see him, but Andréa de' Bellanti declared emphatically that he would die as he had lived. Father Tommaso was then sent for, but he was also refused admittance. It so happened that this was on December 15th, the eve of the feast of Saint Lucy, and Tommaso was inspired to appeal to Catherine, who had a great devotion to this saint. He went to see her and found her at home, but in a state of ecstasy, surrounded by her friends. They told him that in the afternoon Catherine had said that she beheld preparations being made in heaven to keep the feast, and that it was shameful that nothing was being done upon the earth. She was even then preparing to go to San Domenico to ring the bells herself, when suddenly, quite contrary to the season of the year, a storm broke over Siena — and, as the custom was, all the bells of the town began to ring. Thus Catherine's desire was fulfilled and when the thunder ceased to roll and the bells fell silent she heard wondrous singing in Paradise. In the midst of the heavenly choir stood Lucy, purest and fairest of them all. On her bosom sparkled a jewel, a great gem set in pure gold, given her by Our Lord in honour of the feast. Catherine was still absorbed in the contemplation of this vision when Father Tommaso arrived. The priest explained to the Mantellate that he had come to ask for Catherine's prayers for a poor young man, who was in grave peril of dying in a state of impenitence. He then left them.

About ten o'clock in the evening* Catherine awoke from her ecstasy. As soon as her confessor's message had been given her she again gave herself up to prayer and so remained until day-break. "But the 16th day of December had hardly dawned," says Caffarini, "before the rumour of the conversion, the re-

* *Intorno all'ora quinta della notte.* In December the angelus bell rings at five o'clock in the afternoon; "5 o'clock at night" is therefore our 10 o'clock in the evening.

pentance and the Christian death of Andréa Bellanti was spoken of everywhere; presently it came to the ears of Father Tommaso, who was greatly astonished and hastened to Catherine, to learn whether the Sisters had faithfully delivered his message. He saw Catherine herself and questioned her on the subject. She replied that as she had received the message in time she had prayed for the soul of the sick man, and assured him that this unhappy soul had, moreover, obtained forgiveness for his sins. 'But how do you know that Andréa de' Bellanti repented and that he has escaped hell?' the monk asked. 'I am telling you the truth, Father,' she replied, 'Jesus appeared to Andréa, who was seized with contrition and humbly implored His pardon. But Jesus, looking sternly upon him as his judge, declared that his sins were too great and that the hour of justice had come. Nevertheless, He consented to have mercy upon him, on condition that a soul, dear to Jesus, would be willing to suffer in his stead, and I was chosen as this soul, for in no wise fearing to bargain with Our Lord, I said to Him: "Lord, I desire and will that the rigours of Thy justice shall be satisfied in me, to the end that this poor man may be saved, and I am even willing to be condemned in his stead, if salvation can not be obtained for him in any other way. I will not rise from my knees until thou grant me my desire." By the mercy of the Most High my prayer was heard: the face of Our Lord shone and He promised to give to this sinner the grace of repentance and to save him from everlasting damnation.'"

"At the very moment when she ceased from prayer," Caffarini adds, "the dying man, enlightened from on high, begged that a priest might be sent for; to him he confessed his terrible sins and soon after he breathed his last in peace."

All this agreed, and yet, says Caffarini, Father Tommaso was still in doubt; it might have been accidental, it might be an illusion; perhaps Catherine had already heard the news from others. In order fully to convince himself he asked her certain questions about the appearance of the room in which Bellanti had died and she then described to him all that he had observed himself during his fruitless visit: the outward appearance of the sick man, the size of the room, the position of the bed, the material and colour of the curtains and the coverings on the bed, even adding that the dying man had declared to the priest that he had distinctly seen the devil ready to seize his soul, but that at that moment a maiden robed in white had entered, and striving with the Evil One, had driven him out; "after which this maiden prevailed upon me to make my confession without delay if I desired to escape eternal punishment."

Thus the year 1370 ended with Catherine's first apostolic work, the conversion of a great sinner.

Christmas, the Feast of the Nativity, came; then the New Year and the Befana (Epiphany). Winter now made its appearance in Siena; every morning all the fields were white with hoar frost and one day a snowstorm whirled through the streets. The vines, stretching their tendrils from tree to tree, looked like garlands of white flowers; the olives bent under the unaccustomed weight; the cypresses, under their mantles of snow, loomed like seamen's landmarks out of the snowy haze. It was the season of clear and frosty nights. In the morning at the hour of Mass the streets and lanes were lit up by the cold blue light of the moon, and old women carried beneath their cloaks a hot *scaldino* with which they warmed their frozen fingers.

Every feast of the Church was the occasion of new visions for Catherine. On Christmas night she went with the other Mantellate to the Capella delle Volte to sing Matins, but no sound came from her lips, her soul was entirely absorbed in contemplating the radiant Crib before which Mary was kneeling in prayer, adoration and rapture, and she besought the Blessed Virgin to entrust the Infant Jesus to her for a moment. Mary held Him towards her and Catherine cradled Him in her arms, kissing the little silky head, and whispering in the tiny ear the names of all those who were dear to her. During Mass she beheld the Sacred Host transformed into a child so lovely that words could not describe it. From the bosom of this Child sprang (like the branch spoken of by Isaiah) a vine bearing ripe, heavy grapes; on every side big, beautiful white dogs with black spots came running up; they ate of the grapes and pulled off great bunches which they carried out to the little dogs, which, not being able to reach up to the vine, had to be content with what the others gave them. Catherine understood that these big dogs represented all the priests, and in particular her friends the Dominicans,* while the little dogs symbolised the faithful people, and that this vision foreshadowed a great reform in the Church of God. Catherine was so filled with joy at this vision that she received Holy Communion, not only on Christmas Morning, but on the two following feast days (of Saint Stephen and Saint John the Evangelist) and persuaded the other Mantellate to do the same.

On New Year's Day Catherine was again in the Capella delle Volte with the other Sisters. After the Consecration, when the moment for Communion was drawing near, she was so overcome with emotion that she would have fallen, if two hands, at once strong and gentle, had not held her up from behind. She dared not turn round to see who it was, but she felt that it was the Blessed Virgin.

According to her custom she remained very long at her thanksgiving, and when it was over she felt so tired and weak that she wondered how she should be able to walk home. (Since the feast of Saint Lucy she had been in a continual state of ecstasy, without any other food than the Sacrament of the Altar.) But He who had promised never to forsake her was faithfully waiting for her outside. As she went out of San Domenico, Jesus approached, saying to her: "My daughter, lean on Me," putting His arm about her and kissing her tenderly. For several days the fragrance of this kiss remained on Catherine's lips and was perceived by all who came near her.

Epiphany came. Father Tommaso had enjoined upon Catherine to receive Holy Communion on that day, but during the night she was so ill that she could not move for pain. She arose, however, in order to obey her confessor and dragged herself to church, more dead than alive. After having received Holy Communion she remained for some time deeply absorbed in prayer and suddenly saw before her a narrow door, by which no one could enter without having first deprived himself of his own will and become ready to suffer. Catherine went through the doorway and at once a number of saints came towards her: Saint John the Baptist, Saint Dominic, Saint Thomas Aquinas,

---

* "Domini canes," the dogs of the Lord, such was the general interpretation in the Middle Ages of the name of the Order.

Saint Peter Martyr, Saint Agnes and Saint Lucy. All held in their hands as it were white garments, these they held out to Jesus Christ who stood in their midst and who clothed Catherine in them. The names of the garments were: Faith, Charity, Perseverance, Zeal and Humility.

In the evening Catherine broke her long fast; but Jesus took the piece of bread that she was about to eat, put it into the wound in His side and gave it back to her. It tasted like milk and honey.[8]

Visions followed visions, all of them charged with deep meaning. At times it seemed to Catherine that the altar at which Mass was being said was burning, as once the bush on Mount Horeb, and that the priest remained safe and sound in the midst of the flames, like Shadrach, Meshach and Abednego in the fiery furnace. One day she was seized with a doubt of the real presence of Christ in the Blessed Sacrament: the bread is and remains bread; the wine is and remains wine; how then can they become flesh and blood by the mere fact that a priest utters over these species the five words of the consecration? Then, at the moment when the priest was uttering these mighty and mysterious words, she beheld two angels bearing the Body of Christ in a cloth of fine linen, coming down from heaven and placing It on the altar. "Lord," cried Catherine, "this vision was not needed, I would have believed without it." "It is not for thyself that I show thee these things, but because of those whom thou shalt confirm in the faith," replied Jesus. For Catherine was a support not only to all the Mantellate, but to many others among the faithful. Their faith seemed more living when they were near the ecstatic, and many were those who came to kiss the stones in the floor of the dark corner in the chapel where she was wont to kneel.[9]

And so time passed and the feast of the Conversion of Saint Paul came, on January 25th. Catherine, who had just arisen from one of her frequent spells of illness, crept rather than walked to San Domenico. Contrary to her usual cheerfulness she was downcast, a strange faintness seemed to paralyse all the powers of her soul, she felt as if she had no faith, no hope, no charity; impious and unholy, unworthy to enter the house of God. The spirit of the publican, so strong in her, weighed her almost to the ground. She "stood afar off, not daring to lift up her eyes," did not go into the Capella delle Volte to the other Mantellate, but cowered in a corner behind the door, against a deserted altar. A priest came walking from the sacristy to say Mass in the Capella delle Volte — Catherine did not dare to go in. Then one of the Sisters discovered her in her corner, came down the church and fetched her. Catherine followed her and when the moment came to receive Holy Communion she advanced to the altar rails with the others. The priest, though, pretended not to see her and passed her by with the Sacrament: he was not going to have any of those scenes of tears and ecstasies in the church!

Her object unattained Catherine had to return to her place, faring no better when two other priests afterwards said Mass in the chapel. The Prior of the monastery, Bartolommeo Montucci, who was also the spiritual director of the Mantellate, had simply forbidden the priests to give Catherine Communion for the time being.

"But though rejected by the priests she found mercy with the Lord," says Caffarini. For without allowing herself to be angry or scandalised at the disgrace of rejection, she quietly knelt down in her place — the black sheep among the spotless white ones — and suddenly a light from heaven dazzled her, on a golden ground she saw (as on an altar piece by Sano di Pietro or Matteo di Giovanni) God the Father and God the Son side by side on the heavenly throne, above them the Dove of the Holy Spirit, and out of the radiance came a hand of fire holding a white Host, and a voice spoke the solemn words which Our Lord spoke in the night in which He was betrayed, when He took bread in His holy and venerable hands, gave thanks, brake and gave to His disciples, saying: "Take and eat ye all of this. For this is my Body." Bathed in the ocean of light of the Holy Trinity, Catherine received the Sacred Host, felt it like a live coal upon her lips, swallowed it like a drop of liquid fire. . .[10]

The next day a band of robbers was seized in Siena and two of them were condemned to be pinched with red hot tongs and to be executed on the gallows hill (Poggio delle Forche). If, at the present day, you go from the market-place behind the Town Hall down to the old well and washing-place, and turn your steps to the picturesque but dirty Via del Sole, you will have on your right a blind alley. In the Middle Ages this street led (for reasons easy to understand it was called Via dei Malcontenti, "the Road of the Discontented") through Porta della Giustizia to San Stefano a Pecorile, where the place of execution was. On that 8th of February the two miserable condemned criminals were led by this road. The executioners came with them on the tumbril and seized them with red hot tongs, and in this way the sad procession came past the old Saracini palace (now *il Casone*) where Catherine was just then staying on a visit.[11] Alessia was sitting at the window and called Catherine, but as soon as the latter had seen what it was she recoiled, knelt down at the back of the room and began to pray. She had heard the curses, blasphemies and cries of despair of the two who were condemned to death; she had recognised their hardened hearts and now fought for their eternal salvation. She saw them surrounded by ethereal hosts which were only waiting to carry off their souls to hell — yellow, green and red devils as on a picture by Fra Angelico, or as Paolo di Neri's fresco in the monastery courtyard of Lecceto — and she implored her Bridegroom to have mercy on the two miserable sinners. In spirit she continued following the tumbril, like a priest who usually accompanies the condemned to the place of execution, and with tears she exhorted the two sinners to repentance. In vain did the demons attack her, in vain did they threaten to take possession of her and rob her of her reason. Catherine did not yield and did not give up; and just as the tumbril reached the Gate of Justice the Lord heard her prayer. Visible to Catherine, but also visible to the two malefactors, Jesus stood beneath the archway in the figure of the Man of Sorrows, thorn-crowned, with the mock robe of royalty round His shoulders, bleeding from all His wounds, with a look of grief like that with which Sodoma's Christ bound to the marble pillar looks at one. Like a convincing flash this look penetrated the hearts of the two sinners; they saw themselves and were filled with horror; they saw the Saviour and wept; their defiance melted away. They sang a hymn and instead of blaspheming God and His holy Mother, they confessed aloud that for their great sins they deserved a far greater punishment than glowing tongs . . .

and Catherine continued in spirit to go with the tumbril on the long road to the place of execution and did not stir from them until they had breathed their last sigh — then she came to herself, murmuring the words of the Saviour on the Cross: "Today thou shalt be with me in Paradise." [12]

There are those who will say that such things are inconceivable, and that such stories are legends. Perhaps such things really are inconceivable, but that does not make them any the less real. Is it not a characteristic of reality sometimes to be inconceivable? And Catherine's tele-activity is no more legendary than her television. Who will presume to make laws for the ultra-violet rays of the human heart or set limits to the radio-activity of the human will? The cathode light from Catherine's soul penetrated the thickest walls, those of hardened souls; and healed the deepest wounds, those of conscience.

The rumour of the conversions obtained by the dyer's daughter of Fontebranda soon spread beyond the town and she asquired fame as a sort of miracle-physician of souls. People came to her with the most hopeless cases of spiritual and physical disease. Many were the mothers of prodigal sons, many the despairing and unhappy wives, who went to Catherine's cell for advice, or at least for consolation.

In Alessia's house there was plenty for her to do. Her friend's father, Francesco Saracini, an old man of over eighty, was as hardened a sinner as any Andréa de' Bellanti. In all his life he had been only once to confession, during a serious illness, and now he scoffed at any talk of it. All Alessia's warnings were fruitless, and in her need she begged Catherine to come and stay with them for the winter; the daily intercourse, Alessia thought, might more easily afford some opportunity of approaching the old sinner.

It happened to be during the year when the wool-spinners in the low-lying and despised Bruco quarter rose in rebellion (a movement like the *Ciompi* rising in Florence seven years later). For several days the Bruco people were masters of Siena and put seven of their men in the city council. The adherents of the Twelve rose in opposition, supported by the Salimbeni family and a fierce fight on the steep Costa d'Ovile ensued (July 30th, 1371). The other families of the nobility, however, went, as always, against the Salimbeni; the party of the Twelve suffered a decisive defeat, one of the leaders, Francesco di Naddi, was beheaded in the middle of the market-place, another, Nanni di Ser Vanni Savini, was sentenced to a fine of five hundred florins. Those were stormy times and the pious Alessia might well be afraid of old Francesco Saracini coming to a sudden and violent end.

Evening after evening Catherine and Alessia sat by the fire with the stubborn old man. He seems in particular to have had a great hatred of priests — like Folgore of San Gimignano he despised "the mad monks" — "most of what they tell you is lies." [13] And he would rattle off to her, with the passionate contempt which is still to be met with in an old Garibaldist who was at the battle of Mentana, all the sins of Italian priests in general, and those of a certain Sienese prior in particular. "I cannot endure him, and if I ever meet him I will murder him," was the furious old man's invariable refrain.

Catherine did not contradict him; in the course of time she had gained not a little knowledge of the failings of priests and the decadence of the Church. Instead, she began to talk to him about something else, about the great knight and captain Jesus Christ, mounted on the spirited charger of the Cross and fighting against Satan, and of the blood that He shed in the ardour of love, and in which alone we can be saved from all our enemies, the vices and devils. That Blood is in the care of the Church, only the priests have the keys to it, without them we cannot have a share in it. Leave them as they are then, grant even that they are devils incarnate; they are the anointed of the Lord, we have no right to judge them, the Lord has reserved to Himself judgment on them. The strength of the Sacrament is not lessened, even if the hands which administer it be unworthy, and for the sake of the Sacrament we ought to honour them all, the bad as well as the good.[14]

In such ways as these Catherine may have spoken to old Francesco Saracini. It was the same doctrine that Francis of Assisi had preached a century and a half earlier: "I will fear, love and honour all priests as my masters, and not see any fault in them, for I behold in them the Son of God, and this I do because in this world I see nothing else of the Son of the Highest but

His holy Body and Blood, which alone the priests receive and give to us."[15] Catherine persevered in urging this doctrine upon the old man and the day came when she no longer preached to deaf ears. "Tell me what I must do," he said, "I am ready to do anything." "Then go," was the answer, "and be reconciled to that prior who has so grievously wronged you and whom you hate so bitterly. Forgive him, and Jesus will forgive you." Old Saracini promised to do so, and with the thoroughness of Italian piety he took his favourite falcon and put it on his hand to give to his enemy. Thus provided he entered the church to which the prior belonged, but when the latter saw him, he fled, convinced that his last hour had come. Francesco then sent a messenger to the priest, to tell him that on the contrary he came in peace, and wondering, still trembling for fear, the priest accepted the falcon of friendship from the hand of his enemy, hitherto so irreconcilable. With a joyful heart the old soldier then went to Fra Bartolommeo de' Dominici, confessed all the misdeeds of his long life, received absolution of his sins and returned happily to the Palazzo Saracini. During the year still remaining to him he could be seen going to Mass in the Duomo early every morning, having in his hand a rosary, on which he daily said his hundred Our Fathers and a hundred Hail Marys.[16]

It was probably in consequence of this remarkable conversion that another old warrior of the same family, Niccolò Saracini, also repented. His wife had begged him to talk with Catherine, but that he refused to do: "Why should I talk to that young woman?" But she continued to haunt his thoughts. When old Ser Francesco had repented and had begun to go to church, the same thing might happen to him. . . And one night in a dream he saw Catherine, and the next day he made up his mind to go and see her, "only to see whether she looked like that in reality." But from Catherine the road went straight to Fra Tommaso della Fonte's confessional.[17]

It was evident that Catherine had the gift of disquieting souls. One could not remain indifferent about her; one had to love or hate, to follow or persecute. This was realised by one of the proudest and wildest of the young men in Siena, Giacomo Tolomei, who was bursting with brute strength, and

THE IMITATION OF CHRIST

like the German knight, Werner von Urslingen, "an enemy of God, of compassion and mercy." This thoroughly masculine creature, brimming over with vitality, boasted of already having two murders on his conscience, and was furious when he heard while away on one of his campaigns, that the little cloak-sister from the dyer's house at Fontebranda had now also gained an entrance to the dignified old Palazzo Tolomei. His mother, Monna Rabe, had long been "pious," that of course one had to put up with; it was the sort of thing that came with ageing years! But his younger brother Matteo, had also begun to put on sanctimonious airs; and his sisters, his two splendid sisters, Ghinoccia and Francesca, two of the prettiest girls in Siena, they had been persuaded by that little monster to cut off their beautiful golden hair, to throw all their ornaments and rouges on the refuse heap and to join that bleating choir of old maids, who crept about on the floor of the Capella delle Volte! "Take care that you don't get converted yourself, when you come to Siena," said Matteo, who brought this news to his elder brother. "I'd sooner wring the necks of the whole mob of priests," answered the young soldier.

This ferocious animal was also tamed by Catherine and brought into the fold through the narrow door of the confessional. He became a totally different man, living for many years as a blameless husband and father in Siena, and seeming, even in his old age (he died on July 20th, 1406, in Venice), to have been received in the Third Order of Saint Dominic. His younger brother Matteo became a Dominican, and the two young girls, who had before been so worldly, died like saints — "with unutterable joy they went blissfully smiling to the Lord," says Raymond.[18]

And so Catherine's winter in the Palazzo Saracini was passed. "But from September until the beginning of Lent she lived on nothing but a little raw lettuce," Caffarini writes. "And when Lent began, even that slight nourishment was too much for her, and what she had eaten in the morning she had to yield up again in the evening . . . But from Passion Sunday [the fifth Sunday in Lent] "until the joyful feast of the Lord's Ascension it was impossible for her to take any food whatever. . . For fifty-five days she kept herself alive and in health without tasting the very least, either bread or vegetables or any other food. At the same time she suffered unbearable pains, caused by that continual fasting, but the strangest thing about it was that those pains did not hinder her from working with the same ardour and zeal as was ever her wont.

"Some days before Ascension, however, she felt so ill that she thought she could not bear it any longer, and trustfully she turned to God, saying: 'Lord, how long wilt Thou that I shall continue in this pain?' She received the answer that she would be delivered from it on the feast of the Ascension. On the three days before the Ascension, while processions were held to pray for the blessings of heaven on the young growth, Catherine lay in bed and could neither go to church, nor, as she usually did, take part in the processions . . . Then the Lord vouchsafed to her an angel who in white and precious raiment brought her the most holy Body of Jesus Christ. . . And in those three days she could not speak with a single soul. . ." [19]

On the Eve of the Ascension Bartolommeo de' Dominici and five other friars came to visit her in the Palazzo Saracini. Catherine was aware of the serious state of her illness. "I shall either go hence, and that I should desire most," she said, "or else I must from henceforth live in a quite new and strange manner." The next morning she awoke perfectly well, called in a loud voice for Alessia and asked for her cloak and shoes. Together they walked to San Domenico, and after the Mass Catherine's face shone with such radiant joy that the Sisters who crowded about her decided to go home with her and partake of the midday meal. But as Alessia was not prepared for so many guests a pan with boiled beans was brought, with much gaiety, from the convent kitchen to the Palazzo Saracini. Catherine sat down to the table, eating and drinking like the others, and all day long there was an invasion of friends and acquaintances, with whom she even drank a glass of wine, and altogether (as Caffarini says) she was *l'allegra e festosa vergine,* the gay and festive maiden.[20]

VI

"Judge not, that ye be not judged." This saying from the Gospels is among those which made a great impression on Catherine. It occurs again and again in her letters, she uses it as a shield and buckler. Again and again does she complain of those who "judge the servants of God."

"He who is perfect," she writes in a letter to a Carthusian, "never judges the servants of God, nor any other creature whatsoever. Not even if with his own eyes he had seen others sinning should he pass judgment, but he should look upon them with compassion and plead before God, taking upon him the faults of his neighbour. Charity demands this of us and it forbids us to be like the imperfect who are still blinded by self-love. For it seems that these live only to judge others and it is not so much the children of the world that they judge, as it is the servants of God, in that they are scandalised at all those who do not live after the same manner as themselves." [1]

Catherine spoke from bitter experience, she knew what it was to be judged. She was an object of scandal in more ways than one, but there was one thing in particular that gave offence, and that was her gradual and almost complete abstinence from meat and drink. That dinner on Ascension Day had been a mere passing incident, soon it was again as impossible for her as before to take any nourishment. And the talk about it went on. At one time it was said that she was play-acting . . . "Why, my dear, of course she eats when nobody sees it! It looks so holy not to need any food!" Others, her confessor, Padre Tommaso, among them, were of the opinion that it was all imagination and *commanded* her to eat. She obeyed, but was so ill that he had to permit her, as usual, to render up the food again. "My stomach is like that," she explained, "because in my early youth I was so greedy for fruit. God is punishing me now for my gluttony."

"During all the time I was in the company of that holy virgin," Francesco Malavolti testified after her death, "I saw her living on Holy Communion alone . . . But so that she might avoid giving scandal she would sometimes take a little lettuce or other raw vegetables or fruit, and after chewing it, turn away and spit it out. And if only the least solid particle or even a little juice of the vegetables or fruit entered her stomach she had no peace until she had again rendered it up. And such vomiting caused her so great trouble that her face was quite swollen with it. At such times she would retire with one of her women friends, drink some cold water and with the stalk of fennel or a quill pen she would tickle her throat until she had thrown up that which she had swallowed. She called this process bringing up for justice, and when it had to be done she would say: "Let us bring this miserable sinner up for judgment."

Stefano Maconi, who made Catherine's acquaintance four years before her death, gives the following description of her mode of life: "She had a great aversion against meat and wine, sweet things and eggs. Generally her women friends prepared raw vegetables for her, *salad,* as it is called, when it was to be had, or a dish of cabbage in oil. She would eat only the head and tail of an eel. She did not eat cheese, except when it was very old. She really did not eat anything, but would take something in her mouth, afterwards spitting out all the coarse part and often drinking water with it. This she continued to do as long as the others sat at table, then she would rise and say, 'Let us go and bring this miserable sinner up for judgment.'" He tells the same as Francesco Malavolti and adds: "This is the pure truth, which many of us have seen, that so long as there was anything left in her stomach of juice or water or aught else, even so much as a bean, her whole body became ill and quite useless." [2]

Catherine's friends were grieved and shocked at the accusations of hypocrisy directed against her; even after her death Raymond of Capua devotes a whole chapter of his story of her life to defending her fasting. What must it not have been while she lived?

She did not, however, allow anyone to defend her. "Dearest daughter," she wrote later to one of her women disciples, "I must rebuke you because you have not remembered what I have enjoined upon you, not to answer those who might say something about me that was not in my favour. If in future anyone speaks evil of me, then you must only answer them that a great deal more might be said, and that they do not say nearly enough. But you must also ask them to feel as much compassion for me in their hearts as they have on their lips, so that they will earnestly beseech God to convert me and bring me to a better life." [3] "Every thing may be turned to good account," she often said. "Whatever befalls us, whether of joy or sorrow, our first thought should be: my soul shall make use of it! If we always did this we should soon be rich." [4] In this too, the Sienese woman agreed with the pious Umbrian who saw his true benefactors in those who blamed him and accused him, because they made him aware of his faults.

The accusations against Catherine, however, soon became more serious. The pious gossips found new and welcome material in Catherine's growing intimacy with the Dominicans — these long talks in the church — and now lately this dinner, which it seemed had been provided by the monastery! Many an elderly sister in the Lord felt the thorn burning in her flesh and rumours began to buzz. A devout widow named Palmerina, who had given her whole fortune to *Casa della Misericordia,* was the first to set them going; an old, invalid Mantellata, whom Catherine nursed, was the next. It went so far that the Prioress at last sent for Catherine. When the young woman understood of what she was accused, she threw herself at the feet of the Prioress: "By the grace of God, my dear Sister, I am a virgin!" she exclaimed. Nothing further was done about the matter, Palmerina died soon after and Catherine continued quietly nursing the invalid Mantellata, whose name was Andrea.

Meanwhile, we are told by Bartolommeo de' Dominici, the accusations still occupied Catherine's thoughts. She could not believe that anyone could accuse another falsely out of pure malice; there must be a reason; she must have given cause. And conscience began its work of searching. She who had once wept for three hours because she had for one second looked away after her own brother Stefano, she who had for three days and three nights accused herself because she had thoughtlessly told two Dominicans, who came to fetch her for a walk, that she would go with them, although it was not her intention — she would be sure to find out in the end, really and actually, that the devout Palmerina and poor, sick Andrea were right. "Alas, Lord," she complained, "if only I could believe that I suffered unjustly, that I suffered with Thee, I ask for nothing else. . ."

In this great distress of her soul Jesus appeared to her one night. In His right hand He held a crown of gold, adorned with pearls and precious stones; in His left the crown of thorns. "Both these crowns are meant for thee, my dearest daughter!" said the Voice she knew so well, "but thou canst not wear them at the same time! Choose then, whether thou wilt have the golden crown now, but then thou canst not have it later! Or whether thou wilt wear the thorny crown of persecution and suffering, so that I may keep the crown of justice for thee for everlasting life."

Without a moment's hesitation Catherine stretched out her hand for the crown of thorns. Should she not wear it gladly, when she was sure that it came from Him — that it was a distinction and not a chastisement? And Jesus pressed the wreath firmly about her temples, so firmly that ever after she felt the pricking of the thorns on her brow. . .

Next day she went to her nursing with the joy of a conqueror and proud as a young bride; all the time she felt the sweet bitterness of the crown of her Lord about her brows. The days passed, the sick woman was rapidly sinking. One morning a large cancerous sore had opened in her breast, and diffused an intolerable stench. When Catherine got home, the smell was still clinging to her clothes, and Lapa, violent as always, raged about it. *Maladetta figlia!* she screamed (in the official legend by Raymond of Capua she expresses herself more politely, but Bartolommeo is probably right), — "You confounded girl! It is not enough for you to destroy yourself, but you must fill the whole house with stench as well!"

Meanwhile Catherine was not deterred from exercising her labour of love; like the Samaritan in the Gospel she dressed the repulsive sores of the sick woman every day and poured oil and wine upon them. One day she had pressed out a large quantity of matter from the sore into a bowl, and nearly vomited at the sight. Then, as the old narrative relates, she was incited by

THE IMITATION OF CHRIST

such a holy hatred of herself that she put the bowl to her lips and began to drink of its terrible greenish-yellow contents. Many years after, this heroic deed of her youth was recounted by Raymond of Capua. The Dominican shuddered — "Was it not horrible?" he asked Catherine, who was sitting at his feet. "No," she whispered, "I never tasted anything sweeter!" We moderns, and we modern Catholics included, must try to make the best we can of such a deed. We invoke our gods — of hygiene and æsthetics — or whatever they are — and in their name we turn away in horror from Catherine emptying the bowl of pus. But Andrea, poor afflicted, spiteful Andrea, did not turn away. "Daughter, daughter," she cried (calling her *figlia*, as older Italian women generally call the younger ones), "daughter, daughter, do not kill yourself!" And the tears welled up from the hardened heart, she begged Catherine's forgiveness and sent for the Prioress of the Mantellate, so that she might retract all the evil accusations she had made against her young nurse. "The greatest love conquers," says the German poet.

In the night that followed Catherine had a new vision. Our Lord Jesus Christ appeared to her, and putting His pierced right hand round her neck, He bent her head to His breast and guided her mouth to the open wound in His side. With her lips against the open lips of the wounded side of Jesus Catherine drank long draughts of the divine hero and martyr blood with which she desired to fill her own heart.[5] No doubt she had that hour in mind when she wrote later to the Prior General of the Carthusians these words: "Glorious and precious is the blood of the humble and immaculate Lamb! And who can be so unwise or so hard that he does not take the vessel of his heart and go in love to the wound in the side of Christ Crucified, from which the blood flows freely?"[6]

From that time, says Raymond, the fame of Catherine was reported widely, and many journeyed to Siena to see her. A few years ago pious visitors made pilgrimages in the same way to Lucca to see Gemma Galgani, and in the southern part of Germany there is a small village where to this day many go to behold a woman, who in the most literal sense (like Francis of Assisi) can say with St. Paul: "I bear about in my body the wounds of the Lord Jesus Christ." *

One day when Catherine was lying ill in her cell, a "servant of God from Florence," probably a hermit or another devout man, came in and without any preliminaries began to heap abuses and reproaches upon her. Catherine answered not a word while her guest was speaking, only sitting up on her hard couch and remaining seated, motionless and silent, with bent head and arms crossed upon her breast. The devout visitor, who had only wanted to test her humility, went away satisfied. "She is like gold that has been tried in the fire," he said to her confessor, who went to the door with him.[7]

The Franciscan, Fra Lazzarino of Pisa, was a more difficult and redoubtable critic. He was lecturer in theology at the Franciscan convent in Siena and a preacher who drew many listeners to the church of San Francesco. Driven, perhaps by the old rivalry between the two Orders, he began a violent and ruthless persecution of Catherine, calumniated her, both in the convent and the town, and mocked at all who had any dealings with her. He particularly attacked Fra Bartolommeo de' Dominici, who was at that time giving lectures on the Lombard's Sentences, tried to draw the students away from him and at last began a course of sermons against Catherine and her followers. In order to get material for these sermons he decided to pay her a visit, being quite convinced that during their talk she would soon betray herself and show that she was not the pious soul she was said to be, but more likely a heretic.

One evening, it happened to be the eve of Catherine's feast day, November 25th, he came to Fra Bartolommeo's cell and asked to be taken to Catherine. The Dominican, thinking in his guilelessness that the other had at last seen his error, hurried to Fra Tommaso della Fonte and obtained his permission, and then gladly accompanied his opponent to the Via dei Tintori. The two visitors stepped into the cell, where the dusk was already falling, and Catherine asked them to be seated: the Franciscan on her clothes chest, the Dominican opposite him on the couch, while she herself sat down on the floor, according to her habit, at the feet of Fra Lazzarino.

* Theresa Neumann.

There was silence for a while, neither Catherine nor the Franciscan wishing to begin. At length the latter spoke (and Fra Bartolommeo has kept a record of the interview):

Fra Lazzarino: "I have heard so much of your holiness, and that the Lord has granted you insight to understand and interpret the Scriptures. Therefore am I come in the hope of hearing you speak comforting and uplifting words."

Now, independent interpretations of the Scriptures were exactly one of the points on which Catherine could be caught and convicted. It has been stated above how she interpreted in her own way the prayer of Christ in Gethsemane, and it was not the only place which she submitted to an ingenious but free exegesis. Catherine perceived the snare and answered:

"It is a great happiness for me to see you. You know the Holy Scriptures, you interpret them daily for the food and refreshment of souls. Of a truth you have come hither to strengthen and build up my poor soul, and this I beg of you to do."

Catherine had parried the thrust, and for a while they now exchanged remarks like two well-matched opponents, who walk round each other trying their rapiers. Catherine, however, did not expose herself in the least before the captious theologian, and at length the Angelus bell rang and gave the hint for departure to the two ecclesiastics. "I will come again at a more convenient time," said the lecturer as he stood up. Catherine went to the door with him, knelt down before him as he was taking his leave and asked for his blessing, while also recommending herself to his intercession. Fra Lazzarino made a careless sign of the Cross, adding, as pious courtesy requires, "Pray for me too, Sister," and left, with feelings half-way between superciliousness and disappointment. That Catherine had seen through him he did not understand. "Good enough little girl, but not very intelligent," he thought on the way home. With that he went to bed. He had to give a lecture the next morning and had to prepare for it early next day.

But on the next morning he did not wake up bright and gay as usual, pleased with himself and life, but in deep, crushing misery. He dressed himself, but the heavy grief was still there, and before he was aware of it he suddenly began to weep. The lecturer was a man who hated any giving way to feelings, and annoyed with himself he wiped away his tears and fought against weeping. It only welled up all the more; at last he was walking up and down in his cell or standing helplessly leaning up against one of the whitewashed walls, weeping unrestrainedly.

Being a man of reason Fra Lazzarino set to work to examine the matter methodically. There must be a cause for this unreasonable fit of crying and he began to look for it. First in the natural order of things — "did I sit up too late last night with the others, and perhaps drink a little too much? Or is it because I lay down to sleep without drawing my hood up over my head?" His conscience, however, did not reproach him with anything in regard to what he had drunk — and in spite of an Italian's dread of uncovering his head (*tenga in capo* is the first formula of Italian courtesy, urged with anxious eagerness: "do keep your hat on!") he could not believe that a slight cold could make him weep so continually.

The time passed, his weeping did not stop. The lecture had to be postponed and Fra Lazzarino stayed in his cell all day. He now began to look for reasons in the supernatural world. Could this sudden inexplicable grief be an omen, perhaps, that a great disaster had happened to him: "Has my mother died suddenly? Has my brother perished by the sword?" he asked himself. Or had he, unknowingly, seriously offended God?

The day passed and Fra Lazzarino remained inconsolable. The dusk came, and then he remembered where he had been the day before at the same time. He saw the little room before him, where the lamp burned quietly before the Crucifix, and on the mat of rushes at his feet frail little Catherine in her white habit, with the pale face, the dark eyes, questioning and expectant, gazing at him. . . He saw her pale lips open and speak. . .

Then he knew all at once what his transgression had been. He understood who and what Catherine was, that she was the sincere one, who really belonged to God, who lived up to what she believed. And he understood what he was himself . . . the insincere one, the preacher without deeds, the man with the warm words and the cold heart, the man, who in his heart did not believe, who *could* not believe, because in his heart he was always seeking his own. . . He looked round his comfortable cell with its well-filled bookshelves, its broad bed, its comfortable chairs, and reflected that in his comfort he had dared to judge her who lived in honest poverty and genuine imitation of Christ — of her who had so sincerely and humbly commended herself to his intercession and begged for his blessing — and he had made the sign of the Cross over her with three hard, haughty fingers and had carelessly tossed her his "Pray for me too, Sister!"

When Fra Lazzarino had perceived this his weeping began to abate, as when a child has had out its fit of crying in its mother's lap or on its father's knee, and lifting up its face again looks up at two smiling eyes. Happy as a child the learned lecturer dried his tears and now longed for only one thing: to go back to Catherine and tell her what a little self-satisfied and conceited soul he was and to beg her forgiveness because he had dared to judge her.

Early in the morning, before the late dawn of the November day had begun to appear, Fra Lazzarino stood outside Catharine's door. She came and opened it herself and he sank down at her feet. Then Catherine knelt down too and besought him to rise. They both stood up and went into the cell, and Fra Lazzarino would not sit any longer on the couch, as on a lecturer's chair, but sat down on the mat beside her. And there, *in the cell of self-knowledge,* the learned theologian surrendered his whole soul into Catherine's hands. "Hitherto I have only known the shell of Christianity," he exclaimed, "you have the kernel!" A great peace descended upon him, and while the tears welled up again (this time they were tears of joy) he listened to Catherine (the "mother of souls"), who gently but firmly reminded him what his brown habit and bare feet and the cord with the three knots meant, and showed him the way to the spiritual guide whom he had vowed in his youth to follow, but later had left and betrayed — the Poor Man of God of Assisi. "There is the way of salvation for you," said the Dominican Sister. "Despite all earthly riches, do not conform to the world, cast away all money and all unnecessary possessions, follow frugally and humbly Christ Crucified and your Father Santo Francesco."

Brother Francesco went home to the convent, the large, beautiful convent which is now the archiepiscopal seminary, took what he had of money and superfluous garments and gave them to the poor, and out of his large collection of books he kept only some volumes of sermons. Once again a Saul had been turned into a Paul, a persecutor into a disciple.

Fra Lazzarino, though, had to suffer greatly because of this sudden conversion. "Yesterday you attacked Catherine, today you sing her praises," everyone said contemptuously. Finally he retired altogether from his brethren in religion and lived in a hermitage, which he only left when he went about in the country to preach. But his sermons were better than ever before; Catherine strengthened and comforted him in all his adversities, and he felt it as a joy and an honour when they shouted after him in the streets: "There goes *il Caterinato*." [8]

VII

"All the saints of God are one in the bonds of charity. They have a particular communion with those whom they loved here in the world with a particular love. For with that love they grew in grace and increased in virtue, and one caused the other to increase the honour of my name, both in themselves and their neighbour. That love is not lost in life everlasting, they shall always be near to each other, and it is an addition to the joys of everlasting life which is given to all. . . Not so, that their hearts are not full and need to be filled further — they are filled, they cannot hold any more! But there is an exultation, a joy, a sweetness, a happiness which is renewed in them when they see the good which the Lord has worked in the other souls." [1]

Una exultatione, una giocundità, uno giubilio, una allegrezza — the very sound of the words chosen by Catherine, testify to what friendship between souls, love between those of like mind, meant to her. Not even in heaven was it to be forgotten; in that she agrees with the Danish seer: [*] "We shall for ever there in the light speak with friends." How much more must not the friendship of friends, the affection of disciples here on earth be a comfort and sweetness to her and a joy and exultation?

She was happy in the midst of her *bella brigata,* as she loved to call the circle that gathered around her. Her old friends the Dominicans, and her old women-friends — Alessia, Lisa, the two Catherines, Francesca Gori — were joined by a large number of new ones. Among the latter there was only one woman: Giovanna Manetti, married to Nello Cinughi, a member of the Pazzi family so famous in the history of Florence, and generally known by that name. As *pazzi* in Italian means "mad," Giovanna was soon re-christened "Mad Joan," *Giovanna Pazza,* but she returned the compliment by calling Cecca (Francesca) Gori *stolta Cecca,* "foolish Cecca" and Alessia "fat Alexia." These friendly nicknames were also applied by the persons in question to themselves; when they wrote Catherine's letters for her they generally added a greeting on their own ac-

[*] A quotation from a hymn written by Gruntvig.

count and then signed themselves as *Alezzia grassotta* or *Cecca pazza*.² A letter to Bartolommeo de' Dominici and Tommaso d'Antonio di Nacci Caffarini is concluded by Alessia in this way: "Alessia commends herself a hundred thousand times, she is longing to see you again and wonders greatly that you have not written at all. May God guide us all to that place where we shall see each other face to face in the presence of God." She adds further in a postscript: "Alessia the Useless would fain roll herself up in this letter so that she might come to you." ³

The kind of influence exercised by Catherine is perceived when reading the letters written by her to disciples, when journeys took her away from Siena. In the Catholic care of souls, there is, besides the confessor, also another guardian of souls, the so-called spiritual director. One might say that it is he who does the more delicate work, while the coarser is left to the confessor. Catherine was the spiritual director of her whole brigade.

"I, Catherine, your unworthy, miserable mother [she says in a letter to Alessia] desire to see you reach that perfection for which God has chosen you. But it seems to me that if you would get so far, you must walk moderately — and at the same time without moderation. We must love God without moderation, that love must not know either measure or moderation. But if you would attain to perfect love you must put your life in order. And the first thing then, that you must do, is to flee from all communion with creatures only for the sake of pleasure, when love does not require it — love all, but seek intercourse only with few. And those too, whom you love with a spiritual love, you must love in moderation. . . If not, you may easily turn that love which belongs to God alone from Him to creatures, for you love them without measure — which will hinder your perfection. . .

"Be like a concha which you fill at the spring, and from which you draw water and drink while it remains standing by the spring.* Suppose too, that your heart is filled with love

---

* Catherine is thinking of Fontebranda. When the concha remains standing underneath the flow of water, one can draw water from it, as much as one likes, without emptying it.

from God — if it does not remain in God it will soon be empty. And this shall be a sign to you, that you are not drinking your fill in God, when that being whom you love, causes you suffering, and that you grieve then over something else than the offence which may thus have been given to God — then your love is still imperfect and outside the spring.

"You ask me how the imperfect love shall become perfect? In this wise: you chastise and punish the movements of the heart with true knowledge of self, with hate and dislike of your imperfection, because you are so bad, that the love which you owe to God is given to creatures, and love God with moderation, but creatures without moderation. Watch, therefore, that you love all things and all men in God and correct every inordinate affection.

"My daughter, build yourself two cells. First a real cell, so that you do not run about much and talk unless it is needful, or the Prioress has ordered it, or you do it out of love for your neighbour. Next build yourself a spiritual cell, which you can always take with you, and that is the cell of true self-knowledge; you will find there the knowledge of God's goodness to you. There are really two cells in one, and if you live in the one you must also live in the other, otherwise the soul will either despair or be presumptuous. If you dwelt in self-knowledge alone you would despair; if you dwelt in the knowledge of God alone you would be tempted to presumption. One must go with the other and thus you will reach perfection. For of self-knowledge arises hate of the sensual nature, and you place yourself with the sword of hate on the judgment-seat of conscience and bring your feelings up to judgment.

"From this self-knowledge spring also the waters of humility, so that you endure all indignity with joy, all loss of comfort and all suffering, from whatever side they come. The humble soul feels refreshed by persecution and shame seems an honour to her, so that she rejoices in seeing her spoilt sensual self-will, which always rebels against God, punished and herself conformed to Christ Crucified, Who is the Way of Truth.

"In the knowledge of God you find the fire of divine love. Where will you find your joy? On the Cross, with the Lamb without blemish, seeking His honour and the salvation of souls by persevering and humble prayer. In that is all our perfection. There are many other things to care for, but prayer is the chief one. For there we get light, so that we do not go astray in the lesser things which follow from them.

"Let it be your joy, beloved daughter, to become conformed to the indignities of Christ. Watch over your tongue, that it speak not in the evil superfluity of the heart, but melt what is in your heart with hate and contempt of yourself. Be the least of the least, subject to every creature in patience and humility, not with excuses but in saying *mea culpa*. . .

"Have a care of your time. When you have given your body the sleep it needs then say Matins and go to Mass, and do not waste your time in gossip. And when you have dined, retire for a while and work your hands, according as it may be needful. And wait upon your aged mother with great care and attend to her wants; let that burden be yours. More when we meet. Have a care that you do my will. I will say naught else. Remain in the holy and sweet love of God. Sweet Jesus, Jesus Who art love." [4]

Catherine is a good mother but she is also a strict mother. She wants her disciples to do as they are told. Again and again this expression recurs in her letters: "Do this for me" . . . "Be this or that for me . . ." She is a born ruler who feels that she has a right to rule, because she wills that which is right.

In a letter of about the same time to another of her women friends, Caterina di Scetto (or Ghetto), she expands one of her favourite thoughts: the identity between the love of God and love of one's neighbour. "We conceive the virtues in the love of God," she writes, as a woman to a woman — "and we bring them forth in love of our neighbour. When you act thus, that you love your neighbour without guile, freely, with no hidden thought of your own gain, either spiritual or temporal, then you are a true handmaid of God, and return the love of the Creator for you with love of your neighbour — then you are a faithful bride and not a faithless one. You are a bride . . . And as the bride of Christ you should be the handmaid of your neighbour. We cannot be of use to God in our love of Him, we should therefore serve our neighbour with true and heartfelt love."

As we can see, the relationship of a bride to God is purely ethical. The love of God is revealed as love of one's neighbour, the service of God as service of man. It is good New Testament doctrine. "We know that we have passed from death unto life, because we love the brethren. He that loveth not, abideth in death," says Saint John the Apostle.[5]

It was a great joy to Catherine that her mother at length joined the circle. The tie of blood is not always the tie of the spirit — perhaps even seldom. Those who are nearest to each other in the flesh are often furthest apart in conviction, in mind, in their outlook upon life. Jesus was thinking of it when He said that He had come to bring a sword and not peace. "I came to set a man at variance against his father, and the daughter against her mother . . . and a man's enemies shall be they of his own household."[6]

Lapa and Catherine were the exact opposites of each other, the one living in this world, the other more and more in the world to come. Great, therefore, was the despair of both when Lapa (in October 1370) fell seriously ill, says Raymond. The illness seemed to presage death, and Lapa by no means wanted to die. In vain did her daughter speak to her about a priest and the Sacraments. "I will not *hear* of it," said Lapa irritably, "but as you are so holy, as they are always telling me, then go and pray to Our Lord that I may get well!" With a heavy heart Catherine left her, and as she knelt absorbed in prayer her mother suddenly grew worse, and in the presence of her daughter-in-law Lisa Colombini, of Caterina di Ghetto and yet another Mantellata named Agnola di Vannino, Lapa Benincasa breathed her last. . .

"Is that the promise, Thou hast given me, Lord, that none of mine shall be lost?" exclaimed Catherine, when the message was brought to her. On the feast of Saint Agapitus in August in that very year Jesus had expressly given her this promise, and she had received the pain of the wound in His right hand as a pledge. Once again she wrestled with God in prayer. . .

She conquered; Lapa returned to life — and lived far, far longer than she cared to. Children and grandchildren died around her, at last she sat quite alone in her rooms out in Via Romana, forsaken and forgotten by everyone, even by death.

"I think my soul must be stuck crosswise in my body, so that it cannot get out," she usually said.

A change, though, had come over Lapa after that illness. Before long she, too, became a Mantellata; took part, as well as she could, in her daughter's life and accompanied her on the last journey to Rome.[7] The few letters written to her by Catherine are quite short; two of them are evidently answers to her mother's complaints at being so lonely. The daughter points her to the example of the Blessed Virgin, who after the Ascension of Christ did not keep the Apostles back in Jerusalem, but let them go out to preach the Gospel. The disciples, too, would fain have stayed with Mary, but their work called them. As the true disciples of the Lord we must also give up ourselves and think only of the glory of God and the salvation of souls — "for this my Creator has chosen me, I am in the world for nothing else, dearest Mother!"[8]

Catherine's brigade of priests and women was increased by a third corps, consisting of young and elderly men who came in from the world outside. One of the first was Messer Matteo di Cenni Fazi, who with his friend Francesco di Lando put in an appearance out of pure curiosity in order to see Catherine in her state of ecstatic prayer. This sight made such a profound impression upon the two men and made them so conscious of the reality of that unseen world with which Catherine was in such close communion, that they resolved to come again and speak with her. "If the mere sight of her can do this, what must it not be to converse with her and be guided by her?" they said to each other. Both sought her friendship and became her faithful disciples. Messer Matteo, who had until then lived a rather worldly life, but whom Master William Flete in Lecceto had led to other thoughts, devoted himself to works of charity as Rector of the second largest hospital in Siena, *Casa della Misericordia.*[9]

A man of quite different character was Neri (Rinieri) di Landoccio dei Pagliaresi. He was a young man of great refinement and culture, he read Dante and wrote beautiful verses himself, was in a high degree of a poetical temperament, could be raised to a heaven of joy and sink into the depths of melancholy. As Colombini had had his spiritual mother in Monna

Foresia, the Abbess of Santa Bonda, Neri wished to stand in a filial relationship to Catherine. "You have asked me to adopt you as a son," she writes in her first letter to him, "and although so miserable a sinner as I am quite unworthy of it, I have already adopted you and do so with great affection. I also pledge myself to answer for you to God for all the sins you may have committed, or may yet commit."

To bear chastisement for the sins of others was what Catherine desired most; she promised her friends again and again to do this, and Caffarini relates how she often implored God in prayer: "As Thou, Lord, didst bear the pains that we had deserved, so will I bear the punishment for my spiritual children." [10] "Begin a new life," she writes to the notary, Ser Antonio di Ciolo, "and I will take upon me all your guilt and melt it with tears and prayers in the fire of the love of God and do penance in your stead." [11]

This promise, then, she also gave the young Sienese poet. This gave her the right, though, to tell him what she expected of him, that is, "altogether to tear himself away from all conformity to the world. For the world is at strife with God, and God with the world, and they have nothing whatever in common. . . God made Man chose as His lot perfect poverty, insults, anguish of the heart, mockery, contempt, hunger and thirst; despised all human honour and esteem; sought always the honour of His Father and our salvation, persevered to the end with true and perfect patience, and there was no pride in Him, but perfect humility. . . The world is the direct opposite: it seeks honours and glory, pleasure, pride, impatience, avarice, hate, rancour and self-love, and a man's heart grows so narrow that he has no room either for God or his neighbour.

"And yet, how foolish and mistaken are they who conform themselves to this evil world — how are they deceived! They seek honour and find reproach; they seek riches and are poor, for they do not possess the true treasures; they seek pleasure and enjoyment, and they are sad and heavy-hearted because they have not God, Who is the highest happiness. They will not hear aught of death and suffering, and they fall straight into the abyss of death; they wish for a secure life and depart from the firm foundation of the Rock."

As so often elsewhere Catherine appears here as the relentless realist, as one who sees reality as it is, and who cannot evade the great fact that "this world and the form thereof will pass away" — *tutto passa!* In the spirit of the Gospel she now develops further the fundamental paradox of Christianity: "He that loveth his life shall lose it; and he that hateth his life in this world, keepeth it unto life eternal." [12] "The true servants of God," she writes to Neri di Landoccio, "strive with great care not to be in any wise conformed to the world . . . but they choose that which Christ chose as His lot . . . and then they find the opposite. They choose poverty and the lowest places, and they are honoured; they have peace and joy and happiness without any sorrow. I do not marvel thereat, for they are conformed and transformed to the highest and eternal truth and goodness, which is God, in Whom is all that is good, and in Whom all true and holy desires are fulfilled." [13]

Neri left his family and attached himself to Catherine in order to serve her as her secretary. His soul, always volatile, continued to be a prey to changing and contrary moods, his imagination played him continual tricks, so that he saw things larger and different from what they really were. Being very sincere in his piety he was tormented by scruples and severe doubts about himself; it seemed to him, as it did to Luther a hundred years later, that he could not possibly be saved. Catherine had, again and again, to cheer and comfort this soul, which was "like a leaf shaken by the wind." [14] Her letters to him are often short — written casually as an encouragement, such as a friend would write when he knows that the mere sight of his handwriting on the outside of a letter can strengthen and comfort the other. She gives him practical advice: not to neglect prayer, "to keep Easter every Sunday," i.e., to receive Holy Communion,[15] "not to take scandal at anything, to bear willingly the sweet sufferings of the body." [16]

Once only does she deal seriously and in detail with his spiritual struggles. "I wish [she writes] that your despondency may consume itself and vanish away in trusting in the blood of Jesus and in the fire of the ineffable love of God. . . Is He not more ready to forgive than we are to sin? Is He not our physician, and are we not His patients? Did He not bear our iniquities?

Is not despondency a greater fault in His eyes than all others? Yes, assuredly! Dearest son, open the eyes of your understanding and with the pupils of faith behold how you are beloved of God. Be not downcast and disconsolate because you see His love on the one hand and on the other how cold and feeble is your heart. Even if you must recognise that hitherto you have not requited God for all the benefits He has bestowed upon you, then humble yourself so much the more and say with a holy resolution; 'That which I have not done hitherto I will do now.' You know that which I have always told you, that despondency is a leprosy which is hurtful to soul and body and paralyses all holy desires, making the soul unbearable to herself and turning the mind to all manner of fancies and interior unrest; it robs you of the supernatural light and darkens the natural one. And thus the soul is led into great infidelity, in not recognising the truth of God, which is that He has created us for eternal life. With a living faith, with holy desire and with firm trust in the blood of Jesus I ask you therefore to put the devil of despondency to flight." [17]

Neri brought his friends to Catherine, and several of them became her disciples. Among the latter was Gabriele di Davino of the famous house of the Piccolomini; a Piccolomini on the throne of Peter was later to canonise Catherine. It is said of Gabriele that he would not allow anyone to speak ill of Catherine in his presence. His son, Giovanni di Gabriele, became a Dominican and died in the fame of sanctity.[18]

Another friend of Neri was that restless youth, whose relations with Catherine consisted of a continual series of conversions and lapses — Francesco di Messer Vanni Malavolti, of one of the great houses of Siena. Many years after he told the story of his youth himself:

"At that time I was about twenty-five years old, and not a little proud and overbearing because of my birth and my family. I was rich in worldly goods, and spurred on by the desires of youth I lived as dissolutely and licentiously as if I were never to die, and thought of nothing but the lust of the world and the flesh, and was not restrained by any respect if I could but satisfy the demands of the senses. It happened, however, that there was, among the great number of my friends and companions and those of my own age, one who was among my closest friends, a young nobleman named Neri di Landoccio di Messer Neri de' Pagliaresi, with whom I spent most of my time, both because he was pleasant and refined, and because I admired the beautiful verses he wrote. After we had known each other for some time it happened that Neri heard tell of that famous maiden, Catherine, and, unknown to me, visited her several times; I only wondered that he had become so changed in mind and manner.

"Neri, who was grieved at my dissolute life, and who cared for the welfare of my soul more than the health of my body, asked me several times if I would go with him and visit the said Catherine. I waved it aside and laughed at him, and so some time passed. As he continued his importunities, however, I promised at last for the sake of friendship to go with him. I thought to myself, though, that if she began to preach to me or talk about going to confession, I would give her such an answer that she would never talk in that way again." [19]

Francesco Malavolti now learned what so many others had had to confess: "she conquered all who came to her." Or, as one of her disciples of the later years, the papal notary, Tommaso di Pietra, declared: "her radiant countenance and holy smile made everything else seem of no account, save that of doing the will of God." [20]

This was the experience of Francesco Malavolti. He says himself that he came to her like "a brutish and almost devilish man." He began to tremble all over as he sat face to face with her. At the first words from her lips he felt — as Verlaine sings — "a new, clean heart burning in his breast," went to confession and from that hour began to live a new life. In spite of his marriage to a good and beautiful girl of noble birth, he had hitherto roamed about like a faun after peasant girls and young married women. He now gave up even his married life, and instead of running to dancing and carousals with the other members of the *brigata spendereccia,* he spent his time in churches or sat at the feet of Catherine in the circle of pious friends.

Then it came to pass, in the midst of this honeymoon of conversion, that Francesco Malavolti suddenly fell into a grievous sin. He does not say which, but it is permissible to think that he yielded to one of the old temptations. After such a life as his there would be many ties to loosen, perhaps there was some young girl or other who begged him to meet her once more for the last time at the usual trysting-place among the lonely olive-fields around Siena.

But this time Ser Francesco goes home with a bad conscience. The hot kisses on his lips have left a bitter taste behind. And in the evening, in an unhappy state, he turns his steps into the familiar road leading to Catherine's house.

With the eyes of a mother she sees that he is not the same as yesterday — the air about him is different, it tells of the unrest of sin. She makes all the others go out and bids Francesco sit down beside her.

"When were you last at confession?" she asks when they are alone.

"On Saturday," he answers, truthfully enough.

Everyone in the circle around Catherine went to confession every Saturday, and to Holy Communion every Sunday. At the bottom of his uneasy conscience he may have had the intention to confess his sin, and then of course all would be well again.

Catherine, though, did not want the evil to take root, she wanted the tare to be pulled out at once from the young wheat.

"Go to confession at once, my son," was her grave answer.

Francesco still held his ground, still acted the part of innocence.

"Dearest *Mamma*," he said, "tomorrow is Saturday, then I will go to confession as usual."

Then Catherine turned to him with a flaming face.

"How now, my son? Do you really believe that I do not know what you have done? Do you think that my eyes do not continually follow all my children wherever they go? You can *do* nothing, *say* nothing, which I do not know at once! And you imagine that you can hide your misdeed from me? You have done this and that, at that place and in that hour! So go at once and cleanse yourself from so great a misery!" [21]

It was not the only time Francesco failed in his good resolutions. There was a time, particularly when Catherine was away from Siena, when the young nobleman again sought his old haunts. "Dearest, more than dearest son in Christ, sweet Jesus [Catherine wrote to him], it seems to me that the devil has carried you so far away that you will not let yourself be found and led back to the fold. I, your poor mother, go about seeking you and asking for you, and I would take you on the shoulders of my grief and compassion and carry you home. Dearest son, open the eyes of reason, look up from the darkness, confess your guilt, not in despair, but with self-knowledge and hope in God. Behold and acknowledge that you have shamefully wasted your inheritance of grace, given to you by your heavenly Father. Do therefore like the prodigal son: he had wasted his goods and suffered want, and then he returned to his father. So it is with you, you have become poor and needy, and your soul is starving to death. . . Woe, woe, where are all your pious resolutions now? Miserable one that I am, must I look on while the devil steals your soul and all your good resolutions? The world and its servants have stretched out their nets for you with all manner of disorderly joys and pleasures. But do you arise and seek rescue, do not sleep any longer. Comfort my soul and be not cruel to yourself and your salvation. Do not let me implore you any longer, let not the devil deceive you, do not keep away from me, either from fear or from shame. Tear up this sling, come, come, dearest son! Well may I call you dear, for you have cost me many tears and much care and bitterness. Come therefore now and return to the fold." [22]

In this way Catherine pleaded like a good, anxious mother with the prodigal son, and he came, filled with shame, but happy in again sitting at her feet. He came — to disappear again, and the Mantellate who were with Catherine were at last scandalised at this inconstancy and waywardness, this hesitating between heaven and hell. Catherine alone was never scandalised and never angry, was always the same *dolcissima Mamma,* answering the complaints of her friends with the sweetest smile: "He is a wild bird, but he shall not escape from my hands. Just when he thinks I am far away, I will throw a sling round his neck, and he shall never be able to free himself!" "We laughed at these words, both the Sisters and I," writes Malavolti. But after Catherine's death, and after having lost both wife and children, when he sat as a monk in his cell at Mont' Oliveto, he recalled these words and understood what Catherine had meant by the snare in which she would catch him.

Francesco's conversion had of course been a scandal to his former associates: for some mysterious and significant reason he who would live an honourable and decent life is generally out of favour with his old friends, who look upon conversion as something more disgraceful than forgery. There were in particular two of the former boon companions who could not forget Francesco's desertion; they were Neri di Guccio degli Ugurghieri, with whom the Malavolti had intermarried, and Niccolò di Bindo Ghelli. Whenever and wherever they could find an opportunity to do so they raged against Catherine, "and we are not afraid to tell her so to her face," they declared. Francesco offered to introduce them to Catherine, but warned them that it was certain to end in their conversion. "If she were Our Lord Himself in person, she shall not get away with us," the two noblemen boasted.

They went to Catherine, sat facing her, and she began to speak to them in that clear, limpid and purling tongue, still to be heard from the lips of women and children in Siena. Her smile shone upon them, the smile remembered again and again by her disciples when writing about her, and which must have been irresistible. And ere the two sinners were aware of it, their eyes were filling with tears — Catherine was so good and kind — and they felt how evil and unclean they were themselves. Suddenly they fell on their knees before her: "Madonna," they stammered, "tell us what we must do. We will go on pilgrimage for our sins to Rome or to San Giacomo di' Compostella!" Catherine, though, did not ask so much of them, she simply bade them go with Francesco Malavolti up to San Domenico and make their confession to Fra Tommaso della Fonte. Francesco went with them and said to himself, quietly and wonderingly: "There is no one who can escape from the hand of this holy little maiden!" [23]

And so the circle widened of those who submitted to the authority of Catherine's charity.* Among other disciples of that time are the young nobleman Nigi di Doccio Arsocchi; the capable man of affairs, Sano di Maco, often employed by Catherine as the addressee of the letters sent by her to the whole circle of disciples when she was away on her journeys; the influential Tommaso di Guelfacci, who had been one of the friends of Giovanni Colombini; the hermit, Fra Santi from Teramo; the notary, Ser Cristofano di Gano Guidini, who has left us his memoirs of Catherine; finally the painter and democratic politician Andrea di Vanni, to whom we are indebted for the fresco in the Capella delle Volte, depicting Catherine at the age of twenty and (according to tradition) painted on one of the pillars of the chapel while she was in ecstasy. The stigmata and the kneeling woman have been added later and the fresco has now been placed above the altar in the chapel. Taken together with the bust in the Municipal Library of Siena, it enables us to obtain an idea of Catherine's outward appearance.

Catherine had a mother's heart and mind for this large number of disciples. She had Lapa's generous temperament. "I shall continue with tears to bring disciples into the world until my death," she exclaims in a letter. She would nourish them, not with milk but with fire, and again and again she calls them to her, "as a mother calls a child to her breast." She parts from them with *una santa piccola tenerezza* and in her letters she assures them that they are more precious to her than her life.[24]

When they were away travelling she followed them in spirit; often, just as she was sitting in the circle of her disciples, she would get up and go away and pray, saying: "My dear sons are calling me." Generally it turned out that they had been in some great danger, and that it had been warded off by Catherine's prayers.[25] Thus Fra Tommaso della Fonte and Fra Giorgio di Naddo felt that they were delivered from the violence of robbers between Siena and Montepulciano; Stefano Maconi was later to experience the protection afforded in invoking her name in a similar danger; Fra Bartolommeo de' Dominici felt consolation and light irradiating his soul from Catherine's ecstatic prayer before the altar of Saint Peter Martyr in

---

* *Autorità di carità,* an expression of Raymond's.

Siena, one morning when he was praying in a bitter spiritual struggle in the church of Santa Maria Novella in Florence.[26]

Perhaps the most beautiful testimony of what Catherine was to those who were intimate with her is given by Francesco Malavolti in the following narrative:

"While I was still wearing the garments of the world — it was during the early days of my conversion — it happened that I agreed with my friend Neri that we would go together to the monastery of Mont' Oliveto, which is about fourteen miles distant from Siena. But as it was during Lent we resolved that we would take our first meal on the way in a town called Asciano, which is about twelve miles from Siena. And this we did, but when we came to Asciano we had no desire to eat, and therefore we decided to go on and not eat until we could do so at the monastery with the friars, and it seemed to us that we could well bear to fast so long. But we had hardly walked a little over a mile when we felt so weary that we had to sit down and rest, and we were so tired and weak that we thought we could not possibly walk any farther that day. This troubled us for there were no houses near. And as we talked with each other about this, behold it happened (according to the councils of God) that we chanced to speak of that blessed virgin Catherine. And hardly had we uttered her name when we felt marvellously strengthened, and we stood up, and notwithstanding the steep road we walked on for more than a mile, speaking all the while of that handmaid of God.

"In our ignorance, however, we did not suspect whence we had that strength, and we therefore began to talk of other things and no longer of the bride of Christ, and immediately that weakness returned, so that again we had to rest. But the Lord, who would open our eyes, made it so that again we began to talk of Catherine, and when our strength now returned we stood and walked with ease the remainder of the road, and saw that which before had been hidden from our eyes, because we had not understood sooner who it was that was helping us. Then we walked that part of the road still remaining in calling often upon the name of the maiden, and reached the end of our journey without weariness." [27]

The landscape between Asciano and Mont' Oliveto Maggiore

looks to this day as it did in the days of Francesco Malavolti and Neri de' Pagliaresi. It is the so-called *creta* — a peculiar desert country, consisting of nothing but barren heights, furrowed by heavy rains, cracked by the sun, and across which the road climbs laboriously up from Asciano to the little town of Chiusure and to the large, old monastery. Round about Asciano the valley is still green with corn or vines, or, in May, carpeted with purple clover. Soon, though, one is up among the ashen-grey heights, a kind of dunes, but of clay, not of sand, and they look as if they were covered with wrinkled elephant hide. The waves of clay grow more and more bare, their ridges sharper and sharper, the wind blows cold, the heights are desolate, only a lonely farmhouse with a cypress or two and some sparse corn on fields whose cultivation has cost much weary toil. Out beyond rise Mont' Amiata, Monte Cetona, Montepulciano, and if you turn round and look back, you see far away in the blue horizon Siena like a luminous vision, and notwithstanding the distance of seventeen miles, the belfry of the Cathedral and the *Torre del Mangia* of the Town Hall.

One September day I stood among those desolate heights, with the immense outlook over the tawny, lion-coloured *creta* to the distant towers of Siena. Shadows of drifting clouds sped across the endless plain, but Siena still lay shining in the sun. And then I saw so vividly how Francesco Malavolti and Neri de' Pagliaresi came walking up here from Asciano on that day in Lent — the gravely pensive poet with the friend who was so eager for the gaieties of life — he a sombre and Dantesque figure, already stooping a little, the other a broad-shouldered, blue-eyed Tuscan with strong senses, but endowed also with the deep gift of reverence for the beautiful and the pure.

They come wandering up over the ashen-grey heights, eagerly talking and Catherine's name flies to and fro upon their lips. He who loves knows the joy it is to utter the name of the beloved, and how, involuntarily, the talk turns to where the thoughts are, and by a hundred devious ways they seek their goal: to find a reason for speaking that blessed name, in which all light and life seems to be enclosed. Thus did the two disciples speak continually of the daughter of Giacomo Benincasa, and one has hardly ceased speaking before the other begins. They speak of her constant joy, she is always radiant and fresh like a morning in May, never downcast, never sad like the sad children of this world. And never an idle word from her lips, but always the evangelical "yea, yea," and "nay, nay." *Yea* to God and Christ and grace, *no* to the devil and self and the world. "Always does she fill us with her joy, and there is no sorrow so great but that we forget it when we are near her. And never do we speak of things so indifferent or of no matter; she always knows how to make them useful to the soul and to lead the talk towards God; and when she has once begun she does not cease so long as there are any who will listen to her. And notwithstanding all the pains she suffers in her body, she never complains, and if she is ever so ill, if there is anything in which she can help, she rises from her bed and works as if nothing ailed her. And never have we seen her angry, except in the cause of God. Never does she speak a hard word of anyone, except of herself, for she thinks of herself that she is the greatest sinner in the world, and is the cause of all the evil that happens in it, because she has not known how to turn it away. One thing only can make her sad: that is when all is well with her. But do you remember when she had those ugly red sores upon her arms and on her face, and right into her ears; she smiled and said quite cheerfully: 'They are my roses and my flowers!'"

"She is here on the earth, but she lives her life in heaven," Francesco Malavolti exclaims at last, "and it makes a miserable creature like me giddy merely to think of it!"

"But that is why she can be what she is to us, our venerable, joyous and sweetest *Mamma*," says Neri de' Pagliaresi.

The two young men pause and look out across the vast plain towards the towers of Siena, lying in the sunshine far away. Their thoughts go out to her who is now threading her way in those far-off streets between the Cathedral and the Town Hall of Siena. A feeling like homesickness steals over them, a longing to walk in again through the Porta Sanviene, but still more a longing for Catherine, for her little cell, her voice and her smile, her words and her counsel, and slowly they wander on towards Chiusure, eagerly continuing their talk about her who was to them what Beatrice had been to Dante and Monna Pavola di Forese to Giovanni Colombini — their *venerabile e gioconda e dolcissima Mamma*.[28]

VIII

The persecution of Catherine, the criticism upon her, had become quieter, but it had not ceased. At that very time it flamed up with renewed strength and again it came from the Friars Minor, that Order which all through the Middle Ages, notwithstanding all official friendship, stood in sharp and hostile opposition to the Dominicans. "There were at that time" (again it is Francesco Malavolti who relates it) "two greatly esteemed members of the Order. One of them was named Brother Gabriele of Volterra, of the Order of the Friars Minor, Master of Theology, and it was said that in the whole Order there was not a greater scholar nor a more able preacher than he, and he was at that time Superior of the Tuscan province of the Order. The other was named Brother Giovanni Terzo [*] and was likewise Master of Theology, and he was from Siena, of the Order of the Augustinians. These two able regular priests and scholars often talked with each other and murmured against that blessed maiden Catherine, saying: "This ignorant little woman seduces the simple and ignorant with her false interpretations of Holy Scripture, and thus leads many souls with her to hell. May it not be our duty to speak to her so that she may see her errors?"

In consequence of these deliberations, then, the two theologians decided to visit Catherine. As it happened, a large number of the circle were assembled: besides himself, Francesco Malavolti mentions Tommaso della Fonte, Matteo Tolomei, a certain Niccolò de' Mini, called Cicerchia, the old Gésuato Tommaso Guelfacci, Neri de' Pagliaresi, Gabriele Piccolomini, finally Monna Alessia, Monna Lisa, Monna Cecca and several other Mantellate. The Franciscan and Augustinian now stepped into the midst of this circle and having found seats, began to examine Catherine and subject her to a series of questions, each more captious than the last.

Now Master Gabriele, Malavolti relates, lived in his con-

---

[*] Brother Giovanni's family name was Tantucci, the surname Terzo (the third) having been given to him to distinguish him from two other brethren of the Order, of the same name.

vent in the style of a cardinal. He had had the walls taken down between three cells to make himself a spacious room; his bed was provided with curtains and rugs of silk; he possessed books and many other things worth many hundred ducats. Catherine knew this and suddenly she upset all the snares which the Franciscan had prepared for her and told him to be ashamed of the life that he, a son of Saint Francis, dared to live. "How is it possible for you to understand anything of that which pertains to the kingdom of God," she exclaimed, "you who live only for the world and to be honoured and esteemed by men? Your learning is of but little use to others and only harms yourself, for you seek the shell, not the core. For the sake of Jesus Christ Crucified, do not live on this wise any longer!" Her exhortation was so forcible that the learned Franciscan took the keys from his belt and handed them to Catherine, saying: "Is there no one present here who will go to my cell and take everything he finds there and give it to the poor?"

Then the old Gésuato, Tommaso Guelfacci, stood up; he had seen such things before, in the days of Giovanni Colombini, when Frater Cristofano Biagi gave the Gésuati permission to empty his cell and give everything to the poor and nothing was left but a sack of straw.[1] He now went with Niccolò Mini to the Franciscan convent and cleared Master Gabriele's room, and of all his books they left him only a breviary. The learned man changed his mode of life to such an extent that soon after he went to Florence and humbly served at table as a lay brother in the convent of Santa Croce. Master Giovanni Tantucci too, gave away all his possessions and later, poor and contented, accompanied Catherine to Avignon and Rome, and became one of the three confessors who went with her on her mission journeys to hear the confessions of repentant sinners. Francesco Malavolti had two fresh proofs that no one could approach Catherine without becoming better.[2]

Through Master Tantucci, Catherine came into contact with one of the centres of religious life in Siena, that is, with the old Augustinian monastery of Lecceto. "In the province of Siena," says Fra Filippo Agazzari, "there is a monastery of the hermit order of Saint Augustine, not quite three miles from the town, and it is called the forest monastery by the lake (Selva di Lago).

And as I have heard from the old brethren who were in the Order when I entered it, they said that that monastery was built more than three hundred years before all the Augustinian hermits joined together in one community,* and that many pious and exceedingly holy hermits had lived in that place. They said also that the renowned Messer Santo Francesco, during the first part of his life, had lived with them for a time. Then, after the Augustinian Order had been gathered up into one community, a new monastery was built in Siena.† But the holiest and most virtuous brethren continued to live in the forest monastery and they were so austere and zealous in keeping the rule and ceremonies that once the following came to pass: The Prior of the monastery was then an exceeding holy and venerable brother named Fra Bandino de' Balzetti da Siena, and it was immediately after the midday meal, during the hour of rest, when all the brethren were sleeping in their cells. But Fra Bandino was not sleeping and he saw that a thief had stolen the ass belonging to the monastery. Rather than break the silence or permitting any other to break it, he submitted to letting the thief steal the ass. Only he went into the church and fell down before the image of the Saviour, praying earnestly for that thief, that God would grant him true self-knowledge, so that he would repent and save his soul. Meanwhile the thief drove the ass before him and was already near the end of the wood, when the ass suddenly stood still and could not be made to move. Do what he would the ass would not go out of the wood. The thief, who feared to be surprised, then resolved to go away and leave the ass behind. But he fared in the same way, he could not get out of the wood and the air all round him was like a wall. Then he repented sore in his heart and made a vow to God and the Holy Virgin that if they granted him grace to go from thence he would turn back and restore the ass and thenceforth lead a better life. When he had made this vow the ass returned of itself to the monastery and he felt likewise that he was loosened, and he came to the monastery and asked for the Prior, who was that blessed Fra Bandino, and restored the ass to him, confessing his guilt with many tears and begging for-

* This amalgamation took place in the thirteenth century.
† Since 1820 the monastery of San Agostino has been a grammar school.

giveness, and telling of the wondrous thing that had befallen him. The blessed Fra Bandino forgave him and bestowed upon him a generous alms, with much charity exhorting him not to steal any more, but to lead a better life, and the thief gave his word and went his way in peace." [3]

This is only one of the many stories told by Fra Filippo of the brethren in his monastery, and which shows how Italian Christianity of that time was penetrated by the spirit of Francis of Assisi. Exactly thus would *il glorioso Messer Santo Francesco* himself have done with a poor thief who had stolen an ass.

This was the circle into which Catherine now entered. The two names of the monastery: *Selva di Lago* and *Lecceto* (*Ilicetum,* from *ilex,* holm oak) indicate the surroundings — wood and lake. To this day the monastery proper, standing on the top of a hill north-west of Siena, has to be reached by traversing large forests of ilex. At the foot of the hill there is a smaller monastery, San Leonardo al Lago, to which those brethren retired who wished for a still greater solitude and peace than life in a great abbey could offer them. It was down here, on the shores of the lake, under the ilexes, that Master Giovanni Tantucci made Catherine acquainted with a remarkable man who was to become one of her warmest admirers: an English Augustinian monk, William Flete, Bachelor of Arts of the University of Cambridge. Flete had probably been a fellow-student of Tantucci, who had taken his doctor's degree there,[4] and this acquaintance had led him from the green hills of England to the shade of the evergreen oaks at San Leonardo al Lago. Here he lived a life which in more ways than one reminds one of English pilgrims to Italy of a later day — Beckford, Shelley, Browning. . . Trelawney tells in his Memoirs how he found Shelley (*l'inglese malinconico,* as the happy-hearted Italians called him) one day in the pinewood at Pisa, sitting alone on the shore of a gloomy little lake, while his hat, books and loose papers lay scattered around him. "One of the pines had been undermined by the water and had fallen into it, and behind its trunk, almost hidden, sat the poet, gazing at the dark water and so lost in his poetic dreams that he did not hear me coming." [5]

Catherine found William Flete, also sitting like this, only that the books lying around him on the grass were manuals of prayer, and that he was not writing verses "From Ariel to Miranda," but theological or ascetical meditations. In the little chapel which is still shown in Lecceto, and where Catherine usually spent her time during her visits, he was soon after to write down the *Guide to a Spiritual Life,* which Catherine dictated to him.

William Flete did really need guidance. "He spends most of his time in the wood," writes Ser Cristofano di Gano Guidini in his memoirs, "and not until the evening does he return to the monastery." From another source we learn that "He often lives in the said wood in the caves which he has made for himself in dark and trackless places; thither he goes with his books, shunning all communion with men. His path is from the church to the wood and from the wood to the church, and he only speaks when compelled to do so by necessity." That is the lifelike portrait of that splenetic, misanthropic, taciturn Englishman. At last he did not even say Mass any longer in the church, to edify the congregation, but in one of his caves, for his own sole benefit.[6]

Catherine saw that he was a religious egoist and tried to reform him. She exerted herself to drag him out of his life of pleasure in solitude. Self-knowledge," she said, "is the true cell and we take it with us wherever we go. The exterior cell is of no use without the interior one, and if we are in the interior one we do not need the exterior one."[7] She enjoins upon him the duty of loving his neighbour, she admonishes him to show consideration and forbearance with others, she urges him not to live for his own spiritual pleasure and comfort, but to do the will of God and to be of use in the world. "I tell you from Christ Crucified that if your Prior wishes it, you shall say Mass in the church of the convent not only once or twice a week, but every day if it so please him. You do not lose the grace of God because you lose your spiritual consolation, on the contrary, you will find grace with God if you give up your own will. We ought to hunger and thirst after the salvation of souls, and so we ought not to think only of ourselves and our own pleasure, but we ought to have compassion on our neighbour and share his sufferings. If we neglect to do this it is a great fault. I will have you, therefore, to listen willingly to Fra Antonio's complaints and troubles, and likewise I beg Fra Antonio to lend a willing ear to what you have to say. I ask you this from Christ and from myself. Thus you will keep in charity, but otherwise you will give the devil room in your heart. I say naught else, but that I beg and beseech you to engraft yourself upon the tree of life, which is Christ Crucified. Sweet Jesus, Jesus Who is love." [8]

The Fra Antonio (da Nizza) mentioned in the letter is another of Catherine's disciples at Lecceto. They were joined further by the Sienese, Girolamo Bonsignori and Felice de' Tancredi da Massa. On the other hand she does not seem to have known the author of *Assempri* quoted above, Fra Filippo Agazzari, although he lived in Lecceto from 1353 to 1398 and was a diligent writer. "All the cells of the brethren in Lecceto were full of his writings," says Carpellini, who has edited him. Evidently there were circles which continued to hold aloof from Catherine, if not to be hostile against her.

Her efforts to convert the English hermit from the passive to the active virtues did not bring her much happiness. He cherished a romantic admiration for her, he venerated her cast-off garments as relics; after her death he wrote mournfully that he would never receive any more of her letters, never hear her voice in the hermitage by the lake. But during the Schism, when she begged him to come to Rome and join her and the other *servi Dei* in forming a bodyguard round the Successor of Christ, he excused himself and stayed away in his forest solitude.[9] He was a romantic, which is the opposite of being a mystic.

At the present day, Lecceto is no longer a monastery. Dissolved in 1840, it now serves as summer quarters for the students of the archiepiscopal seminary in Siena. Beneath the outer loggia of the church can be seen the frescoes of Paolo di Negri of the year 1343: restless life of the world at play and pleasure is here displayed, *la brigata spendereccia* setting out for the festival of the day in a *carroccio* gaily decorated, Cupid flying above it with his bow stretched, loving couples strolling among flowers, some plucking golden fruits from trees, gamesters sitting at dice-tables. Not Cupid only, though, is busy; demons, too, hover in the air, everywhere engaged on their evil work. This outer court has been intended as a bill of divorcement from the world and a penitential sermon for the children of the world. Its opposite is the innermost *chiostro,* painted in frescoes of the same period as the first, but by an unknown artist. Here, inside, the *monastery* is depicted, as the *world* was outside; the religious life contrasted with that of the world, *la vita religiosa* against *la vita mundana.* They are scenes corresponding to many a chapter in Fra Filippo Agazzari's pious book. Here you see the monks praying, scourging themselves, reading, pondering, weeping, embracing the Cross, conversing, dying, and their souls flying heavenwards. On one of the pictures all the brethren are sitting at a table loaded with good things; only one of the brethren is absent, he has gone out alone into the forest, and out there under the oaks he meets Jesus coming towards him in the garb of a pilgrim, in a coat of camel's hair and with a staff in His hand.[10]

The chapel in Lecceto, in which Catherine liked to linger, can still be seen; the inscription says: "Stay here thy steps, wayfarer, and consider with reverence the temple which Blessed Giovanni Incontri built in the year 1330, and in which the seraphic virgin, Catherine of Siena, received Christ, her Spouse." [11]

By stony paths, through thickets of holly and the laurel-like *albatrelli* — on a summer afternoon the sun flashes in the glossy foliage — you get down to San Leonardo al Lago, William Flete's place of retreat at the foot of the monastery hill. The lake has dried up, only a small pond remaining; the hermitage is a peasant farm and the church (rich in frescoes by Ambrogio Lorenzetti) is kept mercilessly locked up by its owner, a nobleman who lives far away from it. It is a Romanesque church with a beautiful façade, a simple portal in a pure rounded-arch style and having a rose-window above it. The green space in front of the church is surrounded by a stone dyke and here, at any rate, a disappointed pilgrim to places with associations of Saint Catherine is allowed to sit down and rest awhile. The forest extends in all directions, nothing but oaks and *albatrelli;* birds are singing and it is spring time and towards evening: the cuckoo can be heard calling. Catherine was fond of walking in these woods between Lecceto and Belcaro; we are told by Caffarini how she and some of her women friends roamed about in them for three days, at last returning to Siena in pouring rain, wet to the skin but praising God and all his works.[12]   Five centuries and a half have gone by since then, and those enthusiastic young men and women, so eagerly seeking God, have long since rested in their graves of saints.   But he who listens carefully, sending out his thoughts across the centuries, thinks he can still hear a faint echo, as it were, of singing, and the music of lute and viola and holy Laudes blending with the rustling of the leaves about San Leonardo al Lago. . .

IX

"In the names of Christ Crucified and our gentle Mother Mary.*

"Dearest and most venerable Father in Christ, sweet Jesus.

"I, Catherine, servant and slave of the servants of Jesus Christ, write to you in His precious Blood, wishing to see you bound with the bonds of love, as you have become bound as the legate of the Pope in Italy, according to what I have heard. This news was a great joy to me, for I think that you will be able to do much in that position for the glory of God and the good of Holy Church. But it is not enough that you are sent, therefore I said to you that I wished to see you bound with the bonds of love, for as you know we can do nothing to benefit either ourselves or our neighbour without love. Love is that gentle and holy bond which binds the soul to her Creator, it joins God to man and man to God. It was this love beyond price which fastened and nailed the God-Man to the holy wood of the Cross; it is that which brings peace to those who are at strife and re-unites those who have been parted; it enriches those who before were poor in virtue, for it gives life to all virtues; it gives peace and takes away war; it gives patience, strength and long perseverance for every good and holy work; it never wearies and never turns away from the path of the love of God and man, neither from labour and suffering, nor from abuse or insults. It never grows impatient so that it seeks comfort in the pleasures of the world. He who has that love cannot be shaken, for he is firmly established on the living Rock, Christ sweet Jesus, and has learned of him to love his Creator. . . In Him he has read the rule which he must obey and the doctrine that must guide him in his life, for He is the Way, the Truth and the Life, and he who reads in Him Who is the Book of Life walks in the glory of God and the salvation of his neighbour.

"I wish therefore, and desire that like a good servant and son, redeemed by the blood of Christ Jesus, you follow in His

---

* The letter is addressed to the Papal Legate in Italy, Pierre d'Estaing, and the Italian text contains an untranslatable play upon the words *Legato* (legate or envoy) and *legato* (bound).

steps with a manly heart and with willing care, and that you never turn aside from this way, neither for pleasure nor for pain, but persevere until the end. Have a care to uproot all injustice and to punish the many faults that the world commits, and which cast shame upon the name of God. Do what you can to make reparation for so great an injustice. I have great faith that when you keep yourself bound in the bonds of love you will use that office which the Vicar of Christ has entrusted to you in the way that I have said. You cannot use or do your duty as you ought without the bonds of love. I entreat you, therefore, strive to have that love in you. Bind yourself to Christ Crucified, follow in His steps with true and real virtues; bind yourself to your neighbour with works of love.

"But I would, dearest Father, that we should remember this, that if our soul be not stripped of self-love and all pleasure in herself and in the world, she can never reach that true and perfect communion of love. For the one love strives against the other, and so great is the strife between them that self-love parts you from God and from your neighbour, but that other love unites you with them; the one love brings you death, the other life, the one darkness, the other light, the one war, the other peace; self-love shrivels your heart so that there is no room in it either for yourself or for your neighbour; the love of God will make your heart large, so that it can hold both friends and foes and every reasoning creature. . . Self-love is miserable and turns its back on justice and commits every injustice, and it suffers from a slavish fear, so that it dare not do its duty, out of fear of offending others or of worldly loss which might follow from it. This is that wrong spirit of thraldom and fear which led Pilate to slay Christ. And such men do not work justice, but injustice; they do not live justly or honourably, but in injustice and vice and in the gloom of self-love. May such love therefore be far from you, but I desire you to be firmly grounded in true and perfect love, so that you may love God for the sake of God, because He is the highest eternal truth, truly worthy of love, and you shall also love yourself for the sake of God and your neighbour likewise, and not for any personal cause. Oh Father, Legate of our Father the Pope! Thus I will that you may be bound, in the true and ardent bonds of love — my soul desires to see it in you. I say no more. Strengthen yourself in Christ, sweet Jesus, fulfil your duties and be not neglectful in what you have to do, and I can see then whether you are a Legate (or whether you are bound,* that is, with the bonds of love to Christ) and whether you hunger and thirst after seeing the holy banner of the Cross raised up. Remain in the holy, sweet love of God. Sweet Jesus, Jesus, Who is love." [1]

This letter was written by Catherine when she was twenty-five years old, and he to whom the dyer's daughter of Siena writes (early in 1372) is the newly appointed papal legate in Italy, the French nobleman, Pierre d'Estaing, afterwards Cardinal of Ostia. It is the beginning of Catherine's political activity and it is therefore necessary to cast a glance at that political world into which she now entered, and which was to be her chief sphere of activity until her death.

Since 1305 the Popes had resided on the banks of the Rhône at Avignon. As French historians have pointed out, it was by no means anything new in the annals of the Church that the successor of Peter should live away from Rome. During the half century preceding that which has been called "the Babylonian captivity of the Popes," the Eternal City did not see much of the Vicegerents of Christ on earth. Innocent III had already often left Rome, which was always disturbed and rebellious. Honorius III generally lived in Perugia or in Rieti. Innocent IV (1243–1254) is elected Pope at Anagni, is only a short time in Rome, flees from Frederick II in 1244 to Lyons, where he remains for seven years, and when at length he returns to Italy, it is in order to make his home in peaceful Umbria, afterwards in Naples, where he dies. Alexander IV has a predilection for Anagni; he stays only a short time at the Lateran and dies at Viterbo. The Frenchman, Urban IV (1261–1264) resides at Viterbo, Montefiascone and Orvieto; these three towns also see within their walls his successor and fellow-countryman, Clement IV (1265–1268), who also stays in Perugia and Assisi. Not a single document of those issued by this Pope was dated from Rome. Gregory X (1271–1276) goes from Rome to Orvieto, thence to Lyons, where he con-

* *Legato.*

venes the fourteenth General Council. When at length he thinks of returning the journey is undertaken slowly and as it were reluctantly — on the way there is a halt at Orange, Beaucaire, Valence, Vienne; he goes through Switzerland across the Alps and dies at Arezzo. John XXI (1276–1277) is elected at Viterbo but is crowned in Rome; he resides partly in the Lateran, partly at Sutri and Viterbo. Martin IV (1281–1285) is elected at Viterbo, "where the Roman court then resided," and spends his pontificate in Tuscany and Umbria. Honorius IV (1285–1287) is one of the few Popes of that time who likes Rome; he takes up his residence at Santa Sabina on the Aventine and is only during the summer out at Tivoli. Nicholas IV (1288–1292) is elected in Rome, but prefers to reside in Rieti and in Orvieto. Bonifacius VIII (1294–1303) frequently goes out to Anagni, Orvieto and Velletri. His successor, Benedict XI (1303–1304) remains after his election only five months in Rome, has the intention of transferring the Papal Chair to Lombardy, but dies in Perugia.[2]

Nothing absolutely new therefore happened when Bertrand de Got, Archbishop of Bordeaux, after having been elected Pope and taken the name of Clement V, had himself crowned at Lyons and took up his residence in Gascony, or when his successor, John XXII (the Frenchman, Jacques d'Euse), remained in Avignon, where he had formerly been bishop.

It is under this Pope, however, that the name of *Babylon* begins to be flung at the exiled Roman Church. In the thirteenth century the great prophet of Calabria, Joachim of Santa Fiora, had proclaimed his prophecies of the near approach of a new age in the world; after the ages of the Father and the Son, the age of the Holy Ghost was now drawing near, the reformation of the Church was coming and judgment would be passed on all those who in the name of Christ had gathered to themselves the mammon of unrighteousness. These visions and thoughts found a fertile soil in the outermost wing of the Franciscans, in Ubertino of Casale, Pietro Giovanni Olivi and Gherardo da Borgo San Donnino. A zealous son of Saint Francis might well feel cause for scandal on finding that the Vicar of Christ had left a fortune of over half a million florins! Out of his nine years' pontificate Clement V had managed to scrape together this handsome amount, and from his will it appeared that he had lent the kings of France and England 320,000 florins, with which to make war upon each other, and that he had remembered his sorrowing relatives to the tune of 200,000 guilders.

The Franciscan Order, then, under the successor of Clement V, rose in their great struggle against the simonistic Popes in Avignon. Their leaders were Angelo Clareno (1260–1337), Liberato da Loro and above all the highly gifted Ubertino of Casale already mentioned.

Ubertino is the focus of religious life in Italy about the year 1300. Born in 1259 at Casale on the Po he becomes a Franciscan in 1273 at the early age of fourteen. In 1284 or 1285 he visits the deposed Franciscan General, John of Parma, in the hermitage at Greccio, and sitting at his feet, "gazing at his most holy countenance," he hears from "his most holy lips" about the great departed, the faithful lovers and the intrepid knights of the Lady Poverty, Brother Leone, Brother Angelo, Brother Masseo and Brother Rufino, who had lived in this little rock-hewn convent. In the mountain cave John of Parma, whence there is a wide outlook across the fertile valley of Rieti towards the bleak Abruzzi, the young Franciscan receives the baptism of fire of his ideal, which sets an indelible mark upon his soul, and the flame of which was stirred up to greater strength by Margarita of Cortona (1247–1297), Angela of Foligno (1248–1309) and Conrad of Offida (1241–1306). In Siena Ubertino made the acquaintance of the pious tertiary, Pier Pettinaro (d. 1289) and in 1305 he wrote his great work, *Arbor Vitae Crucifixae,* "The Crucified Tree of Life," on Mont' Alverna. This book became a Bible for radical Franciscanism and the General of the Order, Michael of Cesena, supported by Ludwig of Bavaria, stood up against the Pope. Called to Avignon to defend himself and there thrown into prison, the rebellious General made his escape and died in 1348, in opposition to the end. Ubertino himself went so far as leaving the Franciscan Order in 1317 to become a Benedictine; later he left that Order too, and a papal letter of September 16th describes him as "a vagabond roaming about the world." No one knows where and when he died.[8]

It is Ubertino and his circle of lovers and preachers of poverty who fasten the name of Babylon on the papal court on the Rhône. In return John XXII flings his bulls against all "fraticelli, beghines, bizocchi and brothers of a life of poverty (the Bulls *Sancta Romana* of December 30th, 1317; *Gloriosam ecclesiam* of January 23rd, 1318), and those who prove insubordinate are seized by the Inquisition, thrown into prison and burnt alive.[4] Moreover, sixty Sentences of Pietro Giovanni Olivi's interpretation of the Apocalypse are condemned as heretical on February 8th, 1326.

This struggle was continued under the following Popes residing at Avignon. Clement VI (1342–1352) threw the Franciscan Jean de Roquetaillade into prison for preaching the doctrine of Joachim of Santa Fiora, for proclaiming an approaching millennium and condemning the luxurious life of the clergy. Innocent VI (1352–1362) had two Franciscans burnt at Avignon. Meanwhile, instead of the voices that were silenced in this way, another voice was raised: that of Saint Birgitta.

The Swedish seeress was forty-seven or forty-eight years old when she came to Rome; it was in the year of jubilee in 1350. Driven by her mighty spirit she had already, while still in Sweden, sent Clement VI a letter in which, on behalf of Christ, she bade him make peace between England and France and come to Rome to keep the year of jubilee. The Bishop of Abo and Prior Peter of Alvastra had brought this letter to the papal court. "Think of bygone times, when you defied Me so often," Birgitta makes Christ say to the Pope. "You did what seemed good to you, but not what you ought; My hour is now coming when I will make you come up for judgment, and if you do not obey I will humble you as deeply as I have permitted you to rise. Then shall your boastful tongue be silenced and your name be forgotten in the world. . . I shall punish you because by shameful means you have obtained all your dignities, and because of what the Church has suffered in the days when you took your ease. Rise up, therefore, before your last hour comes. But if you doubt whose spirit it is that speaks here, then look into your conscience and see whether I speak not truth."[5]

Clement calmly stayed on at Avignon and his deputy in Rome, Ponzio Peretti, paid no attention to the Scandinavian prophetess. "The earth," said Christ to Birgitta in a vision, "hides heaven from this prelate." In Santa Maria Maggiore she had a revelation which she communicated to Cardinal Annibale Gaëtani. She had beheld the Catholic Church as a building which was on the verge of collapsing; the foundations had sunk, there were deep cracks in the roof, there were holes in the floor; if the Church were not restored soon it would inevitably fall, and the fall of it would be heard all over the world. She declared openly of Clement: "He who ought to cry with Christ: Come unto me and ye shall find rest unto your souls, he cries instead: Come and behold me in my glory, which is greater than Solomon's — come and empty your purses and ye shall find damnation for your souls! Therefore the hour of wrath is drawing near and he shall be punished as one who has scattered Peter's flock. What a judgment will there not be upon him!"

This judgment was not long delayed. During a terrific thunderstorm on December 3rd, 1352, the lightning struck the church of Saint Peter and melted its bells, and in Birgitta's ears rang the words: "Now the Pope is dying! Blessed be that day, but not that Pope!" Three days later Clement VI breathed his last.[6]

Nor from his successor, Innocent VI (1352–1362), could Birgitta obtain anything. The Lateran was burnt down in 1361, and Petrarch, who joined his voice to that of the seeress of Sweden, warned the Pope in vain: "While you lie sleeping under your gilded roof by the banks of the Rhône, the Lateran lies in ruins. When will you come? Will you stand up on the Day of Judgment among the great sinners in Avignon, or among Peter, Paul and Celestine?" (i.e., Celestine V, the reformer Pope, who reigned only five months, from July to December 1294).

For the Vicegerent of Christ was sorely needed at the heart of the Church of Christ. Not only was the material decay of Rome a terrible sight — the churches were falling into ruins, as well as the monasteries — but the priests and monks (Birgitta complains) "break all the laws of the Church, wear short cassocks and swords, and a coat of mail under the cassock; shamelessly they embrace their mistresses and their children; the convents of nuns are houses of ill fame, countless people die without ever having been to confession or Communion — the world swarms with serpents and Peter's fish dare not lift their heads for fear of their venom — Oh, Rome, Rome, I must speak of thee now as the prophet spoke of Jerusalem! The roses and lilies in thy garden are choked by thistles, thy walls are broken down, thy gates have no watchmen, thy altars are destroyed, thy sacred vessels are sold and no smoke of sacrifice ascends from thy sanctuary. The vessels of the Church have been carried off to Babylon, the sword of the fear of God is thrown away and in its stead there is a bottomless bag of money; all the words of the ten commandments have been gathered up into one, and that is: Bring hither the money! . . . Simony is committed openly, without shame, indulgences are an article of merchandise; like Judas they sell Christ; the priests have grown savage like wolves, and shaking like loose stones, like thieves they walk in darkness; they are unclean like pitch and defile all that comes near them, they turn their bare lips to their nether limbs and eat their own filth — the devil is as sure of them as the whale of her young that she keeps alive in her belly. Cursed be their food and drink, it feeds the body for the worms and the soul for hell! Cursed be their eyes and ears, their mouths and their hands — cursed be they by heaven and earth!" [7]

At about this time a bitter and caustic pen composed a Mass in honour of "Our Lady Simonia," "to be sung in the house of Simon Magus, which has now in these times grown larger than the church of the Holy Cross in Rome itself." The Mass is modelled on that of the Assumption of Our Lady (August 15th), but where the latter contains words of joy — *gaudeamus, celebrantes* — this one has words of sorrow — *lugeamus, lamentantes* — and in the Collect it invokes Peter against Simon Magus, Elisha against Gehazi and against all those who buy and sell in the Temple. The Epistle is from the Apocalypse, the verse about the great harlot; the Gospel has been taken ironically from the words of Jesus to his disciples: "Carry neither purse nor scrip — freely have you received, freely give." A verse, travestied from the Psalms, is inserted at the priest's Communion: "If I have not committed nepotism, I shall be accounted just in all my ways," and the concluding prayer wishes for all those who are guilty of simony the same fate as that of Judas. "But

THE IMITATION OF CHRIST

this Mass," the rubric concludes with acerbity, "should be celebrated on the day following the feast of Saint Peter's Chair at Rome." [8]

Birgitta's early hopes of Innocent — "this Pope is of better metal than the former one, and deserves to be painted in the best colours," [9] — were disappointed; in vain did she fulminate, threaten and implore. His successor, the Benedictine Guillaume Grimoard de Grisac, called as Pope Urban V, was the first to set out for Rome. The name he had chosen (from *urbs*) already pointed to the Eternal City. In spite of all the protests of the French King and the French Cardinals, Urban left Avignon on April 30th, 1367, set sail for Marseilles on May 19th and amid the rejoicing of Italy the Vicegerent of Christ again set foot on Italian soil. It was at Corneto, on June 3rd. Urban said Mass in the open air in the presence of an immense and brilliant gathering, "received, not like a human being, but like God Himself," to use the words of Petrarch. Mingling with the crowd and as the delegates of Siena, Giovanni Colombini and his Gésuati, wearing wreaths of olive on their heads and holding olive branches in their hands, stood at the landing-stage and cried aloud their "Praised be Jesus Christ! Long live the Holy Father!" "It was the most beautiful and edifying thing that ever was seen," the old lay missionary wrote home to Santa Bonda.[10]

On October 16th Urban made his solemn entry into Rome; a year after on October 21st Charles IV came to be crowned by the Pope: the two great lights, which in the Middle Ages were sun and moon, the Papacy and the Empire, shone once more in all their splendour. It was but for a short time, however; in 1370 Urban again left Italy and died a few months after at Avignon. On December 29th of the same year Pierre Roger Beaufort ascended the papal throne as Gregory XI. Birgitta, now nearly seventy, had returned from long pilgrimages to Naples, Amalfi, Salerno, Bari, Monte Gargano, and expected great things of the new and young Pope, whose acquaintance she had made in Rome when he was still only a Cardinal; through her confidential adviser, the Spanish Bishop Alphonso Vadaterra of Jaën, she had sent him a pressing demand to come to Italy "before next April" (1372). A copy of the letter was delivered to the Papal Nuncio, the Abbot of Marmoutier, and thereupon torn to pieces before his eyes by Birgitta's messenger. "If the Pope," declared the seeress, "is not in Italy at the time appointed, his countries will be rent asunder in the same manner." [11]

No threat could have been more effective than this. Thanks to the victories of the Spanish Cardinal-Legate Albornoz under Urban V, the See of Rome had become a great Italian power. In the south the houses of Aragon and Anjou ruled over Sicily and Naples; the Papal States therefore extended north of them and were divided into seven provinces (the Campagna with the Roman Maremma; the Duchy of Benevent; the *Patrimonium Petri* proper and the Sabine mountains with the towns of Narni, Terni, Rieti, Amelia and Todi; the Duchy of Spoleto; the Marches of Ancona with the Duchy of Urbino; Romagna; finally Bologna, town and country). The Tuscan republics ran like a wedge into these widespread States. North of Bologna sat the mighty Bernabò Visconti, the tyrant of Milan, of whom Urban had only been able to rid himself by buying him off for half a million florins. Both Bernabò and the Tuscan free states looked with anxiety at the encroachments of the Papal State, and this anxiety was not lessened when the successor of Albornoz, the new Cardinal-Legate, Pierre d'Estaing, took Perugia in 1371.

Such was the position, and this was the man to whom Catherine sent her letter on that day early in 1372. He was not unused to such communications, a copy of Birgitta's threat to Gregory XI had reached him too. Moreover, the thought of the Pope's return to Rome was not strange either to him or his master; in the winter of 1370–71 Gregory had already made it plain to those around him that he intended to go to the Eternal City. It was clear, both to him and the Cardinal-Legate, that the Chair of Peter would have to be raised again in the Papal State, if the latter were not to fall to pieces again. Birgitta had chosen exactly the best argument in her prophecy.[12]

The Swedish saint died in the following year on July 23rd, 1373; Catherine never saw her. She mentions her in a letter in 1374 as "the Countess who died lately in Rome"; at the same time she made the acquaintance of Alphonso of Jaën, and later of Birgitta's daughter Karin, who differed widely in character and energy from her mother, and also from her Italian namesake.* Birgitta's mantle therefore fell, not upon Karin of Vadstena, but upon Catherine of Siena who, by her delicate, firm and virginal hand, her pure, strong and wise mind, led Gregory to Rome. In that letter to Cardinal d'Estaing she puts her hand for the first time on the helm of the Church.

The letter is admirable in its frankness. When Birgitta thundered and threatened, she did so in the consciousness of being the messenger of God, but that was not the only reason of her influence — she also possessed the advantages of social rank. To the Italians she was *la principessa di Nericia,* of royal birth and noble blood; she had occupied an exalted position at the Swedish court and played an important part in Swedish politics; she was *molto ricca,* built monasteries and convents at home in Svezia, while travelling in Italy with her three children (Birger, Karl and Karin) and a large retinue of chaplains, bishops and courtiers. Compared with this awe-inspiring lady Catherine was of no account, a poor dyer's daughter from a little Italian provincial town, without any other visible support than her connection with the Dominican Order, in which she even had constant opponents. And this young girl, without any kind of political training or experience, stands up in front of one of the mightiest men of her time, the Legate of the redoubtable See of Rome itself, and says to him: "I will that you do so and so," "my soul desires to see you so and so," "I will" — *voglio* . . .

This *I will* recurs continually and more and more frequently in Catherine's letters. "It is the will of God and my desire," she writes in one place. In another: "It displeases God and me." To the Bishop of Florence she says outright: "I will!" To the King of France: "Do God's will and mine!" To the Pope: "Fulfil the will of God and the ardent longing of my soul!"[13] This fearless *voglio* is Catherine's magic wand with which she knocks at all doors and all hearts. When the doors and hearts are actually opened — more or less, and some to close again soon — it is simply the result of the *power of truth* in Catherine. Not in vain does she feel that she is in league with God, whom she calls

---

* Karin being a Swedish, contracted form of Katherine. Tr.

by a name that is at once abstract and loving: *la prima dolce verità*. Of all the names of Christ, one in particular had made the deepest impression upon her, the name of "Truth," which He applies to Himself in saying, "I am the Truth." The two loves, which she sees struggling for the mastery in the human soul, are identified by her as two intellectual powers, truth and falsehood. He who loves God and his neighbour abides in truth; he who loves self, in falsehood. Virtue and truth, sin and lies, correspond to each other, they are practice and theory.

On two sides, Catherine says somewhere, there is an invitation to us; there are two who say: Whosoever is thirsty, let him come to me. "Come ye to me, ye who are thirsty." We are all thirsty, the question is only which water we will drink to quench our thirst, the water springing up into everlasting life, or *l'aqua morta* in the dead lagoon of wrath and sin — *la Vie* or *le Néant,* Ernest Hello would say.

To choose the former is to imitate Christ. "He who will go to the Father, who is eternal life, must here on earth be with His Word, which is the way . . . and he who walks in this way, walks not in darkness but in the light of faith . . . and prays: 'Lord, grant me grace to see light in Thy light!' The Word is Truth itself and the soul which follows His doctrine forsakes the falsehood of self-love and stifles it in herself. . . His doctrine is that we shall love Him above all things and our neighbour as ourselves. We must show that love in our deeds, as He did. . . Before God and our neighbour we must prove whether we are true to His teaching. . . We are all called to it. Which of us, then, are bidden? Those who are bidden are they who hunger and thirst after virtue and run like the thirsty with the light of faith on the path made by Christ Crucified. . . With this thirst and this light they will reach the spring. . .

"So does Christ, sweet Jesus, bid us come to the living water. The other who invites us is the devil. . . In him is death, therefore he invites us to the dead water. If you asked him: 'What will you give me if I serve you?' he would answer: 'I will give you what I have. I live without God, and so shall you also live without God. I am in the everlasting fire, in which there is weeping and gnashing of teeth; I am without light, I am plunged in darkness; I have lost all hope; I am with all those who are damned and tormented. That is what I will give you as reward and comfort. . .'

"And what is the way by which we are invited to go? It is the way of lies. Lies bring forth the miserable self-love with which you love inordinately the pomp and splendour of the world and creatures and yourself, without taking thought whether you lose God and the beauty of your soul. In your blindness you make yourself and the world your god: like a thief you steal time. For the time which you ought to use for the glory of God, the salvation of your soul and the good of your neighbour, that you spend in seeking your own pleasure and rejoicing in yourself and in giving the body more comfort and well-being than is pleasing to God. Christ has written His doctrine on His body; He made a book of Himself, with initials so large and so red that even the dullest and most unlearned can see them and read them plainly. The devil puts a book before your eyes and it is your own sensuality, and in it are written all vices and evil inclinations of the soul: anger, pride, impatience, unfaithfulness to the Creator, injustice, ruthlessness, impurity, hatred of your neighbour, pleasure in sin and displeasure in virtue; rudeness against your neighbour and slander, dulness and sloth, negligence and sleepiness and impatience. . . If the will reads all this and learns it and puts it into practice, he follows, like an unbeliever, the devil's path of lies and drinks the dead water to everlasting judgment and damnation." [14]

This was Catherine's message to the world, including that of politics. There are two realms: on the one hand egoism, the world, sin, darkness, death, hell; on the other, love, self-denial, devotion to duty, light, life, heaven. The door to the kingdom of death is self, the *ego,* the door to the kingdom of God is Jesus, the Word. He, who abides in self, abides in that which perishes, and is lost. He, who abides in Jesus is in the eternal and is saved.

The truth of this doctrine was so self-evident to Catherine that she *could* not but proclaim it, early and late, among high and low, "in season and out of season," like the Apostle. "This woman," writes the worthy notary, Cristofano Guidini in wonder, "cared little whether that which she said was pleasing or not pleasing." [15] She regarded politics — like all other human works — as a chapter of ethics, and a statesman, like everyone else, as a follower of Christ.   And she went out among the warring republics, went into the Church which had become worldly, to call men from fighting, brother against brother, to the kiss of peace; from nepotism and simony to conscientiousness and honesty, from the fear of man to the fear of God, from self to Jesus.

There is one word which constantly recurs in Catherine's letters, and that is *manliness*.   Manliness means to her all that Christ was; and everything to which the devil invites and urges man, she calls, regardless of her own sex, effeminacy.   "Be a manly man," she cries to the vague and vacillating Gregory XI, and she speaks sternly against those "who are very loving and compassionate out of carnal affection, just as they are very tender over their bodies."   They are those who dare not act justly and punish injustice out of fear of getting into unpleasantness or incurring the displeasure of others; they have a timid need of living in peace and on good terms with all the world, even where the honour of God demands that they should be at strife and war. "Such persons see those under them sin," writes Catherine, "and make as though they did not see it, so that they do not have to punish them, or if they do punish them, they do it so mildly that it is only a covering up of vice, for they are always afraid of displeasing and getting into strife.   And this comes of their self-love.

Catherine is inexorable in showing how this soft, timid egoism is the opposite of the love of Christ.   He did not come to bring a sultry peace, in which everything grows equally well, or where weeds even flourish exceedingly.   He came with the sword and the scythe and the winnowing fan.   He was the surgeon, who cauterised the corruption of sin with red-hot irons.   As his true disciple Catherine teaches: "Wanting to live in peace is often the greatest cruelty.   When the boil has come to a head it must be cut with the lance and burned with fire, and if that is not done, and only a plaster is put over it, the corruption will spread and that is often worse than death." [16]

In a succeeding letter to Pierre d'Estaing, Catherine develops these principles with all her keen psychological insight, and tries to impart them to the Cardinal.   "I wish to see you as a manly man," she writes with her usual intrepidity, "so that you may serve the Bride of Christ" (the Catholic Church) "without fear, and work spiritually and temporally for the glory of God, according to the needs of that sweet Bride in our times. I am persuaded that if only you know the needs of the Church, you will do it with every care and with no fear or negligence. The soul which fears men will never wholly achieve anything, it will fail everywhere and finish nothing. Ah, how perilous is that fear! It paralyses good resolutions so that they are not carried into action; it blinds a man so that he dare not recognise the truth — for that fear springs from self-love. As soon as men begin to love themselves with sensual self-love they begin to fear."

All those who are a little accustomed to observe themselves know this from experience. While the surrender to the will of God makes one fearless, this striving after egoistic satisfaction at once produces anxiety and dread. We must not lose God, everything else is uncertain and may be lost. Or, as Catherine says with subtlety:

"And why does he fear? Because he has put his love and his hope in weak things, which have neither firmness nor constancy, but pass away like the wind. Ah, self-love, how harmful thou art, both for those who are masters and those who are servants! For the superior does not punish and rebuke out of fear of displeasing his subordinates . . . and does not practise justice and righteousness, but judges according to his own whim or to please men. And thus the subordinates grow continually worse and worse."

Catherine now sets up against this selfish weakness and favouritism the relentless devotion to duty of Christ, which sought only the glory of God and the good of His neighbour. He is our teacher, "we are the scholars, and we have been put in that gentle school."

Now comes the practical application of the principles — politics suddenly proceed from dogmatics (as everything is regarded by Catherine as proceeding from dogma). "It seems to me, dearest Father, that it is time now to give honour to God and our work to our neighbour. It is not the time any more now to care for oneself with sensual self-love and in the fear of a slave, but to work with true love and a holy fear of God. You have now been set in a place where you have power in both temporal and spiritual things. As for that which is temporal, be manly, and so far as may be, create peace and unity in the land."

"The land," here meant Italy to Catherine. Like Dante she was an ardent Italian, and the welfare of her country is revealed again and again in her thoughts and her speech. She is alluding here to the strife prevailing between Bernabò Visconti in Milan and the Holy See. Christians ought to fight against infidels, she says, and not against each other. Perceiving the vocation of the Church more clearly than both the Pope and the cardinals she exclaims: "Peace, peace, peace, dearest Father! Look more at the loss of souls than at the loss of cities, and make the Holy Father see this. God requires saved souls of him more than conquered towns."

Then she concludes as she began: "I am persuaded that if you will put on the new man, Christ, sweet Jesus, and put off the old man, which is your sensual nature, you will attain this, for you will then be delivered from the fear of men. But you will never attain to it in any other way. . . God has placed you where you have no right to any other fear than the fear of God. I said to you therefore, that I desired you to be a manly man, not a timid one. I hope to God that He will grant you grace to do His will, which is also your desire and mine. . . I say no more. Remain in the holy, sweet love of God. Sweet Jesus, Jesus who is love." [17]

Besides Pierre d'Estaing, papal politics in Italy at that time were represented by another French prelate, the Abbot of Marmoutier, Gérard du Puy. Evidently following the old maxim "Divide and rule," he tried to stir up strife where he could manage it. Thus he awoke to new life the old strife between Arezzo and Castiglion Fiorentino, and it was believed that he secretly supported Cione Salimbeni in the feud of the latter against Siena. He was the nephew of Gregory XI and enjoyed the confidence of his uncle; he had been the intermediary between the Pope and Saint Birgitta and now, after the death of the Swedish saint (July 1373), he approached the new star, Catherine.

The saint of Fontebranda answered him in a letter which is kept in terms resembling those in the communication to Cardinal d'Estaing. "Christ Crucified," she says, "is the way, in which we must all walk to come to the Father. There is no other way of doing the will of God than in binding oneself fast to Christ. When we do that we discover that we are in *the fire*. The love of God burns in the soul like a flame on the hearth, it warms and gives light, and it transforms the fuel that is placed in the fire to itself." Catherine is now engaged on her great, everlasting only, first and last subject: the transforming of the soul to conformity with Christ, the perishing of self-will in the holy fire of the will of God. . .

"Oh, sweet fire, that draws us to thyself," she exclaims, "thou drivest away all the cold of vice and sin and self-love! Thou warmest and enkindlest the dry wood of our will, making it burst into flame in bright longings, loving what God loves, and hating what God hates." In that fire the soul is purified, so that it remembers nothing but the benefits of God; its thoughts dwell only on His goodness and the will strains after Him and cares for nothing in the world apart from Him.

After this theoretical and theological foundation, which Catherine never omits to lay down, she passes on to drawing the practical conclusions. "With great joy I have received your letter," she writes, "and it comforted me to see that you think of so mean and miserable a creature. Your three questions I will answer thus: I think it would be well if our dear Christ on earth [i.e. the Pope] would set himself free from two things which cause the misery of the Bride of Christ. The first is his far too tender clinging to his kinsfolk and his far too great care for them . . . the second that he is far too good-natured and merciful. Woe, woe, therefore do Christ's members decay, because there is no one who chastises them! There are three vices which Christ hates more than any others, they are the unchastity, the miserliness and the puffed-up pride prevailing among priests and prelates, who think of nothing but of pleasures and feasts and of amassing wealth. They see devils dragging the souls of their subordinates to hell and care naught for it, for they are ravening wolves themselves and traffic in the divine grace. A strong hand is needed to bring order here, for great mildness is the greatest cruelty that can be imagined. I hope to God that the Holy Father will begin to set himself free from that wrongful love of his family. . . I do not say that the Church of God will therefore not be persecuted, but I believe it will continue to flourish, as it has been promised it shall. But corruption must come down to the roots before all can be well again."

These words of Catherine have by many been considered to be prophetic, as indeed they were. She had that deep insight into the inter-relation of events, that intimate understanding of history, which enabled her to foresee and foretell the development of centuries. "Before everything can be well again, corruption must go down to the very roots." Had she lived to see that devil incarnate (*dimonio incarnato*), Alexander VI, on the Chair of Peter, she would have understood that the hour had now come which she had foretold: "Your hour and the power of darkness," when the Bride of Christ like once Christ Himself was not only to be betrayed by Judas (that has often happened), but even to be denied by Peter: "I do not know this Galilean." [18]

Catherine now goes on to answer the two other questions put to her by the Abbot. He seems to have found it correct to indicate in his letter that he was a great sinner, yet hoping in the mercy of God, and so forth. Catherine takes him at his word. "God does not will the death of a sinner, but that he should repent and live," she says to encourage him. "And I, your unworthy daughter, offer to bear all your sins for you. Together with my own we will cast them into the fire of holy love and there we will burn them up! Be assured that God in His mercy has forgiven you. But you must now endeavour to live a new life."

After this Catherine passes on to the answer of the third question — concerning the Abbot's duties as the intimate confidant of the Pope. "Together with the Holy Father," she writes, "you must work as well as you are able at driving out the bad shepherds, who are wolves and incarnate devils and think of nothing but good living and fine houses and beautiful horses. Woe, woe, that which Christ earned on the wood of the Cross is now wasted on harlots! Though it may cost you your life, I bid you say to the Holy Father that he make an end of so great a shame. When the time comes that he must appoint cardinals and other shepherds of the Church, then beg him not to let himself be led by flattery or do it for money or out of simony, and to take no thought whether those concerned are nobles or commoners, for virtue and a good name ennoble a man before God." [19]

Gregory XI received Catherine's message safely enough, but he did not act very much upon it. On December 21st, 1375 he created nine new cardinals, among them being Gérard du Puy himself, and all of them lacking the qualities demanded by Catherine. The best of them was the Spaniard, Pedro de Luna, later the anti-pope, Benedict XIII.

Catherine, however, persevered in her work. She found plenty to do near home too. The year 1373 was a particularly disturbed one. "It seems," says the old chronicler, Neri di Donato, "as if these times were under the rule of a planet which produces strife and quarrelling everywhere. In the monastery of Sant' Antonio [at Bagni di Petriuolo, near Siena] the Augustinian monks murdered their Prior with a knife. . . In Assisi the Franciscans in the *Sagro Convento* fought each other with knives and fourteen were killed. In Abbadia della Rosa [in Siena, where now stands the church of *la Mustiola*] there was also fighting within, and six of the brethren were turned out. Among the Carthusians too, there was strife, and the General came and moved them all to other houses. Thus all religious were at war amongst themselves, and on the other hand all religious were persecuted and oppressed by the world. It was no better among kinsfolk by blood. . . The whole world was fighting, in Siena there was no one who kept his word, either in his own party or outside it, the people disagreed with their leaders and agreed with no one, and truly the whole world was a valley of shadows." [20]

The old chronicler undoubtedly did not exaggerate: the clergy of those days were an example to the people in worldliness and pugnacity. Catherine, probably through her disciple Nigi di Doccio degli Arzocchi, had come into communication with the parish priest in Asciano, a town south of Siena, Biringhieri degli Arzocchi, and she writes a very serious letter to him. Poet as she was, she begins with an image: when flowers stand too long in water they decay, and no longer give forth fragrance but a bad smell. "You priests are flowers," she says, "flowers in the church of God, flowers on the altar. But when these flowers stand in water in sin and impurity and worldliness they stink — and corrupt others with their stench. Arise therefore, from sleep, slumber not any longer. We have slept long enough [in order to soften the sting of reproach Catherine generally includes herself] and we are dead to grace. But now we have no more time, the bell of judgment has rung and we are condemned to death."

She now begins to ring the bells of the day of doom. She conjures up death in all its deep inevitability — when standing face to face with it neither money nor noble birth (alluding to the wealthy and distinguished kinsfolk of the priest) are of any avail. "How miserable will my soul be then, when it has wallowed in carnal lust like the swine in the mire, and has become a dumb beast, and has wallowed in rotten miserliness, and has often sold spiritual benefits for gifts and favours. . . And a whole life has been spent in seeking honours and feasts and having many servants and good horses instead of helping the poor." "This is to spend one's time in serving the devil. But we are dearly bought with the blood of Christ, we are not our own, we can no longer sell ourselves." "For the sake of Christ Crucified I therefore entreat you, that we may come forth from so great a thraldom. . . My faults are without number. But I promise you that I will take yours and mine and make of them a bunch of myrrh, which I will keep always at my breast with constant bitterness and lamentation." [21]

In Semignano, in the mountains west of Siena, the so-called Montagnuola, there was a parish priest who lived in constant enmity with another ecclesiastic. Catherine writes to him: "I marvel greatly that a man in your position can live in hate; God has drawn you out of life in the world, and by the power of the sacrament made you an angel upon earth, and you have again to do with worldly business. I do not know how you can dare to say Mass! I tell you that if you persist in this hate and in your other faults, the chastisement of God will come upon you! I tell you, no more of this life of sin! Repent, remember that you must die and you do not know when. . . I beseech you: tear out of your heart all mean feelings and above all hate. I will that you make peace! It is shameful for two priests to live in such enmity. Of a truth it is a marvel that God does not let the earth open and swallow both of you!" [22]

In Casola d'Elsa, between Siena and Volterra, the dean and another priest in the same place likewise live in hate and dissension. Catherine writes and preaches a sermon to them about the only hate a Christian is allowed to cherish — the hatred of sin. She begins by showing that hatred of others is in reality a hatred of self, for in hating my neighbour I kill the grace in my own soul and thus I am my own worst enemy. "If anyone has offended me by a bodily injury," she says, "and I hate him for it, I slay my own soul. . . I ought therefore to feel more hatred of my self, who murders my soul, which is immortal, than my enemy who murders the body, which must die, after all, sooner or later, for the body perishes and its summer * does not last, and its only value is in the precious jewel of grace contained in it. When this jewel is gone the body is nothing but a sack, full of filth — food for death and worms."

Foolish then, is he, who because of a bodily insult hazards the life of the soul. Against the unreasonable and sinful hatred of self Catherine sets the true hatred — the hatred of sin, of the will of the senses, the pride of self. That hatred does not urge to blood-feud, but to patience, to forgiveness and to loving our enemies. They who offend us are only implements in the hands of God, rods or scourges with which He chastises us, and it is better to atone for one's sins here than hereafter. "This is the right way to bear things, and there is no other. All other ways lead to death. . . We are in need of forgiveness, therefore we must forgive. . . When you do this you are on the safe road and are true mediators between God and men, and shall at last enter in and see the face of God. Behold, I have had compassion on your souls, I have not willed that you should live in such darkness, and I have come to bid you to that sweet and glorious feast. . . And inasmuch as it seems to me that the way of truth is closed to you because of the enmity that you cherish, and the way of lies is opened wide to you, I will

* *Verdura.*

that you leave altogether this way of darkness and make peace with God and your neighbour and return to the way that leads to life. And I beseech you in the name of Christ Crucified not to refuse me this prayer." [23]

Notwithstanding Catherine's requests for peace the war between the Papal Chair and Bernabò Visconti continued. In the hope of being able to draw the Tuscan republics over to his side, the tyrant of Milan sent an envoy who arrived in Siena in November, 1373. Here he sought an interview with Catherine, to whom he brought greetings, not only from his master, but also from the wife of the latter, the worldly and splendour-loving Beatrice della Scala. In January the Pope had excommunicated Bernabò and Galeazzo Visconti and the two despots now sought Catherine's mediation with the Pope, or the persuasion of Siena, and with it, the rest of Tuscany, to come over to their side. In the reply which Catherine dictated to Neri di Landoccio, she addresses Bernabò as "Revered Father," and begins by pointing out the vanity and transitoriness of all worldly power and greatness. "And if you ask me: Is there no dominion, then, that is lasting here in this life? I answer: Yes, there is, It is the city of our soul. . . We are masters of it, and it is so strong, that neither the devil nor man can conquer it, if we will not so ourselves." But how shall we obtain the strength of will that is needed, how will it be possible not to lose in the fight against the Prince of the flesh and the world and darkness? That is the work of the Lamb without blemish, Jesus Christ — "by His death He granted us life, in bearing insults and outrages He has regained our honour for us, with His hands nailed to the Cross He has loosened us from the bonds of sin; He clothes us with His nakedness, saves us in His blood, by His wisdom He has overcome the malice of the devil, by the strokes of the scourge He has won the victory over our flesh, by His humility He has conquered the pride and lust of the world. We have therefore nothing to fear from an enemy; with His disarmed hand He has overcome our enemies and restored to us our free will."

Catherine is now where she wants to be — at the chapter about *the Church*. We sin daily, daily we need forgiveness of sins. We find this forgiveness in the blood of the Lamb.

which is shed in the Sacrament of Penance. But this sacrament is administered by the *Church,* it is she who has the "Keys of the Blood." "Foolish then, is he, who departs from the Vicar of Christ Crucified, who has the keys of the Blood, or who goes against him." Exactly like Francis of Assisi in his testament she says: "Even though the Pope were Satan incarnate himself, I may not lift up my head against him, but I must always humble myself and beg for the Blood as a mercy, for in no other wise can I obtain a part in it. And therefore [and this is the personal application] and therefore I beseech you no longer to set yourself up against your superior. Give not ear to what the devil whispers to you, that it is your duty to speak against the bad shepherds of the Church. Do not believe the devil, do not seek to pass judgment, where it is not for you to judge. It pleases not Our Saviour, He says: 'They are my anointed,' and the judgment upon them belongs to Him and not to you nor to any other creature." Nay, Catherine goes so far as to exclaim: "Even if the priests took all our goods from us we ought rather to be willing to lose our worldly goods and our lives than to lose spiritual wealth and the life of grace." This is not the spirit of Luther, nor of Wyclif, nor of the Hussites and Huguenots. This is not a heretical spirit, which is a rebellious spirit; this is the spirit of a saint, "meekness and humbleness of heart," "obedience unto death, even to the death on the Cross."

The letter concludes with a fiery exhortation to begin the Crusade. Not until 1373 had Gregory proclaimed the Holy War, and Catherine supports him. "What shame and scandal it is for us Christians to leave that which is ours by right in the hands of shameful infidels!" "In the name of Christ Crucified I demand that you make a true and entire peace with our sweet Father, Christ here on earth, and set forth to fight against the infidels. In doing so, you will have a part in the Blood of the Son of God."

Writing to the proud and worldly Beatrice of the house of Scaliger, Catherine calls her "Dearest Mother and Sister in Christ sweet Jesus." True dignity, she explains to her, cannot be united to love of this world, for the world is lower than the human soul and is not worthy of our attachment. "The soul becomes like the thing it loves, and sin, being naught, my soul becomes naught if I love sin, and nothing can be worse for me. Sin comes of our loving that which God hates, and hating that which God loves, thus loving the transient pleasures of the world and our own self. . . In itself there is no evil in the splendour and magnificence of the world, nor in creatures, the evil is in the love which attaches itself to them. . ."

Fortunately love of the world grants no peace; if we would have peace we must leave the way of self and walk in the way of the Cross. It looks as though the latter is strewn with thorns, but that is only an illusion. Or rather, out of the thorns of tribulation grow the roses of patience. Moreover, he who has drunk of the Blood of Christ is inebriated by it and does not feel where he treads. Catherine wishes Beatrice to have this inebriation, "not only for your own sake, but also because *I will* that you shall be a guide for your husband to the path of truth and virtue. Lead him and entreat him, as far as you are able, to be no longer a rebel against the Holy Father. . . I will not that you be two who are ungrateful for God's gifts of grace." [24]

Catherine seems to have intended to go in person to Milan in order to influence Bernabò. "I would rather show my love for your salvation in deeds," the letter to Beatrice concludes. And it appears, from a letter written on May 30th, 1375, by Bernabò's daughter-in-law, Elisabeth of Bavaria, to Catherine, that the saint had been expected at the court of the Visconti. Elisabeth now expresses her sorrow at learning that the visit will not take place.[25]

Meanwhile Gregory's and Catherine's plans for a Crusade fell to the ground. In March 1374, Cardinal d'Estaing's successor as Papal Legate, Guillaume de Noëllet, a French prelate of the same poor quality as the Abbot of Marmoutier in Perugia, arrived in Bologna. This boded ill for Italy, nor was there a brighter outlook in Catherine's country in a more limited sense. The robber knight Andrea di Niccolò Salimbeni, who, from his castle of Perolla out in the Maremma had long levied extortionate taxes in the countryside around Siena, had at last been seized; but the Sienese supreme judge, the so-called *Senator*, Ludovico da Moligno, had not had the courage to have this high-born chieftain executed. On the other hand, sixteen men of his band had to forfeit their lives. Outraged at such flagrant injustice, the people rose against the Senator; a saddler named Noccio di Vanni sat down in the judge's seat in the Palazzo Pubblico and sentenced Andrea to be beheaded — and this was done.[26] The powerful family of the Salimbeni, however, were enraged, and from their inaccessible fortress-castles in the mountains they fell upon the defenceless country around Siena. At the same time Catherine herself was threatened by a danger: she was summoned to Florence to give an account of her doings and her teaching at the General Chapter of the Dominican Order.

X

It was in Florence, on Saint John's Day, 1374. Saint John is one of the patron saints of Florence and his feast is still celebrated there with great solemnity in the twentieth century. On that 24th June, 1374, High Mass was sung in honour of the saint in all the churches of Florence, and in the Dominican church of Santa Maria Novella, where many friars had remained behind after the chapter meeting lately concluded, Fra Tommaso della Fonte was standing before the altar, assisted by Fra Bartolommeo de' Dominici and Fra Raimondo da Capua. Catherine knelt further down in the church and looked with interest at the third priest, who was a stranger to her. She had long been seeking and praying that she might find a confessor who could wholly understand her, and who by his commanding personality and learning could help her to advance. Suddenly it was clear to her and with the certainty of a revelation that here was the man she was seeking, and it seemed to her that the Blessed Virgin herself stood by her side and gave her Raymond of Capua for her spiritual father and guide.[1]

Catherine was no stranger to Raymond. The Dominican, who was seventeen years older (born about 1330), had heard accounts of her on more than one occasion. Born in Capua of the old noble family of the delle Vigne, the same from which had issued the famous chancellor of Frederick II, Pier delle Vigne,[2] he had entered the Order when quite young and later had occupied important positions in Rome and Bologna. From 1363 till 1366 he was in Montepulciano in the mountains south of Siena, as the spiritual director of the Dominican convent; in the solitude there he wrote a biography of Saint Agnes of Montepulciano whose body is preserved in that convent, probably also the commentary on the *Magnificat,* of which he is known to be the author. Out here in Montepulciano he also received the visits of Fra Tommaso della Fonte, Catherine's confessor, whom he had perhaps sent for to make enquiries of him. For — he says himself in his history of Catherine's life, with a reminiscence of Dante — "I was thinking that it was the age of *'the third beast,'* that we were in the sign of the spotted leopard, by which is meant hypocrisy." [8]

At the Chapter in Florence (which was held in the Cappella degli Spagnuoli) Catherine's case was no doubt thoroughly discussed, and Raymond arrived at the conviction that the young Sienese woman was not "one of those women of whom he had met several, who are easily deceived by the devil and then deceive others." It was therefore he who was chosen by the General of the Order to be Catherine's spiritual guide, a choice which was confirmed by Gregory XI in a letter of August 17th, 1376. Raymond was transferred to San Domenico in Siena and for five years his life became more and more closely connected with that of the young Sienese woman.

Meanwhile Raymond's was not the only acquaintance that Catherine made during her sojourn on the banks of the Arno. "In May, 1374," we are told by an anonymous Florentine author, "a certain Caterina di Giacomo di Benincasa came to this city from Siena; she wore the habit of the Dominican Sisters of Penance, and we regarded her as a great servant of God. With her came three other women, clothed in the same habit, who followed her wherever she went. When I heard of the great fame that there was about her, I sought to make acquaintance with her and gained her confidence so that she came often to my house." [4] This anonymous writer is perhaps Niccolò Soderini, a rich and distinguished Florentine, with whom Catherine subsequently came into friendly relationship, and who, amongst other things, helped her brothers with money. For the three brothers living in Florence were still unsuccessful. Stefano even went on to Rome. When Catherine returned home to Siena at the end of June, Bartolommeo went with her, so that Benincasa was left behind alone in the house by Canto a Soldani. Probably Raymond joined the company of travellers, and we are permitted to imagine the four Mantellate, the Dominican, the worthy artisan and their escort leaving Florence one summer morning by the Porta Romana. The road goes past the newly erected Certosa di Val d'Ema, through Val di Greve and across the vineclad Chianti mountains. Near Barberino is still shown a fountain whose unhealthy waters were purified by the benediction of the saint. Here the travellers reach the familiar Val d'Elsa and again the Siena countryside, less imposing than the country about Florence. The road passes the old abbey *a Isola,* beneath the castles of Staggia and Monteriggioni, of which Dante has sung, "whose ring of walls is crowned by turrets," and well may the wayfarers have been reminded of Alighieri's meeting, in the purgatory of the envious, with Sapia Saracini, who, from her window here looked down in malicious exultation at the defeat of her fellow-countrymen, and at Provenzano's head carried aloft on a pole: "then defiantly I turned my face to heaven and screamed to God: Now I fear thee no longer!" When the Florentine nevertheless found the haughty noblewoman on the way of salvation in the purifying flames, it was not because of her own merit. "Peace did I desire with God, when I lay dying, yet but little had my repentance aided me, had not Pier Pettinaro known of me and helped me by his prayers." [5] Pier Pettinaro, the pious combmaker, lay preacher and tertiary, had stood by the wicked noblewoman in her last hour and brought her from the dark flames of hell into the golden ones of Purgatory. . .

Then the wanderers stood on the heights of Monte Celso and saw below them Siena in the evening glow — like the nest of a bird of prey with all the threatening towers straining upward like naked necks — and highest up the campanile of the cathedral like a white hand lifted in vain to give a powerless benediction. For the land all round was ravaged by Salimbeni's bands, and it was useless for all the keys of the city to be carried up every evening when the bell had rung, and the gates had been closed (as they are still closed every night), to the cathedral and laid upon the altar of Our Lady, the exalted ruler of the city. Our Lady had given them the victory at Monteaperti, and the earthquakes did not dare to venture in under the white cloak which she spread over her town. But the wild Cione di Sandro Salimbeni ravaged the countryside about Montepulciano; Agnolino di Giovanni Salimbeni laid Montalcino waste, and within the city walls there was a worse enemy, against whom no arms were of any avail. When Catherine and her company came in through the Porta Camollia the first sight that met them was a cart loaded with dead bodies and escorted by the black *Misericordia* brethren. By the light of the torches carried by the brethren they saw the swollen bodies and bluish faces of the dead. Then they who had experience of the year 1348, knew what had happened, and with a shudder they whispered to each other: "The Plague."

Siena was terribly ravaged by the merciless epidemic; it is computed that it carried off about a third of the inhabitants of the town. Catherine's brother had only come back to his native town to die (at about the same time that Stefano died in Rome, which the plague had also reached). Catherine's sister Lisa too (not to be confused with the sister-in-law of the same name, Bartolommeo's wife, née Colombini) died, as well as eight of Lapa's grandchildren, who lived with her. Catherine clothed all the little bodies herself, saying to herself as she did so: "These at least I shall not lose!" The same thought was in her mind when she wrote to Alessia Saracini: "God is letting these children die, if they are not to grow up into good men and women." [6]

Together with her tried friend, Matteo Cenni Fazi, the Rector of *Casa della Misericordia,* and her new confessor, Raymond, Catherine now trod the old paths of charity. She was the soul of the untiring little band which from morning till night, from dusk till dawn, went about doing deeds of mercy, tending the sick, consoling the dying, burying the dead. Those who at the present day walk through the narrow, dark and ill-smelling streets in the Ghetto of Siena, can obtain a faint impression of the horrors that the cities of the Middle Ages offered to the senses. Even in ordinary circumstances the only scavengers were the pigs of the Brethren of Saint Anthony, and for that purpose they were allowed to roam freely everywhere in the town.[7] Now, while the epidemic was raging, there were other things to think of than sweeping the streets. Catherine, though, was hardened, she who had drunk the pus from the wound of her enemy, did not shrink from a few bad smells. She had her bottle of smelling-salts; armed with that and her lamp (both can still be seen in her house at Fontebranda) she walked untiringly from hospital to hospital and up the dirty stairs of the houses of the poor.

Her faithful followers went with her: Fra Raimondo, Fra Bartolommeo de' Dominici, the hermit Fra Santi. They knew there was danger, but they trusted in God and in Catherine's intercession. Raymond relates of his experience: "When the plague broke out in Siena I resolved to expose my body to danger for the love of the salvation of souls, and not to refuse to go to any one who was sick, although I knew that the infection spreads through the air and thence to those who stand near. I considered, however, that Christ is mightier than Galen, and grace than nature, and that it was my duty to love my neighbour's soul more than my own body. But inasmuch as I was almost alone in the work, I had hardly time to eat or sleep, or even to pause for a moment, so many messages were there from the sick craving a visit . . . Then it happened one morning, just as I had rested a little, and wanted to get up to say Matins, that I felt a slight pain in the groin, and when I felt it there was a swelling as though from a boil. This caused me no slight fear, and instead of rising I remained lying down and began to think of my passing hence. I longed for the day to dawn, that I might go and seek that holy maiden [i.e. Catherine] before I grew worse. Meanwhile other symptoms appeared — fever and headache; nevertheless I tried, as well as I could, to finish saying Matins."

Aided by one of the friars, Raymond reached Catherine's house, but she was not at home, so they laid him down on a bench. Here she finds him, kneels down by the bench, lays her hand upon his hot, feverish brow and begins to pray without words. It lasted half an hour. Raymond lay waiting for the next symptoms to appear, vomiting and the other bad signs which he had seen so often in others. But they did not come. Instead, while Catherine prayed, a gentle sense of well-being began to permeate the body of the sick man. "It was," he writes, "as if something was being pulled out of me at the ends of all my limbs," and when Catherine stood up from her prayer Raymond was cured. She gave him something to eat, bade him rest awhile longer and then sent him home saying: "Go out again for the salvation of souls and give thanks to the Highest Who has saved you."

Fra Bartolommeo and Fra Santi had likewise an experience of the *Mamma's* power over sickness and health; they saw her too, like her Lord and Master in the house of Simon's wife's mother, "and standing over them and commanding the fever to leave them. And immediately rising, they went to their work." [8] Messer Matteo, the Rector of *Casa della Misericordia*, was also attacked and thought he was to share the fate of his colleague of the La Scala hospital, Galgano di Lolo, who died at his post. He already felt the pains in the groin and the terrible headache, which seemed to split his head into four parts, and the physician told the anxious Raymond that there was no hope — "the patient's water," he said, "indicates great inflammation of the liver, which is usual in this disease, yet we will try tomorrow to purge the blood with cassia." Before the next day had fully dawned, however, Catherine had heard the sad news and hastened to the sick-bed of her friend. Outside in the passage she already cried: "Out of bed, Messer Matteo, out of bed, out of bed, this is no time for you to be lying here taking your ease." And as soon as Messer Matteo heard her gay, cheerful voice he began to smile and got out of bed quite recovered.[9]

The plague was followed by famine, and it was at this time that Alessia and Catherine were baking bread for the poor one day in the house of the former.* Catherine, however, got five times as much bread out of the flour as Alessia, and although the corn had been poor, and Alessia had really thought of throwing away the flour, the bread did not taste bad. Catherine afterwards confessed to Raymond, though, that the Blessed Virgin and many angels and saints had stood by her side and helped her, so that the honour was due to them and not to her.[10]

Soon after the plague had ceased Catherine fell ill, probably from overwork. She would have preferred to die, but Our Lady showed her in a vision all the souls she was called to save, and for whose sake she must live. Someone to whom she told this vision, asked her afterwards whether she would be able to recognise them again, and she answered that she thought she would.[11]

Catherine did not undertake journeys for pleasure, but in any case she must have enjoyed going to Montepulciano in the au-

---

* Which was no longer the Palazzo Saracini. "Alessia," says Raymond, "could at last no longer live without Catherine and therefore hired a house in her neighbourhood, so that she could always be near her." (Leg. Maj. II, XI, 1).

tumn of 1374, accompanied by Raymond of Capua and Alessia, Giovanna Pazzi and other Mantellate. Here, outside the Cyclopean walls of the ancient Etruscan city with the widest view of the Chiana valley right across to Cortona shining pale pink in the blue of the distant mountains, stood the convent in which Raymond had written the life of Saint Agnes of Montepulciano, and the convent was still full of memories of her. Agnes, too, had matured early, at the age of nine she took the Augustinian habit, but discarded it later to become a Dominican. In a dream she saw three ships; in one of them was Saint Augustine, in the second Saint Francis, in the third Saint Dominic, and an angel advised her to enter the last-named ship. Signs and wonders followed her through life: at her birth burning torches appeared in the room; loaves of bread were multiplied under her hand; on ten successive Sundays she received Holy Communion from the hands of an angel in the church of Proceno; when she died infants at the breast in Montepulciano, who had not yet come to the use of speech, began to speak and say: "The saint is dead!" It had been revealed to Catherine that in heaven a chair awaited her by the side of the departed Agnes — *Agnete Politianæ in cœlis compar* — and two golden chairs, standing side by side in heaven, and prepared for Agnes and Catherine, can be admired on one of the frescoes in the convent which has now been transformed into a technical school.[12]

The sojourn of the Sienese saint in Montepulciano was also marked by signs and wonders. When she approached the catafalque in which the body of Saint Agnes was preserved incorrupt, and humbly stooped to kiss the feet of the departed one, many of the nuns present saw that Saint Agnes herself raised her foot to Catherine's lips. At a later visit, when Catherine brought her niece as a novice to the convent, a shower as of manna fell down from the ceiling of the chapel upon the body of Saint Agnes and Catherine praying beside it.[13]

In Montepulciano, and probably through Neri de' Pagliaresi, Catherine found two new enthusiastic friends: the poet Anastagio di Ser Guido da Montalcino and Giacomo del Pecora, belonging to one of the most distinguished families in the town. We are indebted to both of them for poems in honour of Catherine [14] — poems in which they glorify the "divine flame of her soul, in which all earthly desire is burnt to ashes," and on her tear-stained countenance the crimson reflection of that sun which she beheld in ecstasy, and after contemplating which she returned to bear the sins of her neighbour — *trasformata in Jesu tutta gioconda* . . .

That late summer in 1374 seems altogether to have been a time of wandering for Catherine and her little band of faithful followers. There is something about the Sienese landscape that awakens a longing for the far away; heart and sight are drawn involuntarily towards the distant horizon. You stand one bright and sunny afternoon, at the end of harvest time or early in the spring, outside one of the southern gates of the town — Pispini, Tufa, Porta Romana. You see in front of you olive fields where the soil, newly dug and hoed, is reddish brown or blood red, or golden — *terra di Siena*. Behind it lies the undulating country of cornfields and vines and olives, varying from golden green to withered yellow, ribbed like velvet by deep furrows, spotted here and there at regular intervals by the silvery canopies of the olive trees. Beyond them more heights and still more fields, and cypresses in rows or groups, and peasant farms, white or yellow or ochre-coloured or pink, and always having green shutters. Cypresses stand round the farm and large hive-shaped ricks, some half cut into; and round about the country there are little chapels and churches with a belfry on the roof, and here and there, among brownish or violet wooded slopes, there is a convent. Then, towards the south, the elephant grey or tawny *Creta* desert opens out in a mysterious half-light of sunny haze and glints of sun, endless and fascinating. All round the horizon are the mountains — Montagnuola in the west, Chianti in the north and east; white houses shine far away on the heights, a spiral of smoke ascends, and far, far away in the south, behind the hazy, luminous *Creta,* you see the blue, wavy lines of Mont' Amiata, Monte Cetona and the steep, lonely Radicofani which guards the road to Rome.

You stand gazing out upon all this. The foliage of the olives sparkles in the sun, peasants are talking in the fields while they cut the vines, from Siena comes a far-off silvery chiming, as if bells were ringing in the kingdom of heaven. Your heart fills at the sight of so much beauty, it desires still more beauty;

the longing for the far away seizes you, the infinite craving to wander. Out there, far out, there is a little hill crowned with cypresses, you wish you could walk over it! That white point, shining a long way out in the country, is a house — who lives there? You would like to cross its threshold, sit down to a meal with the people in it, break bread with them — that good, coarse *pane casalingo* — drink the ruby wine which they pour out for you from the big *fiasco* in the plaited straw cover which is no longer clean, and hear about their joys and sorrows, share in their lives. . . You feel like that and ere long you have set out for the far away!

Catherine walked with Alessia and Giovanna Pazzi from Montepulciano further on towards the Orcia valley. At the old city of San Quirico with the beautiful Lombard churches the Dominicans and Franciscans had a hospital in common; afterwards it became a fortress castle, but it is still called *Ospedaletto*. We have a letter in which Catherine wrote while there to Fra Tommaso della Fonte, and which is singular, because the tone in it is gentler than one is accustomed to find in that strong-willed young woman. She whose motto is always: "No comfort but that of having no comfort," "No consolation without the Cross," reproaches herself for having swerved, though ever so little, from the thorny path. The autumn days in the Val d'Orcia are so sunny, the moonlight nights so dazzling, in the silent, luminous night the white roads shine across the country, they lead so far, far away to Florence, to Rome, to the end of the world. And Catherine feels as it were a decline in her zeal for the glory of God, a surging up of human longings, of a young woman's heart. Her soul is like a well — there is in it the pure water of heaven, but there is earth as well. "Woe is me," writes this girl of twenty-seven, "that I have remembered so little what you have so often taught me, that I must be dead to my own wrong will. I have not done what I ought and could do, I have not bound my will under the yoke of humility and due reverence. . . I have not set my will to embrace the Cross of my sweetest and dearest Bridegroom, Christ Crucified, but I have sat down to rest in negligence and idleness. It grieves me now, I repent of it and I come to confess it to you, dearest Father, and beseech you in mercy to absolve me." It was perhaps at this time that the following happened: "One day in September," Caffarini relates, "Catherine was weeping bitterly over her sins, and Jesus Christ, who had compassion on her unreasonable grief, said to her: 'Daughter, weep no longer. All thy sins are entirely forgiven.' Catherine answered: 'Give me a sure sign of it. My transgressions are far too many for me to believe it.' Then Christ stretched out His hands over Catherine's head and pronounced the words of absolution over her." [15]

It was during their stay at Montepulciano that Raymond was quite won over to Catherine's cause. Her intensely supernatural life tired him sometimes; he was far more a child of earth than she. One evening when, according to her custom, she sat talking with enthusiasm about heaven, Paradise and everlasting bliss, he actually fell asleep under the influence of her unceasing flow of eloquence. She awoke him scandalised: "I do not intend to sit talking to the wall! It would assuredly do you no harm to listen better!" Raymond had written with admiration about the dead saint, Agnes, but here he had encountered a young, living saint, who was uncompromising in her Christianity and relentlessly forced *her* will upon him as the will of God. "If you really are what you say you are," he said to her one day, "and if you stand in that relation to Our Lord that you tell me you do, then beg of your heavenly Bridegroom to grant me the greatest good of all, that is, the full forgiveness of my sins."

The Dominican was in earnest. "I wish to be as sure," he said, "as if I had received a bull from Rome itself about it." Catherine smiled: "It is well. You shall receive your bull!" It was at dusk and they parted to go to their own rooms.

"The next morning, however," Raymond relates, "I felt rather ill with my usual ailment, and therefore went to bed, and a friend of mine, pleasing both to God and man, Brother Niccolò Pisano,* came to me. We were on a journey at that time, and Catherine was lying ill of fever not very far from our dwelling. When she heard that I was not well she arose from her bed and said to the Sister who was with her: 'Let us go and

---

* This was the same Niccolò da Cascina, who had come to Siena from Pisa, solely to see Catherine.

visit Brother Raymond who is ill.' The Sister answered that there was no great need, and even if there were she, Catherine, was more ill than I. Nevertheless she came and said to me: 'What ails you?' And although a short while before I could not, for sheer weakness, talk with Brother Niccolò, I forced myself and said: 'Why have you come hither? You are more ailing than I.' But she began, as she was wont to do, to speak of God and of our ingratitude if we offend so great a benefactor, and I felt strengthened and arose from my bed — also for the sake of courtesy — but I did not think of her promise of the night before. Then I sat down on a bench beside the bed on which I had lain. Now, as she continued without ceasing to talk as she had begun, a marvellous knowledge of my sins arose in my mind, and it was as clear as if I were standing naked before the eternal judge, and I felt that I must die, as surely as the poor sinners who are led to execution. I beheld also the mercy and mildness of the same judge, in that instead of judging and condemning me as I had deserved, He not only saved me from death and doom, but clothed my nakedness with Himself as with a garment, and bade me to a feast in His house, and sent me out in His service, and in His infinite mercy turned death to life, fear to hope, pain to joy and shame to honour. In this knowledge, or rather, in this clear vision my hard heart was broken, the tears welled up and I fell a-weeping so loudly, and sobbed so much (I redden to say it) that it was as though my heart and my breast were to burst.

"Now that exceeding wise maiden, who had come to me for no other reason, kept silent and suffered me to weep to the end. And while I wept thus, I bethought me of what I had asked of her the day before, and her promise, and I looked up at her and asked: 'Is this the bull I begged of you yesterday?' She answered: 'It is!' And immediately she rose to leave, and if I mistake not, she put her hand lightly upon my shoulder and said: 'Do not forget the benefactions of God,' and with that she was gone."

Raymond was to have one more last doubt about Catherine. They were still in Montepulciano, Catherine was ill and Raymond was sitting beside her bed. As she had told Fra Tommaso della Fonte her visions in the old days, so she now told them to Raymond. In the simplicity of his heart Fra Tommaso had accepted it all as gospel truth and faithfully recorded it, like Clement Brentano, who wrote down all the revelations of Catherine Emmerich. Raymond, however, that highly cultured nobleman, with experience of the world, had still moments in which the supernatural seemed to be too much for him, and when he involuntarily became sceptical. This is genuinely Italian; the same national character which accepts, for instance, the Holy House in Loreto floating down through the air, is capable of suddenly upsetting all its religion and declaring with the futurists: "There are five senses and nothing else!"

Raymond, then, was sitting by Catherine's bed and looking at the pale face with the deep, violet shadows under the half-closed eyes, the flushed cheeks, the narrow mouth with the thin, pale lips which moved unceasingly and told without a break of new visions, new revelations, new heavenly favours, kisses, embraces, drinking of the blood of the heart of Jesus. In between them came her constant urgings to love God alone, to drive out the love of self, of the world, of the flesh, to hate oneself with a holy hate, "for this is the unerringly sure and royal road by which one rises to perfection." Raymond felt how far he was from that ideal, that he certainly did not hate himself as Catherine wished that he should, that a cross and suffering were no joy at all to him, but that he tried to avoid them, if only it could be reconciled with his duty. He felt, in short, like an average Christian, and Catherine's absolutism, Catherine's intransigence, almost irritated him. "I wonder if all that is really true, that she lies there telling me," he thought to himself. And with these thoughts he looked down at Catherine again. . .

But the sight that met him there made him lift up his hands in terror. It was no longer Catherine's face that he saw, framed in the black hood of a nun. It was a man's countenance that looked up at him with two strong, blue eyes, and the man's face was oval and looked about thirty years old, with a short, fair beard — majestic like the Byzantine Christ in the apse of the church of Monreale. "Who art thou, that I see?" exclaimed the Dominican, stricken with fear. And the voice of Catherine answered: "He, who is." At the same instant the vision vanished, but Raymond fell prostrate like Moses before the burning bush, and like Thomas before the Risen One. "Verily, thou art the true bride and disciple of my Lord and my God!" From that moment Raymond stood faithfully by Catherine's side, defended her against all attacks and permitted her that which she so ardently desired: frequent, nay daily Communion.[16]

In a letter which Catherine wrote from Montepulciano to Monna Agnesa di Messer Orso Malavolti in Siena she says: "We could almost desire to make here three dwellings for ourselves, for it is like being in Paradise to live among these holy nuns, and they are so filled with affection for us, that they will not suffer us to depart, and weep if only we speak of it." Francesca Gori, to whom the letter is dictated, adds: "I, Cecca, have almost become a nun and I am beginning to sing the Office together with these handmaids of Jesus Christ." [17]

XI

This life on Mount Tabor, in the white peace of the convent cell, and the rarefied air of the choir, was not to last long; soon the call came to Catherine to come down to earth again and take her place among "this faithless and perverse generation."

This time the request came from Pisa. "It happened at this time," Raymond of Capua writes, "that many persons, both men and women, but in particular certain nuns of the town of Pisa, who had heard of the maiden [Catherine], desired ardently to see her and hear her teaching, which was said to be wonderful. And as many of them could not go to her they entreated her to come and visit them, and to persuade her still more, they told her that by her presence she might gain many souls for the Lord."

Catherine's two friends, Fra Bartolommeo de' Dominici and Fra Tommaso Caffarini were in Pisa at the time, and probably many heard through them of the remarkable young woman and wished to make her acquaintance. In her answer Catherine excuses herself with being in poor health, "yet I hope in the goodness of God, that if He sees that it is to His glory and the salvation of souls, that He will let me come with peace, and that no one will be offended by it. I will then be ready to obey the commands of Eternal Truth and to yield to your request." [1]

Those who could at that time take offence at Catherine's visit were her fellow-countrymen, as the Prior of the Knights of Rhodes in Pisa, with the approval of the Government of that city had taken the Sienese seaport of Talamone and held it in occupation. The relations between the two neighbouring republics had improved during the following year and in February, 1375, Catherine set out northwards, accompanied by Alessia, Lisa, Cecca, Master Giovanni Terzo, Fra Raimondo, Fra Tommaso della Fonte and Fra Bartolommeo de' Dominici. The company of travellers was also joined by Catherine's mother, the ageing Lapa.

In Pisa, Catherine was a guest in the Palazzo Buonconti,* on

---
* A marble tablet has now been placed on the house (No. 11, Via Toselli).

the Lungarno, near the church of Santa Cristina, in that quarter of the town called Kinseca, a name imported from the East. Here she received several visitors, among them being the absolute ruler of the republic, Piero Gambacorti, whose daughter was later influenced by Catherine to take the veil. Catherine began to feel all the joys of fame, but also its anxieties.[2]

For criticism increased with her increasing fame. Even Raymond had to reproach her with permitting those who came to visit her to kiss her hand (as seen on the fresco in San Domenico in Siena). She warded off this criticism by saying that she paid very little attention to the manners of people, and that in particular she did not understand that anyone who was conscious of being only a creature could be given to vanity. As once in Siena (and later in Avignon) she was put to the test in Pisa by a couple of local scholars: the physician, Master Giovanni Gutalebraccia and the advocate, Ser Pietro degli Albizzi. These two tried to catch her with all kinds of vain subtleties, for instance, whether God had a mouth and a tongue, as it was written that He had created the world by His word, and those organs were needed to produce words. It was the situation that is everlastingly repeated in Christendom — the slaves of the letter tempting those who are born of the spirit. Catherine answered that it troubled her little whether God had a tongue or not, but that what was required for salvation was to believe in Jesus Christ and to follow Him. The answer satisfied the two scribes and made them repent; Pietro degli Albizzi even begged Catherine to be godmother to a child he was expecting, to which she consented, afterwards fulfilling her promise.[3]

At about this time a sharp criticism on Catherine was pronounced by the poet, El Bianco da Siena. Feo Belcari relates, together with many other things, that one night, when this faithful disciple of Giovanni Colombini was reading the *Theologica mystica,* he had felt that there was someone in his cell, and that when he looked up he saw a tall, venerable hermit standing before him and advising him not to read the book. El Bianco understood, however, that it was Satan, and forced him to go out of a small window. This man, who was experienced in spiritual matters, had also his doubts about Catherine, and it seemed to him to be particularly suspicious that she took no nourishment. He took upon himself to write a poem to her, in which he admonished her very seriously. "I have heard," he said, "that you pretend to be guided by the Holy Spirit. If this be so, I thank God. . . But have a care not to hold false discourses. . . Already you are called a saint; if you are in truth the bride of Christ, then do not seek honour of men, which is a pestilential for the soul. If you fall, many will lose their faith; have a great care then, you poor woman!" [4]

At first Raymond would not read El Bianco's warning to Catherine, but she insisted upon knowing everything. As usual with her, she regarded those who draw attention to our faults as our greatest benefactors, and she therefore wished to answer El Bianco, to whom she wrote the following:

"Dearest Father in Christ, sweet Jesus. I thank you from my heart for your holy zeal and solicitude for my soul. I am certain that you are persuaded by nothing but your desire for the salvation of my soul, in that you fear that I am deceived by the devil. I do not wonder that you think thus, for often it seems so to me also — and then I tremble with fear. But I trust in the mercy of God and distrust myself altogether, for I know that I can put no faith at all in myself. . . Not only in what concerns eating do I live in constant fear of being deceived, but also in regard to all my life and my work. For I know that the devil by no means lost his intelligence when he fell, and I know that with this intelligence he can easily deceive me. But now I turn to the most holy tree of the Cross, and I do not doubt that if I will suffer myself, in deep love and humility, to be nailed to the Cross with Christ Crucified, the devil can not harm me. . .

"You sent me word that I should pray to God that I might take nourishment. I say to you, Father, and I say it in the presence of God, that I have tried in every possible way to take food, once or twice in the day, and I have prayed constantly and still pray that I may live like others — if such be His will (as it *is mine!*). . . I see no other remedy now than to ask you to pray for me to the highest Eternal Truth that He will grant me the grace (if such be to His greater glory and the salvation of souls) that I may take food, and I am certain that God will hearken graciously to your prayers. You spoke also of a remedy which I might take; I beg you to write of it to me, I will gladly use it if it be to the glory of God. And I beseech you also not to judge anyone lightly, provided you have not received light from God in the matter concerned. Remain in the holy and sweet love of God. Sweet Jesus, Jesus who is love."

El Bianco had wanted Catherine to retire from the world, and to live a life of prayer and penance in solitude like himself. But Catherine was led more than ever in the opposite direction, that of taking part in the struggles of the day and the history of the time. In 1373 Gregory XI had already summoned Christendom to a Crusade, and Catherine had entered with enthusiasm into the agitation for this cause. "The confessor of the Countess who died lately in Rome," that is, Saint Birgitta's confidential adviser and friend, the Spaniard, Alphonso da Vadaterra, had sought out Catherine in Siena with a message from the Pope. "The Holy Father sent me word," she writes, "that I was to pray in particular for him and for Holy Church, and as a sign he granted me a great indulgence. . . And I have written a letter to the Holy Father and entreated him to let us give up our bodies to all manner of pain. May the highest Eternal Truth grant us the grace to be of one mind in yielding up our lives for His holy cause." [5]

Catherine's signature to this letter is "Catherine Martha," indicating that it was more and more the life of a Martha that she had to live. But before she entered upon this new chapter of the short history of her life, and the last and greatest — like Saint Francis on the wild rock, *il crudo sasso,* between the Tiber and the Arno — she was to receive, in a little church in Pisa, the last seals of Christ and bear them during the few years of life remaining to her.

It was soon after her arrival in Pisa, on the fourth Sunday in Lent (Laetare Sunday), which in that year fell on April 1st. Fra Raimondo said Mass and Catherine received Holy Communion in the chapel dedicated to Santa Cristina next to the Palazzo Buonconti. "As usual with her," Raymond writes, "she was for a long time after rapt away from the use of her senses, in that her soul departed as far as it might from the bodily senses. But we waited for her to come to herself that we might, according to her custom, hear some edifying words from her lips. And while we were thus standing around her, we suddenly saw her slight body, which was lying stretched out upon the ground, rise up so that she knelt, and with hands and arms outstretched she remained like this a long while, and her eyes were closed but her face shone. Until of a sudden she sank down as if she had received a mortal wound, and then her soul returned to her body. Soon after she called me and said: 'Know, Father, that by the grace of the Lord Jesus Christ I bear His wounds upon my body.' When I answered that I had suspected this from her movements, and asked her to tell me how it had come to pass, she answered: 'I saw my crucified Lord descending upon me in a great light, and in my eagerness to go towards Him my body rose. And then I saw five blood-red rays going out from His most holy wounds, and they went to my hands and feet and to my heart in my breast. And I understood that which was to happen and cried: Oh, Lord, my God, I beseech Thee, let not Thy wounds be seen outside upon my body; it is enough that I have them within me. And while I was yet speaking, and before these rays had reached me, the blood red was turned to gold, and like rays of the purest light they reached the five places on my body, that is, the hands and the feet and the heart. But the pains I feel are so great, and most of all about the heart, that if the Lord work not a new wonder, I think I can not bear to live in so great pain, but that I must die before many days.'"

The disciples carried Catherine, who was almost unconscious, to her room, and for some days she hovered between life and death. On the following Saturday, however, she had struggled through, and on the Sunday, Passion Sunday, Catherine was again able to go to church, and Raymond gave her Holy Communion. "Are there still pains in your wounds, *Mamma?*" he asked her afterwards. "The pains are still there," Catherine answered, "but instead of tormenting me, they are now refreshment and strength." [6]

Catherine would remember that hour when, two years before her death, she wrote in her book, *The Dialogue,* the following lines about those who have attained to perfect love: "To these dearest children of God all suffering is joy, but all worldly pleasure and consolation is suffering and weariness to them. Like my holy standard bearer Paul they say: 'I glory in reproaches and persecutions for Christ's sake,' and in another place: 'God forbid that I should glory, save in the cross of our Lord Jesus Christ,' and yet again: 'I bear the marks of the Lord Jesus in my body.' They who feel thus love the glory of my name, they hunger after souls and hasten to the table of the holy Cross and in labour and trouble and perseverance they show that they love their neighbour, and they practise and increase all virtues, and the love of the Crucified shines in their bodies." [7]

This was what Catherine of Fontebranda had now become, she had attained to the full stature of Christ, to the ripe age of His manhood. She set forth now to the last surrender, to the perfect burnt offering of her life, pierced by the stinging light from the wounds of Christ.

BOOK III

THE CROWN OF THORNS

> Ueberbildet werden in die Gottheit. — *Suso.*
> beata e gloriosa. — *Santa Caterina.*

BOOK III

THE CROWN OF THORNS

I

"I fill up those things that are wanting of the sufferings of Christ, in my flesh, for his body, which is the church." [1]

These words of the great apostle and mystic [*] might stand as a heading of the last section of the life of Catherine of Siena. Her love of Jesus expands, grows insatiable, infinite, is transformed into love of His mystical Body, of the all-comprehensive, all-embracing Holy Catholic Church.

To many minds in the present day this thought of the identity between Christ and the Church seems remote and strange talk, but the Apostles and the early Church lived and breathed in it. According to the old Catholic doctrine, Jesus of Nazareth is not dead; nay, He has not even departed from the earth. He has a body in which He continues to live until the Last Day, and this body is the Church. The Church is Christ, her voice is the voice of Christ, her commandments are His commandments, her authority is His authority, her power is His power. By virtue of this interior unity of essence the Church also performs all the works of her Lord and Master — heals the sick, recalls the dead to life, forgives sins — and is hated by the world for her deeds of love, is persecuted, tortured, crucified. . .

Hence it follows that the history of the Church is, if not identical, then at least parallel, with the history of Christ. The Church, too, was born in a manger, she was sought by adoring shepherds and by the last of the sages of Greece; during the ages of martyrdom she suffered massacre like the infants of Bethlehem. She had her time of preparation and her temptation in the desert — in the hermit caves of Egypt and the laures of the ascetics, in the Subiaco of Benedict of Nurcia and on Monte Cassino. She had her age of preaching when she strode through Europe proclaiming the glad tidings, century after century, and going as far as extreme ice-covered Thule in the Polar night. She has had her disputes on doctrine both with heretical scribes and with Sadducees who deny the existence of the spirit. She has had her period of triumph, her entry into Jerusalem, when all the civilisation of the West was like one holy city, when

[*] Ep. Col. I 24.

art and poetry strewed all her paths with beauty, and incense diffused its fragrance in the narrow and noisome streets of mediæval cities and the people shouted jubilantly: "Hosannah! Blessed is He that cometh in the name of the Lord!"

Then came the time of suffering — when Nogaret struck the Vicar of Christ in the face — the long, modern age of suffering, when the Church stands bound to the pillar of scourging, or is exposed to the scorn and railing of the people, and the people shout: "We will not have this man to rule over us! Away with Him, and give us Barabbas!"

But in Catherine's time that page in the history of the Passion of the Church had not yet been turned. The morning of Good Friday had not yet dawned; the Church had not yet come to the walk out to Calvary, outside the walls of civilisation and carrying the cross of ignominy; not yet was it the hour of the crucifixion of the Church and the darkness over the earth, and the death of the Church, the laying in the tomb and the three days' rest in the sepulchre. . .

Yet it was already growing dusk before the great darkness "at the sixth hour," and well might the Sienese seeress write in one of her letters: "Now is the time to weep and mourn, for the Bride of Christ is persecuted by her false and corrupt members. . . I therefore pray you, my daughters and sons, that you all pray holy prayers and pious desires before the face of God for Holy Church, for she is sorely persecuted." And yet the good of the Church is the good of mankind — "the exaltation of Holy Church is our exaltation, for in no other place do the souls receive life than in that Church." He who is against the Church is therefore his own enemy: "For the Church is no other than Christ Himself, and it is she who gives us the Sacraments, and the Sacraments give us life." [2]

In the Church alone is there salvation, as there is salvation only in Christ, for these two are one. "The sweet Jesus who would be our way and our teacher and our guide never thought of aught else than the glory of His Father and our salvation, and took our holy Mother the Church for His Bride. . . And in the ardour of His love He has fastened His holy Bride so firmly to Himself and with her all those who stand leaning upon her and are her true sons, that no devil and no man can hinder this venerable and sweetest bride from remaining for everlasting.

"And if you say to me: it looks as if the Church is going back and that she can no longer help herself or her children, then I tell you that it is not so, but that it only looks so from outside. Look within and you will find that strength which her enemies have not.

"You know well that God is power itself, and that all power and strength come from Him. The Bride has the same strength, but her enemies have it no longer, for like corrupt members they are cut off from her body. . . Foolish and absurd, therefore, is he who is but a little member who would rise up against his head, and in particular when he sees that heaven and earth will perish sooner than that head will lose its strength. And if you say: 'I do not know about that! I see that these members thrive and that they prosper,' — then wait but a while — it cannot and will not continue to be so. For the Holy Ghost says in the Scriptures: 'If God keepeth not the city, the watchmen keep watch in vain,' and therefore it cannot be long ere those men perish, for they are without the grace which they need, for God has taken it away from them because they rose against His Bride, in whom God dwells, who is the highest strength." [3]

Catherine has been called a reforming spirit, and this she was. But her efforts at reformation issue from another source than those of Luther or Calvin. The point on which she stood, and from which she would renew everything, was an unshakable faith in the divinity of Christ; it was for her as for the Apostle "the pillar and ground of truth." And this Church, which is really the first article of her creed, is not a vague "congregation of friends of the Lord," no, it is the downright Holy Catholic and Roman Church, whose head is the rightfully elected Pope. He is, as she says again and again, "Christ on earth," *il dolce nostro Cristo in terra;* we do not need to seek any other Jesus either in prayer or in the Bible, we have him living among us. "Even if he were an incarnate devil, we ought not to raise up our heads against him — but calmly lie down to rest on his bosom." [4]

This view of the Church as being absolutely right, and as one before whom, in the case of conflict, we are absolutely wrong, controls Catherine's entire activity, politically and ecclesiastically. One does not understand her, nay, one is altogether mistaken in her, if one does not remember this from the very outset. Read, for instance, the forcible words addressed by her to the government in Florence when it rose up against the Pope:

"He who rebels against our Father, Christ on earth, is condemned to death, for that which we do to him, we do to Christ in heaven — we honour Christ if we honour the Pope, we dishonour Christ if we dishonour the Pope. You can see therefore, that by your disobedience and your persecution — believe me, my brothers, I say it mourning and grieving — you are worthy of death and have become displeasing to God, and nothing worse can befall you than to lose His grace. . . Well do I know that there are many who do not think they are offending God by so doing, but rather that they are doing Him a service by persecuting the Church and her servants, for they defend themselves by saying: 'They are so corrupt and work all manner of evil.' But I tell you that God wills and has so commanded that even if the priests and the pastors of the Church and Christ on earth were incarnate devils, it is seemly that we are obedient and subject to them, not for their sake, but for the sake of God, out of obedience to Him, for He wills that we should act thus. Know, that the son is never in the right against the father, even if the father is ever so evil and unjust, for so great is the good which he has received from the father, that is, life itself, that he can never repay him for it. And we have received the life of grace from the Church, which is so great a benefit, that we can never, by any kind of homage or gratitude, pay the debt that we owe." [5]

Catherine is here maintaining absolute theocracy; in regard to Christ on earth humanity has one supreme duty: to kiss His hand, even when it strikes hardest, as a son kisses the rod. All mere worldly power and authority must submit to this highest authority, which comes direct from God, and in regard to which one duty alone remains: to make our conscience subject to the obedience of faith. It is a further development of that which Francis of Assisi caused to be written in his testament in 1226: "I will fear, love and honour as my masters and will have recourse to the priests who live according to the laws of the Holy Roman Church and are consecrated by it, even though they persecute me, and will see no sin in them, for I see only the Son of God in them, and they are my masters." [6]

All war against the Roman See and the Vicar of Christ is therefore sacrilege. "We are not Jews and Saracens, but we are baptised Christians, redeemed by the blood of Christ. Therefore we ought not, because of any injustice that we suffer now, to lift up our hands against our Father the Pope nor against any fellow-Christian — but we ought to do it against the infidels. For they work injustice against us in possessing that which is not theirs, but which is ours."

These, then, are the two fundamental thoughts in Catherine's policy: the infallibility, not only dogmatic but also purely moral and personal, of the Pope (taking the word in the sense of being considered practically infallible), and what she calls *il dolce mistero del santo passaggio,* "the sweet mystery of the holy crusade." During the five years remaining to her she lives in an increasing enthusiasm for these two great ideas; he who reads her letters feels how the wave of feeling grows stronger and stronger in her, like a fire burning her up, until she dies, consumed by her soul as by a flame. . .

Meanwhile the agitation for the Crusade took most of her time and strength. While in Pisa she sent letter after letter to friends and to strangers — to Joanna of Naples, "the harlot on the throne," as to Bartolommeo di Smeduccio, the despot in San Severino delle Marche; to the republic of Genoa and the ruler over Sardinia, Mariano d'Oristano. "Arise!" she cries in these letters, "let us not slumber any longer in the bed of slothfulness. Now is the time to make good bargains. What are these bargains then? They are to pay with our lives for our God and thus to have all our sins struck off the book. It seems to me that I breathe the fragrance of flowers beginning to open, for our Holy Father, Christ on earth, has proclaimed the holy crusade, and he declares that if Christians will give their lives to winning back the Holy Land, he will help us to the utmost of his power. So has he said in the bull which he has sent to our Provincial and to the General of the Friars Minor and to Brother Raymond, and he has sent it to them with the command to search out the feeling of the people in the whole of Tuscany and all the other places, and then he will set all in order and bid the crusade to go forth. I come now to you therefore, and bid you to the great marriage and eternal life. — I invite you to render blood for blood and to invite as many others as you are able, for one does not go alone to a marriage feast." [7]

Catherine remained in Pisa during the summer (from February till September). Busily occupied as she was, however, with exterior affairs, such as correspondence and political talks, she did not forsake her old love of the cloistered life, and she paid frequent visits to the hermits in the Campo Santo of Pisa; several of them seem to have lived in that place, and we have the names of two of them: Jacopo and Bartolommeo. It is easy to imagine the feelings of the saint when wandering there over the soil of the churchyard, which was soil from the Holy Land, brought home in the galleys of Pisa, or in that wonderful Gothic *chiostro,* where the frescoes of Phaurati still show the devout life of hermits, and where Orcagna has taught the same doctrine with his brush as Catherine with her pen. "*Tutto passa!*" Everything perishes! After the music of viol and lute the tolling of funeral bells, after the bridal veil the shroud!

Catherine, though, went further afield, quite away from the town. Away to the foot of the hills of Pisa and the old olive woods with their greyish-green foliage on the hillsides, where Calci, the Carthusian monastery, is still standing, but at that time it was called *Valle Graziosa.* Being a woman she could not enter the monastery and could not see the large *chiostro,* which is so full of sunshine and the scent of boxwood, and where the water tinkles out of the well among birds' beaks of bronze. She could not go into the little Carthusian houses — one for each of the monks, and in front of each house a little garden with lemon trees in big red terra cotta pots, and vines growing like tunnels over the paths leading to a loggia with a view furthest out, where there are two seats opposite each other underneath a whitewashed arch — *o beata solitudo!* She would pray, though, in the church; its white peace and the solemn power of the night prayers would sweep over her; on sunny days she would walk on the heights of Monte Magno, whence she would see for the first time a silvery grey or a gleaming blue streak in the distance — a streak that was the sea. Out there an island in the hazy sky line rose up like a mountain top on a plain — Gorgona! The island of Gorgona with its Carthusian monastery, from which the Abbot had to flee, driven away in 1373 by pirates, but which had been re-established by Gregory XI in the very year in which Catherine visited Pisa. Catherine wished to go out to this distant island of the white monks — and what she willed was usually done. One day the young Sienese woman took her place under the lateen sail in a roomy boat, and away they went down the Arno, past San Rossore's solemn pine-woods, where the dromedaries grazed — out across the rising and falling waves, glassy clear, of the Tyrrhenian Sea. On the sandy beach of the steep coast of Gorgona, with its watch-tower guarding against pirates, stood the white monks with their newly appointed Prior, Dom Bartolommeo Serafini, bidding the Sienese saint and her escort welcome. As it was evening they took Catherine and her women friends to a hostelry about a mile away, while the Dominicans went home with the monks.

Next morning all the Carthusians came out to Catherine and the Prior asked her to say a few words to them, to which she consented after some reluctance. She spoke about the religious life, its conditions and dangers, and spoke so well and so earnestly, so much from her own experience, that they were all interested. As Dom Bartolommeo said afterwards to Raymond: "I am the confessor of all my monks, and each one has received exactly what he needed to hear." There was even one young monk who was in despair at having been parted from his family, and who was thinking of suicide, who was restored by Catherine to a better frame of mind. Such power and charm emanated from the Sienese guest that when she left Dom Bartolommeo begged her to give him her mantle, as Elisha had received the prophet's mantle from his master when he was carried up into heaven in the chariot of fire.[8]

Catherine continued her labours for the crusade all through the summer. Among others she wrote to the mother of the King of Hungary, Elisabeth of Poland, in order to gain the son through the mother. Then something happened which abruptly destroyed all hopes of a crusade being carried into effect soon.

On June 4th the Papal Legate, the Cardinal of Sant' Angelo,

Guillaume Noëllet, had concluded a truce with Bernabò de' Visconti at Bologna. In consequence of this Sir John Hawkwood and his terrible free-lances became idle and threatened to invade fertile Tuscany. The Papal Legate declared that he was unable to prevent this, unless Florence would lend him 60,000 florins. Besides this he forbade the export of corn from the Papal States.

Florence regarded this as a deliberate attack on the freedom of Tuscany. "First they will starve us," it was said, "then they will invade us and bring us under subjection." Added to this the party of the Ricci wanted to overthrow the Albizzi party, which was then in power, and which relied upon the clergy for support. The old Ghibelline spirit arose in the republic, hitherto so Guelphic, and rather than send the Cardinal the money the Florentines would take Hawkwood and his bands into their pay. Spinello Lucalberti and Simone Peruzzi were therefore sent out to make terms with them, and on June 21st they succeeded in obtaining peace at the enormous price of 130,000 gold florins. Hawkwood and his mercenaries left to seek employment elsewhere.

"On June 28th," the chronicle continues, "he crossed the Arno at Cozano and Mazana and invaded the valley of Calci. Here he ravaged and plundered and took over two hundred prisoners, men, women and children, and more than two thousand head of cattle. He burnt down the houses round the church in Calci and carried off corn and beasts." [9]

Thus the storm was gathering over Pisa and the town, following the example of Florence, purchased its peace. "On July 2d," says the chronicle, "Pisa agreed to pay the English thirty thousand five hundred florins in three portions, and the drum went through the town proclaiming that there was peace and that every man could safely go about his business. And about two thousand of the men-at-arms came into the town to refresh themselves, with no weapons but the sword, and in the evening the drum went again that the soldiers were to leave the town, if they did not the punishment would be two strokes with the cat o' nine tails. On the eighth, Sunday evening, Sir John Hawkwood left Pisa and went towards Siena, and they had

THE CROWN OF THORNS

been in the territory of Pisa thirteen days and six in that of Florence."

It was during those thirteen days that Catherine made a last attempt to ward off the threatened fight by a direct appeal to John Hawkwood. One morning the sentries outside the English camp saw two Dominicans approaching and asking in some trepidation for Messer Giovanni Aguto (the melodious rendering of the stranger's barbarous name). When the two monks were at length ushered into the presence of that dreaded warrior they drew out a parchment: "This is sent to you by Catherine, the handmaid and slave of the servants of Jesus Christ."

The Englishman read the letter or had it read to him:

"Dearest and sweetest brother in Christ Jesus.

"It is high time now that you thought a little of yourself and considered how great are the sufferings you have borne so long in serving the devil. My soul desires that you now change your manner of life and with all your followers enter the service of Christ Crucified, so that henceforth you may be a company of Christ, going to war against the infidel dogs who have possession of our holy places — there where the sweet Truth Himself suffered death for us. I entreat you then, in Christ Jesus, that since you take so much delight in warfare and fighting, not to fight any longer against Christian men, but rather against unbelievers . . . and thus you will prove yourself a true and manly knight.

"This letter is brought to you by my father and son, Brother Raymond. Hearken to his words, he is a true and faithful servant of God — and I beseech you, dearest brother, to remember that your time is short. Remain therefore, in the holy and sweet love of God. Sweet Jesus, Jesus who is love."

The huge condottiere (we see him mounted high on horseback in Paolo Ucello's fresco in the cathedral of Florence, where he lies buried) did not repeat what he had done at the conquest of Cesena, when, imitating the wisdom of Solomon, he clove a nun about whom two of his men were fighting into two equal parts. Perhaps he was content to answer, as he usually answered the greeting of the Franciscans: "The Lord grant thee peace," with "And may the Lord take away the alms you have received! Have I to die of hunger? I live on war as you do on alms!" At any rate he sent the two Dominicans away unscathed. Nay, if a note in the second printed edition of Catherine's letters is to be believed (Venezia 1500) Hawkwood bound himself by an oath to go on crusade.[10] He broke this oath, but later, when he again entered the service of the Pope against the worst enemy of the latter, Bernabò Visconti, it was at a moment when he was again under the influence of *her* who had once called him her "dearest and sweetest brother in Christ Jesus."

All over Italy the anger against the See of Rome was great and the rising general. A conspiracy to deliver up the town to the Pope was discovered in Prato and the furious people flayed a priest alive, dragged him through the streets, tore out pieces of his flesh with tongs and threw them to the dogs. Pisa, Siena, Lucca and Arezzi were asked to join the Florentine-Milanese League. A new authority was placed at the head of the republic on the Arno: the Eight of War" (*gli otto della guerra*, ironically also called "the Eight Saints"), and a heavy tax for defence was levied on priests and church property.[11]

War had not yet broken out, however, and after a short visit to her own town of Siena in August 1375, Catherine, in obedience to Gregory's wish, went to Lucca, in order to prevent the desertion of this republic at least. In her report to the Pope she gives the following description of the position of the small free state: "They are greatly troubled because they receive no help from you, and the other side is constantly urging and threatening them to join them." This statement was no doubt made to Catherine by the government of Lucca — *gli anziani*, "the ancients," but it does not quite agree with the facts. Gregory helped Lucca very generously, but, as Lazzareschi has shown, the small republic played a Machiavellian double game, by which it succeeded in fooling the credulous Pope, who was grieved and indignant when he discovered at length that the government in which he had placed such unquestioning trust had been in league with his adversaries and had really been on their side.

It was not till January that the Pope found this out, and Catherine's mission to Lucca had taken place before that. She had prepared her coming by a letter, of which a part has been

THE CROWN OF THORNS 209

given at the beginning of this chapter, and in which she explains her political doctrine. She uses her customary strong words; holds up to the people of Lucca the awful example of Pontius Pilate to show them to what human respect may lead; declares that she comes to them sent by Christ Crucified (as Jeanne d'Arc felt that she was sent *de part Dieu*).

But, as Lazzareschi justly writes, there are too many real gems in Catherine's crown for her to need any false ones. The historical truth is that the political mission of the Sienese woman in Lucca was a complete failure. "It was naïve to hope that pious warnings would have any influence on the fate of a republic in the fourteenth century."

Catherine then turned to another field: to the work for the salvation of souls. In September, escorted by her friends Caffarini, Bartolommeo de' Dominici, Neri di Landoccio, probably also Tommaso della Fonte, she crossed the chain of mountains separating the valley of the Arno from the basin of the river Serchio, which, Dante says, "causes Lucca to be hidden from the Pisans." September 14th, the Exaltation of the Holy Cross, is a great feast day in Lucca, the *Volto Santo* being unveiled in the cathedral, and no doubt Catherine would on that day be among the worshippers under its Romanesque vaults, before the archaic picture of the thorn-crowned Face. Caffarini relates that the people crowded in the streets to see *la Santa* pass by, and Neri di Landoccio remembers a blessed moment when his *Mamma*, as so often before, put all melancholy in his soul to flight and gave him peace from all doubt and all despair by a radiant promise — that one day he would be with her in Paradise.[12]

As in Pisa, so in Lucca, the devout flocked about Catherine. We know the names of several of her friends: Monna Colomba, Monna Lippa, Monna Bartolommeo, married to a certain Messer Salvatico, Monna Mellina, married to Bartolommeo Balbani, at whose villa in Vicapelago outside the town Catherine is said to have been a guest. Probably all these ladies were Mantellate and Catherine would pray with them in their chapel in the church of San Romano, or they would be gathered around her in the house next to the church where a number of them lived like a religious community. And Catherine's teaching would be the same as always: that one must leave the world, forsake feasts and vanities, put on the love of God,* embrace the Cross, run the race (*palio*) of the good fight.

It was in Lucca that a priest, who did not believe in Catherine's supernatural gifts, tried to deceive her by bringing her, one morning when she was lying ill, an unconsecrated host in solemn procession, with lighted candles, as if it were really the Sacrament of the Altar. Catherine, however, did not show any signs of reverence, and when the priest rebuked her for it, she said, to his great consternation:

"Are you not ashamed, Father, to bring me an ordinary piece of bread, as if it were the Blessed Sacrament, and even to compel me to idolatry?" Was it on this or another of Catherine's mornings in Lucca that the following, related by Caffarini, occurred? "Although she was troubled with much sickness, she tried to get up in time to go to church. But in the counsels of God it happened that notwithstanding all her efforts she could not for utter weakness leave her room. When she saw that it was impossible she resigned herself to the will of God and began to pray in her cell. But hardly had she begun her prayer when she felt herself carried in spirit to a place which seemed like a church, where a great company of the blessed were assembled as if to be present at the holy sacrifice, which was offered in solemn splendour by a pious bishop. There were golden candlesticks on the altar, the acolytes carried torches and she heard beautiful singing. At last it seemed to her that the bishop called her to him and gave her the most holy Body of Christ, which she received with great devotion. Then immediately the vision vanished, but when the holy maiden had again come to herself she confessed and said that in that mystic communion she had received the same spiritual benefit, or, as she was wont to say, *dolcezza*, as when she received the heavenly and consecrated bread from the hands of the priest." [13]

Catherine left Lucca and again returned to Pisa, intending to make only a short stay. But it proved otherwise. Writing to Tommaso della Fonte who was at home again in Siena, she says: "I fear that I must stay here longer than you had per-

---

* "As you put clothes on your dolls," she says later in a letter to the saddler, Giovanni Perotti — with an allusion to the dolls for which Lucca was famous at that time (*Bambini di Lucca*).

mitted me, as the Archbishop [of Pisa, Francesco Moricotti di Vico] has asked the General (of the Dominicans) to let me stay longer. Ask that venerable Spaniard [i.e. Alphonso da Vadaterra] to pray that God will grant us His grace, so that we do not return empty-handed. . . Oh, sweetest Eternal Truth, give us large bites to eat! I cannot do otherwise, Father, than invite you in the name of Christ Crucified to fill your soul with faith and with hunger after souls." [14]

"Faith and hunger after souls," that was the entire content of Catherine's own soul. The hunger had its source in faith: he who really and earnestly believes will involuntarily make the utmost efforts to bring to others the grace of salvation. Catherine *believed in earnest,* and therefore, says William Flete, she could be heard to exclaim suddenly, in the midst of a walk, "I want to eat!" She wanted to consume souls, absorb them into herself, unite them with her personality in order to unite them with that divine Person, in whom alone there is salvation. "She aspired," writes the hermit of Lecceto, "to eat spiritually the whole Church of God and to chew the whole world with her prayers as though with her teeth." [15] In her letters she expresses again and again the wish that she constantly applies to her disciples: "May God make you devourers of souls — *mangiatori delle anime!*"

There was plenty of work for everyone who would bring souls to God and the Church. Towards the end of October, 1375, Donato Barbadori came as envoy from Florence to Pisa to persuade Piero Gambacorti to break with the Pope. He did not succeed, and there is no doubt that it was due to Catherine's influence. On the other hand, she had the grief of seeing her own town, true to its old Ghibelline traditions, making common cause with Florence, against the Pope. This, however, was on March 12th, 1376, after Catherine had left Pisa.

The republic on the Arno now thought itself strong enough to venture on fighting. In December the nephew of the Abbot of Marmoutier had attempted to outrage the wife of a respected citizen of Perugia, and to escape from shame she had thrown herself out of a window and been killed on the spot. Scandalised at this crime, the inhabitants rose in revolt against the French despots. "Death to the princes of the Church!"

they shouted in the streets, and in front of the castle in which the French ecclesiastics had taken refuge, they set up a terrible catapult which hurled red-hot stones into the fortress, and which was dubbed "the priest-killer." At the same time other towns, Città di Castello, Viterbo, Gubbio, Urbino, Todi, Forli, rose in revolt and in ten days no fewer than eighty towns had rebelled against the papal rule. To all of them, as a sign of brotherhood, Florence sent a blood-red banner with the inscription: *Libertas*. A wave of enthusiasm for freedom swept over Italy like that which, four hundred and fifty years later, in the days of the Holy Alliance, streamed through the verse of Byron and Shelley:

> *Yet, Freedom, yet thy banner torn but flying,*
> *Streams like a thunderstorm against the wind.*

During this sojourn in Pisa Catherine lived in a hospital near the Dominican church. Fra Raimondo and his brother in religion, Fra Pietro da Velletri, sought her, terrified, on December 2nd, to bring her the sad news from Perugia. Catherine shared their feelings, but then said: "You begin to weep too soon, save your tears for a better occasion. That which you see now is only milk and honey to what is to come!" Fra Raimondo thought this was but poor comfort and exclaimed: "What can happen that is worse? Will faith in Jesus Christ, then, be openly denied?" Catherine answered: "It is the laity now, that rebels — but after that it will be the turn of the clergy!" Then, in plain words, she foretold the coming Schism.[16]

Shortly after she returned with her little escort to Siena to keep Christmas.

II

"I have been in Pisa and in Lucca and have urged upon them, as far as I could, not to make a compact with the corrupt members who are rebelling against you. . . I beseech you to write very earnestly to Messer Piero,* and to do it with care, and do not delay. I say no more.

"I have heard that you have created cardinals. I believe it would be to the glory of God and more useful if you had a care to choose virtuous men. The contrary is a great disgrace before God and works the destruction of the Church. And it is not to be marvelled at if God afterwards sends his judgments; it is only just. I beseech you to be more manly and God-fearing in doing your duty.

"I have heard that you will promote the General Master of our Order to another office. If this be so, I entreat you, for the sake of Christ Crucified to have a care to give us a good and virtuous Vicar; the Order needs one, for it is full of tares. You can consult Messer Niccolò da Osimo,† and the Archbishop of Tronto, and I will write to them thereof."

It is not the first time the dyer's daughter of Siena writes to the Pope. The young woman, who was barely twenty-nine, had already addressed a letter to the Vicar of Christ which has not been preserved, but which must have been written at the end of 1374 or the beginning of 1375, after the visit of Bishop Alphonso of Vadaterra to Siena.

The election of cardinals to which she now alludes, took place on December 20th, 1375, and on that occasion the Pope created seven French cardinals, as against one Italian and one Spaniard. Catherine was perfectly right in her criticism. At first sight, however, it may cause wonder that she, who demanded such an absolute submission to the Pope, should presume to instruct him herself on his duties. Even in a secondary matter like that of appointing a new head of the Dominican

---

* Gambacorti. Messere was a title reserved for knights, doctors and canons. Members of religious orders were addressed as Padre, all others with "tu" without a title.

† "Our notary and secretary," Gregory XI calls him in a letter of 1376.

Order it is she who gives advice, and advice that he will do well to take. In which case she promises to support him with her influence — "I will write about the matter to those concerned."

It is at this point that a character like Catherine's differs entirely from that of, for instance, Francis of Assisi. She was absolutely sure of herself. It never occurred to her that she might be wrong. Francis of Assisi was a man, with a man's sense of the relative, constantly troubled by the question of whether the others might not be right. When a malicious Dominican had given him a problem of conscience to ponder over, he did not sleep at night. He would come to a general chapter with the deepest feeling of his own incompetence and unworthiness, prepared to agree with his critics, take his leave and stay away for ever. Catherine of Siena is a woman, what she thinks is, of course, right. Hence the unity, the absolutism of her life. Francis founds an Order which contains an interior discord, and is therefore liable to break its bounds at any moment. Catherine leads the exiled Papacy by her firm and fearless little hand back to Rome. For in all the world there is only one competent person, only one who is right — and that one is herself.

There is, one is almost tempted to say, a holy insolence all through this first letter, explicit and well considered as it is, to the Pope. In our own times such a communication, even though ever so well intentioned, would hardly be accepted at the Vatican.

The Sienese woman begins with some polite forms of address: "Most reverend and dearly loved Father," and calls herself "unworthy, miserable, pitiable." Soon, though, she has reached her favourite subject — human respect, which hinders us in fulfilling our duties and is only a form of ease-loving, convenient selfishness — and then she has no respect of persons. "He who loves himself," she writes, "be he a prelate or a subordinate, cannot do anything but evil and all virtue is dead in him. He is like a woman who brings forth dead children. This is really true, because the life of love has not been in him and he has cared only for the praise of men and his own honour, and not the honour of the name of God. I say then, that if such an one is a prelate his acts are wrong, because, not willing to displease creatures, to whom he is chained by his love of them, he suffers holy justice to die in his soul. For he sees those under him erring and sinning and makes as though he did not see it, so that he need not punish, or if he chastises, he does it so feebly that it is of no avail, but only a covering up of vice; and always he is afraid to offend and make enemies. And all this is because he loves himself. But I say that this is the greatest cruelty. For if the sore is not burned with fire when it is needful and scorched with an iron, but only smeared with an unguent, it will fester underneath the unguent."

All this is kept in general terms, but Catherine now turns to the Pope himself, like Saint Paul when he "withstood Peter to the face."

"Woe, woe, sweetest *Babbo mio!*" she exclaims, "this is the reason why all the subordinates are corrupted in impurity and injustice. Oh, human misery! Blind are the sick who do not know their own disease, and blind is the pastor who ought to be the healer, but who never dares to use either the knife of justice or the fire of true love. Of such as these Christ says: When the blind lead the blind both fall into the ditch. And both the sick man and the physician go to hell. Such a pastor is nothing but a hireling . . . and he is that because he loves himself otherwise than in God and does not follow Jesus, the true Shepherd. . . I hope, therefore, venerable Father, that you will quench that wrongful love yourself and not love yourself any more for your own sake.

"Oh, Babbo mio, sweet Christ on earth, follow the example of your namesake, Saint Gregory. That which was possible for him is possible also for you. He was a man of flesh and blood like you and God is the same now as then. Nothing is needed but virtue and zeal for the salvation of souls.

"This is what I would see in you. If you have not hitherto been very firm in this matter I entreat you now to use the time remaining like a courageous man, following Christ, whose Vicar you are. And fear not, Father, all the storms that will come over you . . . fear not. God's help is near. Have a care to find good shepherds and good governors in your cities, for the revolt has come because of the bad shepherds and the bad governors. Go forward and fulfil in deeds the two things that you have begun in holy intention, that is, your coming to Rome and the holy, sweet crusade. Arise, Holy Father, no more negligence! Courage, courage, and come, come and console the servants of God, your children ... we await you with love and longing. Forgive me, Father, all these words, you know that out of the fulness of the heart the mouth speaketh." [1]

At about the same time that this letter reached Avignon, on New Year's Day (1376), Perugia fell into the hands of the anti-clericals, and soon after Pisa and Lucca joined the Florentine league. Gregory XI saw that it was time to act, and on January 6th he issued an encyclical to the Italian states, in which he stated that he would return with the whole Curia to Rome, "and live and die among you, and lighten the heavy burdens which have been laid upon you." This did not prevent him, however, from addressing a summons to the Florentines with an order to deliver up to him all the leaders of the revolt; they had all to report themselves at Avignon before the end of March. Among those who were summoned in this way was Catherine's friend, Niccolò Soderini, who had had a seat in the government during the first two months of 1376, and Catherine seized her pen to plead for him and the other rebels.

"We are in your hands, Father," she wrote on their behalf, "and I know and acknowledge that they are wrong, and they acknowledge it. I do not seek to excuse the sin but will only say that they had to suffer much injustice and many wrongs from the bad pastors and governors, so that at last they knew of no other remedy. You know what the lives of many of your governors [*rettori*] are, that they are infected with sin and are incarnate devils. And therefore I beg for mercy for your children, Father, regard not their presumption and pride * ... but grant peace to your poor children who have offended you. I tell you, sweet Christ on earth, from Christ in heaven, that when you do this, without the heat of anger, they will repent of what they have done and come and bow down their heads before you. Then you will rejoice and we shall rejoice, for in charity you will have led the lost sheep back to the fold of Holy

---

* *Ignoranzia.* At the present day the word *ignorante* is still synonymous, in Siena, with audacious, aggressive.

THE CROWN OF THORNS

Church. And then, sweet Babbo, you will be able to fulfil your holy wish and the will of God, that is, to enter upon the holy crusade, which I beseech you on behalf of God to do soon and without negligence. With great love they will make ready to give their lives for Christ. Oh Babbo, raise up soon the banner of the most holy Cross and you will see the wolves turned into lambs. Peace, peace, peace, that the war shall not still compel us to delay this sweet crusade. And if you would have your revenge, then revenge yourself upon me, wretched outcast that I am, and punish me with every possible torment and suffering, even with death. Of a truth I believe that my faults and sins are the cause of much evil, and much disorder and strife. Take vengeance then, upon me, your miserable daughter, as much as seems good to you. Woe, Father, I die of anguish, and yet I cannot die. Come, come, resist not the will of God that calls you. . . Come, come and sit in the seat of him who sat before you in the chair of the Apostle. . . Come, come, delay no longer; no evil can befall you, for God will be with you. Humbly I entreat your blessing on me and on all my spiritual children." [2]

At the same time Catherine wrote the letter to Niccolò Soderini quoted in the previous chapter, and could therefore hope that she had brought the contending parties nearer to each other. To Soderini she had preached the duty of absolute obedience to the Pope; and Gregory had been reminded that he was above all a father and a prince of peace. Then two things happened: on March 20th Bologna fell into the hands of the anti-papal party, and a week later the papal troops, led by Hawkwood, took Faënza, murdered the men and violated the women under the cry of *Evviva la Chiesa!*

Three days later, the ambassadors sent by Florence, Donato Barbadori and Alessandro dell' Antella, stood before the Pope at Avignon and declared on behalf of the republic that the political leaders who had been summoned were not able to put in an appearance, among other reasons because some of them were in prison. Moreover, the Florentines were of opinion that they had been treated most unjustly by the papal governors, and they did not intend to surrender unconditionally. Gregory answered by putting Florence under an interdict and excommunicating the Eight of War, besides fifty-one prominent citizens, among them being Niccolò Soderini. Donato Barbadori heard the terrible judgment pronounced: all Florentines were henceforth outlawed and could, without any claim to redress, be made slaves; no one was bound to keep his word to them or pay them the debts owing to them; no one could trade with them or help them in any way whatever; all the princes of Christendom were called to arms and to exterminate them from the face of the earth. Thereupon he turned to the image of the Crucified, in whose name the terrible words had been pronounced, and cried with the Psalmist: "Look down upon me, God of my salvation and be thou my help. Forsake me not, for my father and mother have forsaken me." [3]

The Florentines were fully aware of the terrible weight the interdict and excommunication would have, and how their enemies and rivals would take advantage of it to ruin their trade, capture their galleys and not redeem the bills in circulation with them.

"In all the world," Raymond of Capua relates, "Florentines were seized and deprived of their property by the government of the country in which they carried on their trade. They were therefore compelled to seek peace with the supreme Pontiff, with the help of some persons whom they knew to have the ear of the Pope." They were thinking, of course, of Catherine, who was indeed ready at once, and who — to prepare the way and show her good will — sent off Raymond to Avignon at the end of March, accompanied by Master Giovanni Terzo and Fra Felice of Massa, carrying a fresh letter from Catherine to the Pope.

"There are three things," it is said in this letter, "which God requires of you. The first is to reform the Church — to pull up the bad herbs by the roots, that is to say, the bad pastors and governors, who poison and corrupt the garden, and cast them outside, and instead to plant good and fragrant flowers." "How shameful it is that they, who ought to be examples of voluntary poverty, meek as lambs, fathers of the poor, that they live in luxury and pomp and splendour and worldliness, a thousand times worse than if they were in the world. And many layfolk put them to shame by living good and virtuous lives."

The second duty of the Pope was to come to Rome, the third to proclaim the crusade and to organise it. But above all, he must work for peace — "Depart not from the way of peace because of what happened in Bologna . . . I entreat you, Father, hearken to what Brother Raymond and the others of my sons have to say to you; they come from Christ Crucified and from me." [4]

"From Christ Crucified and from me" — the words are great. But not too great; Catherine was really the true ambassador of the gentle Prince of Peace to the men of blood of the world and the Church. A vision strengthened her still further in this feeling of communion with Him who rode into Jerusalem upon the ass, and the colt, the foal of the ass.

"In the night after the first of April," she wrote to Raymond, "God revealed His mysteries to me and showed me His wonderful counsels in such a way that my soul no longer knew whether it was in the body, and I was filled with such abundant joy that my tongue has no power to express it. I received so much understanding of the mystery of persecution which Holy Church must now suffer, and of the renewing and exaltation in the time that is to come; and it was said to me that the present happens in looking to what is to come, that the Church may come to its first state again. The sweet truth from the beginning (*Prima dolce Verità*) was given to me in two sayings of the Holy Gospel, namely: 'it must needs be that scandals come,' and this other, 'but woe to that man by whom the scandal cometh.' As if He would say: 'I permit this persecution that I may draw out the thorns from the body of my Bride, which is full of them, but I suffer no man to think evil of her. Do you know what I do? I do as I did when I was here on the earth and made a scourge of cords and drove out them that bought and sold in the Temple, for the house of God is a house of prayer, but they have made it a den of thieves. Thus do I say to that I do now. For I have made a scourge of men, and with this scourge I drive out the unclean, covetous, miserly and proud pedlars who buy and sell the gifts of the Holy Spirit. . .'

"But as the ardour of holy desire grew in me, I marvelled to see how both the Christian people and the infidels entered into the wound in the heart of Christ Crucified, and I walked into the midst of them in love and longing and entered into Christ sweet Jesus together with my father, Saint Dominic, and the friend of my heart, John,* and all my spiritual children. And then He laid the Cross upon my shoulder and placed the branch of olive in my hand, even as I desired it, and He said to me that I was to go out with it to all people. And He said to me: 'Go and tell them: Behold I bring you tidings of great joy! And I rejoiced and exulted . . . and said like Simeon: 'Now thou dost dismiss thy servant, O Lord, according to thy word in peace.'

"But what tongue is able to utter the mysteries of God? Not mine, not my miserable, wretched tongue! And therefore I will be silent and do nothing but seek the glory of God and the salvation of souls and the renewing and exaltation of Holy Church and in the grace and power of the Holy Spirit persevere in this until death. . . Oh, sweet God, who art love, fulfil soon the desires of Thy servants! I will say no more and I have said nothing. I suffer, I die of desire. Have pity on me. Pray to the divine goodness and to Christ on earth that the cleansing may come soon. Remain in the holy sweet love of God. Drown yourselves in the blood of Christ Crucified. . . Rejoice when you have tribulations, and love, love, love one another." [5]

This vision during the night between the 1st and 2nd April was decisive for Catherine. Shortly before Easter she wrote to the government in Florence that she was willing to mediate between the republic and the Roman See. Raymond sent her good tidings from Avignon and in the beginning of May she arrived in Florence, accompanied by Neri di Landoccio, Fra Bartolommeo de' Dominici and a newly acquired disciple, who was to become one of her most intimate ones: the young Sienese nobleman, Stefano Maconi.

In later days, when he had become Prior of the Carthusian monastery at Pavia, Maconi told about his first meeting with

* i.e. Raymond, whom she liked to call by this name.

his famous townswoman. They were of the same age (both born in 1347), but until the beginning of the year 1376 the young nobleman had not troubled himself much about the doings of the pious Dominican sister. "I was," he says, with an expression taken from Catherine's *Dialogo*, "plunged in the waters of this world."

Moreover, it was a purely temporal matter that caused him to seek her. For two years the Maconis had had a quarrel with the powerful and overbearing family of the Tolomei and they wished to put an end to the strife. The other side, however, would not hear of it, and at the advice of Pietro Bellanti, Catherine's earlier convert, Stefano at last went to seek the help of the maiden of Fontebranda. She received him, not (as he had expected) with prudish and old-maidish airs, no, she met him frankly and cordially, "as if I were her brother who had returned from a long journey." After having enjoined the usual conditions on the young man: to go to confession and henceforth lead an upright life, she declared herself willing to take his case in hand. The opponents really did consent to make peace and a meeting was arranged between the contending parties at the church of San Cristofano. The Maconis came punctually, but not the Tolomeis, although they lived only a few steps away on the opposite side of the street. Evidently this was a fresh insult — they meant to make fools of the Maconis! Then Catherine began to pray, and behold, ere very long she had, by the power of her soul, forced the obstinate family across the square, into the church, and peace was concluded.[6]

From that moment Stefano was an enthusiastic *caterinato*. He sought her early and late, he wrote her letters for her, she became for him, as for the others, the admired, adored, beloved *Mamma*. All Siena spoke of it, but what did it concern him? He had only one trouble — Catherine's approaching journey. And one day the following talk took place between the two:

"My dearest son," said Catherine, "I have some good news for you. Your greatest wish shall be fulfilled."

"Dearest Mamma," answered Stefano, "I do not know myself what my greatest wish can be."

Catherine smiled: "Search your heart, look carefully!"

And Stefano: "In truth, dearest Mamma, I cannot find that I have any greater wish than to be always where you are!"

"That is the very wish that you shall have," said Catherine quickly.

She kept her word. She sent Neri di Landoccio on ahead from Florence to Avignon with a letter to the Pope, but Stefano was permitted to remain near her.

The sojourn in the republic on the Arno lasted some weeks. In her encounter with the Florentine government Catherine maintained unswervingly the theocratic standpoint: "The scribes and Pharisees sit in the chair of Moses," it is said in the Gospel, "all things therefore whatsoever they shall say to you, observe and do; but according to their works do ye not." In the same way Catherine distinguishes between the person and the office. "I know well," she says, "that many think they do God a service by persecuting the Church and its servants, and they say, to justify themselves: 'The priests are so bad,' but I say to you that God will and has commanded so, that even if the shepherds of the Church and Christ on earth were incarnate devils, while the Pope that we have is a good and gentle father — yet we must be submissive to him and obedient, not for what he is personally, but out of obedience to God, because the Pope is the Vicegerent of Christ." [7]

At that time Niccolò was no longer a member of the government; the man in the Signoria on whom Catherine had most influence was Buonaccorso di Lapo. But if they did not wish for peace for supernatural reasons, they wished for it on natural grounds — the material effects of the interdict were most unpleasantly felt, and in the beginning of May all divine worship ceased in Florence. The people were in great despair, large penitential processions went through the streets daily, singing Miserere and scourging their bare shoulders. A group of wealthy young noblemen formed a kind of brotherhood in order to perform good works in common, and when Catherine came to Florence with her escort, the elders of the trade guilds stood at the gate of the city to receive her, as the only one who could help them.[8]

During this short visit Catherine met again the Bishop of

Florence, Messer Angelo Ricasoli, and made several new acquaintances: Monna Laudamia Strozzi, the popular politician already mentioned, Buonaccorso di Lapo, as well as the tailor, Francesco di Pippino, to whom and to whose wife, Monna Agnese, she wrote so often later. The pious tailor seems to have been the centre of a small godly circle, counting among its members the nobleman Bartolo Usimbardi and his wife Monna Orsa, who also became Catherine's friends. In the family of the Canigiani she found very good friends; the two brothers Ristoro and Barduccio put themselves entirely under her tutelage and Barduccio, the younger, became her secretary, accompanying her everywhere and remaining with her to the last. Five of the six original letters from Catherine that we possess were written by Barduccio Canigiani.

The Vallombrosa monk, Giovanni delle Celle, was a prominent personality with whom Catherine also became acquainted at this time. This remarkable man had long been a monk at Santa Trinità in Florence. He had there at first devoted himself particularly to humanistic studies, in the spirit of Petrarch and Boccaccio, but later he began to cultivate the Black Art. Like Dr. Faustus he could summon up the devil, and the latter brought, unobserved by the Abbot, young women into Brother Giovanni's cell. At length these nocturnal visits of ladies within the enclosure were discovered; the guilty monk had to confess and was punished with imprisonment in a dark cell for one year. Having come to the end of his term of imprisonment he retired to a hermitage in Vallombrosa, where he lived a life of austere penance. "That which he had been compelled to do against his will in prison," says his biographer, the Vallombrosan Girolamo, "he continued to do of his own free will — his bed was a little straw on the bare ground, and he slept in his clothes, with only a coarse woollen rug over him." From his life as a hermit he was given the surname delle Celle and he became a factor in the religious movement of the time.[9] Barduccio Canigiani was one of his disciples; to another disciple, a woman, Dom Giovanni wrote to dissuade her from following *la Caterina santa,* who (according to a current misunderstanding) declared that she intended to go on a crusade and asked other women to do the same. In order to defend Catherine against this accusation William Flete intervened by writing on her behalf. The misunderstanding was cleared up and it ended in Giovanni delle Celle himself being added to the circle of the Sienese saint's friends and admirers.[10]

Then, one day at the end of May, Catherine left Florence. Alessia, Cecca and Lisa were with her, as well as Stefano Maconi, Fra Bartolommeo de' Dominici and the three Pisan brothers, Gherardo, Tommaso, Francesco Buonconti. Their journey took them northwards, by the road to Pistoja and Bologna, across the Apennines and beyond the Alps to bring the Cross and the branch of olive to the Pope in distant Avignon.

III

"The sack of avaricious Babylon is full of the wrath of God, and so stuffed with vice that it is near to bursting. The gods they have chosen are not Jupiter and Pallas, but Venus and Bacchus." "A fountain of affliction, a house of wrath, a school of error, a temple of heresy is the false Babylon, once called Rome, which is burdened with guilt. It was founded in chaste and humble poverty, and now, oh shameless harlot, thou liftest up thy horns against those who founded thee." [1]

With such violent phrases as these had Petrarch branded the Avignon of the Popes. In far-off Siena the pious daughter of the dyer had felt the stench of the sins that were committed at the court of the Vicegerent of Christ — stronger and more penetrating than the smell of tanning which to this day fills the streets about Fontebranda. And one midsummer evening (it was on the 18th June) she was approaching this Babel of the West. A small ship bore her and her devout friends, men and women, up the Rhône. They were sailing against the stream and therefore made slow progress, so that there was ample time to see and admire the pearly sheen on the water, the meadows deep and richly green along the banks of the oblong islands, lying like vessels moored in the direction of the current; the low huts of fishermen stood between tall, bright-leaved poplars, children played by an upturned boat on the banks of the river. Then towers came in sight ahead of them, and perhaps someone who knew the town pointed out to the Italian travellers the most important of its numerous churches: Saint Ruf, standing where the first Christians had assembled (Saint Ruf had been the Sant' Ansano of Avignon), Saint Agricol of the eleventh century, Saint Pierre of the twelfth, the new church of Saint Didier, only about twenty or thirty years old, the splendid convent church of the Knights Templars, which was still a-building, the monastery of the Augustinians, the Cistercian nuns' church of Saint Catherine, the Cluniacs' church of Saint Martin, and then, of course, there is the Dominican convent, but you can't see that from here, it stands west of the town, on an island between the Rhône and the river Sorgue. It is very large, over three thousand *toises* square!

Someone acquainted with the locality may have pointed all this out to Catherine, until her glance at last found its way up to Rocher des Doms, to the Pope's castle on the edge of the steep rock, dominating the town and river, *moles miranda,* as Michael de l'Hôpital was to call it; with its mighty towers and crenellated walls it was more like the fortified castle of a feudal lord than the quiet dwelling of a prince of peace. Her glance would follow on to the broken line of St. Bénézet's bridge across the Rhône, the bridge which the poor, little shepherd boy, Bénézet began to build in 1177 at the command of angelic voices; everyone laughed at him in Avignon and the Bishop drove him out, but then he worked the miracle of lifting, unaided, a stone which a team of four large oxen could not stir from its place; and in the course of twelve years the bridge was built, with a sharp turn, because the Rhône swings so abruptly round the rock just here . . . There are nineteen arches, all firmly embedded in the floor of the river, except right in the middle, where the island is, the Barthelasse island, where you dance on the meadows in the evening: *sous le pont d'Avignon, l'on y danse tout en rond* . . .

Where the bridge ends France begins, it is not the Pope's country any longer. Philip the Fair therefore built a watch tower right at the bridge-head, and up yonder, on the hill, stands the castle with the large, round towers, also built by King Philip, but the church of Our Lady over there is newer, and the large Carthusian monastery was consecrated by Innocent VI. Several of the French cardinals also live over there; gradually quite a new town has grown up; they call it Villeneuve-lez-Avignon. . .[2]

Thus may Catherine have had her first sight of the city of the Popes on the Rhône, and when the ship was moored to the quay three dear friends were waiting at the landing-stage and welcoming her with such homelike faces: Raymond, Master Giovanni Tantucci of Lecceto, Neri di Landoccio, with his usual sad look, brightening only for a moment in the joy of seeing his friends again. The two young men, Maconi and Neri, old school friends of the same age, and now both pupils in Catherine's school, had much to talk of, and now they all walked together through the narrow streets and threaded their way through the motley cosmopolitan crowds to the house which had been prepared for Catherine and her escort. It was a cardinal's palace — a *livrée*, as it was called in Avignon — which Annibale Ceccano had built for himself at the beginning of the century; his escutcheon was still over the large main door. Afterwards it had belonged to Cardinal Gaillard de la Motte, son of one of the nieces of Clement V, then to Cardinal Niccolò di Branca, Archbishop of Cosenza. After his death it was now standing empty. It was a tall, massive castle-like building with crenellated walls.[8] As soon as the little company had been installed Catherine withdrew to the chapel on the first floor to pray.

For now she had come to the eve of the decisive day, now she was on the battle-field. On the morrow she was to go forth to fight, not with physical weapons, but with the sword of her spirit and her will, not to fight against flesh and blood, but against the spiritual host of evil under heaven, against the power of darkness, against the prince of hell and his demons who had assumed the likeness of cardinals and wore the Roman purple, as in the abyss they are robed in flames. . . She was on the field of battle and on the morrow she was to carry the cause of God to victory. Up yonder on the rock was the fortress held by the enemy, from which she was to set free the Vicar of Christ, as the angel had set free Peter from amidst the soldiers on guard and walked the length of a street with him, until he stood before the house where the faithful were assembled and praying for his deliverance. She was to achieve this great work, she, Caterina di Monna Lapa, Caterina, daughter of Giacomo of Siena, Caterina, who from her earliest youth had drawn from the well of Fontebranda and drunk of its water — the water that makes one lose one's senses, as men see it, and makes one mad with that holy madness, the madness of art, of poetry, of love of country, the madness of the Cross! She was to accomplish this work which the Swedish princess who had died lately in Rome, had not been able to complete. In all the wide world there was no one but her to undertake it; it was in vain that she looked around her on every side for one who would go in her stead and take the Cross from off her shoulders. Catherine felt the terror that overwhelms the soul when it discovers that it is alone, because it has come up to the heights where no other feet have trod — because it has grown up above all others and can no longer find its equal. . .

Two days later Catherine stood before the Pope. She was received in that vast Gothic hall which competent hands of the present day have restored to its original beauty. The woman of Siena stood before the throne of Gregory and in the pauses, while Raymond translated her Tuscan which the Pope did not understand into Latin, her glance would perhaps rest on the frescoes which her compatriots had painted on wall and arch. She may have read the words which can still be deciphered at the present day, though they are indistinct, on the papyrus rolls of the prophets: Ezekiel's prophecy on the dead bones of Israel, the threat of the Lord by the lips of Micheas: "And I will execute vengeance in wrath and in indignation among all the nations that have not given ear." And the words of Nahum about Jehovah: "The mountains tremble at him, and the hills are made desolate: and the earth hath quaked at his presence, and the world and all that dwell therein."

Below the warning and threatening prophecies of the Last Day are presented the quadrangular graves opening in the middle of the tiled floor of an Italian churchyard — in the clouds of heaven the Son of Man and all His holy angels with Him — and midway between heaven and earth, midway between time and eternity, a solitary angel, hovering solemnly and inexorably in the golden light: to look at him is like hearing the resounding note of the last trumpet . . . *tuba mirum*.

Catherine spoke, Raymond interpreted, Gregory listened. Catherine spoke, we are permitted to think, of the olive branch and the Cross, of coming in peace, not with the sword, meekly riding on a colt, the foal of an ass. We are permitted to imagine the Pope bending forward, listening intently, like the Pope on the fresco of San Francesco in Siena, taking the hands of Louis of Toulouse into his own for the vow of obedience. When Catherine ceased speaking Gregory's short answer was that he left the whole matter in her hands, what she did would be well done, "but she must not forget the dignity of the Church." [4]

"By the grace of our sweet Saviour we came here to Avignon on the 18th June, 1376," Catherine wrote home to friends in Siena, "and I have spoken with the Holy Father and with several cardinals and lay dignitaries. And the grace of God has worked greatly for the cause for whose sake we have come hither . . ." [5]

Nevertheless, when peace was not concluded between Florence and the Roman State, the fault lay with the republic itself. The envoys whom the Florentines had promised to send immediately after Catherine did not arrive, and in a later audience Gregory said to the mediatrix: "The Florentines are mocking both you and me. Either they will not send any envoys at all, or when they do come, they will not have the necessary powers to act." On June 28th Catherine wrote to the Eight of War and reproached them with having levied a tax on the clergy. "I have spoken with the Holy Father," she writes, "and he is disposed to make peace and will be like a good father who does not look too sternly at the misdeeds of his children . . . And my tongue can not find words to utter how glad he is to think that peace may come. After I had spoken with him for some time he ended by saying that he was ready to receive you as his children and to do what seemed best to me. I say no more here. The Holy Father will give no other answer until your envoys have come. I wonder that they have not come yet. When they come I will seek them and after that I will seek the Holy Father, and I will keep you acquainted how matters stand. But you destroy everything for me with your rash increase of taxes. Cease to do this, for the love of Christ and for your own good." [6]

At last the Florentine envoys arrived: Pazzino Strozzi, Alessandro dell' Antella, Michele Castelloni; but unfortunately the Pope was proved to have been right in his fears. Since July 6th a new government had been sitting in Florence, which only sent off ambassadors to quieten the Pope's suspicions, but in reality it was not disposed to peace. Indeed the three envoys curtly rejected Catherine's offer of mediation, saying that they had no authority to treat with her.⁷   Gregory then entrusted the negotiations to the two cardinals, Pierre d'Estaing and Gilles Aycelin de Montaigu.⁸

Catherine now devoted herself entirely to the two great causes which were the chief objects of the journey to Avignon: the return of the Pope to Rome and the call to the Crusade. She spoke to Gregory without reserve of the sins of Avignon, so frankly that Raymond was alarmed, and when the Pope still hesitated she made use of her gift of insight into souls, she reminded him of a vow which he had made while still a cardinal, that if he became Pope he would bring the Chair of Peter back to Rome.⁹

The Italian saint was, of course, regarded with curiosity by the papal court, and soon also with opposition. The curiosity came from the ladies of the court, the beautiful sisters and nieces, the friends and mistresses of the cardinals. It grew to be a favourite sport to be present at Catherine's Communion, and afterwards to verify her ecstasy by pricking and pinching her insensible body. Elys de Turenne, married to the Pope's nephew, even pierced her foot with a long needle so that Catherine could not stand on it for several days.¹⁰ The presence of these ladies of the world also caused Catherine suffering in her soul; she turned her back on one of them and would not speak to her, "and if, as I did, you had felt the stench of her sins, you would have done the same," she afterwards explained to Raymond.¹¹ It was in Avignon that Catherine collected material for the terrible chapters in the *Dialogue* about the sinful lives of the clergy, and her outline of a description like the following, of "the bad servants of God" is based on memories of the papal court:

"Their self-love has made sensuality the ruler of their hearts and the poor soul has become its slave. I, the eternal God, have delivered these My anointed from the slavery of the world, and set them to serve Me alone, and to administer the sacraments of Holy Church. And I have made them so free, that I have not willed and do not will that any worldly power should dare to judge them. And do you know, most beloved daughter, what they give Me in return for so great a benefit that they have received from Me? The return which I receive is this, that they ever offend Me by so many and such abominable sins, that thy tongue could not utter it, and thou couldst not bear to hear it. Yet will I tell thee somewhat, to give thee more reason for tears and compassion.

"It is their duty to eat their food at the table of the Cross with holy desires, and their food shall be souls which they save for My glory. This is in truth the duty of every reasonable creature, but it is above all the duty of those whom I have set to administer the body and blood of My only-begotten Son, Jesus Christ Crucified, and to give you the good example of a holy life. . . . But instead they have chosen to eat at the table of a tavern: they sit there cursing and swearing like men without the light of reason, and behave like beasts, and they are lascivious both in words and deeds.

"They are ignorant of the divine office, and if they do sometimes say the prayers it is only with their lips, and their hearts are far from Me. They behave like ruffians and like the hosts of gaming-houses [*barattieri*]; first they gamble away their soul to the devil, and then they gamble away the property of the Church which has been given to them in return for the blood of Christ. And so the poor do not get what is due to them, the Church is not adorned, and lacks that which is needed for the worship of God. For they have made of themselves a temple of the devil, and therefore they no longer give a thought to My temple. But that which they ought to use in adorning My house, that they use for the adorning of their own houses. And worse still, with the property of the Church these incarnate devils adorn the she-devil with whom they live sinfully and unchastely. Without shame they permit such an one to come and go in the church, while they, those miserable devils, stand before the altar and say Mass. And they permit their unhappy she-devil to come up with other people to bring her offering to the altar, holding her children by the hand.

"Oh, devils, worse than devils — is this the purity I require of My servant when he goes to serve at the altar? This is the purity he offers Me: that in the morning he rises with his soul defiled and his body polluted with having lain in filthy mortal sin, and in that state he goes to stand before My altar. Oh, thou tabernacle of the devil, where are thy vigils with solemn and pious hymns? Where are thy prayers and thy devotion?" [12]

One cannot but think that Catherine, while actually staying in the city of the Popes, would sometimes let fall such utterances as those which she here committed to writing. It was therefore no wonder that she incurred the opposition of ecclesiastics in Avignon, such as she had encountered earlier in Siena. Three theologians presented themselves to the Pope and asked for permission to examine the orthodoxy of the prophetess. They obtained it and called upon Catherine "after the ninth hour, and it was summer," Stefano Maconi remembers, and she received them in the presence of Master Giovanni Tantucci and other members of her spiritual family. The three learned gentlemen now began to question her, called her "a wretched little female" (*vile donnucciola*), closely examined her about her ecstasies, her continuous fasting and ended by suggesting that the children of darkness had often been found to have disguised themselves as children of light. The visit dragged on till rather late now and then Master Giovanni tried to answer for Catherine, though she managed very well in answering for herself. When at last the three stood up to go the victory was won — "but" (the Pope's physician, Francesco Casini of Siena, said next day to Stefano), "if those three had not found Catherine unshakably well grounded she would have been lucky to escape from them!" It was the Inquisition that she had had to face. With his usual vacillation Gregory afterwards told Catherine that if those three should come again she had only to close the door in their faces.[13]

The three inquisitors, of whom one was a Franciscan archbishop, were, however, Catherine's friends from that day. Among other acquaintances of importance that she made in Avignon were the Archbishop of Acerenza, Bartolommeo Prignano, the later Pope Urban VI, and the Spanish cardinal and later anti-pope Pedro de Luna.

Meanwhile Gregory, moved by Catherine's insistence, prepared for his departure to Italy. In order to make him give up this project the French King sent his brother, the Duke of Anjou, to Avignon, and the latter, who soon discovered that Catherine was the real cause of the Pope's resolution, tried to gain her over. Catherine spent three days at his castle on the other side of the Rhône, at Villeneuve; the Duke did not convert her, but she converted him, so that he became an enthusiastic supporter of the idea of a crusade and promised to equip an army at his own expense. Moreover, at his request Catherine wrote a letter to Charles V of France in order to gain him too for *il santo e dolce passaggio*. With a delicate allusion to the King's surname, "the Wise," she asks him to use true wisdom, to despise the world, to exercise justice in his kingdom, to make peace with England and with Navarre, and instead to raise the banner of the Cross against the infidels. "In such wise will you follow in the footsteps of Christ Crucified and do God's will and mine." [14]

Not content with the influence that she could exercise on the Pope by direct speech, Catherine wrote a whole series of letters to him in which she refutes the objections which are continually made by the French against his journey to Rome, and about which Gregory kept her informed, sometimes through Raymond, sometimes through his notary, Tommaso di Petra. He still asked her for her advice and her intercession, and she struggled unremittingly against the egoism in the Pope's nature, which made him irresolute and hesitating and uncertain. "Holiest and most blessed Father in Christ, sweet Jesus," she writes to him, "your unworthy and miserable daughter Catherine strengthens you in His precious blood and desires to see you delivered from all slavish fear. For the timorous soul has no strength to perform his good resolutions and holy desires, and therefore I have prayed to the sweet and good Jesus to take away from you all slavish fear, so that only holy fear may remain. The fire of love burns in you, so that you may not be able to hear the voices of the incarnate devils who, from what I learn, would frighten you and hinder your journey by saying that it will be your death. And I say to you in the name of Christ Crucified that you have no cause whatsoever for fear. Be of good courage and depart, trust in Christ Jesus; when you do that which is your duty God will be with you and none can be against you. Be a man, Father, arise! I say to you that you have nothing to fear. If you do not do your duty, then, indeed, you might have cause for fear. You ought to come to Rome, therefore come. Come peacefully, come without any fear. And if there be some who would hinder you, then say to them what Christ said to Saint Peter, who in mistaken goodness would keep Him back. Christ turned and said: "Get thee behind me, Satan! thou art a scandal unto me: because thou savourest not the things that are of God, but the things that are of men. Or wilt thou not that I shall do the will of my Father?" So do you likewise, dearest Father; follow him as his vicar . . . and say to all the others: 'Though I should lose my life a hundred times, yet will I do the will of my Father!' . . . Let them talk who wish to talk, but keep firmly to your holy resolve. My father, Brother Raymond, said to me from you, that I was to pray to God for enlightenment, whether there was aught to hinder you in coming to Rome. I have prayed now, both before and after Holy Communion, and I cannot see either death or any other danger, such as certain people would make you imagine." [15]

In a letter of about the same time Catherine announces Gregory's departure to Buonaccorso di Lapo as imminent. "Behold, now he comes to visit his Bride," she exclaims, "it is the city of Saint Peter and Saint Paul. Seek him there, go to him with true humility of heart and in sorrow over your transgressions, and you will find peace for soul and body. Thus did our fathers do, and they were less unhappy than we, for we call down the wrath of God upon ourselves and have no part in the blood of the Lamb." [16]

The prayer to which Catherine alludes in her letter to the Pope was written down and preserved by Tommaso di Petra, who on this occasion was the messenger of the Pope and heard her pray. As always, Catherine began by expressing her feeling of profound unworthiness, and her soul was kept down under its crushing weight. "Woe is me," she exclaimed "woe is me, Lord, I am a sinner, have mercy upon me! *Peccavi, Domine, miserere mei.* Oh, eternal Goodness, regard not our misdeeds, but look in thy mercy upon thy Church, thy only-begotten bride, and open the eyes of thy Vicar, so that he love thee not for his own sake or himself for his own sake, but thee for thy sake and himself for thy sake, for if he love thee only from self-love we must all perish, for on him depends our life and our death, but if he love himself for thy sake and thee for thy own sake we shall live, for the good shepherd leads us on the right path. Oh, supreme and most unutterable Divinity, I have sinned and am not worthy to pray to thee, but thou art able to make me worthy. Punish my sins, Lord, and judge me according to my transgressions. I have my body, I give it to thee, I sacrifice it to thee. Here is my flesh, here is my blood — let the blood flow away, let the body be cut to pieces, let my bones be cloven for them for whom I pray. If it be thy will then let thy Vicar tread my bones asunder and the marrow in my bones, if only thou, oh my Spouse, wilt hear me, so that thy Vicar may look upon thy will, may love it and cause it to be done, so that we perish not. Grant him a new heart, a heart ever growing in grace, a heart strong enough to raise the holy banner of the Cross, so that the infidels may obtain with us a part in the fruit of the Passion of thy only-begotten Son in the blood of the Lamb without blemish! Eternal, unutterable, supreme Divinity! *Peccavi, Domine, miserere mei!*"

In a second prayer Catherine expresses similar feelings. "Oh, Divinity, Divinity, eternal Divinity," she prayed, "I acknowledge that thou art an ocean of peace, feeding the soul that reposes in thee with affection and love, and assuming it into the kingdom of love, so that it conforms its own will to thy supreme and eternal will, whose only end is our sanctification. The soul that sees this puts off its own will and assumes thine. Oh, sweetest love, this seems to me the true mark of those who are in thee that they obey *thy* will in *thy* way and not in their own . . . But, poor miserable creature that I am, I have been self-willed, I have sinned, I have loved sin. . . Punish my sins, Lord, cleanse me, eternal Goodness, unutterable Divinity! Hear the prayers of thy handmaid and regard not my many transgressions. I beseech thee, that thou wilt fasten the wills and hearts of all the servants of the Church to thyself, so that they may follow thee, thou poor, humble and gentle Lamb of God, on the holiest way of the Cross, in thy way and not in their own. And let them be like angels upon earth, for they are servants at the sacrifice of the Lamb without blemish, and let them not be like brute beasts, that have not reason. . . Unite them and plunge them in the calm sea of thy goodness, let them delay no longer and neglect the good time for the time that may never come. *Peccavi, Domine, miserere mei.* Hear the prayer of thy handmaid. Miserable creature that I am, I beseech thee to hear my voice. I cry to thee, most merciful Father! I pray also for all the spiritual children which thou hast given me, and whom I love with a particular love, in love of thee, thou supreme, eternal, unutterable Goodness. Amen." [17]

"But after she had uttered these words," writes Tommaso Buonconti of Pisa, who was present, "she remained as at earlier times silent, without movement, rigid and away from her senses. Her hands were stretched out, her arms crossed and thus she remained for about an hour. At last we threw holy water upon her face, called upon the name of Jesus and seized her ungently, until the spirit at last began to stir in her, and she said softly: Praised be God, now, and always more and more." [18]

The Pope submitted to Catherine's will, but not so the Florentines. Her letter to Buonaccorso di Lapo obtained no result. Instead of agreeing to the Pope's proposals for peace Florence sent a messenger and letter to the Emperor, the King of Hungary, the Doges of Venice and Genoa, and urged them to stand together against the papal power, the seat of which was now to be transferred to Rome.

The French cardinals made a last effort to keep Gregory back: they made a person regarded as saintly, probably the Franciscan, Peter of Aragon, write a letter of warning to the Pope and inform him that he would meet his death in Rome. Gregory sent the letter on to Catherine, who sent it back with a fiery note that it was the work of a *dimonio incarnato*. The devout man had spoken of the danger of being poisoned, but Catherine remarked pointedly that "there is probably just as much poison in Avignon as in Rome, and such things can be bought everywhere." She had not in vain lived four months in the Babylon on the Rhône; she also knew that Urban V was poisoned *after* his return from Italy. Had he done his duty and stayed in Rome, he might have lived for many a long day yet! In stronger words than ever she warns Gregory: "Do not be a timid boy, be a man! Open your mouth and take the bitter for the sweet!" And she wishes to see him once more before her departure.[19]

A letter like that quoted above helps one to understand what

THE CROWN OF THORNS

Caffarini says about Catherine, that she inspired all who came into contact with her with "a sort of terror." One admired her and dreaded her, as one would a flame of fire. One felt the consuming will burning in that slight woman; that in her glowing love of Jesus she willed, willed, *willed* to conform all to her dearly loved Spouse, press the crown of thorns down on every brow, pierce every hand and every foot with the sacred nails, so that they could no longer walk any other way than the narrow, painful way of the Cross.

One dreaded her because one felt her power. The beatitude of the Crucifixion radiated from her and drew one to surrender to the great adversary, to deaden self, slay one's will, leave the world and become a martyr to conscience, a burnt-offering like her. We do not know what Catherine said to Gregory at that last audience; we only know that he granted it. And we know that on the morning of September 13th, the Pope came out of the gate of his palace, not to take a pleasant morning ride over the bridge of St. Bénézet, under whose arches the people dance so gaily on the green meadows, but to set out on that journey from which he was never to return, to travel on the long, dangerous road to distant, hostile Rome — *vado Romam crucifigi!* In vain did the French cardinals burst into tears, in vain did Gregory's father, old Count Guillaume de Beaufort, throw himself down on the threshold and implore his son to stay. His soul swelling with Catherine's supernatural energy, Gregory stepped over his father's grey head, while his lips murmured: Thou shalt tread upon the adder and tread down the basilisk. *Super aspidem et basiliscum ambulabis et conculcabis leonem et draconem.*" [20]

IV

"Dearest Mother in Christ sweet Jesus. Your unworthy, miserable daughter Catherine strengthens and comforts you in the precious blood of the Son of God. Ardently have I desired to see you as my mother, not only of my body, but also of my soul, for I thought, that when you had attained to loving the soul more than the body, all inordinate affection would die in you, for then you would not suffer so much in not having me about you, but rather would it console you, in being to the glory of God. . .

"It is true, dearest Mother, that if you loved the soul more than the body, you would be comforted and not comfortless. I will, that you learn of our dear Mother Mary, who to the glory of God and our salvation gave us her Son and surrendered Him to the death on the Cross. And when He had ascended into heaven she remained behind with the disciples. But she gave up that comfort also of being with the disciples and let them go forth into the world to the praise and glory of her Son. I will, dearest Mother, that you shall learn of her. You know that I must fulfil the will of God, and I know that you will that I should so live. It was the will of God that I departed, and my departure was not without His secret counsel (*mistero*), and it has not been without fruit.

"It was His will that I remained here; it was not the will of men; whosoever says so does not speak truth. . . And as a good and dear mother you must be content and not comfortless. . . Remember that when your sons went forth into the world for the sake of worldly gain you did not gainsay them, and now it is so hard for you, now when it is for the sake of eternal life, so that you even speak of dying if I do not write to you soon. All that comes of your loving that part of myself which I have from you, more than that which I have from God — you love the flesh with which you have clothed me. Lift up your heart a little and your mind to that most holy Cross which assuages all pain . . . and do not believe yourself forsaken, either by God or by me . . . We shall come soon, with the help of God, as soon as Neri, who has been ill, is well enough to travel. Master Giovanni and Brother Bartolommeo have also been ill. . . I say no more. . . Remain in the holy, sweet love of God. Sweet Jesus, Jesus love." [1]

It was on the way home from Avignon that Catherine wrote this letter to her mother, who was longing for her. A deeply independent soul, the Dominican nun felt an impatience, almost a resentment, against all who wanted to make claims upon her, cling to her, hamper her in her walk and hinder her work. Sometimes it almost scandalised her to be as loved as she was, and in order to make room for God and her work for Him she would repulse, almost ungently, the affection that was bestowed upon her. She made the great demand of those who held her in affection that they should relinquish her and be satisfied with knowing that she was contented to be where she was. "Love my soul," she cried to them, "be glad that I am glad, and that I am at my work."

There was, however, in Siena a mother besides Monna Lapa, who was also longing for her child; this woman was Monna Giovanna di Corrado, the mother of Stefano Maconi. She, too, wrote and asked about her son, whom Catherine had carried off to Avignon. And Catherine — who, alas! knows so well that a human creature is nothing but love, and that each of our actions, each of our movements, that every step from morning till night is the work of love — seeks to guide the heart of Monna Giovanna. But the counsel is the same as that she always gives: enter into the cell of self-knowledge and the knowledge of God, stand before the Cross where the Lamb is bleeding, learn patience there, learn to love the soul of your child, learn all virtues. "Stand up, dearest Mother, I will not that you slumber any more in the slothfulness of sensitive tenderness, but arise in burning and infinite love, bathe in the blood of Christ, hide in the wounds of the Crucifix . . . and say to Corrado that he must do the same." [2]

Catherine sent these two letters home from Genoa. After she had seen Gregory depart on September 13th to go to Marseilles, to take ship from there to Italy, she had herself started on the homeward journey. The little company made their first halting-place at Toulon. "But hardly had we arrived at the hostelry," Raymond of Capua relates, "when the news was out all over the town that that holy woman, who was returning from the papal court, was inside the walls of the city. And so great was the number of those who came flocking to see her, that we had to admit the women at least to Catherine." [3] Even the Bishop of the town came to visit Catherine, and in order to avoid similar inconvenient honours they decided to continue their journey by sea.

Owing to bad weather, the small ship on which Catherine and her escort had embarked, had soon to seek harbour; during a landward gale they landed at Saint-Tropez, after having barely escaped running aground on the "Golden Isles" of Mistral (les Hyères). It is to this forced landing that an incident mentioned in the biography of the saint by Raymond of Capua must rightly be referred. The vessel was on the point of sinking and the disciples were afraid. But their *Mamma* had no fear. "Have you to take care of yourselves, then?" she asked, using one of her favourite expressions. And after she had prayed a short while, the storm abated and a good breeze came, and Raymond and the other clerics began with renewed calm to recite their prayers, "and we ran into port just as we were singing the 'Te Deum,'" [4] [which concludes Matins]. The little company now took the road along the Riviera, the *via Aemilia* of the Romans, now *la Corniche*. Centuries were yet to pass ere the "Côte d'Azur" was to be discovered and motor-cars whirl up the dust on the way from luxurious hotels in Cannes and Menton to the gaming-hell in Monte Carlo. But the sea was the same then as now, greenish blue where it breaks over the red rocks, further out blue and shining and vast and with red sails scattered here and there over its surface. The road winds along the red mountain sides or goes through woods of stone-pines or through gorges where gorse is in golden bloom, and in front, along the curved coast line, there are white, shining towns that remind one more and more of Italy. A blue promontory juts out into the sea: Cap Estérel; and in the horizon there is an island: *Ile de Lérins,* the *Lerinum* of Saint Honorat with the famous monastery where the white monks still pray this very day, while the wind from the sea roars in the pine woods and the waves of the Mediterranean break against the reefs.

After the icy mistral in Avignon and the bad spiritual atmosphere at the papal court it was probably a relief to Catherine to walk with her friends in the mild September sunshine along the sheltered coast, and perhaps one or two of Stefano Maconi's memories can be traced to these wanderings. "Once," he relates, "our Mamma was seized with enthusiasm at the sight of a meadow which was full of bright red flowers and exclaimed: 'Do you not see that all things praise God and speak of God. These blood red flowers clearly remind us of the blood red wounds of Christ!'" On another occasion she fell into contemplation of an ant-hill and said to the disciples: 'These little creatures have come forth from the holy mind of God, as much as I, and it cost Him no more trouble to create the angels than to create these animals or the flowering trees.'" These are the only two occasions in the whole of Catherine's life, in which she exhibited anything like a feeling for Nature. But she has not the mind of Francis of Assisi; as a true Dominican she immediately goes behind that which is visible — this world can never be for her more than a symbol of something higher. "She never spoke," says Maconi, in the same place, "of anything but God, and that which leads to God." [5]

The Aurelian Way led the travellers through the sunscorched wood of stone-pines of Estérel and through the little towns of Auribeau, Vallauris, Antibes, Cimiez, Eze, which at Ventimiglia would bring them into Italy.* [6] All this part of Provence is strewn with small Romanesque chapels, and more than one has its memories of Catherine. It is not difficult to imagine the saint praying in these little white churches among the cypresses: Sainte Anne at Saint Tropez, Saint Cassien near Cannes or Notre Dame de Vie at Mougins.[7] And just before you get to Ventimiglia you can still at the present day see part of the ancient Via Aurelia — only a few hundred yards, but Catherine's foot stepped on these stones. A little further on, between Porto Maurizio and Oneglia, there is an old tower, standing near the beach; Catherine is said to have slept there one night, and to have been sung to sleep by the gentle lapping of the waves when they sucked back shells and shingle with them, like the trickling of little beads. . .

* Dante (Purgatorio, III, 49) speaks of this "desolate way between Lerici" (in Italy) "and Turbie" (in France).

On the eve of the feast of Francis of Assisi, October 3d, Catherine and her friends reached the little town of Varazze, some distance north of Genoa. At the present day Varazze is a favourite seaside resort and a pleasant Ligurian hamlet, with narrow, shady streets, small pink churches, deep lemon orchards and gardens with fig trees, and round it olive-clad mountains where the cicada sing incessantly and shrilly in the noonday heat. Catherine found the town laid waste by the plague, the grass growing in the streets, and it was difficult for the travellers to find a house where they could spend the night. Varazze was the birthplace of a man for whom Catherine had a particular admiration: Jacopo da Varazze (in Latin de Voragine), author of one of the books most read in the Middle Ages: the *Golden Legend*. Before she left the next morning to go on to Genoa, she advised the surviving inhabitants of the town to erect a chapel in honour of their holy, departed fellow-townsman, which they did, and the plague ceased.[8]

Next day the travellers reached Genoa and received hospitality in the Palazzo Scotti, with the devout Monna Orietta. The Scotti were said to have come from Scotland; two brothers, Gabriel and Amico, are mentioned as early as 1120. The Palazzo Scotti (afterwards Centurioni) was situated in the Via del Canneto, near the harbour, halfway between the famous palace of the Compagnia di San Giorgio — one of the first banking houses in the world and the seat of the government of Genoa — and the cathedral of San Lorenzo.

As indicated by Catherine in her letter to Monna Lapa, the Sienese travellers were afflicted with illness during their stay in Genoa. Possibly it was a result of having spent a night in plague-infested Varazze. Neri was the first, and he fell seriously ill; the doctors declared that he was saved only by the prayers of his *Mamma*. Then Stefano had to go to bed. Catherine had again to use her powers of insistent prayer: Stefano himself tells us that he often heard her say when praying: "I will have it so!" And when she used *that* tone to her heavenly Spouse she always had her way! She spoke in that way to get Stefano well, and she succeeded. She came to his bedside and asked him how he felt, and he answered that he did not quite know. "Hark at that sonny," she joked, "he says he does not know what ails him, and he is in a fever!" After which she touched his brow and declared: "I cannot allow you to do like other sick folk. In the name of holy obedience: be ill no longer. I am quite determined that you shall be well and go and help the others and help them as hitherto." And behold, the fever left him and he got up and did as she had told him.[9]

The rumour of Stefano's illness may have reached Siena; at any rate Catherine had to write a fresh letter to Monna Giovanna. To the anxious mother she again preaches the stern doctrine of self-denial: "Put on the wedding garments, put on Christ. But no one can do that without having put off all sensitive love, whether it be of yourself or your children or any other creature. . . No one can serve two masters." As though suspecting the protest of the mother's heart she continues: "And if you ask me: How then, must I love? I answer you that you may love children and all other creatures for love of Him who has created them and not out of self-love or of love for the children, and one may never offend God for their sake . . . And if you see that God is calling them, then do not resist His sweet will, but if He takes them with one hand, then give them to Him with both hands . . . and be content to see them in that state to which God called them. Often the mother who loves her children in worldly indulgence says: 'I have nothing against my children serving God but that need not hinder them from also serving the world. . .' Such as these would make laws and rules for the Holy Spirit . . . and they do not love their children in God but in sensual self-love outside God and love their bodies more than their souls . . . Dearly loved sister and daughter in Christ, sweet Jesus, this I hope will never come to pass with you, but like a true and good mother you must give them up to the glory of the name of God and thus you will be able to put on the wedding garment."

The choice is given in all its severity: if Monna Giovanna demands her son back from Catherine and from the way in which he will walk there, there is no salvation for her soul. She must give up her son; she cannot otherwise "put on Christ Crucified."

Still calling the older woman "daughter," she adds, defending herself for having kept Stefano a captive in her magic circle, "Be comforted, be patient, do not be troubled because I have kept Stefano so long, for I have cared well for him, and by love and affection I have become one with him . . . and I do not think he has come to any harm with me. Until my death I will do everything I can for you and for him. You, his mother, once gave him birth and I will bear him and you and all your family by constant prayers and by tears and zeal for your salvation." [10]

Catherine's whole consciousness of salvation is contained in this letter. That a mother who loves her son wishes to have him by her side, that is evil. That this son loves Catherine and wishes to be with her is the call of God. For in this love he is to find his salvation; she whom he loves to call his *Mamma* promises to give him birth anew to eternal life.

This mighty self-consciousness was the source of Catherine's apostolic power. She could not be shaken in her conviction that her will and the will of God were one, and she therefore had to bring the will of others into subjection to her own. In this spirit she also exercised an apostolate in Genoa, visited the Benedictines in San Fruttuoso at Portofino, wrote to the Prior of the Carthusian monastery of Cervaia, rebuked a Franciscan tertiary who "had a spiritual friendship with a woman and suffered much because of it." Catherine earnestly warns this man, "who has permitted the devil to catch him with the hook of love under the guise of piety, and has now lost God and the love of prayer, has weakened his will and strengthened his enemies, and at last perdition will be his lot." By means of a parable, she warns the unhappy man in terrible terms that perdition is an inevitable consequence of a natural law: "You have conceived death, soon will come the time to bring forth." We come to the place whither our heart leads us. "And you do not flee from that woman like poison, but follow her and seek her! . . . Woe, woe, let us be men, let us root out that womanish pleasure (*il piacere femminile*) which makes the heart weak and fearful." [11]

Catherine *was* a man, and was soon to have occasion to show it. Gregory XI, who no longer had his guardian spirit by his side, had only with reluctance and after long delay left France,

THE CROWN OF THORNS

on October 2nd. "Never was so much weeping and mourning heard as on that day," says the old chronicle. Leaving the old abbey of Saint Victor, where he had slept the last night in France, the Pope embarked in the galley which the Knights of Saint John had placed at his disposal, and which was under the command of the Grand Master of the Order, Jean Ferdinand d'Hérédia, himself. With tears in their eyes the Pope and his retinue watch the coast of France disappearing from their sight. The papal ship is compelled by gales to seek harbour several times along the coast: at Port Miou (October 3rd), at Saint Nazaire, at Ranzels, at Reneston, Saint Tropez, Antibes, Nice, Villefranche (October 9th). They were nearly wrecked off Monaco and only on the 17th did they reach Savona and on the 18th Genoa.[12]

There bad news awaited the voyagers. Rome was in revolt, the Florentines fought with success against the papal troops in both the north and east. The Doge of Genoa was friendly but wished to preserve his neutrality. A consistory was convened and the majority of the cardinals voted for a return to Avignon.

Vacillating Gregory hesitated again. Nothing decisive had happened yet, he could return. . . Already the gentle hills of Provence rose before his mind's eye, and instead of the harsh dialect of Genoa he heard the soft *langue d'Oc*, babbling and rippling gaily like the Rhône under Pont St. Bénézet and like the Sorgue when it turns the big wheels of the water-mills. Only one thought kept him back: "Catherine!" What would Catherine say if he did it? He knew she was in Genoa, never would she allow him to turn back. And he could not stride across *her* with a text from Scripture upon his lips; on the contrary, if *she* gave him leave to return he would do it with a good conscience. And surely she must understand. . . In any case, he would have to speak with her.

It would not do, though, to send for her. The cardinals would make scenes. He would have to go to her.

It happened, then, one evening that the Vicegerent of Christ, dressed as a simple priest and without an escort, came to the Palazzo Scotti and asked to see Catherine. He was taken to her room, where she fell on her knees, surprised and overwhelmed, at the feet of *il dolce Cristo in terra*. He raised her up and they had a talk which lasted far into the night, after which Gregory left, "strengthened and edified." We can form some idea of the content of their interview when reading the prayer which Catherine, according to the old heading, "said in Genoa to prevent Pope Gregory from turning back, as it had been decided at the consistory that he should, because of the difficulties involved in going to Rome." She compares the Pope's coming to Rome with Christ's coming into the world. "And if the Pope's delay offend thee, Eternal Love, then punish it on my body, which I offer and sacrifice to thee, that thou mayest torment it and destroy it as seems good to thee. . . Cause thy Vicar therefore, oh Eternal Mercy to become a devourer of souls, burning with holy zeal for thy glory and serving thee alone." [13]

Gregory returned to the cardinals filled with new resolution. On October 29th he set sail for Leghorn and at last, on December 5th, he set foot on the soil of the Papal States at Corneto, where Urban V had also once landed. It had grown late in the year and Gregory decided to keep Christmas where he was. It was here that he received a letter from Catherine, full of the mood and the thoughts of Christmas and terminating in the Christmas wish that at length he might "pass from so much war to a great peace." "Peace, peace, most holy Father," she exhorts, as so often before. "Ah, Babbo, no more war, by any means. Go to war against the infidels, that is but right. Imitate the Lamb without blemish, our sweet Jesus, in patience and meekness; remember that you are His Vicar. I trust *in Domino nostro Jesu Cristo* that He will work this in you and fulfil His will and mine, for I have no other wish in this life than to see the glory of God, your peace, the reformation of Holy Church and the victory of grace in every creature that has the gift of reason." She excuses Siena which has joined the league against Rome during her absence; it was done under great pressure, she says, and she earnestly implores Gregory to "fish up the Sienese with the hook of love." "But I beseech you to go as soon as you can to your city, which is the city of the glorious apostles Peter and Paul." [14]

Catherine remained in Genoa some time longer, and the Pope was not her only visitor at the Palazzo Scotti. She was sought

THE CROWN OF THORNS

as a celebrated preacher or lecturer is sought at the present day. Caffarini enumerates all those who mounted the stairs to her room, doctors and masters of theology, professors of sacred and profane science, lawyers, senators and other persons of authority. She received them with all her Tuscan charm, her pale face irradiated by her luminous smile, and yet they all left her strangely impressed, almost awestruck, as if they had stood face to face with something that filled them with dread. It was no wonder, for he who sees Jehovah dies, he who gets but a glimpse of Him trembles, and Catherine was like the bush at Horeb which burned in the flame of the Lord, in the fire which is God Himself! [15]

Catherine and her escort had made the journey from Genoa to Leghorn by sea. From Leghorn they journeyed on to Pisa, whither Lapa had travelled to meet the daughter she had so sorely missed. With her came Fra Tommaso della Fonte and others of those who had stayed at home. Perhaps they brought a message from Monna Giovanna di Corrado; at any rate Catherine sent Stefano Maconi home at once, while she and the others stayed a month yet in Pisa.

The young Sienese unwillingly turned his steps homewards and bade his *Mamma* farewell, though but for a short while. A letter written immediately after his homecoming is entirely penetrated with longing for Catherine. It is addressed to Neri di Landoccio Pagliaresi and reads as follows:

"Dearest Brother, This is to make known to you that we reached Siena happily on the Friday after our departure, though not without great fear, for the road from Peccioli* is rather unsafe, and indeed, several unpleasant things had happened there, and if I had known it beforehand I would not have taken that road. I tell it to you that you may be careful. But it is quite clear to me that we were greatly helped by the prayers of our sweetest *Mamma,* not to say that it was altogether due to them that everything passed so well.

"I have given Sano [di Maco, the bursar, so to speak, of the circle] the letters and all the other things that you gave me to take with me, and I have distributed all the letters and performed all the errands entrusted to me, and all our *Mamma's* sons and

---
* Between Pontedera and Volterra.

daughters have greatly rejoiced and await her with longing, as I do also, and I think she is delaying too long.

"I entreat you for the sake of Christ Crucified that you will not do as you did in Avignon . . . but that you will do what you can to hasten your coming, for if you stay away too long I think I shall repent of having come back, and it may be that I will come and bring you a letter from myself.

"I say no more, save that you must embrace our sweet *Mamma* for me and beg her not to forget what I asked for, and commend me to my Fathers, Brother Raymond, Brother Master, Brother Tommaso, Brother Bartolommeo and Brother Felice, and embrace Monna Lapa, and commend me to my Mothers, Monna Cecca, Monna Alessia and Monna Lisa, and ask them to pray for my miserable self. God knows what I should do if I could not console myself by saying that the parting will be but short."[16]

This letter is dated November 29th, and on December 5th Stefano already writes again, even two letters. On the 8th we again see him at his desk, sending a fresh epistle and message to the dear, distant *Mamma*. As usual this letter is addressed to Neri: "Commend me to our sweetest *Mamma*, a thousand times and more," writes Maconi, "and tell her that I have fulfilled her wish about 'il ridotto.'" The letter is mainly nothing but an enumeration of the circle in which he has lived so long, and whose voices still sound in his ears, whose faces and figures he imagines he has seen at every turn in the street — and alas, it was not they, after all! Above all the letter is a greeting to *nostra dolcissima Mamma* and a wistful, impatient question: "Are you not coming soon?"[17]

In his letter Stefano mentions a *ridotto* which he is engaged in putting in order — "and tell Monna Alessia too, that her cell awaits her, and that it is very nice now." Like all who have to wait, Stefano tries to make the time pass in work. This *ridotto* is explained by Grottanelli as a kind of anteroom; it is rather simply a private chapel which Catherine had been allowed by Gregory to arrange in her home. She was bringing home two papal bulls from Avignon, one granting her the privilege of taking with her wherever she went three confessors for those whom she converted by her words. (The three were Raymond,

THE CROWN OF THORNS

Master Giovanni Tantucci and Fra Bartolommeo de' Dominici.) The other bull gave her permission to have a portable altar, so that she could have Mass said wherever she was. This altar, which is still preserved in San Domenico in Siena, is a square stone, just large enough for a paten and chalice to stand upon it. It is said to have been a fragment of the stone on which Saint Thomas of Canterbury suffered the death of a martyr, and a gift to Catherine from her English friend, William Flete.

Shortly before Christmas, she for whom so many had been longing at last came home. Gregory was still in Corneto at that time and it seemed that the papal cause was faring ill. Ascoli fell into the hands of the anti-clericals on December 14th; Bolsena rose in revolt and an auxiliary army sent out by Joanna of Naples was defeated by the Florentines. A brother of Raymond of Capua, Luigi delle Vigne, was taken prisoner on this occasion.

The main fact, though, was that *Rome* surrendered. On December 21st the keys of the city were placed in the hands of Cardinals d'Estaing, Corsini and Tebaldeschi. On January 13th the papal fleet sailed from Corneto and reached Ostia three days later, and on January 17th, 1377, Gregory made his entry into the Eternal City. He landed at San Paolo fuori le Mura and rode the remainder of the way on a white mule. Round about him the Roman people danced for joy; flowers and sweetmeats rained down upon the cortège from all the windows, balconies and roofs, and when Saint Peter's square was reached at dusk, it shone in the illumination of eight hundred lamps. Even the French ecclesiastics, who were accustomed to festive displays, were impressed. "Never," writes Pierre d'Amely, "had I thought I should see such magnificence." [18]

But Catherine — where was she on this day of glory and victory? Did she walk in the festive procession among the dancers and singers, the lute-players and drummers crowding about the successor of Saint Peter? Was she seen, as on Matteo di Giovanni's fresco, leading the Pope's white steed by the bridle?

Only in spirit was Catherine at Gregory's side.[19] Far from the festive rejoicing in Rome she walked in her usual paths from the cathedral to San Domenico, in the familiar streets between Fontebranda and the hospital of La Scala. In the lonely cell of Via del Tiratoio she repeated again and again, broken with gratitude, her Magnificat, adding to it Simeon's song of praise: "Now lettest thou thy servant depart in peace."

V

"Most holy and venerable Father in Christ sweet Jesus, your unworthy daughter Catherine writes to you . . . with the desire to see you attain to perfect peace. Peace with yourself and with your children. Which peace God demands of you, and He wills that you shall make as much peace as you can. Alas, it does not seem to me that God wills that we should think *so* much of worldly dominion and worldly power, that we do not see how much harm there is for souls, and dishonour to God, in war. But it seems to me that God wills that we shall see the beauty of the soul with the eye of reason, and see the blood of the Son of God, which cleanses our souls, that blood whose servant you are. I have therefore always asked you to hunger after souls. For he who hungers after that which is to the glory of God and the welfare of the flock will gladly give his life to save them from the hand of the devil; and how much more will he not sacrifice his possessions! I know well, Holy Father, that you can say: 'In my conscience I am pledged to preserve and regain the possessions of the Church.' Alas, yes, that is indeed true; but I think there are things of greater value to be considered. The treasure of the Church is the blood of Christ, shed for the redemption of souls, and not for the temporal possessions of the Church. But let us say that you are pledged to conquer and preserve the cities that the Church has lost, then you are pledged so much the more to regain so many lost sheep. . . It is better to relinquish the temporal riches than the spiritual ones. Do what you can, therefore, and you will then be excused before God and men. You will also gain more by the staff of mildness than by the rod of war. . . My soul, which desires so ardently the reformation of the Church and the good of all the world, has not found any better means of attaining this end than peace. Peace then, do I cry to you, peace for the sake of Christ Crucified. Regard not the ignorance, blindness and pride of your children. . . By virtue you will drive out the devil. . . While you can not feel safe for one hour with all this war and unrest!"

These words of Catherine reached Gregory shortly after his

arrival in Rome. As usual she also urged him to give the Church good men as rulers — "neither unclean beasts, nor leaves that turn with the wind of this world." "The Church," she says, "has lost her influence for two reasons: because of the lack of virtue in the priests and because she engages in war." The means against the former fault is "to listen to the true servants of God" (of whom the bearer of the letter, the Olivetan monk, Jacopo da Padova, is one), and the evil of war is to be healed by "holy peace." [1]

As far as she was able, Catherine devoted herself to the work of peace, and in her usual way she was the peacemaker in Siena. In this she did but follow the great traditions of the Middle Ages. The peace which Christ, according to the gospel of Saint John, left to his disciples, was in those centuries not only an interior peace, a peace of the heart, but also an exterior peace, between man and man. Christianity was then above all an ethic. The Christianity of the thirteenth and fourteenth centuries did not consist very much in triduums or novenas with several hundreds of lighted candles, long prayers which nobody understood and nobody listened to, and thick clouds of incense. It had a great deal to do, however, with visiting widows and fatherless. A letter from Giovanni delle Celle makes one understand that very clearly. The wealthy Florentine citizen, Guido di Messer Tommaso di Neri di Lippo, has asked Dom Giovanni for guidance in a Christian life and the monk then writes to him:

"Turn to the holy gospel and behold therein as in a glass five rich men (rich men like you) who were holy men (which you are not). And learn then, of Joseph of Arimathea to take down Christ from the cross, and go to Pilate, the podestà of Jerusalem, and boldly demand His body. You do this when you use your influence to help and set free the oppressed and the cowed; those who have been robbed and crucified; when you help widows and orphans in their tribulations and courageously stand up against their oppressors.

"If this be not to your liking then learn of holy Nicodemus, who came to Christ and spoke with Him at night, but in the day was careful not to be seen with Him. Go with him to anoint the body of Jesus with costly ointments, which you do

THE CROWN OF THORNS

when you visit the persecuted and the crucified in secret and anoint them with words of comfort, and visit the sick or those who are in prison and comfort them by word and deed.

"But if this please thee not, then look upon Saint Zachæus, who with great joy received Christ in his house. And this you do when you give shelter to poor pilgrims and feed them and have a good room prepared for them, and receive them as if they were Christ Himself, and wash their feet and give them water to wash their hands." [2]

As a further example Dom Giovanni presents the Roman centurion at the foot of the cross, and Cornelius, who gave Peter hospitality at Joppa, but the above must be sufficient to show how the Christianity of those days was particularly not something that flourished inside the churches, but above all a reality. In many ways the Italian Catholicism of the Middle Ages reminds one very much of the social and practical Christianity displayed at the present day by the Salvation Army.

"Now at this time there lived in Siena a man who was wise after the manner of worldly wisdom, and sorely bound in the snares of the devil, and his name was Nanni di Ser Vanni," says Raymond of Capua. He was the same Nanni di Vanni Savini who had been heavily fined in 1371 for conspiracy against the government. Whether it was because of this or for another reason, he lived in constant feuds and never thought of anything but hate and revenge. He had made acquaintance, it is not recorded how, with William Flete, the Augustinian monk out at Lecceto, and the latter had spoken very seriously to him and persuaded him to promise that he would go to Catherine and hear what she might have to say to him. Ser Nanni kept his promise, but timed his visit at such an hour that Catherine was not at home. He waited awhile and then stood up to go, saying to the confessor who was present: "I promised Fra Guglielmo to seek Catherine and this I have now done. But I am a busy man and I have not time to wait any longer. Please give her my greetings." He was already near the door, pleased like one who has escaped from a heavy yoke and is out again in the gay freedom of self-will. The confessor tried to detain him and began to talk to him about his enemies — were there no means of making peace? — and so on. Ser Nanni answered: "You are a priest and a monk, and Catherine is a holy person. I will not deceive you and therefore tell you frankly that it is *I* who will not make peace. The others are willing enough, but I will not; and never will I consent to do so. And now that I have told the truth do not plague me any more. I have already done a great deal in saying so much."

At this moment Catherine came back and began to speak with Ser Vanni, "wounding and anointing him at the same time," says Raymond. He held his ground a long while. At last he exclaimed: "Well, there, I am not such a lout that I refuse *everything* you ask me. I have four enemies — I give up one of them to you!" Having said this he stood up to go. But now the sweetness of reconciliation, the peace and joy of goodwill swept over him. "Oh, my God," he exclaimed, "I have never felt like this before. I cannot part from you, impossible for me to refuse you anything." With the exclamation, "You have conquered!" he fell on his knees before Catherine. Raymond heard his confession and said to himself: "This little woman does what she likes with all of us!" [3]

Then it happened soon after that Nanni, who had always been successful in his affairs, fell into great misfortune and was thrown into prison by the *podestà*. Raymond murmured against God: "Is that the reward for his conversion?" Catherine, though, saw this trial in another light: "Before this he was of the world and therefore the world loved him. Now he has left the world and therefore it hates him. But this punishment has been laid upon him by God to save him from everlasting torment." After some time Nanni di Ser Vanni was again set at liberty and showed his affection for Catherine by fulfilling one of her dearest wishes: that of bestowing upon her his castle of Belcaro outside Siena, so that she might there establish a convent of Dominican nuns. She had already obtained the Pope's authority for such a convent, and on January 25th the Sienese government also permitted "the humble servant of Jesus Christ, daughter of Monna Lapa, of the contrada of Fontebranda," to transform the above-mentioned fortified place into a nunnery. The convent was given the name of "Our Lady of the Angels," and was dedicated with great solemnity. The Abbot of Sant' Antimo, Giovanni di Gano, was present on this occasion as the Pope's delegate and the first Mass was said by William Flete, who had come over from the neighbouring Lecceto.[4]

At the present day Belcaro is a castle belonging to the family of the Camaiori in Siena, and in its present form it dates from the sixteenth century. But if you walk round the gallery on the walls around it, you have, beyond the clipped sessile oaks which form a sort of second and broader wall below, the same view that lay before Catherine and her friends. You see the groves of stone-pines on the hills in the near distance, and the olives and vines in the fields; you see ochre-yellow or pink farm-houses with ricks of corn around them and a little Romanesque church with its two bells in the belfry. The land spreads out wide before you, striped in red and green fields dotted with cypresses, and there lie *il Monistero* and Santa Bonda; yonder is Siena, shining in the sun, with the Mangia tower and the cathedral and San Domenico. On the other side, towards the west, is Lecceto with its square, threatening tower on the wooded hill, and *La Montagnauola*, the undulating chain of mountains separating Siena from the Tuscan Maremma. Furthest out, away in the south, is the luminous desert of Siena, the tawny Creta country, in whose fields and clefts Mont' Oliveto lies hidden; very far away is the double summit of Mont' Amiata, dusky blue in the distance, and the mountain cone of Radicofani stands like a watch tower on the road to Rome. Catherine stayed out here nearly all April 1377 — April, which is the most beautiful month in Siena, when the *capinara* sings, and the skyblue periwinkle, and green hellebore bloom on the sunny slopes around Belcaro and in the deep groves of San Leonardo al Lago. Alas! it was not the time to gather flowers with her women friends, or to listen to the singing of birds and enjoy the promise of spring. Terrible things were happening out in the world. Hawkwood and his bands, who were still in the pay of the Church, stormed Cesena and seized it with violent hands, and put four thousand of its inhabitants to the sword. The shudder that ran through all Italy at the news of the fall of Cesena can still be felt as late as in the sermons of Bernardine of Siena. "Women and virgins were violated, houses burnt down, palaces destroyed, all works of art ruined, all handicrafts laid waste; that which could not be carried away was burnt, made unfit for use, spilt on the ground" — thus does the great Franciscan preacher describe the conduct of the mercenary troops. "Not even Nero committed such cruelties," wrote a chronicler of the time. "That is what happens when the men of the Church get the mastery," remarked a Ghibelline.[5]

"From our new convent, which has been given the name of *Santa Maria degli Angeli*," wrote Catherine to Gregory. Untiring as she was she sends the Vicegerent of Christ a fresh warning and reminds him of the Prince of Peace in whose name he rules. She does not speak directly of the blood shed in Cesena, but the word *sangue* recurs in every sentence that she writes: "the blood of the only-begotten Son of God," "the blood of Christ, which we can receive only from your hands," "the blood which is never without fire" (as Cesena was in flames and streaming with blood at the same time). Again she lifts up her voice to a great tragic cry: "Oh, most holy our Father, by the love that you bear to Christ Crucified, I beseech you to follow in His steps. Woe, woe, peace, peace, for God's sake . . . Woe, woe, *babbo mio*, woe upon my unhappy soul which because of its sins is guilty of all the evil that comes to pass — and it is as if the devil has become lord of the world!" She continues her cries of peace a long while, but at last succumbs. "I can say no more. I die and yet I can not die. I say no more . . . Greatly have I longed to stand again before Your Holiness. Many things have I to speak of with you. I have not come because I have been busied with many good matters that are useful to the Church. Peace, peace, for Christ's sake. There *is* no other remedy."[6]

It was not to be long before Catherine was in Rome, and while there she tried to use her influence upon the events of the time. Meanwhile she was content to do good in her usual way nearer home.

One of the most striking instances of the moral revaluation produced by Christianity is the difference between the attitude of mediæval Christians in regard to prisons and prisoners and that of pre-Christian ages. In the Catholic liturgy of Good Friday there is a prayer in which these words occur: "Let us beseech God the Father almighty to purge the world from all

THE CROWN OF THORNS

errors; to take away diseases; to keep off famine; to open prisons; to loose chains; to grant to travellers return; to the sick health; to mariners a port of safety." There are not conditions of any kind, the prayer simply beseeches God to grant liberty to all captives; a thing to which the Roman State could not possibly have agreed. Such was the conception, however, of even the early Church, that was also how the Middle Ages regarded those who lay captive and fettered in prisons or languished in dungeons, a conception shared by Oscar Wilde in "The Ballad of Reading Gaol":

> *This too I know, and wise it were*
> *If each could know the same,*
> *That every prison that men build*
> *Is built with bricks of shame*
> *And bound with bars, lest Christ should see*
> *How men their brothers maim.*

In the year 1377, Holy Thursday fell on April 9th, and in the midst of the spring sunshine and the singing of birds at Belcaro Catherine on that day wrote a letter to "the prisoners in Siena." She calls them her "dearest sons in Christ sweet Jesus," and there is not a word in the whole letter about crime or just punishment. She is intent on one thing only, on exhorting them to be patient. And where do we find patience? In Christ. She then paints a great picture of the patience of Jesus: "He endured pain, ignominy, contempt, abuse; was bound, scourged, nailed to the cross, pierced through hands and feet; was glutted with reproaches, tortured with thirst without any relief; vinegar was given Him mingled with gall and harsh words thereto; and He bore it all patiently, nay, He even prayed for those who crucified Him and excused them." The practical application is direct, the prisoners know what it is to be mocked, jeered at, flogged and tortured, they know the taste of poor and coarse food, served with abusive taunts, and what it is to wait, day after day, for a terrible death. But Christ suffered worse things; as *He* endured so must the prisoners endure. "He was a knight on the field of battle . . . the crown of thorns was His helmet, His scourged body was His armour; the pierced hands His gauntlets; His sword was the spear in His side, and His spurs were His pierced feet nailed to the cross. Behold how gloriously this knight is armed! We must follow Him that in Him we may find consolation in all our trials and afflictions." [7]

In order to bring a poor prisoner this consolation of Christ, and all the comfort that the tenderness of a woman's sympathy can give, Catherine went herself one day during that spring, probably after having returned from Belcaro on April 25th, along the familiar road to the prison of Siena. *Magnifici Domini et Patres Domini Defensores Populi civitatis Senarum,* as the rulers of Siena pompously called themselves, carried on a harsh regime. Agnolo d'Andrea was sentenced to death for having given a big dinner without inviting any of the members of the government, and a young nobleman of Perugia, Niccolò di Toldo, who was in the service of the Senator or *Podestà*, was likewise sentenced to death for an offence against the Defensors. Tommaso Caffarini visited him in the prison and found him in a state of wild despair: "he walked up and down in the cell like a madman and would not make his confession or listen either to a monk or a priest." [8] It is easy to imagine the state of mind of the young Perugian. What! die like that! In the height of spring, in the first flower of youth! Ride in the tumbril of felons to the place of execution at Corposanto al Pecorile and lay his head on the block, while the fields everywhere were white with daisies and the larks carolling for joy under the bright sky and the mountains were blue — the distant blue mountains behind which lay Perugia, the city of his fathers, home, liberty, life? Why did they come to him with their talk and cant about the unsearchable councils of God, and Providence, and fatherly love? It was easy enough for them to talk, those thin priests and fat monks; it was not they who had to die; it was not their necks that would be chopped through in a few days by the executioner's axe (he knew the sound of sharp steel cutting through cartilage and flesh). Let *them* believe in God and love Him if they liked. God was good to them and let them live. . . But the God who sent Niccolò di Toldo to death for nothing, for a few silly words said in the heat of wine and in a spirit of frolicsomeness — that was not a good God, that was not a loving father; it was a devil and a *stupido* into the bargain. And

THE CROWN OF THORNS

the young man broke out in all an Italian's wealth of blasphemy, which is always behind their piety, as doubt is always lurking behind their faith.[9]

Catherine went to this unhappy youth and she has told Raymond about her visit in a letter. "Courage, dearest Father," she writes, "let us not sleep any longer. For I have such news to tell you now that I wish I had neither a bed nor any other comfort any more. I have already received *one* head in my hands, and it was such a sweetness to me that the heart cannot imagine it, nor the tongue utter it, nor the eye see it, nor the ear hear it . . . I went to visit him of whom you know, and it gave him so much comfort and joy that he made his confession and prepared himself well, and he entreated me for the love of God to promise that I would be with him when the hour of execution came. I gave him my word and kept it. And in the morning before the bell had rung * I went to him and it gave him much consolation. I took him to hear Mass and he received Holy Communion, which he had never before received. His will was united to the will of God and submissive to it, only he was afraid of not being strong enough at the decisive moment . . . And he said, 'Stay with me and do not leave me. Then all will be well and I shall die content.' And he rested his head upon my breast. Then I felt such an exultation and a fragrance of his blood and it blended with the fragrance of my own blood which I desire to shed for my Spouse, for sweet Jesus. And the desire grew in my soul, and because I felt how he was afraid I said to him: 'Be of good courage, my sweet brother, for soon shall we enter in to the everlasting marriage feast: you shall go thither, bathed in the sweet blood of the Son of God, with the sweet name of Jesus, which must never pass from your memory. And I await you at the place of execution.' And hearken, oh my father and my son, then there was no more fear in his heart, and his face which had been sad became joyful, and he rejoiced, exulted and said: 'How can it be that such abundant grace is granted to me, that the sweetness of my soul awaits me at the holy place of execution?' So far had he come in understanding that he called the place of

---

* The great bell in the Mangia tower, which was rung to let the citizens know that now they might leave their houses.

execution holy! 'Now will I go thither full of joy and strength, and when I think that you will await me there, it seems to me that I have yet to wait a thousand years.' And he said words so sweet that they could break my heart — God is so good!

"I waited for him then, at the place of execution, and I waited in continual prayer and in the presence of Mary and of Catherine, virgin and martyr.* But ere he had yet come I lay down and laid my head on the block; and I prayed and did violence to heaven, saying, *Mary!* I would obtain the grace that at the last moment She would give him light and peace . . . Then was my soul so full that although there were many people in the place, I could see no one any more, because of the promise I had received.

"Then he came, gentle as a lamb, and when he saw me he began to smile, and he would that I should make the sign of the cross over him. I made it and said to him: 'Up to the marriage, dear my brother; soon shall you be in life everlasting.' With great meekness he lay down and I placed his head aright and bent down and bade him think of the blood of the Lamb. His lips said nothing but 'Jesus' and 'Caterina.' And as he spoke thus I took his head in my hands and I closed my eyes and said: 'I *will!*'

"Then I saw the God Man, and His brightness was like the brightness of the sun, and that soul entered into the open wound in His side, and the Truth made me understand that this soul was saved by pure grace and mercy, without any merit. . .

"And that soul did something that was so sweet that a thousand hearts could not contain it. . . Already it began to taste the sweetness of divinity. Then it turned — as the bride turns at the bridegroom's door and looking back, bends her head in greeting and thanksgiving to those who have attended her.

"But when the body had been taken away my soul rested in quiet and peace and in a fragrance of blood so sweet that I could not bear to wash from off my habit the blood that had sprinkled it.

"Ah woe to me, miserable that I am — I will say no more. How shall I bear to continue living here on earth?" [10]

* Saint Catherine of Alexandria, patron of Catherine of Siena.

VI

"It is fitting that we should labour for the glory of God in the same manner as the holy apostles, for when they had received the Holy Spirit they went each his own way and also bade farewell to the sweet Mother Mary. Let us say that they would gladly have been together, but they gave up that which would be pleasing to themselves and sought the glory of God and the salvation of souls. . . That is the rule that we must follow. I know that my presence is of great comfort to you, but in real obedience you should not seek your own consolation . . . or give ear to the devil, who would make you think that I do not love you. . . Yes, I do love you — but in God, for His sake . . . It is therefore right that we are all together or each one alone, according as required by the times. And now it is the will of our sweet Saviour that we should be parted, for His glory.

"You are in Siena, Cecca and 'Grandmother' are in Montepulciano. Brother Bartolommeo and Brother Matteo are going there or have been there. Alessia and Monna Bruna are at Monte Giovi . . . they are with the Countess and with Madonna Isa. Brother Raimondo and Brother Tommaso and Monna Tomma and Lisa and I, we are at the Rocca among great sinners, and we eat so many incarnate devils that Brother Tommaso says it is making his stomach ill. And yet they cannot get enough. They want more work and find it too, at a cheap price. Pray to the Divine Goodness and ask Him to give them large and sweet and bitter morsels. Bear in mind that there is great comfort in working for the glory of God and the salvation of souls. You ought not to want or wish for anything else. You can do nothing more pleasing to God and to me. Arise, my daughters, and begin to offer up your will to the highest, eternal will of God." [1]

South of Siena, in the wild Orcia valley, beneath Mont' Amiata, storm-swept and cloud-veiled, the most powerful of all Sienese families, the Salimbeni, had an impregnable rock-castle: Rocca di Tentennano.[2] This fortress formed the central point of the domain, gradually grown extensive, which this astute and energetic family of bankers had managed to create at the expense of the republic of Siena. Before the battle of Monteaperti, Salimbene Salimbeni had lent Siena, as a war loan, one hundred thousand gold florins, an enormous sum in those times. When the city found that it was unable to pay the debt it was compelled to surrender to the heirs a number of fortified castles in the south: Tentennano, Castiglioncello del Trinoro, Montecuccori, Selva, Montorsaio.

In Catherine's time the family was divided into two branches: on one side Andrea and Cione di Sandro, both accused of treason during the war with Perugia in 1357 and banished from Siena; on the other, Giovanni di Angelino Salimbeni,* whose second wife was Bianchina Trinci, sister of the absolute ruler of Foligno, the "tyrant" Corrado Trinci. Giovanni di Angelino was for ten years sole ruler of Siena; he died in 1362 after a fall from his horse, just as he was riding out to meet the Emperor Charles IV. His son, Angiolino di Giovanni, carried on the traditions handed down by his father and acquired further castles: Castiglione in the Orcia valley, Pian Castignaio and Monte Giovi on Mont' Amiata, Rocca Federighi in the Maremma, and in the north, in the Merse valley, Boccheggiano. Marriages with other great families increased the power of the Salimbeni still further. Angiolino's sister, Benedetta or Bandeca, was married to a Farnese, and another sister, Isa, married her cousin, Paolo Trinci.

The strength of the family, however, was being sapped by internal strife; a quarrel broke out between the brothers Cione and Angiolino and quickly developed into open war. Their troubles were aggravated by exterior disasters: during a rising in Foligno Paolo Trinci and his uncle Trincio both lost their lives; we have still the letter of sympathy written by Catherine on that occasion to Trincio's sister, Monna Jacopa, of the Este family. Paolo's widow Bandeca married again, but her second husband also met with an untimely death. After that both

---

* The Italian system of giving names in the Middle Ages is exactly like the Russian one of later times. Giovanni di Angelino Salimbeni is an exact parallel of e.g. Leo Nikolaievitch Tolstoi. First comes the baptismal name, then the father's name, finally the family name. Even at the present day, in official Italian documents, the father's baptismal name is always given after the baptismal name of the person in question — e.g., Giovanni fu Giorgio, John, son of the late George.

the young widows resolved to retire from the world and bid its joys and sorrows farewell.

Catherine, to whom they turned for advice, gave her consent with all her heart. To Bandeca she wrote: "Love that good and divine Bridegroom, who has given you life and who never dies. Other men die and vanish away like a puff of wind; you have learned yourself, how short is an earthly marriage." She invites her to seek shelter, "as in the Promised Land" in the new convent which is being established at Belcaro. To Isa she gives the same advice, "and do not think that you are unfaithful to your spiritual Father, Francis of Assisi, in so doing," she adds, the young widow having joined the third order of the Franciscans at Foligno.[3]

With the intention of confirming the two young women still further in their religious vocation, and at the same time making peace between the two contending branches of the Salimbeni family, Catherine set out for south Tuscany in 1377, invited by Monna Bianchina. A number of her spiritual family accompanied her — Alessia, Lisa, Cecca, Tommasina, Raymond, Tommaso della Fonte, Bartolommeo de' Dominici, Matteo Tolomei, Neri, Gabriele Piccolomini, Francesco Malavolti and several others.

On the way Catherine intended to visit Montepulciano and the tomb of her departed friend, Saint Agnes, as she had done three years before. During this visit Catherine made the acquaintance of the poet, Giacomo del Pecora. He was a descendant of that nobleman who had had such a decisive influence on the fate of Margherita of Cortona a hundred years earlier. Like his ancestor the young poet had until then lived a worldly life; Catherine converted him to herself and to God. In his verse he was later to reproach Siena with not sufficiently having appreciated the treasure which had been bestowed upon the town in the daughter of Giacomo Benincasa.[4]

To this sojourn in Montepulciano must also be referred a little incident which gives a vivid picture of the life in the circle of disciples around Catherine. One evening at the gate of the convent of Saint Anne, where she was staying, just as she was saying goodnight to all her escort, she notices that one of them seems to be sad. It was one of those who had most recently joined the circle, the young Sienese, Pietro di Giovanni Ventura. Is it because the night is approaching, is it because he has to part from his *dolcissima Mamma* and be alone? He is very sad. "Mamma," he says, "I beg of you to think of me in the night, that the Lord may send me His comfort." With her sweet smile Catherine promises to grant his prayer, and she is heard. The next morning the young man was able to tell her that she had appeared to him in a dream, accompanied by two monks from Mont' Oliveto — and was it she or one of the monks who gave him Holy Communion?

Leaving Montepulciano Catherine went on to Castiglioncello del Trinoro, the castle of Cione di Sandro Salimbeni. Catherine was already in communication with the wild warrior's wife, Monna Stricca, and was successful in her mission. Cione consented to make peace with his cousin, and with this good news Catherine arrived at Rocca di Tentennano (on modern maps it is called Rocca d'Orcia). From here it was that Catherine, in the autumn of 1377, wrote the letter given at the beginning of the present chapter to her friends Caterina della Spedaluccio and Giovanna di Capo, whom she had left behind in Siena.[5]

Cecca di Gori and Monna Lapa (Grandmother, as she was gradually being called by the circle that called Catherine Mamma) remained behind in Montepulciano, where Cecca's daughter Giustina was a novice in the convent of Santa Agnese. Other disciples — Alessia Saracini and Bruna, otherwise unknown — went to the castle of Monte Giovi, which stands on the slopes of Mont' Amiata and belongs to the Salimbeni. Their headquarters, however, were, as said before, Rocca di Tentennano; there Catherine sat with Raymond of Capua, Tommaso della Fonte, Lisa Colombini, Neri di Landoccio, Francesco Malavolti and several other disciples; here they indulged in common in Catherine's favourite occupation, that of "eating devils," i.e. converting sinners, and with such great success that Raymond complained that he could not manage to hear all the confessions that Catherine procured for him. And yet he was not alone in the work; besides Tommaso della Fonte and Bartolommeo de' Dominici he was helped by four others.[6] This fight with the powers of darkness sometimes assumed the most intense aspects. Francesco Malavolti tells how Catherine, during her stay with the Salimbeni, not only converted sinners, but actually drove out devils. When she was sitting among her friends "on the terrace which is called *lo sprone*," the possessed from the surrounding country would be brought to her, bound on hands and feet, foaming with rage, so that fourteen strong men could hardly hold them. Her cure was always the same. "What has the poor creature done?" she exclaimed, "that you keep him fettered like this? In the name of Jesus Christ I bid you loose him!" At Catherine's word they dared to loose the madman, and behold, the raging man grew as meek as a lamb and Catherine (who according to her habit sat on the ground, not on a bench or in a seat of honour) took his head on her lap and wept over the poor soul like a mother over her child. Then all disease, nay, even the lice, that the possessed creature had been infested with in his uncleanliness, left him and crept away along the floor of the room, so that the disciples standing round exclaimed in horror: "Oh, Mamma, do you not see that this man is filling us all with vermin." With her beautiful smile she answered: "Do not care about it — they will not stay long on you!" Nor did they.[7]

Catherine took as a revenge on the part of the underworld certain strange attacks of illness from which she often suffered, and every accident that happened to her. "It is strange to say," writes Raymond of Capua, "especially in our times" (apparently "our times" were particularly enlightened even then!) "that not once, but many times, it happened that invisible hands suddenly pushed Catherine over. Thus she once fell on to the fire and Lisa, Alessia and Francesca rushed to her and raised her up, but she had not taken any harm."

Another time — it was on a journey and they had come near to Siena — the ass on which Catherine was riding suddenly stumbled and fell with its rider into the mud. Catherine fell so awkwardly that one of the animal's hoofs struck her side, just where she always had a pain. She only laughed and said: "It is Malatasca who is at his tricks!" By Malatasca (an expression which can be found in Giovanni Colombini's letters, and which was probably used by the Benedictine nuns at Santa Bonda) the saint meant the evil one — he who has a bottomless pocket for lost souls.[8]

Catherine stayed four months in the Orcia valley. She spent part of this time at Sant' Antimo, near the great abbey which was founded by Charlemagne, and whose abbot, Giovanni di Gano, was a friend of Catherine's. It was he, for instance, who had recently consecrated Catherine's convent of Belcaro.

She walked here in the steps of Giovanni Colombini, but was more successful than he in her missionary labours. It is of the sojourn at Sant' Antimo that Raymond writes: "More than once I saw over a thousand people, men and women, coming as if they had been summoned by an invisible trumpet and descending from the mountains and from the towns about Siena to see and hear Catherine. And not even her words were needed, did they but see her they were seized with repentance over their misdeeds and ran weeping to the confessors, of whom I was one." As usual with him, Raymond does not state exactly where this happened; it is Malavolti who says that it was at Sant' Antimo.

Among those whom Catherine converted here was the notary and poet, Anastagio of Montalcino. Like his brother poet in Montepulciano he gave vent to his enthusiasm for the saint in verse: "She is a hedge, she is a strong wall, a deep pit, she is the safe fortress, where the sinner can take refuge . . . Oh dear, gentle and venerable Mamma, I see thee still as I saw thee then, at the foot of the altar!" "Oh gentle maiden, oh soul of fire, thou hast led us all to love and forgive, so that every one of us now embraces him he once hated most!"[9]

If Catherine thus had enthusiastic and devoted friends, she had also enemies who tried to make her hated. Her long visit to the worst enemies of the Sienese republic, the Salimbeni, must of necessity rouse its suspicion. Might not she and the influential abbot of Sant' Antimo, as well as the highborn Dominican Raimondo, be hatching a political plot out there at Rocca di Tentennano? Catherine indignantly answered in two letters — one of them written at Montepulciano, the other at Sant' Antimo — to "the Lords Defensors and the Captain

THE CROWN OF THORNS

of the People of Siena," * another to an influential citizen in the town, the goldsmith Salvi di Messer Pietro. "I have not come hither," she writes, "for anything but to eat souls and to save them from the claws of the devil. And if I had a thousand lives, I would give them all for the sake of that cause. I have necessary things to perform for the convent of Saint Agnes, and I must speak with the nephews of Messer Spinello to make peace with the sons of Lorenzo [10] . . . and I do not wish this matter to be delayed any longer . . . It grieves me that my fellow-citizens think and speak so ill of me; one would think they had nothing else to do but to throw logs of wood at me." "If I am persecuted and slandered I will answer with tears and constant prayer, as God gives me grace thereto. And whether the devil will or no, I will spend my life for the glory of God and the salvation of souls, for the good of all the world and in particular for my native town. The citizens of Siena should be greatly ashamed to think or imagine that we are with the Salimbeni to make secret compacts." [11]

In reality Catherine was only pursuing her work for peace. "Pietro" (di Giovanni Ventura, who brought letters to Siena) "can tell you by word of mouth the chief reason why I remain here." [12] This reason was not small, it was nothing less than the reconciling of the See of Rome with Milan. Opportunity for this was given her, for just at this time, in the autumn of 1377, the great *condottiere* John Hawkwood came to south Tuscany and pitched his camp in San Quirico d'Orcia, a little to the north of Rocca di Tentennano. It is impossible to think otherwise than that Catherine would again try to approach the redoubtable warrior. Original sources say but little about it, but we suspect what took place when we read in Raymond of Capua, that at Catherine's order he had to leave Rocca d'Orcia to go to Rome and lay before the Pope "several proposals which would have been useful for the Church of God if they had been understood." And in a letter

* *Il Capitano del Popolo* was the leader and spokesman of democracy in times of peace; in times of war he conducted *il Carroccio*, the war chariot with the banner of the republic. In contrast to the *Podestà*, who had always to be a stranger (for the sake of impartiality) the office of "captain of the people" could only be held by a Sienese. In September–October 1379 Catherine's disciple, the painter Andrea di Vanni, was *Capitano del Popolo*.

written on February 3rd, 1378, in San Quirico, we see Hawkwood ask the government of Siena for safe conduct for the papal envoys, who were on the way to him and from there were to go on to Milan. In other words, Hawkwood had been gained for Catherine's idea of peace, and when he could not carry it through it was because one of the two parties, probably Bernabò de' Visconti, refused to agree to it.[13]

Thus Catherine remained behind alone, as she says in a letter, in the castle of the Salimbeni "as on an island with the storm raging on every side." (He who has climbed the mountain, on which the ruins of Rocca di Tentennano are still standing, knows how stormy it can be up there!). The loss of Raymond pained her deeply. During the three years they had known each other the learned Dominican had become her most intimate friend and her best support, *il mio Giovanni Singolare,* as she liked to call him, with an allusion to the disciple whom the Lord loved. And in particular there was one very important point on which he understood her so well and responded to her — it was her need of receiving Holy Communion daily. "Sometimes," Raymond writes, "Catherine desired Communion so ardently that if she could not receive it that day she suffered more in her body than from a fever lasting many days... Wherefore, when I was present, and her soul was ardently longing for Holy Communion she was wont to say: 'Father, I am hungry, for the love of God, give my soul food.' In particular I remember a time after coming home from Avignon, when we had visited some servants of God outside Siena, so that we might edify each other in the Lord. On the feast of Saint Mark, April 25th in the morning, we returned to the town and when we reached her house it was already past the third hour (after nine o'clock). But she turned to me and said: 'Oh, Father, if you knew how hungry I am!' And understanding what she meant, I said: 'It is almost too late now to say Mass, and I am so tired that I can hardly prepare for it.' On hearing this she was silent, but after a while she again said that she was very hungry. I was willing then to yield to her and going into the chapel, which she had been permitted by the Pope to have in her house, I put on the vestment for Mass and in her presence I said the Mass of Saint Mark. For her Communion I had consecrated a small host, and after I had made my own Communion I turned to give the absolution, as the custom is, and then I saw her face like the face of an angel, bright and shining, and it seemed to me as if it had become another face, so that I said to myself: 'This is not Catherine's face.' But in my soul a voice answered and said: 'Yes, of a truth, Lord, this is thy dear and faithful bride.' And pondering on these things within myself, I turned to the altar and said inwardly: 'Come, Lord, to thy bride.' And how I came upon such a thought I know not, but it had hardly arisen within me when the sacred Host, before I had yet touched It, moved of Itself and came towards me, a distance as much as the breadth of three fingers and more, until It reached the paten which I was holding in my hand. . . But whether the Host ascended on the sacred paten of Itself, or I laid It there, I know not." [14]

Others had already observed similar phenomena. If Tommaso della Fonte is to be believed, the Host actually flew of Itself into Catherine's mouth; the same thing was seen once by Brother Gregory of Rimini and all those who were present, when he gave Catherine Communion. Bartolommeo de' Dominici felt as it were, the Host moving between the two fingers with which he held It, as if with impatience for the virgin's mouth, and Francesco Malavolti once saw how It flew like an arrow in between the lips of his *Mamma*.[15] After she had received the Sacrament her soul was no longer aware of anything earthly. The body then sometimes followed the spirit on its heavenward flight and hovered in the air, "for the space of a *Miserere*," and was then raised so much above the floor that one could place one's hands under her. It is here a question of more than pious superstition, for Catherine herself describes this state of ecstatic levitation: "Often," she writes, "the body is lifted up from the earth by the perfect union (with God) which the soul has consummated in me, as if the heavy body became light. It is not because the weight is taken from it, but it is because the union with God into which the soul in me has entered is more perfect than the union between the soul and the body, that the power of the soul lifts up the heavy body from the earth." [16]

The strangest of all these incidents is perhaps that related by Raymond, again from his own experience. Once when he was saying Mass in the Cappella delle Volte, and according to the ritual had broken the Altar Bread before receiving It, a small particle of It disappeared and was not to be found again. Raymond was greatly troubled at this, he searched everywhere, was interrupted in his search by a visit, went back again to the altar to continue his search, but still without success. Until he understood at last and Catherine made a partial confession that it was she who in a miraculous way had received the vanished particle, without leaving her place at the other end of the chapel.

This occurrence is related by Raymond with great particularity and keen psychological description. It is confirmed by Catherine herself in her book, *The Dialogue*. Speaking of herself in her usual way in the book, that is, in the third person, she gives the following account:

"On a certain occasion that soul had a great longing to hear Mass and receive Holy Communion, but because of sickness she had not been able to go to church in time. When she came it was already late and the priest was at the words of consecration (i.e. she arrived just at the moment when the priest was consecrating). And he was at one end of the church and she was at the other . . . and in great sorrow she said to herself: 'Oh, my miserable soul, are you not thankful for the grace you have received, that you are in the holy temple of God and have seen His servant before the altar, though you have deserved hell because of your sins?' Yet her longing would not be satisfied, the more she descended into the valley of humility, the higher was she lifted up, because God in His goodness made her understand that the Holy Spirit would attend her and appease her hunger . . . And it came to pass in this wise . . . when the priest was to give himself Holy Communion and therefore divided the Host, a little piece fell down (*moccolino*) and by the permission of God It left the altar and moved down to the other end of the church where she was. And believing that this which had happened had not been visible, but that it was invisible, and feeling that she had received Communion, she thought that it had happened this time as it had happened several other times, that is, spiritually. But the priest thought not so, feeling greatly troubled when he did not find that particle, until the Holy Spirit in Its mercy had enlightened his mind and told him who had received It. Yet he was still in doubt, until he had asked her about it."

We have here two first-hand testimonies, independent of each other, of an occurrence which may well give food for thought. In order to understand the whole extent of what has been told here it must be remembered that according to Catholic doctrine the altar bread (the wafer or host) is transsubstantiated at Mass into the Body of Christ by the priest's repetition of the words instituting the Holy Supper. Before Communion this Body is broken into three parts, but all the three parts must be consumed by the priest himself, other, smaller Hosts being used for the Communion of the congregation. It was one of these fragments which, according to the accounts of both Raymond and Catherine, disappeared from his altar and passing through the air sought her lips — as a bee seeks the flower.[17]

During her long sojourn at the castle of the Salimbeni Catherine, according to Caffarini, was suddenly able to write. One day she found in a room a little pot of cinnabar which had been used for drawing initials, as well as a pen and parchment. She sat down so that she might try to practise this wonderful art too, as she had so often seen her disciples doing, and "as we may venture to believe, driven by divine inspiration," she wrote down "in a plain and clear hand" the following lines of verse — which may have been composed by herself, or may have been remembered from elsewhere:

> *O Spirito Santo, vieni nel mio cuore,*
> *per tua potenzia trailo a te, Dio vero,*
> *concedimi carità con timore,*
> *custodimi da ogni mal pensero,*
> *riscaldami e rinfiamma del tu' amore,*
> *si che ogni peso mi paia leggiero.*

*Santo mio Padre e dolce mio Signore,
ora aiutami in ogni mio mistiero.
Cristo amore! Cristo amore!*

In English:

*Oh, Holy Spirit, come into my heart.
Draw it by thy power to thee, true God,
Grant me love with fear of Thee.
Guard me from all evil thought,
Warm me and inflame me with thy love,
Holy my Father and sweet my Lord,
Help me now in all my labours.
Christ who art Love, Christ who art Love.*

"It must not be thought," adds Caffarini, "that this leaf was the only thing she wrote with her own hand . . . For the reverend Don Stefano Maconi, who with many others served her as her clerk, has told me that with her own hand she wrote a letter to the aforesaid Don Stefano . . . in which she assures him that this is the first letter she has written herself. He has also seen her write many times with her own hand, and besides several letters which were urgent, many pages of the book which she composed in Italian." [18]

We do not know which letter Catherine wrote with her own hand to Stefano Maconi. On the other hand we know very well what Caffarini means by "the book in Italian." It was Catherine's great work, *Il Dialogo*. She may have begun to write it at Rocca di Tentannano. Bianchina Salimbeni was later greatly interested in this work, perhaps because she had seen its beginning.[19] Catherine herself says, at the end of one of her letters to Raymond of Capua: "This letter and another, which I have sent to you, I have written with my own hand at *Isola della Rocca*" (i.e. the isolated castle of the Salimbeni). She continues: "So that I might have something wherewith I might soothe my heart and keep it from breaking, Providence has made me able to write. I am not yet to be taken away from this dark world; then the ability arose in my mind in the same way as when a teacher shows a pupil what he must do. After you had gone I began at once to learn it, as if in sleep, and present were the glorious evangelist John and Thomas Aquinas," [20] she tells Raymond. Some time had already passed since the parting which had been so painful to both of them. The Dominican, who was held in high esteem, had been kept back in Rome by the Pope as Prior of the monastery of Santa Maria sopra Minerva, a position which he had already occupied in 1369. For three years Raymond had been Catherine's faithful friend and judicious adviser, who with his undisputed authority had helped her to prove herself. It was hard and sad to be parted from such a friend, and Catherine's letters of that period show how difficult it was for her to submit to the will of God — "the bitter will of God," as Claudel has said.

Meanwhile, being heroic, she chooses to live her life in her pain, as the souls in purgatory choose and desire the chastening flame. In Raymond she had given up her last and perhaps her greatest earthly consolation. Now only naked suffering remained to her, only the crown of thorns and the way of the Cross leading on to death. Catherine stayed on with the Salimbenis through Advent and a tone of dark wintry protest against all spring and all earthly longing for happiness seems to ring in the lines she writes from there to her faithful friend, Alessia Saracini.

"I wish to see you follow the teaching of the Lamb without blemish," she writes to her friend, who was now thirty years old, "your heart free, deprived of every creature, clothed only with the Creator. Go every day anew into the garden of your soul, with the light of faith, pull out every thorn which might choke the good seed, and dig up the soil. Which being interpreted is: unclothe your heart every day."

In this Catherine only preaches what she herself practises. Looking back at the bitter parting from Raymond (gone, gone, the evenings on *lo sprone,* where they sat in the circle of friends and looked out across the Val d'Orcia, looked across to Mont' Amiata) she adds: "It seems to me that my Spouse, Eternal Truth, has willed to put me to a sorely sweet and royal proof . . . He has strengthened me in the midst of the trial, so that no tongue can utter it." Then she sings the praises of suffering — for what was left to her now but to suffer, suffer in memory, suffer in longing, suffer in hopeless dwelling on that which was lost and would never return.

"Suffering shall be my food and tears my drink; suffering shall prosper me, suffering shall heal me ; suffering shall grant me light, suffering shall give me wisdom, suffering shall clothe my nakedness, suffering shall take away from me all self-love, both of the spirit and the flesh. Rejoice, rejoice on the Cross with me! On the Cross our souls shall rest as on a bed." [21]

To a woman with such feelings, however, a man actually dared to lift his eyes in earthly love at this very time, during the sojourn at Rocca d'Orcia. Catherine liked to associate with men, she was so virile herself. But the men she attracted were often of the gentle feminine kind: the melancholy poet, Neri di Landoccio; the gay, talkative Stefano Maconi; the undecided Francesco Malavolti who was swayed by his moods; the gentle Pietro di Giovanni Ventura, who was so much in need of consolation.

In none of these young men did their feelings for Catherine pass beyond a romantic and admiring friendship. But in the anonymous treatise, *Miracoli di Santa Caterina,* there is an account of a monk who wanted to be her disciple and became one, "and after some time he was deceived by the devil and turned his holy zeal for her and his admiration of her devout life into a sinful love, and was altogether consumed in this unclean flame. But inasmuch as she continued her holy life and never gave him cause for any but pure and holy feelings, and he grew day by day more inflamed, he had at last come so far that he thought of killing her in the church. Howbeit, as he went towards her, God made it so that a man was present in the church, and he saw it and prevented the misdeed. Not long after that monk put off the garments of his order, and returned to his place, a castle far from Siena, and there he passed his life in despair. And she, who knew of the matter, entreated God to have compassion on that soul. . . But he persisted in his despair, and at last he hanged himself." [22]

Raymond of Capua relates a similar story of "a miserable wretch, whom I knew well," but tells only of hatred of Catherine, the attempted murder in the church and the suicide. "Like a second Judas he hanged himself in the wood." He was found sitting strangled at the foot of the tree round which he had placed the rope, and his body was buried under the dung-heap "such as was fitting." [23]

The Dominican did not know, or refused to know, that unrequited love was at the root of the hate, the despair and the death by his own hand out in the chestnut woods of Mont' Amiata. There are, however, two letters in Grottanelli's collection of letters from Catherine's disciples, which may have been written by that unhappy soul. They were written in that autumn to Neri dei Pagliaresi and are answers to communications from him. In the first he says: "I wonder greatly that you remember such a miserable soul as I, seeing that God has changed me into a vessel of dishonour. I perceive no longer the good odour that nourished me heretofore; I am outside every good path. But know that if it were still in the good time, in the days that are gone, I could not resist but would write to you oftener. Now I am ashamed to write to you or to any other of the servants and friends of God, because I know my own misery. May God keep you in His grace, you and your *Mamma*. F. S.

There is a strange ring of despair in this little letter. The writer of it had once been on the good path and now feels that he is chosen as a vessel of dishonour and looks back at the times when he thought he was among those who are elected for salvation. He is not in the least an unbeliever, not at all rebellious, he is only conscious of being irretrievably damned and wishes for the others the grace that is not for him — "you, Neri, and your *Mamma*" (alas! no longer mine — and nevermore mine — for *her* path leads to heaven, mine to the abyss!).

In the next letter this gloomy tone has grown still more gloomy. "It is already a long while since I was certain that I am condemned," he says. "I am blotted out of the book of life . . . Call me not brother, therefore, any more, count me no longer among your dear friends and brothers. And do not wonder that I do not write to you any more . . . I have been far from the good way for so long now, that I think it is impossible that I can ever find happiness in that which once gave me joy, or find peace anywhere. . . I have been driven away from the table because I have clothed myself in darkness. I have no more any desire or hunger for what is good. This letter has neither beginning nor end, for in myself there is neither beginning nor end. I do not sign my name, for I do not know what name I bear. May God give you grace and perseverance and a holy death." The letter is addressed below: "To Neri di Landoccio. At Rocca di Tentennano." That is where *she* is, where the others can still rejoice in the light of her countenance; it is where he shall never go any more . . .[24]

One who has been banished from the world of light and peace speaks in these letters, one who through his own fault has fallen into the power of a murky passion who knows neither rest nor peace, one who (as Hello would say) has given himself up to *la passion du malheur*. He is unhappy, but he will not let go his unhappiness. He *will* have his despair, *will* have his damnation, *will* persist in that restless and devouring distress of mind, which goes through his being like a dark stream, hindering his work, robbing him of rest, destroying his life — and which, alas! is dearer to him than health itself.

Gardner is probably right when he reads the signature to these two letters as F(ra) S(imone) — the Fra Simone of Cortona who was harassed by scruples and went in ceaseless fear of being numbered among the damned. Other *Caterinati* suffered from the same terrible obsession: in a letter to Catherine Lazzarino of Pisa confesses: "It seems to me that I am hopelessly separated from all that is holy, and that I am irredeemably repudiated by God."

Catherine knew how to help her spiritual children in their distress of soul and to save them from what Angela of Foligno calls "false humility." Taking up Fra Simone's disconsolate designation of himself, she writes to her "dear brother Nameless" and explains to him that it is the devil who inspires him with this fear of being condemned, and that if he will bathe in the blood of Christ *he can win back his name.*" [25]

Fra Simone came back to the light; Catherine gives vent to her joy over it in a letter to Raymond of Capua.[26] But who was

THE CROWN OF THORNS

that unhappy disciple who died by his own hand? We do not know, but was Catherine thinking of him when she wrote in a letter to Neri di Landoccio: "And do not fear that God will permit that to happen to you which happened to that other." For Neri's melancholy poet soul also fought against the law which was in his members — *la puzza della lege perversa* — Catherine wrote forcibly — and was still far from having attained to that ocean of peace where no doubt separates us from God any more," which his *Mamma* promises him, and in which her own soul rests.* [27]

---

* It seems as though Catherine, after Raymond's departure, had left Rocca di Tentennano to visit a number of convents and little towns on Mont' Amiata: Montenero, Monte Giovi, Potentino, Seggiano, the Benedictine hermitage of San Biagio, the Franciscan convent of Colombaio, the convent of the Camaldolenses at Vivo. After her return from this missionary journey the saint lived in the town of Rocca d'Orcia at the foot of the castle; a house in which she is said to have lived is still shown here, and the church in which it was her custom to pray (San Simone).

VII

"If it should happen, dearest Father, that you are called to the presence of His Holiness, the Vicegerent of Christ, our sweetest and holiest Father, then commend me humbly to him and say that I repent of all the negligence of which I have been guilty before God and my indifference towards my Creator, who enjoined upon me to proclaim him with all my power . . . and to stand by the side of His Vicar in word and by my presence. I have committed all manner of countless faults and I believe it is for that reason that he and Holy Church have been so severely persecuted, because of my many transgressions. Therefore, if he complains of me, he is right, and if he punishes me for my faults it is with good reason. But tell him, that so far as I am able I will strive to correct myself and to perform his will perfectly and be obedient to him." [1]

It can be seen from this letter, which was written by Catherine to Raymond in the winter of 1377–78, that a disagreement had arisen between her and Gregory XI. She could not write directly any longer to him whom she had once called *Babbo mio dolce*. It is possible that Gregory regretted having come to Rome; his life on the banks of the Tiber could not exactly be called a happy one, and on his death-bed he is said to have reproached himself bitterly with having listened to the visions of Birgitta and Catherine and to have forfeited his happy and peaceful Avignon. Moreover, it is possible to think that the Pope felt it as a kind of treachery that Catherine seemed to leave him to himself and instead of continuing to support him spent her time in reconciliations and conversions in Italian families of whom he knew nothing and felt completely indifferent. In any case, it was only by a roundabout way that Catherine could gain his ear, and she made use of it. The letter to Raymond contains a whole section which is intended to be read to the Pope, and in it she speaks directly to him:

"Holiest Father," she exclaims, "punish me, but punish me in reason, not in anger. With whom shall I take refuge if you forsake me? Who else will support me? To whom shall I go if you banish me? My persecutors hunt me and

I flee to you and to the other children and servants of God. And were you to leave me and no more to care for me, but to be angry with me, I would hide myself in the wounds of Christ Crucified (you are His Vicar); and I know that He will receive me, for He wills not the death of a sinner. And when I had been received by Him you would not send me away, but we would stand together, each in his own place and fight courageously with the weapons of virtue for the sweet Bride of Christ. In her will I end my life, with tears and sighs and labours; for the Church I will give my blood and the marrow in my bones. And though the whole world should drive me out, I would not reck aught of it, but I would repose with many tears and much endurance on the breast of the Bride. Forgive me, holiest Father, for having offended God and your Holiness. Let the Truth excuse me and make me free — the eternal Truth. Humbly I beg your blessing."

In reality Catherine had nothing to reproach herself with in regard to Gregory XI. It was a peculiarity with her, however, that she always felt as if it was she who was in the wrong and she is therefore always ready to acknowledge her accusers to be in the right. It seemed to her that she was to blame for everything evil that happened in the world, for if she had done thus and thus at the time, *that* would not have happened, and *this other* would not have happened, and then everything would have been different! On looking back at her life it seemed to her that there were so many missed opportunities of doing good; everywhere she saw herself as she who had failed, who had not been equal to the task, as she who had sought her own satisfaction instead of the will of God, and who was therefore, strictly and exactly speaking, *cagione d'ogni male,* "the cause of all the evil that happened in the world." It was under the weight of this feeling that she continually, when praying, abased herself with the cry: *Peccavi, Domini, miserere mei,* "I have sinned, Lord, have mercy upon me!" and impelled by her over-sensitive conscience, as by a spur of pure silver, she now came to the Pope and begged without cause for pardon.

Catherine's repentance reached the foot of Gregory's throne at a moment when he was in great need of her. His position was in fact really desperate. The peace with Florence which Catherine had tried to obtain had never been made. The Florentine envoys returned in October, 1377, from Anagni, where they had sought the Pope, but the terms of peace which they brought home were unanimously declared to be unacceptable. It was decided to carry on hostilities, the Eight of War were re-elected for a year, and it was resolved that the interdict should not be kept. New taxes were imposed upon Church property and the religious orders, and on October 18th solemn High Mass was sung on the Piazza della Signoria.

At the same time Gregory had quarrelled with Siena, whose envoys came to him with a letter of recommendation from Catherine herself, but whom he nevertheless caused to be thrown into prison, at the same time that the papal troops occupied Talamone, the port of Siena, and harried the Sienese Maremma. John Hawkwood had left the service of Gregory and was again in the pay of Florence; the leader of the papal army, Rodolfo Varano di Camerino had been defeated at the end of October, 1377, by Bartolommeo di Smeduccio. The Pope's only support was Queen Joanna of Naples, morally more than defective, to whom he wrote pitiable begging letters.

There was one ray of light in this gloom, and it came from Catherine. Her influential Florentine friend, Niccolò Soderini, had come over to Siena one day, shortly before Raymond's departure for Rome, and had had an important conversation with the Dominican. Florence was really in favour of peace, Soderini assured him; there were only about half-a-dozen people who wished to continue the war. These few men could easily be rendered harmless if all who were amicably disposed joined together, and the others were sentenced to be banished. As those who were best qualified to take the matter in hand the Florentine mentioned the leaders of the Guelphic party, the so-called *Uffiziali* or *Capitani della Parte Guelfa*.[2]

The road to the Florentine Guelphs, however, did not go via Fontebranda — it was Catherine, and she alone, who could be of help. Raymond tells how, one Sunday morning in Rome,

THE CROWN OF THORNS

after he had been preaching, he was sent for by the Pope and had to report himself immediately after his midday meal. "It has been written to me," Gregory told the Dominican, "that if Catherine of Siena went to Florence, peace would be made." "Not only Catherine, but all of us are ready to suffer even martyrdom, if Your Holiness commands it," was Raymond's evasive answer. "I do not want you to go to Florence," the Pope answered, "they will treat you ill. But I do not think they will harm Catherine, in part because she is a woman, and in part because they revere her." The audience concluded in the Dominican being told to report himself all ready the next morning with the bulls and required papers for Catherine's mission.

In this way Catherine went to the republic on the Arno for the third and last time. It was in December 1377. This time she had only a small escort: Alessia Saracini, Cecca Gori, Caterina Ghetto, Neri, Stefano Maconi, and later, when the last-named had returned home, Ser Cristofano di Gano Guidini. "In this year," writes the Florentine chronicler under the year 1377, "there came to Florence a woman named Caterina, daughter of Jacopo Benincasa . . . she blamed the adversaries of the Church. Those who governed the Guelphic Party received her with joy, in particular Niccolò Soderini, who had prepared a room for her in his house, where she had lived before, as well as Stoldo di Messer Bindo Altoviti and Piero Canigiani; they lauded her to the skies. And it is true that she understood ecclesiastical matters, both because of her natural gifts and because of what she had learnt, and she expressed herself well in speech and writing. Piero Canigiani had a dwelling built for her at the foot of San Giorgio and collected money for it from all his party, both men and women, and bought stone and wood and brought it thither. Either of herself or at the instance of the said men she often came to the meetings of the party and maintained that it was right to send into exile" (*ammonire*, admonish, or rather, proscribe, the technical term for to banish) "so that the war might thereby be ended. Those who belonged to the party regarded her as a prophetess, others thought that she was a hypocrite and a bad woman." [8]

Catherine came to Florence shortly before Saint Lucy's day,

December 13th, and she had not forgotten the love of her earliest youth for this saint. It was on the eve of her feast that once in Siena she had seen the heavens open and heard the angels sing in honour of Saint Lucy, and in the midst of the choir of holy virgins stood the saint herself, fair and pure above them all, and on her breast she wore a precious jewel of enamel and gold . . . Tommaso della Fonte knew about this vision and had written it down in his records; she therefore wrote to him now, after long silence, and told him of what she had again experienced on a feast of Saint Lucy. "On her feast day she permitted me to taste the fruit of her martyrdom, and in my longing I was carried to the table of the Lamb, and He said to me, miserable creature that I am, 'I am the table and I am the food upon it!' And the hand of the Holy Spirit gave me to eat . . . And I saw therein so much truth that my soul now confesses that I have never loved God . . . And I felt such a new grace in my soul that my tongue is not able to utter it. Woe, woe, I will say no more, but I pray to that sweetest *Luce*, that she will soon lead us to be rent asunder and slain for the cause of the truth. Marvel not, Father, that I can not have enough of sacrificing myself." [4]

Urged on by this impulse, Catherine came to the meeting of the Guelphic party. Its leaders were well aware of the value that Catherine's name held for them, and that in its shelter they could satisfy their own private revenge, for the "halfdozen" men mentioned by Soderini to Raymond of Capua were not the only ones to become the victims of Guelphic ostracism. Catherine's sense of justice, usually so wakeful, seems to have slumbered on this occasion.

That which interested her was that the Florentines, as the first overture to peace with the Papal State, had begun to keep the interdict. In a letter of this time to her friend, William Flete in Lecceto, she says, "Let us hope that God will have mercy upon the world and upon His sweet Bride and will disperse the darkness from the minds of men. And it seems to me that the dawn is coming, for Our Saviour has enlightened this people, so that they do not offend God any more by compelling the priests to celebrate the sacred mysteries.

THE CROWN OF THORNS

But by the grace of God they keep the interdict and are beginning to show obedience to their Father." In similar terms she writes to Alessia: "The dawn has come, the darkness is gone, which arose from all the mortal sins that were committed at the public service . . . and the interdict is kept. Thanks, thanks be to Our Saviour, who despises not the humble prayer and the tears of His servants and burning desires . . . Therefore up! Sleep no more! . . . Let prayers be said in the convents and tell our Prioress" (of the Mantellate in Siena), "to let all the Sisters pray especially for peace, so that God may have mercy upon us, and that I may not return to Siena without peace having been concluded." [5]

During her sojourn in Florence Catherine found, as everywhere and always, new disciples; thus Giannozzo Sacchetti, a converted minstrel (whose pious Lauds were sung at the religious meetings which had to compensate for the church services during the interdict), and the lovable Barduccio, the youngest son of Piero Canigiani, who during these last years of Catherine's life became what Stefano Maconi had been earlier — the favourite disciple, the secretary who accompanied her everywhere, the Benjamin of her mother heart, as Stefano had been her Joseph. . .

Meanwhile politics went on as usual, and after much going to and fro a meeting between the representatives of the belligerents was at last fixed, and Sarzana chosen as the place of meeting. Three French cardinals represented the Pope; Florence sent five envoys; Venice, Naples, France were represented by ambassadors; Bernabò Visconti and Otto of Brunswick came in person. Then Gregory XI suddenly died on March 27th, 1378 — the Florentine chronicle asserts that at the same hour there was a knock at Porta San Frediano and a voice was heard to cry: "Open quickly to him who comes with peace!" For the present, however, the death of the Pope brought new strife. The congress at Sarzana was dispersed without a result, and in Rome a new Pope was elected (April 8th), Urban VI, under whom the great schism was to break out.[6]

It is not intended to relate here the story of the schism. It is well known that the election by which the Neapolitan, Bartolommeo Prignano, hitherto Archbishop of Bari, was placed in the Chair of Peter, was made under great pressure on the part of the Roman people. The conclave met late in the afternoon of April 7th, and the cardinals in their cells heard the threatening shouts of the assembled crowds in Saint Peter's Square: *Romano lo volemo!* "We want a Roman!" During the night some of the mob broke into the cellars of the Vatican "to drink of the good papal wine"; another part of the mob rushed to the belfry and began to ring the tocsin, which ringing was answered from the Capitol. The night was full of sinister forebodings and the cardinals, shut up in their cells, had no knowledge of what was happening in the town outside. At the suggestion of the Spaniard, Pedro de Luna, the Archbishop of Bari, who was present in Rome, was elected — it was a kind of compromise at least to elect an Italian — and the election was carried by thirteen votes out of sixteen. The rebellion of the people in the square outside, however, had reached such a pitch of fury that the cardinals dared not announce the result of the election. In order to save their lives they now had recourse to the ruse of clothing old Cardinal Tebaldeschi, who was a Roman, in the papal robes and presenting him as the newly elected Pope. In spite of the old man's loud protests, this farce was performed; the bells rang *a gloria,* a *Te Deum* was sung, after which the cardinals fled with all haste from the Vatican. Not till the next day was Bartolommeo informed that it was he and not Tebaldeschi who had been elected. The Romans contented themselves with at least not getting a Frenchman. On Easter Day, April 18th, Urban was crowned and rode in solemn procession on the traditional ride on a white steed to the Lateran.

The new Pope was in every respect a contrast to Gregory XI. If the latter had been vague and hesitating, Urban was strong and stern. One of the first tasks that faced him was to set a limit to the luxury displayed by the cardinals; next he sent home all the bishops who preferred staying in Rome to looking after their dioceses, and introduced a number of other reforms of a similar kind to those of Pius X of later times. In character he was violent and hasty; he would sometimes

THE CROWN OF THORNS

say "Hold your tongue" to the cardinals or make use of such words of abuse as *pazzo* and *ribaldo* to them. A sermon which he preached on the text, "I am the good shepherd," was nothing but a long attack on the exalted ecclesiastics. He was kind to the poor, but the clerical nobility did not find that it was received with the consideration to which it was accustomed. The Prior of the Carthusian monastery at Gorgona wrote in a letter to Catherine: "From what is being said, this new Holy Father is a terrible man and he fills people with terror by his manner and his words. He seems to have great confidence in God and therefore fears no one, and it is evident that he is striving to root out the simony and the craze for splendour prevailing in the Church of God." [7]

During the months of May and June, however, no open opposition had arisen against the new, strict Pope. The college of cardinals in a common letter inform the six cardinals still remaining in Avignon of the election of Urban, and also write to the Emperor and other Catholic sovereigns. But after the arrival of the prominent French cardinal, Jean de la Grange, in Rome, the resistance against Urban obtains a leader and an organiser. Jean de la Grange prevents the Castel Sant' Angelo, which had been occupied since Gregory's death by Pierre de Cros, brother of the cardinal of Limoges, from opening its gates to the new Pope. When the heat of summer came all the dissatisfied members of the Sacred College left Rome, and assembled, thirteen in number, out at Anagni.

In vain did Urban, who at last suspected mischief, send out the three Italian cardinals Orsini, Brossano and Corsini in a deputation. The Pope's delegates had to return without having achieved their object, and in August the Frenchmen send Urban a letter in which they call him "Bishop of Bari," and assert that they elected him under the influence of fear and therefore invalidly. This communication was followed by a document, the so-called *Declaratio,* in which they go over the events of April 8th and declare that they only elected Prignano to satisfy the Roman people and to avoid certain death. In consequence of this the thirteen cardinals (August 9th) excommunicate Urban as an unlawful Pope and place themselves under the protection of Count Onorato Gaetani of Fondi, who had been mortally insulted by Urban.*

While all this was happening Catherine was still in Florence. The election of Urban to the papal throne had not brightened the prospect of those efforts for peace to which she had devoted her strength. The Prior of Gorgona, who had his information from Pietro Gambacorti's son Andrea, who had newly come home to Pisa from Rome, wrote, on the contrary, in the letter quoted above: "Our Holy Father says everywhere that he desires peace, but a peace honourable to the Church, that he does not care about money and that if the Florentines want peace they must come to him with the truth, without any suspicion of lies. And from what he says he will not be satisfied with that which Pope Gregory wanted, for which cause there is no hope of peace, but rather may we look for a great war."

In Florence a "great war" was expected and it soon broke out, for the Guelphs continued their ostracism and at last they dared to strike Giovanni Dini, one of the Eight of War, and two other very influential men. A new Signoria was elected in May, and Salvestro di Medici held office in it as Gonfaloniere della Giustizia. This prominent Guelph endeavoured to stop his partisans in their arbitrary course and obtained a promise that no one should be "admonished," unless he was a notorious Ghibelline, and that when an "admonition" had not been carried after being put three times to the vote it was to be regarded as void. This promise was broken a few weeks later when the captains of the Guelphs had a vote tried twenty-two times within closed doors, until they succeeded in getting two of Salvestro's adherents "admonished."

This led to civil war. Salvestro di Medici stirred up the people against his fellow officials and partisans. The guilds assembled in the Piazza Signoria on June 22nd, armed and with their banners, and set out on a train of revenge and plunder in the town to the palaces of prominent Guelphs. Palazzo Strozzi was plundered at Porta Rossa, at San Piero Maggiore Palazzo

---

* He had been the Pope's vicegerent in the Campagna and in the town of Anagni; Urban had deprived him of both dignities and entrusted them to his bitterest enemy, Tommaso Santa Severina.

Albizzi. With the cry *Viva il Popolo!* the rebels then crossed Ponte Vecchio to the left bank of the Arno. They reached the little Piazza Santa Felicità where the column stands commemorating the sermon of Peter Martyr in Florence against the Patarenes — and then they remembered the Dominican nun. "Down with the hypocrite Niccolò and his Santa Caterina!" they roared. Up and down the narrow Costa S. Giorgio they went, between tall stone façades and walls, down which hung the foliage of the gardens inside. "Where is the witch?" they shouted. "If we find her she shall be burnt, or we will tear her in little pieces!"

They found her. She was out in the little garden belonging to the house and which to this day climbs up the hill in terraces; you look out across Florence, you see Giotto's campanile and Santa Maria Novella. Here they found her, surrounded by the Mantellate and in the midst of her circle of friends; Neri was there and Barduccio and Ser Cristofano di Gano. Together they looked out across the town, which to Catherine seemed "as though overshadowed by swarms of devils." Wildly shrieking the crowd rushed in, and like her Lord and Master in Gethsemane Catherine went to meet them, bravely and alone. "My eternal Spouse played me a great trick," Catherine says in her letter to Raymond about what occurred. "And well may I weep because my transgressions are so many, that I do not deserve to shed my blood and thereby grant light to blinded souls and reconcile the sons" (Italy) "with the Father" (the Pope) "and with my blood place a stone in the mystical body of Holy Church. For it was as though the hands were bound on him who would strike. And I said: 'It is I. Take me but let these go!' But these words were like knives that went through his heart. Oh, my Father, feel in yourself a wondrous joy, for never have I with such great joy felt such mysteries. It was the sweetness of truth that I tasted, it was the gaiety of a pure and good conscience, it was the fragrance of God's gentle providence; it was the new age that has dawned, the age of the martyrs which (as you know) has been foretold by the Eternal Truth. No tongue can utter the sweetness that my soul felt. And I think that I am so deeply in debt to my Creator, that even though I gave my body to be burned

I could not fully repay the great grace which I and my beloved sons and daughters have received.

"I do not tell you all this to make you grieve, but that you may rejoice and be glad, and that you and I together may begin to mourn over my imperfection, for because of my sins nothing came of so great a good. How blessed would have been my soul if I had been vouchsafed to shed my blood for the sweet Bride and for love of the blood and for the salvation of souls!

"I will say no more of this thing. Cristofano can tell you of this and other matters. Only this will I say, that you beseech Christ on earth, that he will not hesitate because of this to conclude peace, but that he will do it very quickly, so that he can begin to work the other great things he has to do for the glory of God and the reformation of the Church . . . Entreat him to act soon; beg him to do it for the sake of mercy, for the countless offences against God can thus be removed. Tell him that he must have compassion and pity on these souls, who live in much darkness, and tell him that he bring me out of prison soon, for it seems as though I cannot go away until peace is concluded; and I desire greatly to go to Rome to taste the blood of the martyrs and see His Holiness and to see you again and tell you of the wondrous things that God has worked in these times — all in the gaiety of the mind, in the joy of the heart, in new hope and in the light of holy faith." [8]

This was Catherine's own account of that moment when she was nearer than ever to reaching the highest goal of her desires, of becoming like Saint Lucy, "who full of love and in a manly spirit went forth to offer up her body" and on whose feast in the previous December Catherine had prayed for the grace of being "slain for our sweet Saviour." On the basis of Cristofano di Gano Guidini's account, Raymond has given a more detailed description in his biography of that dramatic moment and then adds: "But although that rebellion subsided, the holy virgin and her companions were not safe on that account, and so great was the fear in all the inhabitants of the city, that no one dared to receive her in his house . . . until at length they found a worthy and God-fearing man, who without dread took her into his house, although secretly, because of the people and the rebels. And after some days *Mamma*, as well as her spiritual sons and daughters went outside the town, though not outside its territory; and went to a lonely place where hermits used to live." [9]

The "worthy and God-fearing man" mentioned here by Raymond, who gave Catherine shelter at a critical moment, was no doubt the tailor, Francesco di Pippino, in whose humble dwelling in the corn market Catherine would be well hidden. The "lonely place" was probably Vallombrosa.

Out there in the Casentino valley she again lived for a while the convent life that was so dear to her, and there she breathed the strong, crisp air of the High Apennines and the healthy peace of the mountain forests. Devoutly she would stand by the giant beech, said to have been planted by Saint John Gualbertus, the saint of peace, who was reconciled to the murderer of his brother on a Good Friday, and to whom the Crucified by the wayside bent His head in approval. And assuredly she would often look across towards La Verna, the mountain on which Saint Francis a century and a half earlier "received the last seals of Christ." . . .

But soon she is back in Florence where peaceful conditions reigned again. From there she wrote her first letter to Urban, whose personal acquaintance she had made, though only slightly, in Avignon, while he was still only bishop of Acerenza.

At first she preaches her usual stern gospel. "Only he," she says, "is grounded in love, who is ready to die for Him and for the salvation of souls, for such an one no longer loves himself. But he who loves himself is not ready to give his life; nay, he cannot bear the least unpleasantness, for he is always afraid to lose his life and its comforts. Therefore everything that he does is done imperfectly and badly, because at heart his feelings are corrupt, and it is through feelings that one acts."

There is, then, no perfect performance of duty without perfect self-denial. He who fears the displeasure of others will always be inclined to reduce his demands or make a compromise, or, as Catherine says in her forcible and illustrative language: "put ointment on the sore instead of burning it out." And the depravities of the time are of such a kind that only a red hot iron can heal them. On the basis of experiences at Avignon, Catherine outlines a gloomy picture of the decay of the Church and especially of the vices of the clergy. "They behave like drovers, they throw dice with their anointed hands, they sell the blood of Christ and spend the money on the children of their concubines." The servants of God look at all this with loathing and horror — they are like to die of the pain of it — and yet they cannot die. Now, therefore, they put their hope in Urban, they expect of him that he will surround himself with a brigade of holy men who do not fear death. . .

Next the Sienese saint pleads earnestly for the Florentines. "Forgive them, *Babbo mio,*" she says, "and you will see that they will prove themselves better sons than all the others. And I greatly desire to leave . . . Show me the grace, me, a wretched and miserable creature, who comes and knocks at your door. . . Then, when peace has been concluded, raise the banner of the Holy Cross against the infidels." [10]

This letter reached Urban at Tivoli, where he sat alone with his four Italian cardinals, while the opposition was holding a council at Anagni. And now he delayed no longer in concluding peace. On Sunday afternoon, July 18th, the Pope's messenger rode into Florence carrying an olive branch in his hand, and soon the news was all over the town: "The olive branch has come! Peace has come!" The great bell rang from Palazzo Vecchio and the olive branch was fastened beneath one of the windows of the Town Hall so that everyone could see it. The square was crowded with jubilant people, the Priors came out on the balcony and had the papal document read aloud, and in the evening the town was illuminated. Filled with joy Catherine wrote the same evening to Sano di Maco and the other disciples in Siena: "Oh, dearest children, the lame walk, the deaf hear, the blind see and the dumb speak and shout with a loud voice: 'Peace, peace, peace!' " Inside the letter she lays a leaf of the blessed olive branch.[11]

This peace too, though, was but short-lived — like *all* peace in the Middle Ages. Only two days later, on Tuesday morning, the 20th July, the terrible labour revolution, known as the *tumulto dei Ciompi,* broke out. It was, to use a modern expression, the unorganised workers, who had no political rights in Florence, who now suddenly rose and marched through the town, burning and plundering. The anarchy lasted three days and all who could fled from Florence, the Palazzo Vecchio was at the mercy of the rabble. Until at last the wool carder, Michele di Lando, again restored the town to peace and order with dictatorial authority.

Then, on July 28th, peace was signed between the republic and the Pope. The Florentines were to pay a fine of 250,000 gold guilders, repeal all laws hostile to the Church and restore the property of which the Church and the religious houses had been robbed. In return the interdict was raised (on October 23rd) and the Bishop of Volterra, together with the Franciscan, Francesco da Orvieto, received papal authority to loose the town from the ban of excommunication.[12]

Meanwhile, before this Catherine had already gone home to Siena. She left Florence on August 2nd. What her feelings were can be learned from the letter which she wrote, after coming home, to the Priors and Gonfaloniere di Giustizia of the town, and in which she says:

"It was my intention to visit you and together with you to celebrate the feast of the holy peace for which I have laboured so long . . . and then I wished to return to Siena. It seems now, that the devil has sown so much unjust hatred against me, that I have not wished to be the cause of new injustice . . . By the grace of God I have therefore departed . . . comforted because I have worked that which I had set out to do when I came to your city, that is, not to leave it until I saw you like good children at peace with your Father, even though it should cost me my life." [13]

VIII

Catherine came back to her native town during the first days of August, to rest a short while after the period of rude trial in Florence. She accompanied her sister-in-law after the flesh, but her sister after the spirit, to spend the warm summer time at the farm, La Canonica, belonging to the latter at San Rocco a Pilli. In order to get there you leave Siena by the Porta San Marco, pass over the ridge of hills on which are situated Santa Bonda and the ancient abbey of Sant' Eugenio, go through the little town of Costalpino and then turn to the left, out to La Montagnuola, the low chain of mountains which separates the country about Siena from the Tuscan Maremma. You pass small churches with old, Romanesque façades — a castle-like villa behind black cypresses like a Böcklin picture looks threateningly down from a height — and all the while you have wide views across green vine and silvery grey olive country to the gentle double undulation of Mont' Amiata in the bluish hazy distance. Nothing is now left of Lisa Benincasa's farm; a new and modern *fattoria* stands on the site. But in the wall out to the road there is a majolica bust of Catherine, with a green wreath about the brown locks, and below it can be read these lines:

> *Santa Caterina da Siena vergine*
> *Tu che questo suolo un giorno*
> *Possedendo calcasti, ora dal cielo*
> *Rendilo pur di ogni dovizia adorno.*

In English: "Catherine of Siena, holy virgin, you who once as owner walked on this soil, work now from heaven that it may be adorned with the gifts of God."

It is doubtful whether Catherine walked about out here with particular feelings of ownership; in any case we know of quite different things that occupied her mind during her sojourn at San Rocco. Caffarini relates that she was ill for a day and a night with the usual pain. In the morning she dragged herself up to the church standing on a hill at the other end of the town, rather far from La Canonica. She stopped, though, outside the church door, overwhelmed with the deep feeling of guilt that was the bitterest torment of her soul. Again the thought assailed her that all the evil that came to pass in the world, and especially the threatening schism, which she could not doubt would come, was all *her* fault. She had not done her duty; she ought to have spoken far better, written far more and far more forcibly, above all prayed more earnestly and more ardently. She had not thrown enough suffering and tears and self-denials into the scales of God's justice, and behold, now the other side, the scales of darkness, was growing the heaviest, and the devil laughed, the devil mocked at her crucified Lord! Overwhelmed with pain Catherine collapsed on the stone flags outside the green-painted church door. "Lord," she moaned, "I am not worthy to enter under thy roof, I am not worthy to receive thy holy body with my useless lips and upon my tongue which has not pleaded thy cause. *"Io miserabile, cagion d'ogni male! Peccavi, Domine, miserere mei!"*

Now as she was thus bending lower and lower she suddenly felt as if she were being bathed in fire, as if flames were sweeping over her, or was it burning blood? And purified in the flames she went into the church, up to the altar and received the body of Christ.[1]

It may have been on that day that she wrote to Monna Ludovica di Granello the letter dated August 27th, 1378, in which she says: "You ask me how and where you are to find the love that is so needful and likewise so blithesome. I answer you in few words: Love is gained only with love. But neither can it be found without light, for if we walk without light we seek for love where it is not and thus we walk in darkness. It is therefore needful that we remove that which takes the light from us, and that is self-love, which is a cloud that prevents us from seeing what we ought in truth to love. Self-love is the cloud that makes us love in darkness and outside God, not with reasonable but with sensual love. It is good to drive away that cloud, and to disperse it with displeasure and hatred of that law of the flesh, which is always warring against the spirit and leading to this wrongful and inordinate love. When the eye of reason is clear and sees by the light of faith, it looks upon nothing but that unutterable love which God has vouchsafed to us by the Incarnate Word, and it sees how that sweet and loving Lamb without blemish has shown us His love by His blood. In that blood the soul is inebriated, for it sees with what fire of love it was shed. In that blood the soul knows eternal life, and sees how God, to lead us to the end for which He has created us and to consummate His truth in the soul, permits the world and the devil and the unruly flesh to torment us, only so that our feelings may not seek their end in the world or in our senses, but that they may rise above the dark thorns of this world, above the joys that perish and are like prickling thorns and that rush along like the wind." [2]

Gradually, as Catherine's life draws towards its close, those fundamental feelings, which were also her fundamental thoughts (because her whole existence was founded on experience) grow more and more marked. Another month yet and her philosophy is finally and decisively expressed in her book — which she and her disciples simply called *Il Libro* — the book which was her spiritual testament. Strange it is to see how the virgin who had vowed herself to God, who had never lived in the world, has so profound a knowledge of what that world is, and is able to express it so clearly. Only the perfectly truthful soul is able to do this, and it shows the deep kinship between holiness and genius: they are both grounded on the pure love of truth. And being a poet and a saint Catherine says what all poets and all ascetics have always confessed and preached: *Tutto passa*. The petals of the roses fall and only the sharp thorns remain. And more than that: even the beauty of the roses is like a sting, smarting in the soul and poisoning it and filling it with gloomy unrest. To this day the peasant sings among the trailing vines about San Rocco a Pilli as he sang in Catherine's time:

> *Amore, amor! Perchè si loda l'amore!,*
> *L'è una catena che non ha mai fine*
> *l'è una carcere oscura e una prigione.*

"All speak of love. All sing the praises of love. Why? It is an unending chain, it is a prison cell, a gloomy prison."

Catherine sang too, when she walked, hurriedly as always, the long way from Siena to San Rocco, singing in her clear voice (Caffarini writes), so that the Sisters who accompanied her wondered and thought she had become quite another person. But she did not sing melancholy *stornelli* of the pain and pining of earthly love; she sang hymns and *laudes,* psalms and spiritual canticles. As a frequent visitor to Santa Bonda she could not help knowing Colombini's songs and to know them is to love them. Like his disciples, the Gésuati, she would also sing: "Beloved Jesus Christ, he that truly loves thee, the more thou dwellest in his heart, the greater is his longing for thee — ever does he gaze upon thee and never enough. For love of thee I wander through the world singing and rejoicing!" [3]

> *Diletto Giesù Cristo, chi ben t'ama*
> *avendoti nel core sì ti brama,*
> *te sempre contemplando non si sfama:*
> *cantare e giubilar vo' per tuo amore.*[3]

William Flete remembers that Catherine often sang a song beginning: "The bride of God have I become, the bride of God, for maid am I." She sang this in Latin, but in Italian that song of exultation which she had composed herself: [4]

> *Angeluzzo piccolino*
> *che in Belleem è nato*
> *non ti paia così fantino*
> *ch'è gle re incoronato.*[4]

> *Little darling angel-child*
> *who art born in Bethlehem,*
> *here on earth thou art a child,*
> *but in heaven a crownèd king.*

Like Francis of Assisi, Catherine was a wandering minstrel of God; she was, like him, a poet, but had a greater, richer and more varied mind, and a deeper, less naïve spirit. She possessed especially the chief poetic gift, the gift of creating the perfect image, the parable which expresses exactly that which has to be expressed, neither on one side or the other of the truth, like a chemical or mathematical formula, in a way that is perceptible to the senses.

Her letters abound in such images, those already given contain more than one example of them (e.g. the great parable about Christ as the knight in armour, in the letter to the prisoners in Siena). Her comparisons are often humorous, as when she calls the breviary the priest's wife, because he always walks with it under his arm. Of temptations she says that they are like flies in the kitchen, they do not go near the pot that is boiling. She makes a beautiful comparison of the heart with a lamp: it is narrow below, wide above, narrow in egoism, but wide open to God, and the oil which keeps the lamp alight is humility, patience, meekness. Nourished by this oil the lamp diffuses the light of self-knowledge in the soul, but the hand that must hold it is the fear of God. Virtue is likened to a flower, but when flowers stand too long in water they stink instead of being fragrant, and so it is with the virtue that wants to live amid worldliness. The soul is like a city or a castle; the watch-dog, conscience, keeps guard at the gate and barks at the approach of an enemy. What is the food and drink of this dog? It drinks blood and eats fire, the blood of Christ and the fire of the Holy Spirit. Catherine has a whole series of images of the blood of Christ — the bath in the blood kills the vermin in the soul — the blood gives fresh colour to Adam's pale face, the blood wells up from the side of Christ like a spring, or it is sold in the tavern of the Church, standing on the middle of the bridge leading to heaven. This wound in the side of Christ is always open too — or it is a cell into which the soul withdraws and finds the knowledge of God and of itself. To Catherine as to Angela of Foligno and Henry Suso the crucifix is the book of life, the great book, lying wide open, in which all can read the love of God and the horror of sin, and in that book the five blood-red wounds of Christ are the red initials. The Cross is our staff on the road to heaven, but it is also (grotesquely) the roasting-spit on which the Paschal Lamb of the New Covenant was roasted at the fire of suffering; or it is the charger on which Christ, the noble knight, rode out to fight against the old enemy. Jesus is a lovely rose which bore fruit on the Cross, and the three nails become the keys to heaven.* The body of Christ is a cask of wine, it was tasted at the circumcision, but at the crucifixion it was broached when Longinus pierced it with his lance. At the circumcision a ring was taken from the flesh of Christ, and with that ring God betrothed himself to man. In Christ God descended upon earth as a chariot of fire, for God is fire and loads the ship of the soul with a cargo of fire and blood. To that sacred fire the city of the soul must surrender and perish in its purifying flames.

The soul is a city — or a garden — or a vineyard. The *city* has three gates, the three faculties of the soul, and the gate of the will alone is wholly in our power for it is guarded by freedom (*libero arbitrio*). No devil and no other creature can open that gate without the consent of the guard, and so long as it has not been taken the soul has not been conquered. Moreover, the watch-dog, conscience, lies outside and with its barking it rouses slumbering reason. In the *garden* or the orchard the gardener is the free will; like a good gardener he sets to work turning over the soil of the feelings, pulling up the weeds and thorns and planting good, fragrant herbs. Round the *vineyard* there is a wall, and in the wall only one gate, that of the will, and in the midst of the vineyard the heart is like a well. How hideous many souls are, they are neglected and they resemble most of all a wood that is full of poisonous weeds, of the thorns of pride and the wild growth of anger and impatience, and the fruits they yield are so bitter that no one can eat them. Then the vineyard has run wild, the garden is a wilderness and a stable for unclean animals.

These images of Catherine's often seem far-fetched, as in the constantly recurring comparison between Christ Crucified and the roasted Lamb, or when she says that "one must have the teeth of patience in the mouth of longing." Often, though, they are profound and delicate, as, when alluding to the Pauline text, that on the Cross the indictment against sinful humanity was nailed to it for ever: "And the indictment was written on

---

* The Italian text contains a play upon the words *chiovi* (nails) and (*chiavi*) keys — which cannot be rendered in English. The nearest rendering is to be found in the French, *clous, clefs*. Tr.

lambskin." Heretics interpret the Apocalypse and other difficult books in their own way, "but the eternal truths," says Catherine, "are like the stars, they can best be seen from the depths of the well of humility." They who "are always learning and never come to a knowledge of the truth" are described by her as "leaves turning with the wind," an expression which she shortens, so that at length she simply describes people of that kind as *uomini da vento* — "men of wind." The love that bursts into flame in the Master's presence, like Simon Peter's, making great promises, is often but a fire in straw, quenched by the first shower of rain, "and nothing but black smoke is left." So is it with straw and dry wood, but when the green wood — which is the strong, convinced mind — takes fire, it weeps tears of devotion, such as one may see in the evening on the hearth, when fresh firewood has been used.

As many of these expressions show, Catherine was well versed in Holy Scripture. She read it in Latin, as may be seen from Caffarini's letter, in which he explains to her the difference between the two words *ablattatus* (weaned from the mother's milk) and *adlattatus,* which he interprets as the believer who absorbs the grace of God as the nursling does the mother's milk. She read the Scriptures, in the form in which the Church gives them into the hands of her children, that is, in the Missal or the Breviary. The above-named place (in which, by the way, the correct reading is *ablactatus*) is, for instance, from the 130th Psalm in the Vulgate and occurs among the psalms for Vespers on Wednesdays. Catherine was familiar with the New Testament through the Epistles and Gospels for Sundays and holy days; Caffarini refers in the same letter to the parable about the wise and foolish virgins, "such as you know them from the Gospel on the feasts of confessors and virgins."

She often quotes the words of Our Lord Himself: "He that shall humble himself shall be exalted," "to have faith as a grain of mustard-seed," "And I, if I be lifted up from the earth, will draw all things to myself," "in my Father's house there are many mansions," ". . . my Father will love him, and we will come to him, and will make our abode with him." She is acquainted with the saying about the narrow gate, with the testimony of Jesus about Himself as the Way, the light of the world, as the water for thirsting souls. She hears His cry of woe over Jerusalem. She knows the parables: of the cockle in the wheat, of the wicked servant, of the great supper; "the parable of the buried talent," "hidden in the ground," i.e. coveting earthly things, is her ingenious interpretation; she is glad to remember the gentleness of the Saviour towards Zachæus and the Canaanite woman. She knows that the blind cannot lead the blind; and she knows how the true disciples of Jesus can be recognised. One saying of Jesus had made a deep impression upon her: "No man putting his hand to the plough, and looking back, is fit for the kingdom of God." This saying sounds like another one that was also dear to Catherine: "Let the dead bury their dead." It is a judgment upon all sentimentalism, upon all morbid brooding over the past, over a longing for a time that is gone, which was a time of sin and sorrow, but which one loves because it was one's own — "my own life in evil and good, my own life in nothing but this," the poet sings in false and beautiful verse (Ernest Hello has written a chapter about it that cuts into the very bone and marrow — *laissez les morts ensevelir leurs morts*). Not to linger among the dead, not to long for the world of shadows, not to look back, but bravely to put one's hand to the plough and guide its iron-sheathed edge on through the golden-brown soil in the morning sun, under the dewy wet foliage of the olive trees — that was Catherine's ideal, duty, life. It recurs, therefore, again and again in her letters: "do not stand still, do not turn back, do not leave hold of the plough," or, as she finally shapes it (and those who have seen an Italian workman stand contemplating his tools thoughtfully and undecidedly will understand her): "Do not turn your head to look back at the plough!"

In this determination to advance she feels her kinship with Saint Paul, the vessel of election, and the vessel "full of fire" (like the thurible before the altar), Paul who was in love with Jesus, Paul, the standard bearer (but the standard is the Cross), he who has taught her that a Christian's life is a *palio*, a race that has to be run — *Paoluccio* "my little Paul," as she calls him, intimately and affectionately. In him she finds salvation for her soul, "for he sees himself in the eye of God as in a mirror," from him she learns to put off Adam and to put on Christ, to be conformed to Christ, to glory in nothing but the Cross; like him she knows that the sufferings of this present time are not to be compared to the glory that is to come; with him she rejoices because nothing shall separate her from her Lord, neither hunger nor thirst, nor persecution, neither fire nor sword, neither things present nor things to come, neither angel nor devil, "if only I will it not myself."

Catherine mentions but few of the Fathers of the Church: *Agustino* (as she generally writes it), Jerome, Gregory the Great, as a rare instance Saint Bernard of Clairvaux. She mentions Thomas Aquinas, the great Dominican philosopher (she had seen him sitting in the seat of honour on Taddeo Gaddi's fresco in the *Cappella degli Spagnuoli* in Florence — even Moses and David, Paul and John, had to make room for him). It is certain, though, that she can never have read him, the similarities to be found between her and him depend on the identity of their fundamental thoughts. Saint Thomas says: "Men apprehend things in different ways, according to the disposition of their souls. He whose soul is just sees them as they really are; he whose soul is turned to error, sees them in confusion and falsely." This, as will be shown below, is Catherine's entire doctrine about the ethical basis of knowledge, of the knowledge of the truth as a function of conscience. "Everyone apprehends according to his capacity," she says in the *Dialogue*, and by capacity (*capacità*) she means the moral disposition, the pure, unalloyed will to the truth. But this does not by any means signify that she has studied the *Summa* of Aquinas.

Did Catherine know Dante? In the year after her death one of her less intimate disciples, Bonagiunta di Grazia, wrote a letter to Neri di Landoccio — who was then in Siena in his father's house near Porta San Maurizio — in which these words occur: "If you can send me that piece of Dante's (*quello pezo del Dante*) which I left behind, I shall be very grateful to you if you will do so." Neri dei Pagliaresi was, as we know, a poet, and from the letter it is seen that he had borrowed from the other some poem or other of Dante, a canto of the *Divnina Commedia* or the *Vita Nuova*. It is also probable that the

THE CROWN OF THORNS

verses of the great Florentine would be read aloud in the circle around Catherine. To this day it is a delight to hear the youth of Tuscany recite long "pieces of Dante": *Vergine madre, figlia del tuo figlio, umile ed alta più che creatura, termine fisso d'eterno consiglio* — etc., etc., for half hours at a time.

It is possible, and also probable that a single memory, some apt image or other, may have clung to Catherine's mind and slipped into her pen later when she was writing. There is, for instance, the parable about the fresh wood which sheds tears when put on the fire; it occurs in both of them, but the Sienese saint had seen that sight so often that she would not need to obtain the image from anyone else.[5]

For Catherine was a poet on her own account. She who heard the ravens cry: *cras, cras!* "Tomorrow, tomorrow!"— like the lazy, she who saw the key to heaven, rusty with sin, become clean and shining in the blood of Christ and knew that one must bend one's head humbly to enter in at that gate — she possessed wealth enough in her own imagination. The soul is a tree, *un arbore d'amore,* a tree of love. "Oh, dearest daughter," she exclaims in a letter, "do you not see that we are a tree of love, for it is love that has created us? God has given this tree a gardener to tend it, that is, free will. And the tree has the gift of reason so that it can use the free will, and it has the eye of understanding which knows and sees the truth, if only it is not hidden by the mist of self-love. By that light the soul sees where the tree should be planted; for if it did not see it and had not the sweet gift of reason the gardener could excuse himself and say: 'It is true that I was free, but I could not see where I ought to plant my tree, high up or low down.' But this he cannot say for he has intelligence (*intelletto*) which sees, and reason (*ragione*) which binds the soul to love of the right, and by which the tree can be grafted on the tree of life, Christ sweet Jesus. The will must therefore plant its tree in that soil which it has seen and perceived with the eye of understanding will make it grow and bring forth the fruit of life, Dearest daughter, if then the gardener, free-will, plants the tree where it should be planted, that is, in the valley of true obedience and not on the mountain of pride, it will bear the fragrant flowers of the virtues and above all, the most beautiful of all the flowers, the glory of the name of God. God keeps that flower for Himself but He wills that the fruits should be for us, for He has no need of our fruits. He is He who is, whilst we are those who are not, and it is we, therefore, who are in need. We do not exist for ourselves but for Him, for He has given us our being and every other grace that is added thereto. . . . And because the highest and eternal goodness sees that man does not live on flowers, but only on fruits (for we should die of the flowers but we live on the fruit), He takes the flower for Himself and gives to us the fruit. And if the creature in its ignorance would nourish itself on flowers, that is: if it would take for itself the glory and praise that it ought to give to God, it loses the life of grace and dies the everlasting death. But when our tree is planted in the right place it grows until its top, which is the feeling of the heart, can not be seen any more by men, but has been united in love to the infinite God." [6]

In these lines the poet Catherine already makes way for the thinker, as indeed it is impossible to separate these two, and for the Sienese saint it was but natural for her to give her philosophy a poetic form. She was, in fact, preaching a philosophy which was entirely her own, derived altogether from the profound knowledge of humanity of her truthful and intrepid spirit.

The essence of the soul, Catherine teaches us, is *amor*, love or will. The will can go in two directions, outwards or inwards. The will goes out in love of creatures, of the world, of the flesh; it is "die falsche Minne," as Henry Suso said, selfishness, pleasure-loving self-love. The will goes inwards in love of God and one's neighbour, in self-denial, renunciation, self-sacrifice, and that is true love, that which alone has a right to this name. These two directions of will lead by two ways to two opposite worlds: one to egoism and unrest, darkness, passion, everlasting restless disquiet and impatience, in other words, to hell; while the fruits of true love are peace, light, joy; that is to say, heaven.

The choice between these two ways would be a foregone conclusion (for who does not want to be happy?) if man could see clearly and judge impartially. But as the will, *amor*, is the primordial faculty in man and the intellect only an instrument, the latter is dependent on the former. In other words: the recognition of truth is also an intellectual faculty. Here a dual psychological affinity asserts itself: the egoist feels an antipathy against truth, is in sympathy with illusion, and vice versa. Catherine expresses it in this way, that self-love (*amor proprio*) darkens the eye of the itellect like a cloud, so that the egoist, as such, is incapable of arriving at a knowledge of the truth. To separate the true from the false is for Catherine not a purely intellectual function, it is also dependent on the moral attitude and is impossible where certain ethical qualities are lacking. One knows what one deserves to know. *Corde intelligitur*.

As the mental attitude which is inaccessible to truth, egoism is the same as pride. Its opposite is humility, which removes the interior hindrances and inhibitions due to egoism and thus qualifies it to receive knowledge of the truth.

So long as man remains in the world of self-love he is unblessed, lost in the most literal sense, without happiness, without light, without joy. Salvation consists in passing from this dark, restless and tormented existence in which the worldly man lives, to life in truth, to that in which it is really worth living. This change of spirit becomes possible through experience, the bitter experience that everything is transient. *Tutto passa come il vento,* "everything rushes on, everything flies away." And *tanto si perde con dolore, quanto si possiede con amore,* "the more one has loved something, the greater is the pain of losing it."

This is really the weak spot in every outlook that takes only this world into account. Catherine therefore directs her logic to this vulnerable point when she wants to convert the lovers of this world. It all perishes, she cries to them, and what else have you in the end but a handful of withered leaves? If Catherine Benincasa had lived in the nineteenth century she would have agreed profoundly and cordially with her compatriot of a later date when he, crushed under "the vanity of everything," sang to his heart:

Non val cosa nessuna
i moti tuoi, nè di sospiri è degna

la terra. Amaro e noia
la vita, altro mai nulla; e fango è il mondo.* ⁷

To Catherine, as to Leopardi, life on this earth, regarded in itself and by itself, was nothing but "gloom and bitterness," "hideous," "dark and unclean, full of stench and filth." ⁸

But — and in this the saint of Siena differs from the poet of Recanati — this miserable life is not the sole prospect open to man. Beyond all this transitoriness there is something imperishable, ever green and incorruptible that she calls with predilection *la vita durabile,* the life that never ceases. To enter into that life only one thing is really needful: to turn round. Man's will must turn quite round and turn its back on the world. At the very instant that its glance is no longer blinded by the mists rising from the marshes of self, the eye of the intellect grows clear and the middle of that eye is what Catherine calls "the pupil of faith." The contrast between faith and knowledge is so non-existent to Catherine that she regards faith as simply the consummation of knowledge, as a natural consequence, as soon as the soul is no longer interested in denying. It is because of egoism that one does not believe. When egoism has been overcome faith makes its appearance quite naturally, because from being blind one has received sight. *Corde creditur.*

What, then, does the liberated soul see? Two things, Catherine answers. It sees itself and it sees God. It has entered into the cell of self-knowledge, which is also that of the knowledge of God. It is in "the double abyss" (as Angela of Foligno said). There it sees itself as *he who is not,* and God, as *He who is,* and from whom man derives his being. In other words, man recognises himself as a creature, which is the basis of all Christian philosophy. Not pantheistic, as part of a great whole, nor monistic, as part of a great nothingness, but simply as a creature that literally owes God everything. Creation, according to Catherine, is God's first benefaction, and that from which all others arise.

From this beneficent act of creation is derived above all the

---

* "There is nothing that is worth loving, this earth is not worth even a sigh. Life is bitter and loathsome; the world is filth." (Leopardi).

second great act of God: the redemption. Creation must arouse gratitude in us, the redemption calls for our love. The Cross is raised in the cell of self-knowledge; in the cell "we find the blood." The Incarnation, the Passion, the Death on the Cross, bear witness to the love of the eternal Being for His creatures. As He hangs upon the Cross He is held there not by the three nails but by the will of His own love, Christ, *il Pazzo d'amore*. He sheds His blood with fire, and in that blood man in his old state dies and the new man is born.

But the new life begins with a feeling which Catherine likes to compare with a two-edged knife, a dual feeling, of which one edge is love of the God that has saved us and of all that He loves, and the other is hatred of all that opposes God, and above all self, the flesh, the world. On the one hand is love of God, love of one's neighbour, zeal for souls; on the other, hatred of self, of the ego, of the world. This is the pruning-knife that must be used in the vineyard of the soul. Armed with this weapon man, the regenerated, takes a holy revenge upon the Adam, the son of the earth, that he was before. These two feelings sit like two angels in white garments at the grave of the man that was.

Now we cannot live without love. Asceticism, penance, is not enough. Fire can only be quenched with fire. Love of the world can only be overcome by a new and greater love of eternity. And when the choice has to be made between these two kinds of love, it is really impossible to understand that anyone can choose the inferior one. It is so easy to see from their fruits what both are worth. Self-love makes a man cruel, makes one impatient, makes one unbearable to oneself and others; it whimpers, is childish, always wants to be pitied, it is timid and shudders at the mere movement of a leaf, it clings to persons and to things and therefore lives in constant fear of losing them. It is like one unceasing and unendurable torment in the soul, nay, it is really the same as "the worm that dieth not and the fire that shall not be quenched." "This kind of love not only gives no strength, but takes away from us the strength we have, and so mean and wretched is it, that it leads man to the most complete slavery and makes him a servant and slave of that which in itself has no continuance, and robs him of his dignity and greatness." This is the love that gives death, this is the dark love that leads to sin, "for we can not love or see anything outside God, that does not bring us death; that which we love we must love in Him and for Him."

As the opposite of this *amor mortale, amor tenebroso,* Catherine places the true love which does not seek its own, but seeks the glory of God, which delivers man from human respect, rejuvenates and strengthens the soul, inspires us with dislike of ourselves, dislike of the world and love of the Cross. This true love clothes us in the will of God, for he who loves does not displease the Beloved; it chooses as its device: To God glory, to my neighbour love, to myself hatred and contempt. And thus the soul is filled with a foretaste of heaven. Take away self-will and you will be at peace. In the midst of trials we are secure, in the midst of dangers without fear. To be servants of God is to be masters. "He who believes is free, and is no longer the slave of his senses, which he has trodden under foot, despised and slain with the knife of hatred and love, that is to say, the hatred of vice and love of the good. In that sweet servitude the soul has become king and lord, for it has not sought itself for its own sake, but itself for God's sake . . . and its neighbour for God's sake, not for the sake of its own gain.[9]

"What tongue can express the peace of the believing soul? It is not that the waves of the sea and that storms do not reach it, but its will is at peace because it has become one with the sweet will of God. Therefore the storm is like calm to it, for it cares not for itself. It serves its Creator, whether He will that it shall be in war or in peace, and war and peace are both dear to it, for it sees with the light of faith that both come from one hand . . . And as the servants of God we shall rule in this world by grace and be lords over the world, the flesh and the devil; in freedom we are bound with the bonds of love, in patience and meekness, and with true and holy patience. But at last we shall rule in the life that never ends. . .

"Courage, dearest children, run in that race,* and whoever among you wins the prize, you have all won it, for your hearts are one. And so that you may run the better you must refresh

---

* *Palio.* An allusion to the great Sienese popular festivals on July 2d and August 16th.

yourselves, inebriate yourselves, in the blood of Christ. That blood demands of us that we should run for the prize of victory, and it makes us so full of courage that no one turns his head from fear of the enemy, for he trusts not in himself but in the blood of Christ Crucified." [10]

In a hymn of praise to the blood of Jesus, Catherine sums up all her philosophy. "With His blood He washed the face of our soul, with the blood which He shed with the fire of so great a love and with true patience He created us anew in grace; the blood covered our nakedness, for He clothed us with His grace; the warmth of the blood melted the ice and heated the tepidity of man; in the blood the darkness vanished and the light was born; in the blood self-love was consumed as surely as the soul which sees that it is beloved unto blood, ought to rise from its miserable self-love and love its Redeemer, who with the fire of so much love gave His life, and hastened to the ignominious death on the Cross. The blood has become drink for us and the flesh has become our meat if we but will; and in no other wise can the hunger of man be satisfied and the thirst of man can only be quenched in the blood. For even though man owned the whole world, he can not be satisfied with it, for the things that are in the world are less than he and cannot satisfy him. Only the blood can satisfy his hunger, for the blood is filled with the eternal divinity, the spirit whose nature is greater than the nature of man." [11]

The blood and the fire, those are the words in which Catherine finally concentrates her message to the world. Salvation is to drink the blood, to bathe in the blood and to perish in the fire. In the blood all selfish and worldly thoughts are melted away, all earthly or merely natural feelings. The fire consumes the dry wood of our self-will and the damp wood of our natural senses; it consumes everything in the soul that is not purely and entirely the "sweet will of God." In that fire we are hammered into likeness to Christ, until we are in perfect union with Him, in union with the fire, so that those words of Jesus, which are not to be found in the Gospels, but which Catherine knows that He has said, may be fulfilled: "I am the fire, you are the sparks!"

This is Christianity: "we lack so much of Jesus as we keep

of ourselves." There is no way to heaven except this: "to lose oneself," "to seek the glory of God, the salvation of souls, the peace of the nations." "And a miserable woman like me has been sent into the world for nothing else." [12]

IX

In the country round Siena there are many small churches and chapels. You see them sometimes in a field of olives, right in the middle of the golden-brown ploughed earth, the silvery grey foliage hanging over the simple façade; its two flat pillars at the corners, supporting a triangular front gable, remind one of an antique temple — a little heathen shrine, dedicated to the gods of the fields.

Or such a chapel may stand high, on the top of a rounded hill, its whitewashed walls glinting out between a close guard of broad, black cypresses; and if you sit down on the withered winter grass in the sunshine by the chapel wall you look far, far away, out across the country; you see farms with large, hive-shaped ricks around them; down in the valley a bridge across the river Tressa, and far away several little cypress-crowned hills. Furthest out the undulating and motionless desert land of the tawny Creta, and the atmospheric blue lines of Mont' Oliveto and Santa Fiora and Mont' Amiata.

Or you find such a chapel some afternoon when you have gone out for a walk and hear the bells ringing somewhere not too far away. Those little Italian bells, hanging so picturesquely in their belfry, and whose silvery voices can call with such wonderful urgency, so hurriedly and eagerly, as if it was at the eleventh hour — now, now, you must come! You walk along a road between walls, get a peep into gardens with fig-trees and medlars and olives, and under the trees there are beans and large-leafed pumpkins. Then a stone-paved, climbing road turns off at one side, that is the way up to the church where the bell is ringing. At the top of the hill there is a little pink church and next to it a whitewashed presbytery with green shutters half hidden by trailing vines, and there is a neglected churchyard with a wall round it and a huge cypress in one corner. You sit down on the low wall and look down into the olive trees in the fields below, and if it happens to be on a day in spring last year's leaves stand like blackish-green flecks in the new silvery grey foliage, which gleams in the sun and bears such unpretentious, such modest yellow clusters of blossom.

In such places one dreams hermits' dreams. Ah, to live here, far from everything, from the disturbing pleasures of the world and the eye, to live quietly and frugally, going to Mass early in the morning in the little chapel, working faithfully in solitude through the day and holding the rosary in one's hand when that difficult hour comes, when the western sky flames like gold and blood and all the vast valley turns blue in the dusk and is like a bowl of violets; when a golden fire burns up far away in the mountains, and a voice rises from the darkening fields, singing a wild and yearning *stornello,* in which *dolore* rhymes with *amore, canto* with *pianto.*

So does the child of the twentieth century dream day-dreams, but the men and women of the Middle Ages were not content merely to dream. In the fourteenth century the whole country round Siena was full of hermits and the government considered it an honour to provide for their wants. Quite a colony of hermits had settled down between Porta Camullia and the Anteporta; the so-called Apostolini lived outside Porta Tufi; after the death of Catherine of Siena her disciple, Neri dei Pagliaresi, became a hermit "in Gromaggio's hermitage outside Florence"; another hermit, while she was living, was Brother Santi of Teramo, who had earlier been a friend of Giovanni Colombini and of the saintly Carthusian in Maggiano, Pietro Pietroni.[1]

We do not know where Brother Santi's hermitage stood. Perhaps it was outside Porta Tufi, where Saint Bernardine tried a quarter of a century later to become a hermit, but gave it up after a trial of half a day. Perhaps it stood on Buccianino's hill between the cypresses, not far from *La Certosa,* where Dom Pietro had lived in prayer and penance, and in the hour of his death struggled through all those agonies of hell that the great sinner, Boccaccio, ought to have suffered. We do not know. But we do know that in October, 1378, Catherine wrote her book about the way of salvation — "The Book" — in Fra Santi's hermitage.

In his memoirs Ser Cristofani writes of Catherine's literary work:

"And the said servant of Christ did yet another thing that is worthy of remark, namely, that she wrote a book which is of

THE CROWN OF THORNS

the size of a Missal, and it was written while she was rapt in ecstasy and had lost the use of all her senses, except that of her tongue. God the Father spoke in her and she answered and asked questions, and she repeated the words that God the Father had said to her and also her own that she said, and the questions that she asked were in Italian* . . . She spoke and there was one who wrote down the words, now Ser Barduccio (Canigiani), now Don Stefano (Maconi) and now Neri di Landoccio. When one hears such a thing told one can scarce believe it, but they who wrote it down and heard it think otherwise, and I am among them." [2]

We have Stefano's own words that he was one of those to whom Catherine dictated her book; it was he, too, who afterwards translated it into Latin, so that it could be read by the whole Catholic world.[3] And, as Père Hurtaud has pointed out with acumen in his introduction to the French translation, the fairly big book (400 pages in the latest Italian edition) was written in the course of only five days: from the 9th to the 13th October 1378.[4] There is nothing at all impossible, nothing miraculous in this; Nietzsche, for instance, wrote the second part of "Also sprach Zarathustra" in ten days, from June 26th to July 6th, 1883. And Catherine did not even need to hold a pen, she had only to dictate, and we know that her speech was like a rushing torrent.

In a letter to Raymond of Capua Catherine herself has told how the book came into existence, and given a short outline of its contents.

First she thanks the absent friend for a kind letter with good news which she has received from him; it came just on the feast of Saint Francis of Assisi (October 4th). And speaking as usual of herself in the third person as "a handmaid of God," she continues:

"And by the grace of God she was filled of a sudden with desire and joy above all measure. And it was the day of Mary" (i.e. Saturday) "and she was waiting for the morning to come that she might go to Mass. And when the hour for Mass had come she went to church and knelt down in her place with true self-knowledge and was ashamed before God of her im-

* *Volgare*, as distinguished from Latin.

perfection. And in her ardent longing she rose above herself and beholding the eternal Truth with the eye of understanding, she prayed for four things and made an offering of herself and her spiritual father (i.e. Raymond) for the Bride of Truth.

"First she prayed for the reformation of the Church. And God being moved with compassion for her tears, and constrained by her desire, said: 'My dearest daughter, behold how the Church has defiled her face with impurity and self-love, and behold how it has swelled up because of the pride and avarice of those who have been nourished at her breast. But take thy tears and thy sweat, which have sprung up from the fountain of my love in thee, and cleanse thou her face. For I say to thee that she shall not regain her beauty, either by the sword or by cruelty or by war, but by peace and by constant and humble prayer and by the sweat and tears of my servants. If thou wilt persevere I will grant thy desire, and never shall my providence fail thee.' "

In this the salvation of all the world was really assured, but Catherine's prayer, nevertheless, went more into detail, extending to prayer for each and all. Then God showed her how great was the love with which he had created man, and He said: "Behold, my daughter, how they all strike me. Behold, my daughter, with how many, and all manner of sins they strike me, and above all with that miserable and most abominable self-love with which they have poisoned the whole world. You, who are my servants, make reparation with all your prayers, and thus you will soften the wrath of the judgments of God. And know that none can escape from my hand. Open the eye of thy understanding and look in my hand." Then she lifted up her eyes and beheld the whole world in the closed hand of God. And God said: 'I will that thou shalt know that none can be taken from me. Whether they are under my justice or under my mercy they are all mine. And because they are all gone out from me I love them unutterably and for my servants' sake I will have mercy upon them.'

"Then the ardour of her longing grew and she was full of joy and of sorrow at the same time (*beata e dolorosa*) and she gave thanks for the goodness of God because she understood that He had revealed the faults of His creatures to her, to con-

THE CROWN OF THORNS

strain her to be more faithful to duty and more zealous hereafter. And the fire of holy love grew so great in her that the sweat which poured from her seemed to her poor and to be despised, so great was her longing to see all her body sweat blood. And she said to herself: 'My soul, thou hast wasted all thy life and therefore so many evils and plagues have come upon the world and upon Holy Church . . . and I will that thou make reparation now and sweat blood.' Then did her soul lift up itself higher yet, inspired by holy desire, and opened the eye of the spirit and gazed upon the divine love."

It was then that Catherine saw the *bridge* — the only one leading across the river of the world to the shores of life. . .

In the old legend about one of the two patron saints of Siena, San Galgano (Sant' Ansano is the other), we are told that as a young man he had a vision. The holy archangel Michael appeared to him and said to him: "Follow me." "Then Galgano arose with great joy and followed in the footsteps of the angel, until he came to a river, and across the river there was a bridge. And the bridge was very long, and one could not walk over it without great toil. But under the bridge, it seemed to him in the vision, there was a mill, and its wheel kept turning round, and it signified the earthly things that are ever in movement and without any constancy, and that are vain and perish. And he walked over the bridge and came to a beautiful meadow full of flowers." [5]

San Galgano died in 1181 and all the people in Siena knew his legend. There can be no doubt that Catherine had often heard it told, as it is still told at the present day, and especially in Galgano's native town, Chiusdino. That illustration in the saint's vision — the river which drives the wheel of this world (the wheel which the apostle, Saint James, had already used as a symbol of the ever-changing temporal life), and beyond the river the fair Paradise with its flowers and meadows — that illustration could not but make an impression on Catherine's mind. She takes it up, transforms it and elaborates it, but the main thought is the same: the river of the world and its deceitful water (she has no use for the mill and leaves it out), the water alone is symbol enough of changeableness, and across the water the bridge, the narrow bridge, the narrow way. This becomes the chief thought in her book and it coincides with another old Christian thought, that of the three degrees in the life of piety, or the three ways — *via purificativa* or the way of purgation, the cleansing from earthly things, *via illuminativa,* the illuminative way, or enlightenment about the things of heaven and *via unitiva* or the way of union with God, with eternal love.

These three degrees are already found in the detachment from the ego and the world in oriental mysticism, in Saint Basil; later, in the West, in Saint Bernard of Clairvaux. The latter describes the three degrees in the form of three kisses: the kiss on the foot, on the lips and on the heart wound of Jesus, *osculum pedum, oris, cordis.* The same doctrine is preached by Saint Bonaventura under the figure of the three pairs of wings of the Seraphim, and we meet with it in a legendary form in the forty-eighth chapter of the *Fioretti,* in which Brother John of La Verna is permitted to kiss, first the feet of Jesus, then His hands, finally His breast, "and from the mouth of Brother John, who had drunk of the fountain of divine wisdom in the breast of the Saviour, proceeded wonderful and heavenly words which converted the hearts of all those who listened to them and gave much fruit to souls." German Dominican mysticism is penetrated with this thought and Henry Suso concentrates it into a formula in the three sentences standing as mottoes of the three parts of the present book: *entbildet werden von der Welt, gleichgebildet werden mit Gott, überbildet werden in die Gottheit.* It is the old doctrine of Saint Paul, not to be like this world any more, but to be conformed to the likeness of Christ, and thus to obtain a part in God and His everlasting life. It is the teaching of Saint John, the Evangelist: "Love not the world or the things that are in the world." It is the stern, strong saying of Jesus Himself: "Whoso will come after me, let him take up his cross." The world is the broad way of death, the cross is the narrow gate of life, the ladder with the blood-stained steps. Such are the conditions; there are no others.

This is the monastic ideal, the ideal of the religious life — and therefore the Christian ideal. The monk is the perfect Christian. Everything that is not the cell is the world, that which is not *claustrum* is *sæculum.* And Jesus "prays not for the world." One must therefore be in the world "as those who are not in it," as "pilgrims and wanderers." "We have here no abiding city, but seek that which is to come." Our place or "city," as the Vulgate has it, is that Jerusalem which is above — *civitas Dei*.

The two cities to which one comes, the two ways by which one goes, the two loves, which lead, each by its own way to its own city: *amor proprio* and *caritas,* the false, dark "Minne" and true charity. As in all her letters, as in the spiritual testament (*documentum spirituale*) which she dictated on the 7th January 1376, to her English friend and disciple, William Flete in Lecceto, Catherine also inculcates in the *Dialogue* the great fundamental truth by which she has lived. "Self-love," it is said in the Englishman's notes from Catherine's dictation, "is the cause of all evil and the destruction of all good . . . But the man who is really spiritually minded loves God alone, and for His sake he wills the salvation of souls. He uses all other things with this object before him . . . and he judges all things according to the will of God" (i.e., from the standpoint of God) "not according to the will of men." When one consolation or another is taken from him he thinks immediately: "This happens to me with the permission of God, according to His providence, as in all things that befall me, all tribulation that He sends me He wills only one single thing, my sanctification." And this thought makes all bitter things sweet.[6]

The letter continues in this strain and gives an outline of the thought dominating the *Dialogue*:

"My third prayer was for the salvation of your soul. Eternal Truth answered me and said: 'Daughter, I will that he seek it with much care. But neither he nor thou nor any other can do aught without suffering much persecution, according as I permit it. Tell him that as truly as he desires the glory of my name, so truly must he desire to suffer and persevere with true patience. Therein shall I see that he and my other servants do indeed seek my glory. Then shall he be my dearest child and find rest upon the bosom of my only-begotten Son, for He is the bridge which I have built, so that ye may all pass over and enjoy and receive the fruit of your labours. Ye must know, little children, that the way was broken by the sin and disobedience of Adam, so that no man could reach the goal any more, and thus my will was not fulfilled, for I had created man to my image and likeness, so that he might have everlasting life and part in me, who am purest joy and eternal goodness. From that sin grew thorns and thistles and many tribulations; they are like a river whose waters flow without ceasing, and therefore I gave them my Son as a bridge, that ye might pass over the river and not be drowned. Open the eye of thy understanding and behold that it reaches from heaven to earth; therefore it could not be built of men, for earth cannot stretch so far, it could not reach across the river. . .

" 'Ye must therefore pass over by that bridge, giving glory to my name by seeking the salvation of souls, enduring all tribulations and following in the footsteps of the sweet, loving Word. Ye are my labourers, whom I have sent out to work in the vineyard of Holy Church, because I will show mercy to the world. But have a care that ye do not walk *under* the bridge, for the way of truth is not there. Dost thou know who they are who walk under that bridge? They are the sinners, the unjust. Ye must therefore pray for them, ye must weep for them, ye must labour for them, for they are lying in the darkness of sin unto death. They follow the river and will end in everlasting perdition. . . There are some among them who are seized with fear and seek refuge on the shore, and flee from the state of sin . . . And if they are watchful and do not fall asleep in self-love, they cling to the bridge and begin to climb up by practising virtue. But if they continue in self-love and negligence they will fare ill. They are not persevering and when the wind blows from another quarter they return to the place whence they came, like the dog to its vomit.'

"After having seen in how many different ways the soul was drowned she said to herself: 'Now I will contemplate those who go across the bridge, which is Christ Crucified.' And she saw many who walked without any trouble, because they were not weighed down by self-will; they were the true sons of God, who had given up themselves and sought only one thing: the glory of God and the salvation of souls. Aided by this desire they had trodden down the thorns under their feet so that they could not prick them, and the river flowed on beneath them, which is, being interpreted, that they gave no heed to the thorns of adversity, and they accepted with patience the prosperity that is so full of peril for the soul and brings death to everyone who gives himself up to it with inordinate affection. They despised prosperity as if it were poison, and cared for naught but to rejoice with Christ on the Cross, for it was He whom they sought.

"Others walked more slowly. And why did they walk slowly? Because their eyes were not fastened upon Christ Crucified, but upon the consolation which He bestowed upon them, and therefore their love was imperfect. . . And when they no longer see the Beloved, and no longer feel any consolation, and persecutions come, and temptations from the devil or from creatures or from their own weak-hearted need of love . . . then they hesitate and fail and turn away from Christ Crucified. For in Christ they have wanted to follow the Father and taste sweetness and consolation, for the Father does not suffer, only the Son. Therefore I say that they follow the Father. . . But Eternal Truth has said: 'No one can come to me but by my only-begotten Son, for it is He who has prepared the way that you must go. . . And thus they know my truth, and having acknowledged it they follow it and thus they receive everlasting life (*vita durabile*). . . Every other way is full of torment, for that which causes pain in us is self-will, whether it be spiritual or worldly. Therefore he who has no will is free from all punishment and all pain. . .

"Others I saw who had begun to ascend, and they are those who began to acknowledge their sin, but only because of the punishment that follows upon guilt, and for that reason they had left sin, from fear of punishment, which is a slavish fear. Now many did I see passing from slavish fear to the fear of God, from imperfect fear to perfect fear, and they advanced from the first step to the second and the last. But there were many others who sat down in negligence at the entrance to the bridge . . . and stayed there in their lukewarmness. The sweet Truth said of them: 'Behold, daughter, it cannot be otherwise but that those who do not advance in virtue go back. And this is the reason: the soul cannot live without loving, and it strives to love and serve better that which it loves. If it does not know and recognise itself it will not come to a knowledge of the riches and abundance of my mercy, and as it does not know me, it does not love me, does not serve me. Being thus it is deprived of me, and not being able to live without love it turns back to its own miserable self. Such as these are like the dog which vomits after it has eaten and eats that which it has thrown up, feeding on uncleanness; thus have those lukewarm souls that fear punishment cast their sins away in holy confession and have begun to walk in the way of truth. But as they do not advance they must go back. And they turn to look at that which they have thrown up, not seeing the punishment any more, but seeing the sensual pleasure, and then they fear no more, but swallow what they have thrown up, nourishing their feelings and desires with their own uncleanness. . .'

It is the unworthy ecclesiastics, in particular, who are the subject of this description of souls in whom the good seed falls on stony ground and quickly withers. "They are like flies," the description continues, "that settle now on a sweet-smelling flower, now on stinking refuse. . . Thus do they leave the altar and let their souls and their bodies sink into such great uncleanness that even the devils are filled with loathing at so miserable a sin . . ."

And in this way these wretched souls sink from the rescuing bridge down into the bottomless water and the deceitful world. They extinguish the light of reason and yield themselves up to be guided by their senses alone — those *five unsatiated senses* whose absolute dominion Carlyle also feared with his puritanical and heroic spirit. "They are like the blind, who would judge of good and evil by the hand alone, or sometimes by taste or by the sound of a voice, in their weak and limited powers of judgment, and will not be guided by him who has light to see by, but walk like one who is mad, guided only by feeling and by the hand, which errs because it cannot distinguish colour. Taste deceives too, for it sees not the unclean animal that has settled on the food. The ear is deceived by the harmony of sound and sees not him who sings, and that the singer may cause his death. Like the blind, without the light of reason, they feel the joys of the world with sensual hands, and they seem to them full of pleasures. They see not that the pleasure of the world is a cloth interwoven with many thorns. . . The soul is led astray by the sound of sweet music and falls into the pit and

THE CROWN OF THORNS

is bound in the bonds of sin and is in the hands of her enemies. Blinded by self-love, such as these trust in their own strength and their own knowledge and do not keep to me, their way and their guide; to me, who am life and light, and whosoever is guided by me cannot go astray and will not walk in darkness. They do not trust in me, who will nothing but their sanctification, sending and permitting everything out of love alone. They are always scandalised in me, and I tolerate and bear with them in patience, for I have loved them without being loved. They pursue me constantly with much impatience, with hate and murmuring and much faithlessness, and in their blindness they would search out my unsearchable judgments which have all been passed in justice and with charity. They do not know themselves and therefore they err. For he who does not know himself can not in truth know me nor my judgments."

Catherine's third prayer to God was for Raymond of Capua and the salvation of his soul; but she had still a fourth prayer to offer up. There was one who had fared as described above; he had saved himself out of the river, he had stood at the entrance to the bridge, then he had turned back, had sunk back into himself and his past, had sunk beneath the waters and perished. We do not know who that soul was whom Catherine singled out with so great a love. Was it perhaps that unhappy disciple of the previous autumn, the suicide of Mont' Amiata? It is hardly probable, for the consolation which the voice from heaven brought her was that that soul was saved, in spite of everything, saved "because he had not forgotten to honour and love my gentle Mother Mary."

With this Catherine received answers in prayer to the four questions that she had at heart. As a last cry Lapa's daughter heard the command: "Conceive and bring forth! Bear a generation of mankind that hates sin, and which loves me with a love that faints and dies!"

Fainting and dying she writes down the last lines of the letter: "Oh, dearest and sweetest Father, so much did I hear and see of the sweet Truth from the beginning [*la dolce prima Verità*], and it was as though my heart should burst. I die and can not die. Have pity on such a poor woman as I, whom it sorely torments to see God so greatly offended, and who has no one to whom she can pour out her heart, but the Holy Spirit comforts me and in His mercy has helped me in letting me write to you." [7]

The Book is written on the basis of these thoughts, in this passion for the glory of God. Its content is the same as that of the letter, but more detailed, fuller and interwoven with all Catherine's experiences of the last few years.

The work, such as it is presented, is divided into different sections (tracts): an introduction, which goes from Chapter I to Chapter VIII, then *Tractato de la discrezione* (IX–LXIV), *Tractato dell' orazione* (LXV–CXXXIV), *Tractato della providenza* (CXXXV–CLIII), *Tractato dell' obedienza* (CLIV–CLXVII). This introduction is not original, it replaced another one, of which only few traces remain, as when Catherine in one place mentions *Tractato della resurreczione* as a section of the book or alludes in a letter to *Tractato delle lagrime*.[8]

The division of the book is of minor importance, however; the whole work, like the outline of the letter to Raymond, is borne up by one connected train of thought and wave of feeling. The first chapters lead us to the church, one Saturday morning. Catherine has received the sad news of the schism (the election of the anti-pope Clement VII at Fondi, on September 20th, 1378), and during the Mass she offers up the four prayers: for herself, for the Church, for peace among Christians and for that unknown one, whose everlasting welfare she had so much at heart. She prays also for Raymond — "she always presented this father of her soul before the throne of divine goodness."

These prayers, which are questions, are set forth in the first two chapters of the book. Will she herself, will the Church, will Christendom, will her confessor, will that single soul find mercy with God? After that the whole book is nothing but a great promise of mercy. Mercy for Catherine, if she knows herself and knows God, and if she uses the double-edged knife of holy love and holy hate and does not take her hand from the plough to look back. Mercy for the world, to whom God has given Christ, the Bridge to heaven, by which man can walk over the waters of death. Mercy for the Church, when her priests repent and live worthy of their calling. Mercy for all through the charity of God's providence. And the book rings out in a great prayer of praise and thanksgiving to the God who is "mad with love of His creatures."

"Oh abyss, oh eternal divinity, oh deep ocean! What couldst thou give me more than thyself? Thou art fire, ever burning and never burning out; thou art fire which in its heat consumes all the self-love of the soul; thou art fire which drives away all cold; thou givest light and in thy light thou hast let me see thy truth; thou art light above every light. Thy light gives a supernatural light to the eye of the soul, so full, so perfect, that the light of faith grows bright to me and I see that my soul has life in that faith, and in that light it receives thee, oh Light! In the light of faith I gain wisdom from the wisdom of thy Son; in the light of faith I am strong, firm, persevering; in the light of faith I hope and do not grow faint on the way. That light guides me on my way, without that light I should walk in darkness; therefore I said to thee, eternal Father, that thou must give me the holy light of faith.

"Verily, that light is an ocean, for it nourishes the soul in thee, thou ocean of peace, eternal Trinity. That water is not unclean . . . it is clear, it shows the hidden things . . . it is a glass, and when I hold it with the hand of love and look into it, it shows me myself, thy creature, in thee, and thee, in thy taking upon thee the nature of man, united to me. In that light I know thee and see thee before me. Thou highest and infinite good, incomprehensible good, inestimable good, beauty above all beauty, wisdom above all wisdom! Thou, who art the food of angels, hast given thyself to mankind in the ardour of thy love. Thou, the garment that covers all nakedness, in thy sweetness givest food to all that hunger. Sweet art thou, and without any bitterness. Oh, eternal Trinity, in thy light which thou hast given me, and which I received in the holy faith, I have known the way of high perfection, so that I might serve thee with light and not with darkness, to be an example of a good and holy life and repent of my miserable life hitherto. For by my own fault I have hitherto served thee in darkness. I have not known thy truth, and therefore I did not love it.

"Why did I not know thee? Because I did not see thee

with the glorious light of holy faith; because the cloud of self-love obscured the light of my soul. And thou, eternal Trinity, didst drive out the darkness with thy light. Who can ever attain to thy height and thank thee for a gift so exceeding great and for the countless benefits which thou hast bestowed upon me, for the doctrine of the truth which thou hast given me . . . ? Answer me thyself, Lord, thou hast given, give thou thyself the thanks in giving me the light of grace so that I can offer thanks to thee with that light. Clothe me, clothe me in thyself, eternal Truth, that I may come to the end of this mortal life with true obedience and in the light of holiest faith — the light in which thou dost inebriate my soul anew!" [9]

Catherine ceased speaking, and there was dead silence in the hermitage of Fra Santi. The quill no longer twittered over the parchment, on which it had at last scarce been able to follow the ecstatic words of the seeress. She was on her knees, her countenance radiant. They approached her, sprinkled holy water on her face, and with a great sigh she came to herself, softly breathing a "Thanks be to God!" *Deo gratias!*

Amen, answered the disciples, and the writer concluded the book: *Deo gratias! Amen.*

X

"You have written to me, and from your letter I understand that you are suffering and that your suffering is not slight . . . You would like to leave your convent and go to Rome. Give up your wish altogether to the will of your heavenly Spouse, and if it be to His glory and your salvation He will provide the way and the means, such as you could never have imagined. Leave it all to Him, let go of yourself, lose yourself on the Cross, and you will find yourself entirely . . .

"Let us not slumber any longer, let us rise from the slumber of negligence, let our prayers roll on without ceasing like the roaring of the beast of prey over the mystical body of Holy Church and over the Vicegerent of Christ.* Let us never cease from praying for him, that he may gain light and strength to resist the incarnate devils who love themselves and would corrupt our faith. It is a time for weeping.

"In so far as my visit to you is concerned, pray to the highest eternal goodness of God that He will ordain that which is to His glory and the salvation of souls, above all now, when I must journey to Rome to obey the will of Christ Crucified and of His vicar. I do not know which road I shall take." [1]

This letter to Catherine's disciple in Orvieto, Sister Daniella, was written in October or November, 1378. A note of November 4th to the tailor, Francesco di Pippino in Florence, allows us to see Catherine busy with preparations for her journey: "By the goodness of God and at the command of the Holy Father I am thinking of journeying to Rome about the middle of the present month, a little sooner or later, and I shall travel by the road. . . I beg you, Francesco, for the sake of Christ Crucified, to take upon yourself the trouble of delivering the letters sent with this. . . Go therefore to Monna Pavola" (in Fiesole) "and tell her, that if she has not obtained what she wished at the [papal] court, to write it to me, and I will care for her as I would for my own mother. . . Seek also Niccolò, the beggar of Romagna, and tell him that I am going now. . .

---

* In the Middle Ages it was a generally accepted belief that the lion was able by its roar to awaken its dead cubs to life.

Barduccio" (Canigiani, who writes the letter for Catherine) "asks you to give his letter to his father and brothers and to tell them that they can give to you what they would send to us, and then send it to us or bring it yourself, if you are coming here." [2]

As the letters given above clearly show, it was the Pope who desired Catherine's presence in Rome. His wish responded to her own longing. "If matters were as I could wish them I should not remain here long," she concludes a letter to Urban. "I have had enough of words, it is my desire now to go out on the field of battle and fight by your side until death for the cause of truth." [3]

This is a warrior spirit, like that of Jeanne d'Arc later, and there was need of it in the times through which the world was passing then. The Great Schism had broken out on September 20th (*venti settembre* — five hundred years later again a decisive date in the history of the Church!). The cardinals hostile to Urban, who would have preferred to see the papal chair moved back to Avignon, assembled in conclave at Fondi and elected Cardinal Robert of Geneva Pope. Robert took the name of Clement VII and was solemnly crowned in the cathedral of Fondi.

From this moment the whole Catholic world was divided into two hostile camps: the Urbanists and the Clementists. The supporters of the anti-Pope were, first and foremost, France under Charles V; the French King's brother, Louis of Anjou; Joanna of Naples; besides Savoy, Piedmont, Monferrato. The rest of Italy was on Urban's side, as also the new German emperor, Wenceslaus (Charles died on the same day that the antipope was elected). Bavaria, Luxembourg, Kurmainz, on the other hand, sided with Clement; Scotland likewise; while England under Richard II was definitely Urbanistic, as well as Flanders, and also King Ludwig of Hungary and Poland. Pedro IV of Aragon and Henry II of Castile were neutral.[4]

While in Florence and later in Siena, Catherine had done what was in her power to ward off the disruption of the Church. She had written to Cardinal Pedro de Luna, whom she had met in Avignon, and with all her forcible energy she had pointed to self-love, *amor proprio*, as the source of this and all other evils. "I will, dearest Father, that you shall be a column that cannot be shaken by any persecution. . . But if you have not put off the love of self, there is no doubt that you will be weak, and weakness will make you fail. . . I have been told that there is disagreement between Christ on earth and his disciples . . . but for the sake of the blood of Christ I beg of you never to stray from virtue and from him who is set over you. . . Be a man and a column that does not give way!" [5]

Pedro de Luna was at that time still on Urban's side; later Catherine had the grief of seeing him desert and become a chief supporter of Clement. She did not apply to him any more; on the other hand, after the election at Fondi had taken place, she wrote a thundering letter to the three Italian cardinals who had taken part in it: Orsini, Corsini, Brossano. The truth is, she exclaims, that "Pope Urban VI is truly a pope, elected at a regular election and not out of fear, more by divine inspiration than by your human shrewdness. This you have proclaimed to us yourselves, and it was the truth. . . But now you deny this truth and would have us believe the contrary, in saying that you elected Pope Urban out of fear. Which is not true, but he who says so (I speak to you without reverence, for you are not worthy of it!), is a liar. For he, whom you pretended to have elected could be seen of everyone who would see him, for that was the Cardinal of Saint Peter" (Tebaldeschi) . . . "And how do I see that you have lawfully elected Messer Bartolommeo, Archbishop of Bari, so that he is now rightfully Pope Urban VI? I see it by his crowning, which you performed with much solemnity, and you did homage to him, you asked him for favours, of which you have made use. You cannot deny this truth except by lying!"

Catherine now gives full vent to her indignation:

"You fools, a thousand times worthy of death! You are like the blind who cannot see their own disease . . . you make liars and idolaters of yourselves. Even if it were true (which it is not, but let us suppose it), you lied to us when you said that he was the pope, and you have falsely paid him homage and reverence, and have committed simony in obtaining favours from him and using them unlawfully. This is true. And now they have elected an anti-pope and you have joined with them, in having been present when the devils elected a devil."

Their guilt is even greater than that of the foreign cardinals — "for, humanly speaking, Christ on earth is an Italian, and you are Italians, so that you were not even urged by patriotism like those beyond the Alps. Therefore I see no other reason for your action than self-love." [6]

Catherine repeats the same arguments in a letter to Joanna of Naples. "They threw Saint Peter's cloak about Messer di Santo Pietro," she says, "but he confessed himself that he was not the Pope, but that the Pope who had been elected was Messer Bartolommeo, Archbishop of Bari." Otherwise why all the subsequent repetition of the election, the coronation, the homage? Otherwise why proclaim to "us sheep" that Urban VI was the true Pope? Catherine reminds the queen of Naples of how she has always been faithful to the Church, and emphasises that the faithful can obtain the food of sound doctrine and right living from the Church alone. But Joanna seems to her to have lost the taste for the right spiritual food, it seems that she prefers "the doctrine and the customs of unrighteous egoists, for if such were not the case you would not go with them, not favour them and help them, but depart from them." She also writes to the Count of Fondi and tells him frankly that when he cannot see the truth in this matter, it is because his mind is obscured by anger and hate. "How can you do that which you are doing?" she exclaims boldly. "You know full well in the depths of your heart that Urban is a true and real pope, and whoever says otherwise is a heretic, rejected by God, and not a believing or Catholic man, but a renegade who denies the faith."

In a later letter to Joanna of Naples Catherine exclaims: "What manner of man is that whom they have elected antipope? A holy man? No, an unrighteous man, a devil! And therefore he does the works of the devil!" [7]

She had not forgotten — and no Italian had forgotten it — that the son of the Genevan Count Amadeo III had only two years earlier, as papal legate, ravaged Romagna with his English and Breton hordes. She had not forgotten Cesena.

It was Catherine's desire now to fight against this devil in human form. "I have heard," she wrote to Urban, "that the incarnate devils have put an Antichrist into the world against

THE CROWN OF THORNS

you, Christ on earth. . . Forward, holiest Father, go without fear into battle!"[8]

Urban, too, was longing to see Catherine by his side and through Raymond he sent her a letter begging her to come. Then something very human, very feminine happened: at the last moment Catherine had her misgivings, was afraid — of the talk about her in Siena. She who had stood before the Pope and the cardinals, who fearlessly went to meet those who would murder her in Florence, she is troubled at the thought of what will be said in Siena when she again goes on a journey. She, at whose door Gregory XI knocked one night of doubt in Genoa — she is, to the women along Costa Sant' Antonio, still only Caterina di Lapa, sister of the debt-laden dyers down at Fontebranda, who had at last to retire to Florence when they could not get on any longer in Siena. . . "And the girl would certainly do much better in keeping house for her brothers than always gadding about, now to Pisa, and now to Venione[*] or goodness knows where. . . Besides, all those journeys must cost an awful lot . . . especially as she must needs always travel with a big escort, both of the other silly women and then these secretary fellows that she takes with her. . . They say the Maconis are so grieved because young Messer Stefano is always hanging on to the skirts of *la Benincasa* — why, the boys in the street actually shout it after him! And I suppose you've heard that Monna Rabe Tolomei wrote a properly sharp letter to the lady when she was staying with the Salimbenis at their Rocca and got her son Matteo home from there. . ."

Thus the tongues would wag in the town, as they wag to this day in Siena about a young woman who differs from the others in her conduct. Catherine knew them and wanted to protect herself against them. She wrote to Raymond: "Father, many of the citizens here and their wives, and also my sisters in the Order have been scandalised not a little by my journeying so often (as it seems to them) hitherto, as I travel hither and thither, and they say that it is not seemly for a virgin who would serve God to travel so often. And although I know in myself that I have not offended in this, for whithersoever I have gone, it has only been to obey God and His Vicegerent and for

[*] Avignon.—*Translator.*

the salvation of souls, I do not wish of my free will to cause scandal to anyone, and therefore I cannot resolve to depart. But if it be the absolute will of the Vicegerent of Christ that I shall come, then his will be done and not mine. But if it be so, then cause his holy will to be made known to me in writing, so that those who are scandalised can see clearly that I do not undertake this journey of my own will." [9]

Catherine received from Rome the categorical command which she had requested, and she could set out on her journey. For the present she left her ageing mother behind in Siena, in the house in Via Romana, to which Lapa had moved from Via dei Tintori. Stefano Maconi also remained behind, his place nearest the saint being taken by Barduccio Canigiani — "my son Barduccio," as Catherine affectionately calls him. Others in her escort were the faithful friends Alessia, Cecca, Lisa, Giovanna di Capo, the two friends Neri di Landoccio and Gabriele Piccolomini, the Dominican Fra Bartolommeo de' Dominici, Master Giovanni Tantucci of Lecceto and the hermit Santi, in whose hermitage she had written the *Dialogue*. "Several more would have come too, if she had not forbidden it," Raymond writes.

And so they set out from Siena, out of Porta Romana — for the last time, but Catherine did not know that. It was in the middle of November, and it is permissible to think that the Sienese pilgrims to Rome would choose a bright and sunny day to begin their long journey. In the fields the peasants are busy gathering the black, ripe olives; rustic vehicles with a body of wickerwork come slowly up towards Siena, drawn by large white oxen with huge horns; far away Mont' Amiata looks blue in the distance. Down yonder on the left, towards Porta San Viene, the Carthusian monastery of San Maggiano raises its campanile — her friend and disciple, the pious Don Pietro di Viva, is now going about his peaceful work there in the little garden belonging to his house — *o beata solitudo!* Up there on the hill stands the old church of San Mamiliano and a little further on, on the other side of the road, the convent of *Bethlehem*. . . Then Catherine passes San Lazzaro, where she once in her youth (such a long, long time ago — and yet so near!) nursed wicked Tecca, and when she was dead, buried her with her own hands, those hands in which the pain of the wounds of

THE CROWN OF THORNS

Christ now glow and burn day and night. . . Over yonder lies Santa Bonda, where she has prayed so often at the grave of Giovanni Colombini in the convent church, and where she once tasted in ecstasy the deepest sweetness of heavenly love. Further away, on the next hill, stands the castle of Belcaro, where they are still working at putting everything into monastic order; as they are displeased with her over so many things, they have also murmured at her taking so little charge of this matter herself. She therefore wrote from Florence to Sano di Maco "and all the other sons in Siena," that "good children take more pains when their mother is not present, so that they may show her afterwards all that they have done while she was away."

And now the wanderers pass the little inn of *la Coroncina* — "the Rosary." When the executioner and his men come to it with those who are to be executed they begin to say the rosary for the dying — it lasts exactly the time it takes to get to the *Albergaccio*, "the evil inn," where the condemned man sleeps his last night. Over there, on the left of the road, is the *Albergaccio*. In one of its rooms Niccolò di Toldo slept his last sleep — or did he watch all the night in prayer? From here they led him out, the few hundred steps to the place of execution, up on the hill on the right, *al Pecorile*. It was up there that Catherine stood waiting for him on that morning in spring while Sister Lark sang high up in the blue sky, and all the white daisies of April dotted the new grass; and she knelt beside the block. She bent her head over his round neck and the black, young hair, she spoke into his ear: "My sweet brother, soon you shall be seated at the everlasting heavenly feast!" She held his head so that it should not fall into the executioner's basket; she closed her eyes when the axe flashed, she heard the sound of steel through bone and cartilage. "I will," said her lips and her hands held firmly, oh, so firmly. . . Then she felt the splash of hot blood, and when she opened her eyes she had the pale head in her hands, and all her white habit was sprinkled with blood, like the grass with flowers — *fratello mio dolce!*

Then the road goes down towards Malamerenda; the towers of Siena could not be seen any longer. The vast, desolate desert country lay spread out before the wanderers, tawny in the sunshine, far away were bluish Mont' Amiata, Monte Cetona, Radicofani, and down behind all the blue mountains was Rome, where "Christendom lay dead." Catherine hastened her steps so that the others could hardly keep up with her — "I am hungered," they heard her murmur, "I die and yet I cannot die." The flame of life and the flame of death burned in her, the hunger for souls, the will to give up her life for the Bride, which is Holy Church.[10]

The road — Via Francigena — led from Siena to San Quirico, and Catherine saw the Orcia valley again. It is probable that, as she had half promised, she visited Sister Daniella in Orvieto. On November 28th, 1378, the first Sunday in Advent, she arrived in Rome, where she was to see Raymond of Capua again for a short while.[11] At the beginning of the following year Maconi wrote from Siena to Neri di Landoccio in Rome, and in his letter he sent a greeting to *la Nonna,* that is, Lapa, who must therefore have gone to Rome later, to join her daughter.[12]

Catherine was at once received in audience by the Holy Father. Messer Lando di Francesco Ungaro, who (according to the old account books was paid "a salary of 126 lire by the city of Siena in November, 1378, for thirty days' sojourn in Rome as envoy to the Pope, to obtain the restitution of Talamone") wrote home to his government: "Caterina di Monna Lapa has come hither, and our Master the Pope has had pleasure in seeing her and listening to her. But it is not known what he has asked of her, only that he has gladly seen her." [13]

What Urban had asked Catherine to do was to undertake a political mission to Naples. He had received her in public audience, surrounded by the cardinals, and Catherine had spoken and made the deepest impression upon them by her faith and her courage. "This little woman (*donniciuola*) puts us all to shame," Urban exclaimed, when she ceased speaking. "We are troubled and afraid, while she, who belongs by nature to the timid sex, is fearless; nay, she gives us others consolation." Then, with enthusiasm, he added: "What can the Vicegerent fear when Christ the Almighty is with him? Christ is stronger than the world, and it cannot be that He will fail His Holy Church."

THE CROWN OF THORNS

Like so many others Urban had felt the presence of Christ in the frail little woman — like the Host in the tabernacle. With her by his side he would go forth into battle; he had found his attending spirit.

Catherine was ready to go to Naples, as she had been ready to go to Florence. The Pope, however, did not want her to go there alone; he wished to send another Catherine with her — Saint Karin of Vadstena, the daughter of Saint Birgitta, now forty-six years old. Karin knew Naples, knew Queen Joanna, she had been there with her mother nine years earlier and again on the journey to and from the Holy Land in 1372 and 1373. Karin knew Joanna and she remembered the avid glances that the beautiful queen had cast upon her brother Carl; she remembered how the Lady Birgitta would rather see her son dead than in the arms of a loose-living woman. She remembered how Carl had suddenly been seized with fever, as his mother had wished, and had died, and they had buried him by the shores of the blue gulf. Karin would never again look into the big, brilliant eyes of Queen Joanna, would not meet again the cruel smile about those strong, full lips. She, the virgin wife of Sir Eggert, feared the revenge which a sensual woman might find in her heart to take upon her and the maid of Siena.

Raymond of Capua agreed with Karin. He, too, feared the malignity of Joanna and shuddered at the thought of seeing his friend come back to Rome dishonoured and shamed. He went to Urban and prevailed upon him to give up the plan. When Catherine was told of it she exclaimed: "If Agnes, Margherita, Caterina and the other holy virgins had been so timid they would never have won the martyr's crown. Have not all good virgins a Spouse, mighty enough to defend them and preserve them? These doubts arise rather from little faith than from wise virtue."

The decision was made, however, and Catherine remained in Rome. At first she lived in a house in *Contrada di Colonna,* at the foot of Monte Pincio, afterwards "near Santo Biagio, between Campo di Fiori and Santo Eustachio," in Via del Papa (now Via Santa Chiara) not far from the Dominican monastery of Santa Maria sopra Minerva, of which Raymond was Prior. The size of household varied, yet it never numbered less than sixteen men and eight women, sometimes the number might rise to thirty or forty, as Catherine's house naturally became a place of meeting for the Sienese who came to Rome. She obtained for them what they wanted at the Vatican (audiences, letters of indulgence and the like) and she gave them food and houseroom. "And although she possessed no worldly goods," Caffarini writes, "she possessed all things, as the Apostle writes. And because her heart trusted so greatly in God, He cared for her and her children in Christ in many wonderful ways, and they received what they needed. And even though the times were hard and there were thirty or forty at table, and sometimes more, they never lacked anything, but if there were fewer there was not more left for that reason, at which many greatly marvelled. God cared for them according to their need, with gifts of alms and in other new ways, wherefore Catherine was wont to say with holy trust and living faith: 'And though I were here with a hundred persons, nay, with a thousand, I make no doubt but that my heavenly Spouse would provide for us.' And we constantly saw that indeed it was so. But so that everything might be done in order, and each of her women companions might have leisure for her pilgrimages and her visits to the churches in Rome to gain the holy indulgences, that wisest of virgins decided that each of them should have charge of the kitchen and the table a week in turn. When bread or wine or any other necessity was needed they were to tell her of it the day before, so that she might procure it, either by going out begging herself or sending some one in her stead.

"Now it happened once that one of her companions, by name Giovanna [di Capo], whose turn it was to work in the house, forgot to tell Catherine that there was no bread, and she did not think of it until they were going to table. Then, greatly ashamed and sorrowing, she came and confessed that there was no bread in the house. 'May God forgive you, Sister, how comes it you have let it go so far?' And she reproved her. Then she asked her: 'Is there no bread at all?' The Sister answered: 'Yes, there is, but so little that it is as good as nothing.' Then Catherine said: 'Tell the whole family from me to sit down at the table and to begin eating what little there is until God provides for us in another way.' Having said this she went up to pray. The family, who were hungry after having fasted long, gladly began to eat. All ate the little bread there was, both before the soup and with the soup and all were satisfied, and still there was bread enough on the table so that they all wondered greatly. And as they questioned each other it was said that Catherine was praying very earnestly. Then they understood clearly and concluded that that wonderful multiplying of the bread was wrought by the power of her prayers. For that bread sufficed not only for the first table (that of the men, who dined first and by themselves), but also afterwards for the women's table, and a large portion of it was also given to the poor." [14]

XI

Urban now had Catherine by his side, and without delay he hurled the bull of excommunication against "the children of loss" from Santa Maria in Trastevere, whither he had fled from the Vatican, which was too near the ever threatening Castel Sant' Angelo. The bull is dated November 20th, 1378, and pronounces the great excommunication, first upon Robert of Geneva, then upon the cardinals of Amiens, Marmoutier and Sant' Eustachio, upon the Patriarch of Constantinople, the Archbishop of Cosenza and a number of other prelates, finally upon the Count of Fondi, the protector of the schism and upon the three leaders of the schismatic army, the Condottieri Jean de Malestroit, Bernard de la Salle and Silvestre Budes. The three Italian cardinals, who were sitting out in Tagliacozzo — Corsini, Orsini and Brossano — are still mentioned, on the other hand, as "reverend brothers and beloved sons," nor has Pedro de Luna been struck.

The next question was the winning back of the two renegades, Naples and France. The plan of sending Catherine down to Queen Joanna had been given up by the Pope, but not by herself. As late as on September 18th of the following year, Fra Bartolommeo de' Dominici writes that his "Mamma" has thought several times of going to Naples, "but it does not seem to be the will of God, nor has his Vicar consented to it, so for the present it is better not to think any more about it." At about this time she had sent down two of her disciples to influence Joanna — Neri di Landoccio and the Abbé Lisolo (Eligio?), otherwise unknown. She supported them by an extensive correspondence, not only with the Queen herself, but with a great number of ladies of rank at the Neapolitan court: Countess Johanna d'Aquino, married to Count Sanseverini of Miledo, Terranova and Belcastro; Monna Lariella, married to Francesco Carraciolo; Monna Catarina Dentice, Monna Catella, Monna Cecia. Other letters are addressed to the Carthusian, Dom Cristofano, of the famous Certosa San Martino above Naples, to "Madonna Pentella, a married woman in Naples," whose husband had a female slave living in his house as his mistress; to "Peronella, daughter of Masello Pepe," to "three spiritually-minded women in Naples," to "a lady at the court of the Queen," perhaps the wife of the chamberlain Giacomo Arcucci.[1]

Neri went to Naples and Raymond of Capua to France. Catherine had scarcely had time to see her spiritual father, guide and friend before she had again to bid him farewell, and this time it was for ever. "After that it seemed good to the Pope," Raymond writes, "to send me to Gaul, thinking that by the aid of envoys he could tear away Charles, who was then King of France, from the error of the schism, which he had begun to support. But it was in vain, for he had hardened his heart more than Pharaoh. When the Pope's intention was made known to me I spoke of it to Catherine, who, though she was unwilling to let me go, yet urged me strongly to obey the Pope's command and wishes. Among other things she said to me: 'Be assured, Father, that he is the true Vicegerent of Christ, whatever the schismatic slanderers say, and I want you to preach and defend this truth, as you preach and defend the Catholic faith itself.' And although I was already convinced of this truth, these words strengthened me so much in my resolve to fight against the schismatics, that until this day [towards 1395] I cannot grow weary of defending the true Pope with all my might, and in all trials and tribulations the memory of those words strengthen me still. I therefore did as she wished and bent my neck under the yoke of obedience."

Then came the last talk between Raymond and Catherine. He had had so many of them in the past, and sometimes he had valued them so little that he had fallen asleep while she was speaking. But this was the last; she had drawn him into a corner of the room so that no others could hear them, and she talked — talked — talked. He saw before him the little pale face, of which every line was familiar, every wrinkle, even the very pock-marks in the white skin. She talked, talked — the large black eyes were radiant, the delicate lips moved unceasingly, forming the words firmly and beautifully, and now and then she took his hand, smiling that luminous smile which none of the disciples ever forgot, that smile of which nothing now remains but the few teeth spaced out in the mouth of the skull behind the gilded grating above the altar in Sodoma's chapel in San Domenico. . .

"When we had talked thus for many hours," Raymond writes, "she said at last, 'Now go, and God be with you, for I think we shall never talk with each other again in this life.' Which indeed came to pass . . . And as I think, it was for the same reason that she wished to bid me the last farewell, and when I was to embark on the galley she came to the place where the galley was,* and as soon as we began to sail she knelt down and with her hand made the sign of the Cross, and she wept. It was as though she would say: 'May the holy sign of the Cross protect you, my son, but you will never see your mother again on this earth.'" [2]

Besides Raymond, the Pope's envoys were the Bishop of Valence, Guillaume de la Voulte, as well as the Papal Court Marshal Giacomo di Ceve. In spite of the hostile galleys cruising in the Mediterranean they came, first to Pisa, then to Genoa. Thence they continued the journey by land, but at Ventimiglia Raymond was informed that it would be dangerous to go on. "If we had travelled on a little further," he relates, "we should have fallen into the snares which the faithless schismatics had prepared for us, and above all they sought my life." By permission of the Pope, Raymond stayed in Genoa to preach there against the schismatics, but Catherine was little pleased with the timidity of the Dominican. "You were not yet worthy to go into battle," she wrote to him, "but you were turned back like a boy, and you were glad and willing to escape. Oh, bad little Father [*cattivello Padre mio*], how happy your soul (and mine) would have been, if with your blood you could have fixed a stone in the wall of Holy Church. Truly we must weep when we see that our poor virtue has not merited so great a good.

"But now let us shed our milk-teeth and instead get the strong teeth of hate and love. Let us put on the breast-plate of charity and take the shield of holy faith, let us like grown men run out on the field of battle, let us stand firm with one cross in front and another behind so that we cannot flee . . . and so that God may grant you and me and the others that

---
* I.e. on the banks of the Tiber, near San Paolo Fuori le Mura.

grace, let us from today begin to pray for it with tears and with sweet and anxious longing. . . Destroy yourself in the blood of Christ Crucified, bathe in the blood, drink your fill of the blood, inebriate yourself in the blood, clothe yourself in the blood, mourn over yourself in the blood, grow and strengthen your weakness and blindness in the blood of the Lamb without blemish. . . I say no more." [3]

In the spiritual loneliness that fell upon Catherine after Raymond's departure she began to work at the realisation of the other great plan of her life: *the Crusade*. She had completed her first task, the Pope had been brought back to Rome. It was now a question of "the sweet mystery of the holy crusade."

It was a crusade indeed, not against Mahomet, but against the anti-pope, not against the Crescent, but against the fallen Morning Star. It became a spiritual crusade, with no other weapons than the spoken and written word, prayer and fasting.

Catherine had already for a long while cherished the thought that the Pope should above all gather about him a staff of "friends of God," of *"servi Dei."* "Our wrestling," she felt (like the Apostle), "is not against flesh and blood; but against the spirits of wickedness in the high places." Catherine's great plan now was to assemble a chosen company of men of prayer in Rome, to surround Urban's throne with a guard of saints. Her life had brought her into contact with all the prominent men of the time in the sphere of religion; now she calls to them, summons them to a meeting in the Holy City.

The Pope himself approved of her thought. She had written to him: "Your hope and your faith must not rely on human help, which may fail, but only on the help of God which can never be taken from you." [4] Urban now takes Catherine's advice. In a bull of December 13th, 1378, he invokes the help of the pious and declares that he now trusts "more in the prayers and tears of the just than in armed power and worldly wisdom," and like Peter on the waves he looks only to the Saviour's hand for rescue.

Copies of this bull with accompanying letters from Catherine are now, during the days before Christmas, sent out to the friends of God in Italy. It is a call to arms of the picked troops of the Church; the servants of God "must come out of their hiding-places, preach the truth and work for it, for now is their time." "Come, come, do not delay! Put aside everything else, no matter what it is. Now is the time to lose oneself and to care for nothing else but the glory of God with much labour." Such are Catherine's words in her letters to Giovanni delle Celle, to the Prior at Gorgona, Dom Bartolommeo Serafini, to Stefano Maconi, to Fra Tommaso di Nacci Caffarini. There are notes in these letters sounding as if the Last Day were not far off: "He that is on the house-top, let him not come down to take anything out of his house;" is the warning of Jesus in the Gospel; "he that is in the field, let him not go back to take his coat." For Catherine, too, all earthly business was over and useless, one thing only is needful: "to die the death that gives the soul the life of grace," the death of love in the embrace of the Bride, who is the Church — *spasimato in questa dolce sposa*. . .

Catherine writes to the friends in Lecceto, to the English Augustinian, William Flete, and his brother in religion, Antonio da Nizza. She lets them know that what is needed at this time is practical Christianity; it is time "to come out of the wood," where they sit saying all their hymns and their "many Paternosters," time to "leave oneself and go out on the field of battle." Besides, there are "both woods and thickets in Rome," if they needs must have them.

She writes also to the hermits on Monte Luco at Spoleto, to the Carthusian, Dom Pietro da Milano, again to Stefano Maconi and again to Lecceto, and to Raymond, who at that time had got no further than Pisa, and whom she wished for a moment to see "back in this garden to help in pulling up the thorns." "The martyrs of Rome are calling for you," she cries to all of them; "cut through your bonds, do not untie them," she commands Maconi, who was kept back by family considerations — "do not hesitate, act at once, act forcefully, for our sweet God is pleased with few words and many deeds." As if she would obey this principle herself, she breaks off her letter with the exclamation: "Be silent, then, my soul, and say no more." [5]

Others of the disciples disappoint her as Raymond had done, above all her learned friend, William Flete, B.A., of the University of Cambridge. After her death he mourned her sentimentally: "Where shall I find you now, most holy Mother, where is the place in the wood beside the lake where you eat the Paschal Lamb with your disciples?" [6] While she was living, though, and he could still find her merely by going to Rome, he preferred to stay beside that lake, in his woods, sitting on a boulder with his books in the shade of the sessile oaks, and studying or praying, just as it suited him. Deeply offended, Catherine wrote to the Englishman's friend and fellow-Augustinian, Antonio da Nizza: "It seems, from the letter that Brother William has sent to me, that neither you nor he will come. I do not intend to answer him, but I am very much pained by his simple-mindedness, which renders but poor service to the glory of God and the edification of his neighbour" — William Flete having pleaded as his excuse that he prays better in Lecceto, while the tumult of Rome would disturb him. "It appears," the Sienese saint answers caustically, "that God can only be found in the wood, and not in other places, where He is perhaps really needed more." Brother Antonio changed his mind and went to Rome to Catherine. Flete, on the other hand, stayed where he was, though he tried by letters and tracts to influence his own country, and it was due in no small measure to the scholarly hermit in *Selva di Lago* near Siena that England remained true to the cause of Urban.[7]

During this labour Christmas was drawing near, Catherine's first Christmas in Rome. She had always been fond of sending gifts to her friends. In her youth, when she was unknown and had no influence, she had to be content with the posies and crosses of flowers that she tied together herself. She was now able to do more, now she could give her absent friends pleasure with ecclesiastical favours and letters of indulgence. She thought of the Pope too and sent Urban a gift of five oranges which she had gilded with her own hands, and the dainty gift was accompanied by the following ingenious words:

"Be a tree of love, grafted on the tree of life, Christ sweet Jesus. From that tree comes forth a flower when you feel the love of virtue, and a fruit when you bring forth virtue into the world in works, with hunger for the glory of God and the salvation of your flock. At first the fruit tastes bitter in the mouth of concupiscence, but it grows sweet when the soul has resolved to persevere until death, for the sake of Christ Crucified and for the love of that which is good. As I have seen sometimes, one lays oranges in water to draw out the strong and bitter taste, afterwards filling the peel with sweet things and covering the outside with gold. Where has the bitterness gone? It has remained in the water and in the fire. So is it, holiest Father, with the soul that conceives love for all that is good. At first virtue seems bitter, for the soul is still imperfect. But there is a remedy for this in the blood of Christ Crucified, which gives a water of grace, and that water draws out of us all the bitter, sensual self-love that makes us sad. And inasmuch as the blood is never without the fire (for it was shed with the fire of love), it can be said in truth that the fire and the water draw out the bitterness, emptying the soul of that which was in it, that is, the love of self, and filling it instead with strength, with true perseverance, with a patience that is sweetened with the honey of deep humility. . . When the fruit has been thus filled, the gilding is put on the outside. The gold is the gold of purity, and it is the flaming gold of mercy which shows itself in true patience for the benefit of one's neighbour, whose faults we continually bear with heartfelt meekness, and we have no other pain than the sweet bitterness which we should have when we see God offended, and that souls suffer harm." [8]

XII

"Oh, eternal Father, how came it to pass that Thou didst create us? Greatly have I marvelled at it, and I can see only one reason. Thou wert constrained to it by the fire of Thy love, although Thou foresawest all that we would do to offend Thee. The fire compelled Thee, and although in Thy light Thou foresawest all the wrong that Thy creation would commit against Thy infinite goodness, Thou madest as though Thou didst not see, but closed Thy eyes to it, so madly wert Thou in love with the beauty of Thy creation, which Thou hadst drawn from Thyself and brought into the world in Thy image and likeness. Thou, eternal Truth, hast taught me Thy truth — and that Thou didst not look upon the offence we would cause Thee, but Thou didst not regard it because it had to be, and looked only upon the beauty of Thy creation. Thou didst remain in charity, for Thou art nothing but the fire of charity, Thou art mad with love of Thy creation. And because of my faults I have never rightly known Thee. But give me, Thou sweetest my love, the grace that my body may shed blood for the glory of Thy name, and that I may not be clothed in myself. Receive him, eternal Father, at whose hands I have received the precious body and blood of Thy Son. Unclothe him of himself, loose him from himself, clothe him in Thy eternal will, bind him to Thyself with a knot that can never be loosened, that he may be an herb of sweet odour in the garden of Holy Church. Holiest Father, give Thy sweet and everlasting blessing and cleanse the face of our souls in the blood of Thy Son. Love, Love, I beseech Thee to grant me death. Amen." [1]

It was on February 18th, 1379, that the disciples heard this prayer from Catherine's lips, and one of them (Neri or Barduccio) wrote it down. That which the saint had prayed might be given to the priest who had that morning given her Holy Communion was what she prayed might be given to herself and to all others, that they might put off the old man and put on the new, the core of Christianity from the days of Saint Paul to the end of time, the narrow way, the strait gate, the Cross. Only he who has taken up his cross can pray for death as the consummation of his love — *Amore, Amore, la morte ti addimando!*

Not yet, though, was it the hour of death for Catherine; even though she felt that her heart was dying, the body did not die. Life had still to be lived upon the earth, and life was work, and her work was a more and more extensive, more and more important correspondence. Catherine's house in Rome became one of the centres of the church-political life of the time. When Catherine had heard her Mass in the morning, had received the sacred Host, had said her prayers, the hour came for writing letters. Walking up and down the floor, stopping, walking again, she dictated without ever seeking for words and the writer could hardly follow the rapid stream of her speech. It was as though this slight little woman was conscious that she must hasten in accomplishing what she wanted to do. *Premit hora.* Sometimes, we are told by Francesco di Vanni Malavolti, she dictated several letters at the same time; thus he remembers how Neri, Stefano Maconi and himself sat together, each writing his own letter. "One of us was writing a letter which was to be taken to the now late lamented Pope Gregory XI, the second was writing a letter which was to be sent to Messer Bernabò who was at that time Lord of Milan, the third was writing a third letter which was to be sent to a gentleman of rank, whose name I do not now remember. But she dictated, now to one, now to another, now hiding her face in her hands, now looking up to heaven with her hands crossed, and at every moment she was rapt in ecstasy, yet she continued dictating. But now it happened that she said some words addressed to only one of us, and each of us thought that they were addressed to ourselves in particular and we all wrote them down. When we became aware of this it seemed to us that we had written in error, and we therefore asked her to which of us she had said the words in question. . . She answered kindly and said: 'My dearest sons, be not troubled about it, for this has come to pass by the working of the Holy Spirit. When the letters are finished we will see how these words fit into the rest of the letter and will do what is needed.' As already stated the letters mentioned were addressed to different persons and were concerned with different matters. But, strange to say, when we read the words mentioned above, which each of us had written down, they fitted so well into the context that none of the letters would have been complete without them, from which it can be clearly seen how wonderfully the Holy Spirit worked in that virgin." ²

Those who are well acquainted with Catherine's letters, with their constant repetition of the same thought, need not see anything supernatural in what Francesco Malavolti tells us here. An incident of a similar kind to that related above occurred on May 6th, 1379, when Catherine in one day and probably at the same time dictated four letters: one to the Condottiere Alberigo da Balbiano, one to Joanna of Naples, one to the King of France and the fourth to the Government in Rome — *ai Signori Banderesi e quattro buoni uomini mantenitori della Republica di Roma*. These letters were, according to the rubric in the old manuscript, "composed in ecstasy." ³

The letters already quoted in a previous chapter to the three Italian cardinals, who were hesitating, wavering to and fro between Urban and Clement, and to Joanna of Naples, were written in the first months of the new year, 1379. On the whole Urban's cause was not doing badly; England, the Roman Empire, as well as Hungary and Poland, were on his side. From Siena, too, Catherine had good news. "I do not think," wrote Ser Cristofano Gani on January 14th to Neri, "that in all Siena there is anyone who does not believe and maintain that Pope Urban is the true shepherd of Holy Church, and if envoys from the anti-pope come hither they will not be heard." In Siena the centre and place of meeting of the Urbanists, among whom Catherine's disciples were the most fervent, was provided by the pious confraternity of the *Compagnia della Vergine Maria dello Spedale,* who had a chapel underneath the vault of the Scala hospital. "All the brethren," the same letter continues, "send you greeting. Tell our *Mamma* that we are very disunited and that she must give us a bond which we must obey out of reverence for her, and which will now and then bring us together in remembrance of her. Beg her also to write to us some day and to remember her straying sheep." On the following day Stefano Maconi writes a detailed letter, also addressed to Neri di Landoccio dei Pagliaresi, as they never wrote to Catherine herself though it was really meant for her.

"Praised be Jesus Christ Crucified and His most gentle Mother Mary.

"Dearly loved brother in Jesus Christ.

"Great joy have I had from the two letters that you have written to me after your departure from Siena, and great consolation have they been to my mind, and I have not been content to read them but once or twice. But that which you write about our sweet and revered *Mamma* causes me no wonder, nor do I doubt thereof, for I should believe much greater things of her than those you write of; I know and confess it here that our *Mamma* is a splendid *Mamma,* and it is my firm hope that I may day by day believe with greater knowledge and confess with greater strength that she is a *Mamma*.

"The other and great news that you tell me, of the exaltation of Holy Church and of the true successor of St. Peter, Pope Urban VI, verily Christ on earth, has all seemed to me like a soothing ointment for the sufferings I have felt and still feel. And although it has been a great relief to me to learn all this, I shall not recover altogether until I sit again at the feet of my dearly loved *Mamma*."

So strong were Stefano's feelings for Catherine that even the great church-political events of the time were of only secondary importance to him; that which really occupies him is his *dilettissima Mamma,* she who is *benignissima Mamma;* not until he is again at her feet will the longing that is gnawing at his heart cease, the emptiness he feels every morning on awakening be filled up at last. Letters are only like cooling ointments, but the wound still burns under the ointment, every pulse-beat causes pain. Only in one place is there a healing to be found for his suffering, in her presence, gazing up into her face, whose every line is so dear and familiar, and solemnly, reverently, kissing the hem of her white habit. For Stefano, Catherine is the real meaning of existence, she alone makes life worth living for him, and everything else is only of value if she cares for it and in relation to it.

He has therefore taken pains to obtain for her all the political news that she has asked for and now sends it to Neri, so that the latter "can tell her and inform her about it." It is good news that he sends, the feeling in Siena is unanimous for Urban and against the "anti-demon of Fondi" (as Stefano, with some confusion of ideas and a mingling of the words "anti-pope" and "demon," calls Clement, who had been elected in Fondi); Urban's Nuncio, the Bishop of Narni, Giacomo di Sozzino Tolomei, had been very well received in Siena; and together with his friend Pietro Bellanti (he, who once brought Maconi to make Catherine's acquaintance) Stefano had paid him his respects. The envoy of the anti-pope, Alderigo Interminelli, is said to have been in Pisa, but the council in Siena had given orders not to admit him. And if he did get inside the gates it would be worse for himself as he would be stoned by the boys in the streets! So "our poor little town" (*questa nostra città tapinella*) is exceeding well disposed.

"I say no more to you this time, except that I beseech you, my sweet brother, not to forget me, but that you will carefully pray to God for me, which I sorely need, and above all for the grace that I may know how to deliver myself from the corruption of the world, so that I may always do His will, such as may please Him most. Two things shall be a sign to me that you have not forgotten me — the first, that you commend me often to our venerable, sweet and delectable Mamma, and I beg you to begin with it at once before you lay down the letter, so that you do not forget it; the second is that you write often to me and for that I ask you as urgently as I can. . ."

The letter concludes with greetings to and from common friends and the signature is worded: "Given in Siena on the 15th January, 1378 [our 1379, the year being reckoned from March 25th] by your useless and unworthy brother Stefano, alone [*soletto*] and poor in all virtue." [4]

Stefano did not appeal in vain to Catherine's maternal heart on behalf of himself and the other disciples. Though the eight letters that she wrote to him are brief (her letters to Neri are also brief), they are full of kindness and wisdom. True to her principles she tries to draw the young Sienese away from his exaggerated desire for consolation; she enjoins upon him that he "must eat the hard and old bread of tribulation." "God makes sport with us," she teaches him, "to lead us whither He would have us. When the sweet medicine and the soothing ointment do not avail he burns out the sore with fire so that it may not fester." She admonishes him and the other disciples to perseverance in the war between spirit and flesh; there must be irreconcilable enmity between reason and the senses, for the senses are in conflict with grace, they rob us of God and keep us down in the constant bitterness of earthly life. We must leave the world and run to God, who is "waiting for us with open arms."

Thus the letters to Maconi. In a long letter to "The Brethren in *Compagnia della Vergine* in the Hospital in Siena" she develops once more to all the disciples her teaching about the labour in the vineyard: first in the vineyard which is one's own soul, then in the vineyard of charity to one's neighbour, finally in that of the Church. And only he who works well in the first of these three vineyards cares to work in the other two, for, as Catherine says elsewhere with delicate psychology, "He who has renounced the light of faith [notice the striking expression: *renunzio al lume!*] has become without strength, without moderation, without wisdom; he has become unrighteous, he hopes in himself and with dead faith he believes in himself, he trusts in creatures and not in the Creator; he is without love and without goodness, for they forsook him when he was seized with love of his own frail self; *he has become cruel to himself and therefore he cannot be good to others.*"

As she always does, Catherine goes to the root of things. There are two main currents in life: on the one hand love of God, faith, love of one's neighbour, zeal, peace; on the other, self-love, lack of faith, indifference to others, worldliness, torment. There is the kingdom of Adam, and the kingdom of Christ. Catherine has therefore come into the world to lead the children of Adam through the gate of the Cross to the peace of Christ.[5]

These are the thoughts and feelings which with their fire glow in the prayer that the disciples wrote down from the lips of their Mamma on the last day of the Carnival (February 22d) 1379. It was on this day, now twelve years ago, that Catherine had celebrated her mystic betrothal to Jesus (only twelve years — they seemed so long — so much had happened in them). It is permissible to think that Catherine would always remember that day as a particular anniversary; how could it be otherwise, but that her thoughts must go back to the little cell in the house at Fontebranda, and to that which happened on the Shrove Tuesday in

1367! In the midst of the Roman carnival the bride of Jesus, now as in her youth in Siena, prayed: "Oh, eternal God, compassionate, merciful Father, look in mercy upon us, for we are blind and without any light, and most of all, I, wretched, miserable creature that I am! And therefore have I always been cruel to myself... Oh, sweet, gentle Light, oh beginning and ground of our salvation, with Thy light Thou hast bestowed light upon us, and Thy light enters into every soul that opens the door of the will, for the will stands at the door of the soul, and as soon as it is opened the light comes in, like the sun that knocks at the closed window and comes into the house as soon as it is opened. Thus it is right that the soul should have the will to know Thee, and with that will it opens the eye of reason and then Thou comest in, Thou true sun, into the soul and enlightenest it with Thyself. And when Thou hast entered, Thou light of mercy, what dost Thou work in the soul? Thou drivest out darkness from it, Thou givest light to it; Thou drivest away the mists of self-love and the fire of Thy love gives warmth to the room.* Thou makest the heart free, for in the light from Thee it has seen and known how great is the freedom Thou has bestowed upon us, in having delivered us from the thraldom of the devil, into whose hands mankind would have fallen by its cruelty. Therefore the heart now hates the cause of this cruelty, which is compassion with our own sensuality, and instead lets it have compassion with reason and become cruel to sensuality. In locking the door upon all the faculties of the soul, may it shut out the memory of the misery of the world and its vain pleasures, and instead remember Thy benefits. Let the will close it, so that it loves nothing but Thee, but loves Thee above all things and all things in Thee, according to Thy will, and wishing only to follow Thee. Then it will truly have compassion on itself, and when it has compassion on itself it will also have compassion on its neighbour and be ready to give up its life for the salvation of souls."

As in everything that has been preserved for us from Catherine's lips — her letters too, her book is dictated — one admires

---

* *Rimane il fuoco della tua Carità.* I translate somewhat freely, but there is no doubt that Catherine was thinking of one of those large charcoal pans which in Siena are simply called "a fire" (un fuocone), with which the Sienese drive out the chilly dampness of their rooms during the long rainy winter.

the honest love of the truth, bordering on mercilessness, in words like these. The identity between faith and the will to live, unfaith and the will to die, is relentlessly recognised and expressed. We are given the choice between the worlds of love and cruelty; he who accepts faith gives himself up to life, he who rejects faith offers himself up to death. Unfaith is an act of cruelty against myself; I kill my soul and *know* that I am killing it, and *will* to kill it, will it deliberately and with evil and despairing delight. But neither can I, who do not love myself, love anyone else, and I feel that I am of the kind of *him* who is cold *non-love*. . .

Faith is the inevitable condition for attaining to that love which saves the soul from the kingdom of death, and this faith has (as Catherine always maintains) one chief article: it is faith in the Blood. The God of nature, the almighty and incomprehensible sovereign who drowns human beings in His deluge and crushes us in His earthquakes, as a thoughtless boy destroys ant-hills — that God does not appeal to our love. But there is another God, whom we see with the eye of faith, when it has not been darkened by the cloud of self-will (for self-will would rather not see Him) — that is the God of the Cross, the God who suffered for His creatures, the God in whom there is salvation.

"What father," cries Catherine, "ever gave up his son to death for the sake of his slave! Thou alone didst it, eternal Father! Thou didst clothe Thy Word in our flesh, and our flesh bore the suffering, and now we receive the fruit of it, if by Thy grace we walk in the way Thou didst walk Thyself." And then the seeress is overwhelmed by the greatness of the Redeemer's act, the almost incredible witness to God's nature in the doctrine of redemption makes her ashamed of her tepidity and weakness in self-denial. "Fleeing from myself I seek refuge in Thee and complain of myself, eternal Truth. Pass judgment upon me, for I am cruel to my soul and full of pity for my own sensuality. I have sinned, Lord, have mercy upon me. Oh, compassionate cruelty,* which treads the senses under foot in temporal life that it may exalt the soul in eternity! . . . I beseech Thee to grant this feeling to all Thy creatures and in particular to those whom Thou hast given me, and whom I love with a particular love. Make them compassionate, so that they may have the perfect

* *O pietosa crudeltà!*

cruelty with which to kill their spoilt self-will. It was this compassionate cruelty that Thou didst teach us, oh Truth, when Thou saidst: 'Whosoever comes to me, and does not hate his father, mother, wife and child, brothers and sisters, and even his own soul, cannot be my disciple.' The last seems to be difficult, the children of the world often do the other, though not from virtue. . .

"Oh, eternal Truth, fragrance above all fragrance, generosity above all generosity, goodness above all goodness, justice above all justice, Thou rewardest each one according to his deeds. Thou dost therefore permit that the unjust man can not endure himself, for he has given up himself to coveting that which is lower than himself, in coveting worldly pleasures and riches. For all created things are lower than man, they are created to serve him and not because he is to be their slave. Thou alone art greater than we, and therefore it is Thee whom we must desire and seek to serve. Thou dost also justly permit the righteous already to taste everlasting life here in this world, with peace and rest of the soul, for they have put their affection in Thee, who art true and highest rest. . . Thou art eternal and infinite goodness and none can comprehend or know Thee, except so much as Thou dost make us comprehend. And Thou givest us so much as the vessels of our souls are ready to receive. Oh, sweetest Love, I have never loved Thee, in all the days of my life I have never loved Thee. I surrender to Thee all my sons and daughters whom Thou hast laid upon my shoulders; alas — and I must waken them from sleep and slumber myself. Sweet merciful Father, do Thou waken me so that the eyes of their souls may be always fastened upon Thee. *Peccavi, Domine, miserere mei.* God, come to our aid, Lord, make haste to help us." [6]

During the Long Fast, or Lent, which begins on Ash Wednesday, in 1379, Catherine prayed with more fervour than ever. "Oh, eternal Blood," she says in a prayer written down on March 1st. "Oh, sweet Blood, Thou givest strength to the soul and givest it light, in Thee it gains the nature of an angel, so that it forgets itself altogether and can see nothing but Thee. . . Oh, miserable creature that I am, I have never followed Thee, Thou true learning, and therefore am I so weak that I fail at the least trial." Two days later it was her prayer that as the light from above falls like a dew of rest upon the soul, so may the prayers of the pious descend upon the world like a dew of peace. On Lady Day (March 25) Catherine earnestly invokes Mary: "Thou art the book in which the rule of our life has been written down," that is, when the Virgin of Nazareth opened her will to the eternal Word, who willed to become Man in her, and spoke the great consent: "Be it to me according to Thy word," that consent for which the Eternal is also waiting outside the door of your soul and mine. . . "Oh, Mary, blessed art thou among all women *in sæculum sæculi*, for today thou hast given us bread of thy flour which the Deity has laid and baked."

Returning to the fundamental doctrine which Jesus had taught her in the early days of solitude, the Sienese saint exclaims: "Oh, Truth, Truth, who am I, that Thou givest me Thy truth? I am she who is not. It is Thy truth, then, that knows and speaks and works all things, for *I am not*. Oh, Deity, Deity, who art love, what can I say then about Thy truth! Thou Truth, speak truth, for I can not speak truth, I speak only darkness, for I have not followed Thee to the Cross and obtained its fruit, but I have followed only darkness and tasted darkness. . . We have blinded ourselves, for we have laid upon our eyes the cloud of cold and damp self-love, therefore we do not know Thee or any true goodness, but we call good evil and evil good, and thus we become exceeding ignorant and ungrateful. And it is worse for us to lose the light because we have known the truth, for a false Christian is worse than an unbeliever. Such are they, Lord, who persecute the fruit of Thy cross, which is Thy blood, for they do not follow Thee, crucified Christ, but persecute Thee and Thy blood, and this they do especially, who resist the master of Thy cellar, he who has the keys of the cellar in which Thy precious blood is kept, and the blood of all the martyrs is kept, but the blood of the martyrs is of no value except in the power of Thy blood. This rebellion and all sin have come because they have lost the light of Thy truth, which is obtained by faith. But they are foolish and do not understand this, because they judge from the shell. . . Oh, thou foolish creature, who makest thyself like the animals. Knowest thou not that those who are like the beasts shall go to the everlasting punishments of hell?

THE CROWN OF THORNS

In those punishments man becomes naught, not as concerning his being, but as concerning grace. For grace is a consummation of nature, and that which does not reach its consummation may be said to have become naught." [7]

The season of Lent — March and April — is also the season of spring in Rome, and there can be no doubt that Catherine and her friends would follow the Roman custom of going each day in Lent to one of the so-called *station churches*.

In the Middle Ages a certain church was appointed for each day in Lent and all the Roman ecclesiastics of each parish walked there together in solemn procession to hold the service. These churches are called *stationes* and their names can be found in the Roman Missal. At the present day this custom has not yet quite been given up. On the days of the stations the churches in question are adorned as for a festival, the pillars being draped with scarlet and the mosaic floor strewn with twigs of box, and the acrid odour of the leaves blends with the fragrance of the incense from the altar, where the candles burn in bright golden flames while High Mass is sung.

Catherine would go on these pilgrimages. On Ash Wednesday they would be to Santa Maria in Cosmedin down by the temple of Vesta and then up the Aventine hill to Santa Sabina. Santa Sabina in Rome is the mother church of the Dominicans; in the adjoining monastery the cell is shown in which "the holy men, Dominic, Francis and Angelus the Carmelite spent the nights conversing of the things that belong to the kingdom of God." Here Catherine would be profoundly reminded of the great Father of her Order, here she would be so close to his life as never before, here she would be able to pray where he had prayed, to kiss the floor on which his feet had trod, and in the garden she would stand before the orange tree which the Spaniard had planted with his own hands, and she would think of "the tree of love," planted in the good soil, bearing fair blossoms for God and fruit useful to man.

Each day in Lent would take her to fresh holy places. She would go to San Giorgio in Velabro, "in the bog," down by *Forum boarium* beside the temple of Janus, which is no temple, but the arch of honour built by the Roman money changers to

Septimus Severus and his sons; but Caracalla, who in his rancour had his brother Geta's name erased from the arch, here also had his image hewn away.

On another day the goal of the pious walk would be San Gregorio Magno, where the paternal home of the great Pope once stood, and where his room can still be seen — like Catherine's room in Siena, which was later the object of visits, but at this time she was still living and standing on the mosaic floor of the basilica, an ardent life in the midst of the darkness of existence. There are three chapels; in one of them is still preserved the marble table at which Gregory daily received twelve poor guests. Crosses, hewn into the table, mark the twelve places. One day a thirteenth poor guest came and Gregory fed him too, although he was unbidden. But when the stranger had received his food from the hands of the gentle Pope, he had radiant wings and had become an angel.

In this way the Sienese saint and her spiritual family would go through all the ancient churches of Rome. They would visit Santa Pudenziana, Santa Prassede, San Cosma e Damiano, San Lorenzo Fuori le Mura. They would stand in San Clemente and look up at the mosaics in the apse, where the Cross is represented as the tree of life, from which grows the true vine, and in Catherine's mind there would assuredly be a re-echo of the words that recur so often in her letters: "grafted on the true tree of life." Twelve white doves rest on the arms of the cross; they signify the twelve apostles. So would Catherine have apostolic souls resting nowhere but on the hard wood of the Cross.

In San Sisto out in Via Appia Catherine would again tread in the footsteps of "the sweet Spaniard," for there stands the convent of nuns founded by Saint Dominic himself. A fresco, evidently painted soon after Catherine's death, still testifies to the Sienese saint's presence here. And one day in Lent — spring is already showing her green about the brown city wall of Aurelian — she would stand by the Latin gate; in the old church of San Giovanni *ante porte latinam* she would see the place where Saint John the Apostle, under Domitian, was tortured in boiling oil but could not die the death of a martyr and was taken out alive from the deadly bath. There she, too, would groan: "I die and cannot die!" *Muoio e non posso morire!*

THE CROWN OF THORNS

There was reason enough for her groans, for the adherents of the opposing party were still contending against "the cellarer of the Blood," against the true host of the *bottega* of the Church, standing on the middle of the bridge of life. The Castel Sant' Angelo still defied the Romans loyal to the Pope; a Clementine army, led by a kinsman of Robert of Geneva, Louis de Montjoie, was advancing on Rome, and on April 17th, 1379, the anti-Pope issued a bull in which he conferred the greater part of the Papal States as a fief on Duke Louis of Anjou, Catherine's friend of Villeneuve lez Avignon, with a request to him to take possession of his fief.

At this time the Condottiere Alberigo da Balbiano was in the service of Urban, and the end of April brought two great victories for the papal cause: on the 27th Castel Sant' Angelo capitulated, on the 30th Alberigo defeated the Clementine army at Marino in the Alban hills and took the leaders themselves prisoners, both Montjoie and Silvestre Budes, as well as Bernard della Salle. The victorious Romans marched into Castel Sant' Angelo and began to raze the threatening fortress to the ground (as in the French Revolution the Bastille was pulled down) and Urban, who could now return to the Vatican again, walked barefoot in the procession of thanksgiving from Santa Maria in Trastevere to Saint Peter's.

Under the impression of these great and happy events Catherine wrote four significant letters on May 6th: one to Alberigo da Balbiano and his Compagnia di San Giorgio, to congratulate them on the victory, one to the Roman government (the seven Banderesi, one for each *rioni* in Rome, and the four *"good men"*), one to Joanna of Naples, and lastly, one to Charles V of France. She explains to the papal soldiers that they are fighting the good fight, "the Master whom you serve is Christ Crucified," and therefore they can fight "with a good conscience in defence of our faith, of Holy Church and the Vicegerent of Christ." Five hundred years later the same thought inspired the papal Zouaves — until history wrote its unmistakable commentary on the words of Jesus: "Put up thy sword in its sheath, for whosoever draweth the sword shall perish by the sword." Nineteen hundred years were needed before Peter, compelled by necessity, learned the lesson which the Master taught him in Gethsemane "in the night in which He was betrayed." And a too zealous disciple still wonders that Jesus stretches out His hand and heals the wound of His enemy instead of completing Peter's work and cutting off Malchus' other ear. . .

The Queen of Naples is warned by Catherine "to have compassion on her own soul. Egoism is in reality the opposite of egoism — one believes that one loves oneself, but one is one's own worst enemy. "Oh, how happy my soul would be," Catherine exclaims, "if I could come down to you and give up my life to give you back heaven, which you have forfeited, and earth, which you have lost — take from you the knife of cruelty with which you have slain yourself, and instead give you the knife of piety which kills vice, so that with holy fear of God and love of truth you might clothe and bind yourself in His sweet will."

She admonishes the Roman government to be grateful. She tells these rulers that "God has done this, which you, with all your human cunning, could not do. He turned the eyes of His mercy upon us who were in such great peril, and it is therefore to Him that we must ascribe our rescue. Our Father, Pope Urban VI, gives us an example of this, and as a sign that he acknowledges that mercy comes from God, he humbles himself and does what no one has done in times beyond memory: walks barefoot in procession. Let us therefore, my sons, follow in our father's footsteps, that is, acknowledge that this comes from God and not from us. I would also, that you should be grateful to the Company (i.e. *Compagnia di San Giorgio*), who have been the instrument of God, and help them so far as you are able, in particular the poor wounded . . ."

The Roman senator, Giovanni Cenci, had taken an active part in bringing about the capitulation of Castel Sant' Angelo, but this was forgotten, now that his help was no longer needed, and Catherine censures this neglect. "It seems to me that Giovanni Cenci is being treated with great ingratitude; with great zeal and faithfulness and with a sincere heart, only to please God and come to our aid he gave up everything else to deliver you from the scourge that Castel Sant' Angelo was, and now you not only show him no gratitude or even thank him, but envy and ingratitude make people murmur against him and cast venomous aspersions upon him. I will not that you so treat anyone who has rendered you services, for it is an offence against God and it is harmful to yourselves."

Finally, she explains to the King of France her usual teaching, that self-love is the root of all evil. "It corrupts the taste of the soul, so that good things taste ill and bad things taste sweet." Self-love makes one unjust, so that we serve creatures for the sake of favours and gifts, and for the wages of pleasure; it makes us oppose God and His earthly organ, the Church. Catherine fears that Charles too, suffers himself to be led by this self-love. "It seems to me from what I hear [with her immense interest she *heard* everything that happened all over Europe!] that you are beginning to suffer yourself to be led by the evil councils of the men of darkness, and you know that when the blind lead the blind they both fall into the ditch. . . I wonder exceedingly that you, a good Catholic, who would fear God and be a man, permit yourself to be led like a child, and that you do not see how you bring destruction upon yourself and others, in obscuring the light of holy faith by the counsel of those who are clearly limbs of the devil and rotten trees . . . Open your eyes and see that they are arrant liars." She then repeats all the arguments proving the legality of the the election of Urban and again emphasises the psychological element, that the cardinals would not have done homage to a pope whom they know not to be pope rightfully, or asked him for tokens of his favour. "They adhered to the truth," she declares, "so long as he would not correct their faults; when he began to do that they rebelled against him." And now they are not to be shaken in their error, "they are as obdurate as devils."

The letter, which hovers between hope and fear, concludes with a suggestion that Charles can consult the Sorbonne — "You have the source of wisdom there." "Forgive all these many words. Rather would I say it to you by word of mouth, in your presence, than by letter."

As the last lines of the letter indicate, Catherine had entertained the thought of going to Paris herself. Nothing came of it, nor would it perhaps have been of any use.[8] The University of Paris, which had at first stood by Urban, declared itself on May 30th in favour of Clement. In the following year

Charles V died, a partisan of the Schism, yet with a reference to a coming general Church Council as the authority to which he would willingly submit.

Meanwhile, and probably at Catherine's incentive, Urban asked Raymond once more to attempt a mission to France. The Dominican was to go by sea from Genoa, where he was still staying, to Barcelona, and thence to cross the frontier. Detailed instructions were worked out; they are still preserved in the archives of the Vatican. Then came the news that the King of Aragon, at the request of Pedro de Luna, who was now wholly on Clement's side, had thrown Urban's two envoys to Spain into prison. Raymond's courage failed him again; he stayed where he was.

This fresh defection of the disciple, this repeated denial of the Master, was hard for Catherine to bear. She rebuked him sternly for his lack of faith, and according to her usage she included herself as if she suffered from the same fault. "Our love is measured by our faith, our faith by our love," she writes. "He who loves is ever faithful to the beloved and serves him unto death. From that I can see that I do not truly love God, nor all creatures for His sake, for if I did I would be so faithful to Him that I would suffer death a thousand times a day if it were needful and possible . . . and my faith would not cease, but I would be sure that God is my defence and my protector, as He was of the holy martyrs who went joyously to their torments. If I believed I would not fear, but I would be assured that what God was for them He would be also for me . . . But because I do not love Him I do not really trust Him, and my fear shows me how lukewarm is my love, and how obscured the light of faith, so that I am faithless to my Creator and trust only in myself. I confess and do not deny that this root has not yet been pulled up from my soul and therefore the work that God would have me to do is kept back and hindered, and that which I begin to do does not reach that bright and fruitful end that was God's aim. Woe, woe to me, Lord, woe to me, miserable that I am. Must I really continue to be thus, always, everywhere, however my life is ordered! Shall I always close the ways of thy providence with my unfaithfulness? Nay, I will continue to do so, if in thy mercy thou dost not break me asunder and create me anew again and again. Then break me to pieces, Lord, break

THE CROWN OF THORNS

my hard heart, that I may no longer be an implement which thou canst not use!"

The reproaches against Raymond do not here become self-reproach as a mere matter of form; one feels how Catherine is almost in despair at the sight of *her* own defection. After so many years of life in prayer and penance, she too, must repeat the old, bitter confession: "The good that I would, I do not." She too, must learn how difficult it is for flesh and blood to believe, really believe in earnest. For *if* it is true, true like the shining of the sun and the stars, like the sea and the thunder, if it is true like the earth itself and like the rocks, that Almighty God became Man, suffered, allowed Himself to be crucified for us and died for us, for our salvation, then indeed, how *can* there be room in the soul of man for anything but that boundless, bloodstained Cross? Then must every heart become a Calvary, and the eye must find no joy in any flower but the five red roses in the enclosed garden of the body of Christ. Then can no other love be permitted but that for the Bridegroom — "His pierced right hand under my head, his bleeding left hand shall embrace me." Never, perhaps, has Christian poetry sounded greater depths, than when it confessed how powerless is the thoughtless, the hard human heart to give so great, so entire a love that demands everything. At times it is as though Christian experience sums up its inmost confession in a hopeless sigh: "We can not give it! It is beyond our powers!"

But Catherine determines to persevere; to the last she will strive to reach the ideal. She wills the cross for herself, she wills the cross for others. In the letter in which he told her of his altered decision, Raymond expressed his fear that she would now abandon him and that the *amor stretto particolare,* that particular bond which had hitherto bound them so closely together, would now be torn apart. She answers:

"So far as I have understood your letter, you have, by the cunning of the devil and your own fault, had many difficulties to contend with, and it seemed to you that a greater weight than you could bear had been laid upon you. And it did not seem right to you that I measured you with my own measure, and therefore you were in doubt whether I had not decreased in my love and kindness to you. . . But could you ever believe that I desired aught but the welfare of your soul? And where is now that faith which you are always wont to have and ought to have? . . . You have known how to find a way of casting your burden upon the ground. . . If you had been faithful you would not have wavered and would not need now to be troubled about what God thinks of you and what I think, but like a good and willing son you would have done what you could. And if you could not have walked upright, you could have crept; if you could not have gone as a Dominican you could have gone as a pilgrim; if you had had no money you could have begged your way on. This faithful obedience would have worked more, both before God and men, than all earthly prudence. It is because of my sins that this did not come to pass."

Again she urges him to die the mystic death.

"Forsake yourself, let go all your own joy and consolation," she exclaims. "We have offered up ourselves as dead in the holy garden of the Church, we have offered up ourselves to Christ on earth, the Lord of the Church. Let us then be as the dead. The dead neither hear nor feel. Strive to slay yourself with the knife of hate and love, so that you do not hear the words of abuse, the insults and reproaches with which the persecutors of Holy Church overwhelm you. The eyes see naught that seems impossible, for with the light of faith they see that we can do all things in Christ Crucified, and that God does not lay greater burdens upon us than we can bear. . . When we conceive love of suffering we lose the sensibility of the senses, and dead, dead, we will live in that garden, and when I shall see it I will bless my soul. I tell you, sweetest Father, that whether we will or no the time we are living in enjoins upon us to die. So do not live any longer . . . you have been a man of your word, do not be womanish when you must keep your word." [9]

Gradually Catherine became reconciled to the thought of Raymond's defection; that, too, must have been foreseen in the councils of God, *non senza misterio*. Her last letter was written to him. In a letter from Rome to Neri di Landoccio, of December 3rd, 1379, some lines are written in a quite pleased and homely note of every-day: "We have good news from Brother Raymond; he is well and is working very much for Holy Church. He is Vicar of the province of Genoa and has soon to take the degree of

Master of Theology." [10] Catherine had understood at last that Raymond's place was in the valley, in the vineyards, among the other labourers, and that he did not belong to that exalted solitude, on the freezing snow-clad heights of perfect self-abnegation.

XIII

In the fourteenth century the house of the Misericordia Brothers stood on the site where the Academy of Arts in Siena now stands, in Via delle Belle Arti. Those who have visited Siena will remember the black-hooded brothers, who with a crucifix and lighted torches, come at eventide to fetch the dead and carry them through the darkening streets to the Misericordia cemetery outside Porta Tufi — to the place where earlier monks of Oliveto had a monastery, and where Bernardo Tolomei died in the year of the plague in 1348, a victim to his zealous Christian charity. The origin of the Misericordia confraternity goes right back to the thirteenth century; it was founded about 1240 by the pious Sienese nobleman Andrea Gallerani who laid upon the brothers the twofold task of nursing the sick and burying the dead. After Gallerani's death the hospital became the property of the State, and the government of Siena appointed the rector of the house, who in Catherine's time was the oft-mentioned Matteo de' Cenni Fazi, her good friend and disciple.[1]

On account of the difficulties which Stefano Maconi, as a zealous *Caterinato,* still had with his family, Messer Matteo had offered him hospitality in his house, so that Stefano always had a room standing ready in the house of the Misericordia brethren, where he could stay both day and night, and where he considered himself as belonging to the house.[2] One day in June (the 22d) 1379, he was sitting in this room and writing to Neri Pagliaresi and to the whole "family" in Rome.

"Dearest Brother in Jesus Christ.

"Yesterday I received a letter from you, written on the feast of the Ascension, with much and great news of the true successor of Saint Peter and the true vicegerent of Christ, Urban VI, that he is faring well, and of the defeat of that anti-devil [!], at which I have rejoiced exceedingly and still rejoice. And although I have for several weeks known part of that which you write to me, yet not so fully, it is as though I feel a fresh joy over it. But the other good news that you tell me, of certain great lords, of whom the opposite had hitherto been believed, at least of the greatest of them, as to that I beg divine charity to enlighten

THE CROWN OF THORNS

their hearts and the hearts of all others so that the truth be not darkened to them, neither that they be the cause of obscuring the truth in others, so that there may not be too much schism and separation among Christians."

Ascension Day in that year fell on May 19th, and the good news which Neri had sent to his friend in Siena was of course first and foremost the fall of Castel Sant' Angelo and the victory at Marino.

More than that had happened, however. After the defeat at Marino, Clement had decided to seek protection with Joanna of Naples, who had received him well and given him Castello dell' Ovo as a residence. The Archbishop of Naples, however, was on Urban's side, and the people sided with him. In a wordy strife in the open street between Urbanists and Clementists a nobleman had struck out the eye of a carpenter, who was speaking in favour of Urban and against the Queen, and suddenly the whole population of Naples rose against Clement. Furious crowds rushed down to the harbour, down towards Castello dell' Ovo — "Death to Clement, death to the antichrist, long live Pope Urban!" were the savage shouts. Clement left Naples in terror on May 13th, and Joanna sent an ambassador to Rome to declare her submission to Urban. On May 22nd Clement left Italy altogether and did not stop until he reached Avignon, where he arrived on June 20th.

It was important for Urban to follow up his victory, but for that two things were needed: soldiers and money. Or rather, one thing: money, for money meant soldiers as well. Catherine endeavoured to help him in this sphere too, and appealed first and foremost to her native town. In a letter to *"i Signori defensori,"* she reminds them of all the Pope's benevolence. He set them free from excommunication, and owing to his mediation Siena and not Pisa obtained the seaport of Talamone. Meanwhile the Pope had not yet received the sum which had then been decided upon (eight thousand guilders) and Catherine writes: "I beg of you in the name of Christ Crucified, that you will no longer let Christ on earth be content with mere words, but give him deeds and return to him that which he has himself restored to you." [3] In support of her appeal she wrote a letter at the same time to the influential *Compagnia della Vergine*. There is a sign, she explains, by which one may know the good labourer in the vineyard, and that is that he supports Pope Urban "spiritually and temporally. Spiritually, with humble prayer; temporally in doing what you can to obtain the help of the government for him, which is but reasonable. Do you not see that by giving such help we are helping ourselves? Do we love our faith so little that we will not defend it, and if needful, risk our lives for it? Are we so ungrateful after having received so many benefits from God and from him? And do we not know that ingratitude dries up the piety in us?" [4]

Maconi now writes in his letter on behalf of the Company, of which he was a member, and on behalf of Siena altogether:

"I repeat," he writes, "that so far as I know and can judge, nine persons out of ten are for Urban, and the few who think otherwise are pointed at as thieves and robbers. In spiritual matters he will be obeyed as a true shepherd, but in temporal affairs they excuse themselves with their great poverty and the misery into which they have sunk." In order to protect themselves against being plundered by straggling lansquenets, Lucca, Siena, Perugia and Florence had in common to pay a considerable sum to the Condottieri John Hawkwood and Lucio di Lardo. Stefano pleads this as an excuse for his fellow-countrymen: "Every month the soldiers have to be paid six thousand gold florins, and the day before yesterday they even demanded fifteen thousand, and yet it is inevitable that the Maremma and other parts of the country will be pillaged. I do not say this, though, in order to excuse them. I have also spoken several times to the lords in the government about it, both in the town hall and elsewhere, and I have said that we might pledge some of the property of the town, and that if we cannot send many soldiers, we can send a few, and the Holy Father will be content when he sees that we are doing what we can."

Stefano then passes on to certain items of local gossip, speaks of "that affair with the archpriest," a story which no one knows anything about any more, of "a tanned goat-skin," which he has procured for Neri, and which the joiner Francesco del Tonghio's son has now taken with him to Rome, and he hopes it will be found satisfactory. Finally he sends many, many greetings. "Messer Matteo looked in at the door just now; when he heard to whom I was writing he told me to beg you to say to our Mamma that he has written a long letter to her. . . If I had time, by the way, I could tell you a story that would make you laugh; even Messer Matteo laughed at it so that he nearly put his jaws out of joint." To this day the Tuscans are experts in funny stories, and it is a pity that we do not get that "Novella" which had caused so much hearty laughter on that day in June, 1379, in the house of Misericordia in Siena — even the dignified Rector could not help laughing too.

Yet after so much that is serious and so much gossip the usual sigh from the heart does not fail to come. "Greet Pietro [di Giovanni Ventura] and Francesco [Malavolti] and all the others in the little family, in which I have not been found worthy to be present in the body, because of my sins, but in my heart I am always with you; and gladly would I take upon myself the trouble of a journey if God would grant me the grace of sitting once more at the feet of our venerable Mamma." [5]

As with Siena, so with several other towns which were amicably disposed towards the Pope; they had promised willingly, but found it difficult to keep their word. This was so in the case of Perugia, whither Catherine therefore sent Neri di Landoccio with a letter to "the Lords Priors of the People and commune of Perugia." In this letter too, Catherine tries to show how "the fear of God holds promises also for this present life." By supporting the Pope, the Perugians are really supporting themselves. "How? I will tell you. The times, as you see, are such that we must be prepared for great tribulations and our country will suffer under the coming of great lords [she is thinking of Louis of Anjou, whom Clement had called into Italy, and of Ludwig of Hungary and his cousin, Charles of Durazzo, to whom Urban had applied for help], and we are as fragile as glass because of our many faults and our mutual disunion. When, therefore, we depart from our Father, and he does not support us, we are in danger. . . Let us therefore seek to help him, so that in the hour of need he can help us in return. It is clear to you also (for you are not more stupid than other people!) that although the arm of the Church may be weakened it can never be broken, and after weakness it gains new strength, and so also does he who leans upon it." [6]

Florence, too, had hesitated to help Urban, and in a long letter Catherine admonishes "the Lords Priors of the Guilds, and the Standard-bearer of Justice [*gonfalioniere di giustizia*] of the People and Commune of Florence." Once more she still preaches her political gospel, which is the same as her religious one, that self-will is the root of all evil. If the selfish man is a subject he is disobedient; if he possesses rank and office he is unjust, or exercises justice only according to his whim and pleasure, for his motives are always personal, and he pronounces judgment either to be avenged on an enemy or to oblige a friend or finally to serve his own interest. "Hence it is that holy justice is everywhere absent, and the lords have become tyrants. The Commune nourishes the subjects, not with justice and brotherly love, but everyone seeks his own welfare with deceit and lies, and not the common good. Everyone wants to rule for his own profit and not for the good estate and government of the town." [7]

Il buono stato e reggimento della città — "the good government," which Ambrogio Lorenzetti had painted on the wall in "the Hall of the Nine," in the town hall of her own city of Siena — this is also the subject of Catherine's letter to Messer Andreasso Cavalcobuoj, who was was at that time senator of the city. "Dearest Brother," she addresses this highly-placed official, "sleep no longer, but see that you awake. Let us return to ourselves and not wait for a more convenient time, for time does not wait for us. Time is so short that we cannot realise it at all, and I would that we should break the bonds with which we are bound. For he who is bound cannot walk, and we ought to walk in the path of virtue and follow the doctrine of Christ Crucified (He is the Way, the Truth and the Life, and whosoever walks with Him walks not in darkness but in the light). Therefore we must walk in that sweet and straight path. But how shall we cut through the cord? With the knife that is called hatred of vice and love of virtue; and in confession we throw away the cord." Then, when he has been loosened from the bonds of sin, he should again bind himself to the service of the Church, "which is greatly pleasing to God and more particularly so when she is in such great need. . . Beware of taking part in the public prayers and in the Mass, that you may not heap guilt upon guilt." [8]

As the last remark shows, Siena had not yet been loosed from the interdict; the settling of this matter was one of the reasons for the presence of the papal legate, Giacomo Sozzino Tolomei, in the republic. Pious people, who were unwilling to be deprived of their daily attendance at Church, found various ways out of the difficulty; thus Stefano Maconi and several others of the circle had, merely as a matter of form, become members of the Legate's household, which was of course exempt from the interdict, and could freely be present at the Mass of that ecclesiastic. Catherine did not approve of this application of the principle that "the end justifies the means." "If I had known about it you would not have done it," she writes to Stefano, "but you would have waited humbly and patiently for peace . . . It seems to me that the expression 'household' can only be understood of those who are really in his service. And even though I pretended to belong to his house, I do not, nor would I do so."

"If I am not mistaken," she says in the same letter, "the dawn is already appearing, and soon the bright day will come, soon the sun will rise." For a time Urban's cause really seems to be attended by victory; Marino surrendered in the beginning of June and Giordano Orsini submitted to the Pope. It is true that the conversion of Joanna of Naples was but short-lived, but the King of Poland and Hungary was advancing from the north, and Charles of Durazzo, who was married to Joanna's niece, Margherita, bestirred himself to the conquest of both the Sicilies. It was at this time that Neri, who had returned home from Perugia together with the Abbé Lisolo, was sent to Naples by Catherine with a last appeal to Joanna. The tone of this letter is stronger than ever before; she speaks to the sensual and passionate queen of the body, says that it "is a sack full of corruption, stinking on every side," that it is "an instrument giving out no sound but that of sin" — and alas! why will Joanna not admit it? But she is blinded, and because she is blinded she has chosen to serve the false pope — they are well matched! Does she really not see what misfortune she has brought into the world; that it is her fault that strife is now raging between Urban's men with the red rose on their shields, and the Clementines, whose rose is pale and white? "Woe, woe, how unhappy is my soul! Do you not see that we are all created by that purest rose which is the eternal will of God, and re-created to the life of grace in that glowing red rose, which is the blood of Christ, in which men are cleansed by holy baptism and admitted to the garden of the Church? Neither you nor any other has bestowed that bath of roses upon mankind, it has been given only by our holy mother the Church, by the hand of him who holds the keys of the blood: Pope Urban VI."

Catherine reminds Joanna of her submission not long ago — and now her apostasy! "This is so great a pain to me that a greater cross can not be found for me to bear on the earth. When I think of the letter which I received from you, in which you acknowledge that Pope Urban was the true high priest, and that you would obey him — and now I find the opposite." Catherine continues a long while making an insistent appeal to the heart of the worldly queen. She reminds her of the memory she will leave behind her if she dies as a heretic; she threatens her with death. "Death is at the heels of all of us, but above all those whose course of youth has been run. From death none can escape, and no one can defend himself against it. The judgment of death was pronounced upon us at the same moment that our mothers conceived us; it is a debt that we must all pay. But our death is not like that of the animals. We are created in the image and likeness of God, and when the body dies the soul does not die. Its essence does not die, but it can lose the life of grace when it dies in mortal sin. . . Be merciful, then, to yourself and not cruel. God is calling you, be not slow to answer Him, that you may not one day hear the bitter words: 'Thou didst not think of Me in thy life; now I think not of thee at thy death.' " [9]

Catherine's letter made no impression, or only a fleeting one. Joanna's soul, which had long swayed restlessly hither and thither, had now at length come to rest. She had made her choice; she had determined to belong to that world of the body, of passion and pleasure in which she had spent most of her life, and which had afforded her such deep and glowing enjoyments. Life was not yet over for her; her fourth husband, Otto of Brunswick, who was living and loved her, was on the way to her with an army to help her. Joanna sent Catherine's disciples away and did not answer the letter of the Sienese saint. The time was finally past when saints could make an impression upon her.

In April of the following year Urban pronounced the greater excommunication upon the Queen of Naples, absolved her subjects from their oath of allegiance and bestowed her kingdom upon Charles of Durazzo. Louis of Anjou was occupied in France with his position as guardian of young Charles VI and could not come to her aid; Otto of Brunswick was defeated and taken prisoner. In June, 1381, Charles of Durazzo was crowned king of Naples and Jerusalem in Saint Peter's, and in July of the following year Joanna was murdered in Castello di Muro, without being allowed to shed her blood, suffocated between the pillows in the bed where she had found her highest joys. . .

Meanwhile Catherine, seeing her envoys return with their mission unaccomplished, also took her stand *against* Joanna. She now wrote to King Ludwig of Poland and Hungary and asked him to draw his sword in defence of Urban. "Will you permit Antichrist and that woman to lay waste our faith and to spread about darkness and confusion?" she exclaims. She now calls her *una femmina* whom she had hitherto addressed as *Carissima e reverenda madre*.[10]

With all this the year was drawing to a close, Advent was approaching. In the autumn Catherine had the happiness that one of her disciples, the painter Andrea di Vanni, whose portrait of the saint is to this day to be seen on the wall of Cappella delle Volte, had been made *Capitano del popolo* in Siena. She writes to him and reminds him of the dangers connected with a high position — the storms of great temptations rage on the mountains, but there is complete calm in the valley of humility. She urges him to frequent Communion and not to stay away from the Holy Table under the pretext that he is not worthy: only they who imagine that they are worthy are really unworthy and go to Holy Communion in the cloak of pride. "And I beseech you, dearest son, that in your position you will mete out equal justice to both great and small, and not distinguish between rich and poor, but treat each one according to his deserts — as holy justice requires — yet tempered with mercy. I am persuaded that you will do this; I urge it upon you as far as I am able; and I beseech you, in this sweet season of Advent and at the holy feast of the Nativity, to visit the Crib where rests the meek Lamb. There you will find Mary, a stranger and an exile, in such great poverty that she has not garments in which to clothe the Son of God, or a fire to warm Him who is life itself, but the beasts warmed Him with their breath. We may well be ashamed of our pride and our luxury when we see God so deeply abased." [11]

During that autumn Stefano Maconi was taken prisoner by John Hawkwood's troops while on one of his journeys in the country round Siena, and he only saved his life by invoking Catherine, of whose name the English soldiers still stood in perhaps superstitious awe. He informed his *Mamma*, of course, of this, and she answers him in these words:

"You write to me that you were taken prisoner, and that it was not in the night but in the daytime. And by the inspiration of the Holy Spirit the dawn arose in the hearts of those incarnate devils and they let you go.

"Consider, dearest son, that so long as you remain in the night of true self-knowledge you will never be taken prisoner. But if passion would decoy you into the day of self-love, or the soul would enter into the daylight of the knowledge of God, without having passed through the night of self-knowledge, it will soon be seized by its enemies. . . . Presumption and pride, passion and the luxury of life, the devil and the flesh will at once have it in their power. I would therefore have you rest constantly between night and day, that is, that you know yourself in God and God in you . . . I would have you find consolation, dearest son, in this hour of dawn, for soon the sun will rise. . .

"Your neglectful brother Barduccio [Canigiani, to whom Catherine is dictating] says that you must come soon; he has to do something with which you must help him, and he does not think he can do it unless you are with him." [12]

XIV

"The hour of the dawn" — but for Catherine the hour of the evening glow. "In Thy nature, eternal God, I perceive my own nature," Catherine says in one of her prayers at this time. "And what is my nature? My nature is fire." [1] This interior fire parched her more and more, day by day, so that, as we are told by Caffarini, "the skin rested on the bones without anything between. Her stomach no longer received any food and she could not even swallow a refreshing drink of water. It was as though she were burning interiorly, her breath struck against one like a flame of fire." [2] She had become one entire glow, one entire flame. A few months yet and she was burnt to ashes.

The year 1380 brought new dangers to Urban. "The old serpent," Raymond writes, "began to sow dissension between the Roman people and the Pope, and it went so far that the people openly threatened him with death. On learning this Catherine was profoundly downcast, and as usual had recourse to prayer, and with all her heart she implored her Spouse not to permit so great a crime." [3]

We possess several of the prayers which arose from Catherine's heart and lips in those disturbed times, and which the disciples wrote down. Cardinal Niccolò Carraciolo, in her time the friend and admirer of Saint Birgitta, and now of Catherine, had asked the latter, on New Year's morning, to pray for the Pope. "I cry to Thee today, Thou my love, eternal God," was heard from her lips, "to have mercy upon this world, to grant it light to acknowledge Thy vicar, and to grant him light, so that the whole world may follow him. Reveal Thy goodness in him, so that his manly heart may ever burn with holy zeal and be prepared (*condito*) with Thy humility and with goodness and love and purity, and Thy wisdom appear in his deeds, so that he may draw the whole world to himself. Enlighten also his adversaries, whose uncircumcised hearts resist the Holy Spirit and war against Thy omnipotence. . . Invite them, rouse them, oh inestimable Love, and on this day of grace let their hardness of heart be ended. Let them be led back to Thee that they perish not. And

369

because they have sinned against Thee, God of mercy, punish their sins upon me. *Behold, here is my body,* which I have received from Thee! I offer it to Thee. Let it be the anvil on which Thou breakest their transgressions asunder . . . Let all self-love be taken from those Thy enemies and from Thy vicar and from us all, so that we can forgive them when Thou hast broken their hardness and they come in humility to offer their submission. *I offer thee my life,* now or whensoever it may please Thee; I will yield it up for Thy glory; by the power of Thy passion I beseech Thee for yet one more thing, that Thou wilt cleanse Thy Church, sweep out the old vices and delay no longer. I know that Thou strikest at the crooked tree, which is the iniquity of Thy enemies, so long that at last it becomes straight, but hasten, oh eternal Trinity, it can not be a hard thing for Thee to change one thing into another, for Thou hast had the power to create all things from nothing." [4]

She was, William Flete [5] wrote after Catherine's death, like a gentle mule that bore the burden of the sins of the Church without resistance; thus had she in her youth borne the heavy sacks of corn from the street door up to the loft. To the Sienese saint this thought of bearing for others, bearing for sinners, bearing for the Church, gradually assumed a definite symbolic form. Daily she visited Saint Peter's to pray at the tomb of the Apostle. Saint Peter's was still the old basilica, whose façade can be seen on Raphael's fresco of "The Burning of Castel Sant' Angelo," and beneath its portico Catherine would contemplate the same mosaic by Giotto which has been preserved in the new porch, and which represents *la Navicella,* the ship of the Church, the bark of Peter. Catherine's thoughts were gathered more and more about this symbol; there visibly before her was the burden she would bear, *la Navicella.* The word recurs constantly in the prayer which she said on the feast of the Chair of Peter (January 18th). [6]

Then came Sexagesima Sunday, which in that year fell on January 29th. During her prayer Catherine saw "all Rome full of demons" inciting the people against the Pope. And then they rushed upon her with terrible voices and shouts and said: "Cursed be you, who are always seeking to hinder us, we will be revenged upon you and will make you die in great trials and torments." Then she prayed yet more earnestly and the Lord answered her: "Give it up, my daughter, let this evil people commit the great sin that they desire and threaten to commit, so that my justice may punish them as they deserve and the earth can open and they can descend into hell while they are still living." She then prayed with yet more fervour, and for several days and nights she did not sleep and was so unhappy and so exhausted that she was a pitiful sight, for she dragged herself through the chapel like one who could no longer stand upright, and when she stood up she fell down again, and if God had not encircled her body as though with iron bands, it would have broken and burst." [7]

It was in one of these nights of despair that Catherine offered herself like an anvil under the hammer of the wrath of God. While she had earlier, Raymond says, not been able to get up to go to Mass before nine o'clock, she now heard Mass and went to Communion early in the morning and then, with her usual hurried steps, walked the long way from Via del Papa out to Saint Peter's to pray. We can imagine her kneeling before the grille to the Apostle's tomb, that grille through which Francis of Assisi, in his first demonstrative piety, had flung a handful of coins so that they rang again! She kneels there, a little, thin, white-robed figure; the two great black eyes are burning, the deadly pale face is luminous, the delicate lips of the slightly protruding mouth move softly in prayer, like leaves quivering in a slight puff of wind. The thin folded hands are like the motionless flame of a candle upon the altar, her whole figure is white and luminous and aflame like a blessed candle. Her women friends are kneeling by her side, they are praying too, but always watching anxiously over their beloved spiritual mother, *la dolce venerabile Mamma*. Suddenly they see her collapse, as if crushed beneath a burden that is too heavy, see her sink into herself like a building tumbling into ruins. They try to raise her up but it is almost impossible, she has become like one palsied, for Jesus has laid *la Navicella* upon her slight, weak girl's shoulders, laid upon them the whole ship of the Church with all the sins that it has on board. They lead her home, broken, tottering under the weight of the burden which her Spouse has laid upon her, and which henceforth rests upon her like a yoke, like the heavy hand with which the lover bends the neck of his bride, and she loves him all the more for his strength, and because his love breaks her and cows her and permits her to suffer. *Gesù dolce, Gesù amore!* [8]

This happened, Barduccio Canigiani relates in the account which he wrote after Catherine's death of her passing, at the hour of Vespers on Sexagesima Sunday, "and from that time she did not regain her health. The next day, towards evening, I wrote a letter for her, and she then had a second attack, so terrible that we all wept over her as one dead, and she lay thus a long while without giving any sign of life. Then she came to herself and one could not have believed that it was she who had but now lain like that." [9]

The letter dictated to Barduccio and addressed to Urban is quite short, one perceives the weariness and effort in it. Yet once more — it proved to be the last time — the Sienese saint wished to advise and guide her *dolce Babbo, Cristo in terra*. She puts before him the example of Gregory the Great, wishes him insight and wisdom, "which are always needful, but above all in our times." She advises him to deal gently with the rebellious Romans: "You know your Roman children, that they are more easily led by gentleness than by force or with harsh words. You know too, how needful it is for you and for Holy Church to keep this people in obedience to Your Holiness, for here is the source and beginning of our faith." She then enjoins upon the Pope to have great trust in Providence; God will watch over the ship of the Church, which is also the ship of the Pope: *la navicella della Santa Chiesa e della Santità Vostra*. "Be a man in all things, with a holy fear of God, an example in words, in conduct and in all your works. May they all shine before God and before men, like a candle that is set in the candlestick of the Church, to which all Christian people must and ought to look up."

Finally she reminds him of the destructive effect of the bad papal government upon Italy, and warns him against "the bad governors, because of whom the Church of God has suffered persecution. But I know that this is known to you. May Your Holiness now have a care to what must be done. Be of

THE CROWN OF THORNS

good courage, God will not despise your good will and the prayers of your servants. I say no more. Remain in the holy, sweet love of God. I humbly beg your blessing." [10]

These were Catherine's parting words to a man who after her death became one of the most merciless tyrants known to history. In his energy he became relentless, in his firmness harsh, in his ruthlessness cruel. When he discovered a conspiracy among the cardinals in 1385, he had the guilty ones examined under torture, and while they lay on the rack he walked to and fro outside the window of the torture chamber, reading his breviary to the accompaniment of the screams of the tortured. At the intervention of Richard II one of the cardinals, who was English, escaped with his life. By Urban's orders the other five were either thrown into the sea or suffocated, their bodies being buried in slaked lime. Four years after he died himself in the Vatican, half mad, forsaken by all, hated and loathed as but few have been.

All that terrible future, however, was hidden from Catherine's eyes. In an impressive prayer she again offers her life for the salvation of the Church. It was probably Barduccio who on that Monday evening of January 30th wrote down "certain words which she said in prayer after that dreadful attack, when all her family mourned her as dead."

"Oh, eternal God, oh, good Master, Thou hast created and formed our body from earth! Oh, sweetest Love, from such humble things hast Thou formed it and laid in it so great a treasure as the soul which bears Thy image, eternal God. Thou art the Master who breaks and creates anew, break Thou the vessel of this my body and form it again as may seem good to Thee. To Thee, eternal Father, I again offer my life for Thy sweet Bride. As oft as Thou wilt I entreat Thee to draw me out of the body and lead me back to it, with ever greater torment each time, if I may but see the reformation of Thy sweet Bride, the holy Church.

"I commend to Thee Thy Bride, oh, eternal God. I commend to Thee also my dearly loved sons and daughters, and I beseech Thee, supreme and eternal Father, that if it please Thy mercy and goodness to take me away from the body and let me return no more, that Thou wilt not leave them fatherless, but visit them with Thy grace, and grant them true and perfect light so that they may live as though dead. Bind them together with the bonds of love, so that they may die like lovers in the embrace of Thy sweet Bride. And I beseech Thee, eternal Father, that none be taken from me, and forgive us all our transgressions, and forgive my great ignorance and negligence which I have committed in Thy Church, in not having done what I could and ought to have done. *Peccavi, Domine, miserere mei!*" [11]

Che muoiano spasimati in questa dolce sposa — "that they may die the death of love in that sweet bride." That was Catherine's wish for her disciples; it was fulfilled in herself. "From that hour," Barduccio Canigiani continues, "fresh trials and torments began to afflict her body. But when the season of fasting began she gave up herself with such fervour to prayer, notwithstanding her illness, that we marvelled at all the humble sighs and the bitter weeping that broke from her heart. Her prayers were so fervent that one hour spent in praying tired her poor little body more than prayer for two whole days would have tired another. Every morning after Communion she was in such a state that those who did not know better must think that she was dead, and as one dead she was carried to her little, low bed. But one or two hours after she rose again and we went to Saint Peter's, a distance of a mile, and there she began to pray and continued until Vespers, and at last she returned home so exhausted that she looked like one dead." [12]

Barduccio's faithful pen has noted down one or two of the prayers which Catherine thus stammered forth during the daily ecstasy after Communion. Again and again she cries to God for the Church, for the Pope, for the coming of the reformation. Again and again she humbles and accuses herself: "Oh, eternal Trinity, I have sinned all the days of my life. Oh, my miserable soul, hast Thou ever remembered thy God? Verily no, for if thou hadst, thou wouldst long since have been consumed in the flame of His love. Eternal God, grant health to me, who am sick, life to me who am dead, and grant to us all a voice so that we can cry to Thee with Thy own voice. . . I cry to Thee for the whole world, but in particular for Thy vicegerent and for his supporters (the cardinals) and for all those whom Thou hast given me, and whom I love with a particular love. I am sick, but I would see them whole; I am imperfect, but I would see them perfect; I am dead, but I would see them living the life of grace." And turning her glance from the others upon herself, she again utters in the most impressive terms the great fundamental feeling of the Christian life — that consciousness of sin which increases with the increasing light from above, and which can at last lead the soul to the verge of despair, because the goal which it strives to reach seems to recede further and further away, the more eagerly it tries to reach it. "Thou art life, eternal God, and I am death," Catherine exclaims, writhing under the supernatural clearness of self-knowledge like a worm in a flame. "Thou art wisdom, and I am folly, Thou art light and I am darkness. Thou art infinite and I am finite. Thou art perfect righteousness and I am a twisted tree. . . Who can reach up to Thy heights, eternal Godhead?" [13]

Again and again in her ecstasy she sees the two kingdoms into which existence is divided, and between which there is a deep gulf: the kingdom of light within the border of faith, and as soon as one goes outside it, the world of darkness of self-will, in which one becomes like a brute beast. With horror the seeress feels that darkness still has power over her, that she is still a child of Adam, a daughter of Eve, wearing the garment made from the skins of animals, which the Lord God made and gave to them who were driven out of Paradise — "the stinking garment of my own perverted will." She has recourse to the old invocation of her early days: "I am she who is not, and Thou art He who is. Then give me Thyself that I may glorify and praise Thee." [14]

In a long letter to Raymond of Capua, the last, Catherine herself gathered together all that she had experienced in spirit during these full weeks from Sexagesima Sunday to the 15th February, when the letter was written.[15]

"Father, Father and sweetest son, wonderful mysteries has God worked from the New Year and until now, so that the tongue has not power to utter them. But let us leave all the bygone time and let us begin with Sexagesima Sunday. As I now will briefly write to you, those mysteries of which you shall hear, came to pass on that Sunday, and it seems to me that never have I borne a burden like to this one.*

"So great was the pain that I felt in my heart, that I tore my garment and writhed in the chapel like one who is beside himself, and if anyone would have held me he would have killed me on the instant. Then came Monday, and in the evening I felt driven to write to Christ on earth and to three cardinals, wherefore I asked for help to go into the study (*studio*). And when I had written to Christ on earth it was impossible for me to write, so much had the pain increased in my body. And when a little time had passed the devil began to attack me and fill me with fear so that I came near to losing my senses: they raged against me as if such a wretched worm as I had been the cause that they had now lost what they had so long possessed in Holy Church. So great was my dread, together with the bodily torment, that I would have fled from the study and gone into the chapel — as if the study was the cause of my torments. I stood up then, and as I could not walk I leaned upon my son Barduccio. But at once I was thrown to the ground, and when I was lying on the ground it seemed to me that my soul had already left my body. Not in the same way as that other time [that is during her *mystic death* in 1370] for that time my soul tasted the joys of the immortals, and together with them I received the supreme good. But now my soul seemed to be like a thing apart, it seemed to me not to be in the body, but saw the body as if it were that of another. And my soul saw that he who was with me [that is, Barduccio] was troubled, and I wished to say to him: 'Son, be not afraid,' and I could not move my tongue or any of my limbs, so that I was like a lifeless body. I then left the body for what it was and let my spirit gaze upon the depths of the Trinity. My memory was filled with the remembrance of the needs of Holy Church and of all Christian people and cried to God, beseeching His help trustfully and offering Him its ardent desire, and imploring Him by the blood of the Lamb and by the torments of Christ and all the saints.

* I read: "giammai una simile *peso* (not with Tommaseo: *caso*) non mi parbe portare." Catherine alludes to *la navicella*, which on that day was laid upon her shoulders.

And it seemed impossible to me that He could refuse my prayer, so fervently did I pray.

"Then I prayed for you all and besought Him to fulfil His will and my wish in you. I then prayed to Him to deliver me from everlasting perdition. And thus I continued a long while, so that the family [this always means the friends, the disciples] mourned me as one dead. Meanwhile the devils and their terrible onslaughts had vanished, and the meek Lamb of God came and stood before my soul and said: 'Doubt not! I will fulfil thy desires and the desires of My other servants. I will that thou shalt see that I am a cunning potter, who breaks the vessel and creates it again according to his pleasure. I am able to do both, and therefore I take the vessel of thy body and form it anew, and differing from what it was, in the garden of Holy Church.' And eternal Truth gathered me to Himself with many comforting words which I pass over. And the body began to breathe a little again and to show that the soul had returned to her vessel. I was full of wonder. And my heart was in great pain, is still in pain. All joy and all consolation and all nourishment were taken from me. I was carried upstairs, but the bedroom seemed to me to be full of devils, and they began to war against me, worse than I had ever known them to do, and they would have me believe and comprehend that I was no longer she who had been in my body, but that I was an unclean spirit. I did not shink from fighting, but gently I prayed for help from above and said: '*Deus, in adjutorium meum intende, Domine, ad adjuvandum me festina.* Thou hast permitted that I am alone in this fight, without comfort from my spiritual father [i.e. Raimondo] who has been taken from me because of my ingratitude.'

"Two nights and two days were passed in these storms. Yet the spirit and the longing did not suffer under it, but was always turned towards God; the body, however, seemed to be powerless. On Candlemas Day (February 2d) I wished to hear Mass. Then all the mysteries were renewed, and God showed me how great is the need, for Rome has been about to rise in revolt and the talk of the people was full of insults and irreverence. Yet God has now poured His balm upon their hearts and I believe that all will end well. God then laid upon me the duty, through the holy season of fasting, of offering up all the prayers of my family and having Mass said for this one intention, that is, for Holy Church, and of hearing Mass early every morning — which, as you know, is impossible for me, but all things are possible for obedience. And so greatly has this desire filled me, that now I think of naught else, see naught else and wish for naught else.

"Not that I neglect, for that reason, the things here below, but my business is in heaven among those who dwell in Paradise. The soul neither can nor will partake of their joy, but I can share in the hunger which they felt while they were still pilgrims and wanderers in this world.

"In this, and in many other ways of which I cannot tell, my life is consumed and absorbed in that sweet Bride. The martyrs gave their blood, I offer myself in this manner. I beseech God soon to let me see the redemption of His people. At nine o'clock in the morning I leave home after Mass, and then you can see one who is dead walking to Saint Peter's. I go into the *navicella* of that holy church to labour in prayer. There I remain until the hour of Vespers, and if I could I would not leave that place either day or night, until I saw this people a little reconciled to their Father. My body lives without any food, not even a drop of water, and I have as many dear bodily pains as ever, so that my life is hanging on a thread. I do not know what God in His goodness intends with me, but I feel as though He will now consummate my martyrdom and then take me to Himself in the Resurrection and put an end to all my misery and my agony of longing. Or it may be that He will continue as hitherto to afflict my body. I have prayed and still pray that He will consummate His will in me, and that He will not leave you (and the others) fatherless, but that He will keep you in the way of Truth, and this I am persuaded He will do.

"Now I beseech and emplore you, my Father and my son, whom the sweet Mother Mary has given me, that if you feel that God has looked graciously upon me,* that you will renew your life, and being dead to all other feeling, throw yourself into the *navicella* of Holy Church. And be ever prudent in your relations with others. You cannot be much in your cell, but I

---

* I read: *volse*, not like Tommaseo: *volla*.

would that you should always abide in the cell of the heart and bear it about with you. For, as you know, if we are enclosed in it, enemies can do us no hurt, and all that we do is ordered by the will of God. I beseech you to ripen your heart with true and holy prudence; let your life be an example to the children of the world, and never conform yourself to its spirit. The open hand which you have always had for the poor I beg you to maintain; take upon you the poverty that you have freely chosen with renewed good will and with true and perfect humility, and to whatever rank or station God may raise you, go ever deeper into the valley of humility, and sit gladly at the table of the Cross, taking there your food. Embrace humble, faithful perservering prayer like a mother; keep vigil often; say your Mass daily, when not prevented by necessity. Shun useless and idle talk, be grave in speech and in all your dealings. Cast far away from you all compassion with yourself and likewise all slavish fear, for the Church has no need of such, but of persons who are cruel to themselves and have compassion on her.

"This is what I ask you to strive to keep. I beg you also, together with Brother Bartolommeo [de' Dominici] and Brother Tommaso [della Fonte] and the Master [Giovanni Terzo Tantucci] to have a care of the Book [*The Dialogue*] and of what writing you may find of mine, and do with it as seems to you most to the glory of God, and ask the advice of Messer Tommaso [Buonconti, in Pisa]. To me it was a consolation to write those things.

"Furthermore, I beseech you to be a shepherd, as far as you can, of my family [always meaning the disciples] and preserve them in mutual love and perfect unity, so that they may not be scattered like sheep without a shepherd. And I believe that I shall be able to do more for them and for you after my death than in my life. I will pray to the eternal Truth, to rain down upon all of you all that fulness of grace and all the gifts that He would grant to me, so that you may be like a candle in the candlestick. I beseech you to implore the eternal Spouse that He will let me do my duty manfully to the last, and to forgive my manifold transgressions. And I beseech you to forgive me all my disobedience, my lack of respect and my ingratitude, and all the sorrow and bitterness I may have caused you, and the little care I have had for the salvation of us both. And I entreat you to give me your blessing.

"Pray much for me and have prayers said, as Christ Crucified is dear to you. Forgive me, if I have said anything in bitterness; I do not write to hurt you, but because I am in doubt and do not know what God in His goodness will do with me. I wish to have done my duty.

"And be not grieved because we are parted in the body. It would be a great consolation to me if you were here, but it is my greatest joy and consolation to see that you labour for Holy Church. And now I beseech you to labour with more care than ever, for never has she been so much in need of it. And whatever may betide, do not leave your post without permission from your master the Pope. Rejoice in Christ sweet Jesus without any bitterness. I say no more. Remain in the holy, sweet love of God. Jesus, sweet Jesus who is love."

Here ends the letter of February 15th. Catherine, though, had not yet written down her whole testament to Raymond, and she wishes (as she says herself) to have done her duty to the last. Next day she therefore continues dictating to Barduccio.

First she inculcates on Raymond that article of faith which had gradually become the first and most important one to her — faith in the Church. Her whole gospel is finally summed up in this: the Church alone gives light and bestows peace. *Extra Ecclesiam nulla salus* — to Catherine this old sentence was not chiefly a dogma or doctrine; it was an experience, a fact. "No one," she lets Barduccio write, "can attain to joy in the beauty of God in the depths of the Trinity without the help of that sweet Bride, for we must all pass through the gate of Christ Crucified, and that gate is found nowhere but in the Church. That Bride gives life, for it has so much life in it that there are none who can kill it; and it gives strength and light and there are none who can weaken and darken it, for its fruits never fail but ever grow and increase."

"The Church, then, is both the intellectual and ethical centre of existence; it is the solution of the riddle of life and its essential value. In a world of relativities it is the only absolute. Therefore it is well worth while living, fighting and dying for her, nay,

THE CROWN OF THORNS

it is necessary, 'for the fruit of the blood (i.e. salvation) belongs only to those who pay the price of love to obtain it.'

"My pain and my desire increased like a flame, and I cried to God and said: 'What can I do?' In His goodness He answered: 'This: offer thy life anew and never permit thyself to rest. To this I have called thee and now call thee again, and all those who follow thee and will follow thee . . .' In this way the day passed and evening came. And my heart was drawn by the power of love, so that I could not resist, but had to go to the church. And I felt the same as at that other time, I was dying and I threw myself down with many reproaches against myself because I served the Bride of Christ in much ignorance and negligence, and was the cause of others doing the same. And as I arose with that thought in my soul, God became present to me in a new way (for He is always present to me, all things being in Him). It was as if memory, understanding and will no longer had anything to do with my body. And that truth was so clearly reflected in my mind that the mysteries of Holy Church were renewed in it, and all the gifts of grace which I had received in my life — those in the past and the present ones — and I lived again in that day when I was betrothed to God. But the fire increased more and more in me and all that faded away and I had only one thought: what I could do to offer up myself to God for Holy Church and to deliver those whom God had given into my hands from ignorance and negligence. Then the devils shouted death upon me and would * hinder and repress my desire which filled them with terror. And they struck hard at me, but my desire grew freer and stronger, and I cried: 'Oh, eternal God, accept my life as a sacrifice for the mystical body of Holy Church. I can give nothing but what Thou hast given me Thyself. Take the heart then, [the heart which Christ had once given her in exchange for her own, and which she therefore does not call "my heart"] take the heart and press out the blood of it over the face of the Bride.'

"Then God looked in mercy upon me and He tore out the heart and pressed it out over Holy Church. And He seized it with such force that if He had not at once girded me about with His strength — for He would not that the vessel of my body

---
* I read *volendo*, not: *vedendo*.

should be broken — I should have passed hence. Then the devils shrieked worse than before, as if they suffered intolerable pain, and they sought to fill me with terror and threatened that they would prevent me from praying oftener in this manner. But hell has no power against the strength of humility and the light of holy faith; I collected my thoughts the more and laboured as though with glowing irons; before the face of God I heard words so sweet and promises that filled me with joy. And because it was all so hidden my tongue is no longer able to speak of it.

"Now I can only utter a thanksgiving. Thanks be to the supreme and eternal God who has sent us out like brave knights on the field of battle to fight for His Bride with the shield of holy faith. We have gained the victory and the field is ours, for the devil, to whom mankind belonged before, has been defeated. We shall conquer the devil, not by the suffering itself borne by our bodies, but by virtue of that fire which is divine and exceeding ardent and inestimable love. *Deo gratias, Amen. Gesù dolce, Gesù amore.*"

XV

February ended and March began. Springtime and Lent had come round again, but Catherine could not, as she had done the year before, make pilgrimages to the Stations with her "family"; no more, leaning on "her son Barduccio," was she to climb up from Santa Maria in Cosmedin to Santa Sabina and Sant' Alessio; she was not to see the peach trees in blossom yonder by the old brown walls of San Saba, when looking down from Santa Prisca on the far side of the valley which separates the two heights of the Aventine from each other. During the last eight weeks of her life, Caffarini writes, she was obliged to stay in bed, and her sufferings were so great that it was a wonder she could bear them. "But with a brave heart she bore everything gladly and willingly, as if it were not she who was suffering. And how calmly and gently she spoke! Never did the least murmur escape from her holy lips, but she said that everything was a slight matter. Nor was she ever heard to utter a needless word, but everything was for the glory of God and the good of her neighbour. And although, as said above, she was sorely afflicted with pain, her face always shone with a holy and pious joy, like the countenance of an angel." [1]

Barduccio Canigiani confirms this testimony: in the midst of her sufferings he saw her looking up to heaven, her parched lips softly whispering: *Grazie, grazie!* She was suffering for her Spouse, suffering for the Bride.[2]

No one could any longer be in doubt that the end was near. "In all Rome," Tommaso Petra writes, "it was rumoured that although Catherine's mind was still clear, her bodily health was so broken that the end could not be far off." The papal protonotary, who had met the saint in Avignon, and had renewed acquaintance with her in Rome, hurried to her bedside. "I found her lying on a hard board in a room which was arranged as a sort of chapel in the house of Paola del Ferro. I spoke frankly to her. '*Mamma,*' I said, 'it seems that your divine Spouse is calling you to Himself. Have you thought of putting your affairs in order before you pass away?'"

At first Catherine seems to have thought that the lawyer was thinking of a testament of a worldly kind. "What affairs can a poor woman like me have to put in order?" she answered. "I do not possess anything." She soon understood, however, that it was a spiritual testament that was requested of her, whom they liked to call a "mother of thousands and thousands of souls" — a testament like that left by San Francesco to his disciples and by Giovanni Colombini to his. This she was willing to make and Tommaso di Petra was able to write down her last will in the presence of all the members of her little family.

She began by confirming once more the fundamental thought of her life and teaching. She had understood from the very beginning, she said, that if one wanted to surrender oneself entirely to God and possess Him altogether it was above all needful to detach one's heart and feelings from all natural (*sensitivo*) love of any creature whatsoever and from all created things, and to love God alone. For the heart cannot give itself wholly to God when it is not free and open, without a divided mind and any ulterior thought. And she said that from the beginning she had striven most to do this and had resolved to attain to God by the way of suffering.

Naturally she must needs choose a way of suffering, and a way in which it was impossible to walk without a faith that could not be shaken. One can only give everything when one believes as an unutterable truth that there is One who returns it a hundredfold, who bestows the *centuplum* promised in the Gospel, *quel dolce cento,* which Catherine also promised to her disciples.[3] The testament therefore continues:

"She said further that she closed the eyes of her mind in the light that came from the faith." One had to be blind to the joys of this world to walk in the way of suffering, and only the light of faith is so strong and dazzling that it can give one that holy blindness. "She firmly believed that everything that happened to her or to others came from God and was born of that great love which He had for His creatures, and not of hate. In this belief she obtained and conceived a love of holy obedience and a readiness to obey the commands of God and of her superiors, believing that all their commands came from God, either because it was needful for her salvation, or because it was good for the growth of virtue in her soul. And she added: By the grace of God I have never sinned the least in this matter!

"Next she said that God made her see that she could never reach perfection or obtain any virtue without the help of humble, faithful and persevering prayer. Prayer is a mother who conceives and nourishes all virtues in the soul, and without it they all become weak and fail. She urged us very strongly to be very diligent in prayer and she distinguished between the two forms of it, that is, vocal and interior prayer. We ought, she said, to practise vocal prayer at fixed times, but interior prayer ought to be practised constantly, in striving always to know ourselves and the great goodness of God to us."

Now follows a very important clause in the testament. Those who have frequented devout circles will have noticed in how great a degree sitting in judgment on others is the besetting sin of these circles. The moral effort seems to be directed outwards, against others, rather than inwards, against one's own ego: one is so Christian and in one's charity so eager to take out the mote from one's neighbour's eye, and through the hushed whispering between the pews and in the sacristies can be heard the same words that were spoken in the days of the Gospel: "Look, what a glutton and wine-bibber, a friend of publicans and sinners!" Or this: "He neither eats nor drinks, he has a devil!" [4] Here the demon of envy is often at work; one grudges others the good things that one has unwillingly to do without oneself, and one seeks revenge in being scandalised.

In few instances has Catherine shown greater moral greatness than in this; her renunciation was genuine and there was no looking back at the abandoned fleshpots of Egypt. Because of this she was never scandalised and never wanted to pass judgment.

"She said, moreover," the old account continues, "that if one would attain to purity of mind it was needful to abstain altogether from every judgment on one's neighbour and from all empty talk about his conduct. In creatures one should always look only for the will of God. With great force she said: 'For *no* reason whatsoever ought we to judge the actions of creatures or their motives. Even when we see that it is actual sin we ought not to pass judgment on it, but have holy and sincere compassion and offer it up to God with humble and devout prayer.'"

As Catherine was free from a scandalised spirit of censure, so she was also free from the censorious desire for revenge. She really obeyed the commandment, "Love your enemies," and she wished to teach her disciples to do the same. "She said of herself that whatever she had suffered from persecution or attacks, or slander or wrongs or malice, either in words or deeds, she had never thought anything about it except that those who had so acted or spoken had done it out of love for her or from zeal for the salvation of her soul. She therefore gave thanks to the infinite goodness of God who had given her light to deliver herself from so dangerous a thing as judging her neighbour.

"Finally she said that she placed exceeding great hope and exceeding great trust in the providence of God, and she exhorted all of us to do the same. . . And she added: 'You have seen so many proofs of this, and even though our hearts were harder than stone they must melt. My children, love therefore that sweet providence which never forsakes him who trusts in it, and which above all watches over you.'"

As a last injunction she gave them the words of Jesus in the gospel of Saint John: "Love one another, as I have loved you, that you also love one another. By this shall men know that you are my disciples." Then she spoke of the reformation of the Church and testified of herself that during the last seven years — that is, since 1373, since the first political letters — her efforts for this end had been her leading passion and her chief suffering. "And more especially at the present time it seems to me that my sweet Creator has permitted the devils to plague and torment me as once they tormented Job, and I can not remember that I have ever borne so many sweet pains and sufferings as I am bearing now. Thanks be to His infinite goodness, which has granted me permission to bear and endure this for the praise and glory of His name in His sweet Bride. And now at the end I feel that it is the will of my sweet Spouse that my soul shall go out from this dark prison and return to her Creator. I am not sure of it, but it seems to me that it must be so."

With great force she added: "My dearest, sweetest children, be assured that when I die now, I have in truth offered up and given my life in the Church and for the Church, and this is a very particular grace. You ought not to be sorrowful but to rejoice exceedingly, in considering that I am passing hence from so many sufferings to rest in that ocean of peace which is God eternal, and to perfect union with my sweetest Spouse. And I promise you that I will be with you altogether and be of more help to you in the life beyond than it has been given to me to help you in this world, for I shall have left darkness and passed into everlasting light." Then she said: "Nevertheless I yield up life and death to the will of my Creator. And if He sees that I can be of use to anyone here I will not refuse either to work or to suffer. For His glory and for the salvation of my neighbour I am ready to give my life a thousand times every day, with greater and greater suffering if it were possible."

Catherine ceased speaking and Tommaso Petra wrote down the last sentences. The disciples wept in the quiet sickroom, the women sobbed. How they recognised her in these burning words, which were not mere words, but on which she had acted every day of her life. She was still the same as when in the days of her early youth she had wanted to be laid like a door over the descent into hell, nay, she had even been ready to suffer everlasting loss, if only no other soul might be lost. She was still the great mother whose love was boundless, whose readiness to offer up everything and whose power to suffer was endless; she was *woman* in all the purest, deepest, most ardent beauty of womanhood, the voluntary burnt offering on the altar of life, the white lamb of sacrifice which is slain from the beginning in the garden of Paradise, — whose blessedness is found in self-surrender, in being entirely consumed, the bride who "is not" as opposed to the Beloved who alone "is."

"When she had ended her exhortations to them all," Caffarini relates, "she called her disciples to her one by one to tell them what she thought would be best for them after her death. To some of them she explained that it was the will of God for them that they should submit themselves to the discipline of the religious life and put on the habit of some monastic order or other. Thus she commanded Stefano Maconi in the name of holy obedience to enter the order of the Carthusians; Francesco Malavolti was to retire to Mont' Oliveto and become a monk there.

Others were enjoined to become hermits, and others again to choose the ecclesiastical life. She gave the Mantellate Sister Alessia as their mother and superior, but the men were told to seek Padre Raimondo when needing counsel and guidance." [5]

Neri di Landoccio was among those whom Catherine appointed to the life of solitude. The notary Ser Cristofano di Gano Guidini was advised to become a serving brother at the hospital in Siena, under the rule of Saint Augustine. "And each one of us," says the old account, "reverently received her commands. Then she humbly asked pardon of us all, if she had not been the example in her life and had not prayed as much as she could and ought to have done for us, and if she had not cared for our wants as she was pledged to do, and to forgive every suffering and bitterness and discomfort which she might have caused us. And she said: 'I have done it in ignorance, and I confess before the face of God, that I have always had and still have an ardent longing for your perfection and salvation.' And at last we all wept, and as she was wont she gave us all, one by one, her blessing in Christ." [6]

Among those who were present on that occasion Caffarini mentions Stefano Maconi. He had at last, as Catherine had so often urged him to do, shaken himself free, at last he had understood what she wrote to him, that "a man's household can be his enemies." [7] The legend says that while he was praying in the church of the La Scala confraternity in Siena he heard a voice, which warned him: "Go to Rome, do not delay any longer, for thy *Mamma's* passing is drawing near." He came, and came in time. "While she lay dying," he relates himself, "she told several of them what each had to do after her death. Then she turned to me, pointed at me with her finger and said: 'In the name of God and by the power of holy obedience I command you to enter the order of the Carthusians, for that is the order to which God has called you and chosen for you.' But when she gave me this command [Stefano continues; he had then long worn the white habit, and was now sitting in *la Certosa di Pavia* as the General of his Order, when writing these words in 1411] I must confess to my shame that I had as little thought of entering the Carthusian Order as of entering any other. But after she had passed hence, my heart was filled with so fervent a desire to obey her commands, that if the whole world had been against me I would not have been troubled . . . It is not the time now to tell what and how much Catherine did and still does for one of her sons, notwithstanding that he is so useless and unworthy. But I can not pass over in silence that after God and the most Blessed Virgin Mary I feel more indebted to the holy virgin Catherine than to any other creature in the world, and if there has ever been any good in me I owe it to her." [8]

At Catherine's dictation Stefano Maconi had written a letter for her, the last service he was permitted to render her. The letter was to Fra Bartolommeo de' Dominici; it has not been preserved, but probably it contained a request to him to come to Rome. He arrived on Easter Saturday (March 24th) in the evening and immediately hastened to the house in Via del Papa. The sight he saw there was a shock to him. Catherine was lying on a bed consisting of boards, fenced on all four sides by wooden boards, so that it looked as if she were already lying in her coffin. "I went up to her bed, thinking that I could speak with her as usual. I drew near and saw her poor little body so emaciated that one could count every bone and every nerve. And she was so brown that it looked as if she were sunburnt . . ." [9]

The Dominican heard Catherine's confession, but had to stoop quite down over her to catch her low whispers. In her soul he found nothing but gratitude — "I am well, thanks be to our Saviour," she answered, in reply to his questions as to how she felt. The next day, March 25th, Easter Day, was also her birthday; she was thirty-three. Fra Bartolommeo said Mass in her room and by a last superhuman effort she succeeded in rising from her bed, going to the altar and receiving the sacred Host. The Dominican spent the few days that he could still stay in Rome at Catherine's bedside, and in talking with the friend of her youth she seemed to regain some of her old energy. She had strength enough to tell him herself to go back to Siena and ask him to support Raymond of Capua when the latter, as she foresaw, would ere long be elected General of the Dominican Order.[10]

XVI

IL TRANSITO

*From the letter of Barduccio Canigiani
to Sister Caterina Petriboni
in the Convent of San Piero at Monticelli
near Florence*

"Thus was that body consumed then, until the Sunday before the feast of the Ascension, but then it looked indeed, like a dead body such as one sees it painted. I speak not of the face, for that was as ever like the face of an angel and filled one with reverence, but of the rest of the body and of the limbs, of which nothing could be seen but the bones, covered lightly with skin. From the waist downwards she had become paralysed and could not stir the least, not even from one side to the other.

"In this way the night came of the Sunday already named, and two hours or more before daybreak there was so great a change in her that we thought that now the end had come. The whole family was then called in and by a movement of her head she made those standing nearest understand that — humble and pious as she was — she wished to receive the holy absolution from guilt and punishment, and it was given her by Master Giovanni Terzo.[*] Then her strength slowly decreased and we remarked no other movement in her than a constant, weak and painful breathing. It seemed reasonable, therefore, to give her Extreme Unction, and it was given her by our friend, the abbot of Sant' Antimo, while she was lying as though unconscious.

"But after she had been anointed she began to change altogether and to give various signs with her face and her arms, and it looked as if she was enduring severe attacks by devils, and she remained in this struggle an hour and a half, and after three quarters of an hour she began to say, *Peccavi, Domine, miserere*

---

[*] This is not the absolution given in the sacrament of penance, but the papal blessing given *in articulo mortis*.

mei, and this she repeated I think sixty times, and every time she lifted her right arm and let it fall heavily on the bed. Then she said, the same number of times, but without lifting her arm, *Sancte Deus, miserere mei.** In other humble ways like this she came to the end of the time named before, and then her countenance was transfigured, and if but now it had been dark it had become like an angel's, and her eyes which had been dull and full of tears became bright and happy, so that we could not doubt that she had risen, as it were, from a deep ocean and come back to herself, and this softened our grief not a little, for we, her sons and daughters, were standing deeply downcast around her.

"Catherine was leaning on Alessia's breast and she was able to raise herself and with a little help she could sit up, leaning against Alessia. Meanwhile we placed before her a small portable altar, on which were laid many relics and several images of saints, but her glance sought only the crucifix which was set in the middle, and she began to adore it and interpreted in words her deepest feelings of the goodness of God, and while she prayed she accused herself in general of all her transgressions, and in particular she said: 'Eternal Trinity, I confess my guilt, that I have shamefully offended Thee by my great negligence, ignorance, ingratitude, disobedience and many other faults. Miserable am I! I have not kept Thy commandments, neither those which Thou hast given to all, nor those which in Thy goodness Thou hast given to me! Oh, how wretched am I!' And saying this she struck her breast, as when one says the *Confiteor,* and added: 'I have not kept the commandment which Thou gavest me, that I should always seek Thy glory and give my labours for the good of others. I have even avoided my duty, and most when I was most needed. Oh, my God, didst Thou not command that I was to cast away all care of myself and look only for the glory of Thy name and the salvation of souls, and find contentment only in eating this food at the table of the Holy Cross? But I sought my own consolation instead.

---

* Raymond of Capua relates that during that interior struggle Catherine exclaimed again and again: "No, never my own glory, but the glory of God!" It is clear that at the hour of her death she was tormented by doubts of her motives whether she had not, after all, sought her own glory and human admiration in her activities.

Thou didst invite me to bind myself to Thee alone, with holy and loving and ardent desires, with tears and humble and constant prayers for the salvation of the whole world and the reformation of Holy Church, and Thou didst promise me that Thou wouldst have mercy upon the world and grant Thy Bride new beauty. But I, so miserable a creature am I, did not answer to what Thou didst expect of me, but remained in the bed of negligence, sleeping peacefully. Ah, unhappy me! Thou didst give me souls to guide. Thou didst send so many dear sons and daughters to me, that I might love them with a love more than common and lead them to Thee on the path of life. But in me they could only look in the glass of human weakness; I have not had a care of them, I have not stood by them in constant and humble prayer before Thy face, I have not sufficiently given them a good example and I have not guided them with the fruitful exhortations of a good teacher. Oh, how miserable am I! With how little reverence have I received Thy countless gifts and all the many sweet sufferings and trials which in Thy mercy Thou wouldst heap on this frail little body, and I have not borne them with a will so ardent or a love so fervent as Thine in sending them. Woe, woe, Thou my love! Thou didst choose me for Thy spouse from my earliest childhood, but I have not been faithful enough, no, I was unfaithful to Thee, for my soul was not filled with Thee alone and with Thy great benefits, and I had other thoughts besides Thee, and I loved not Thee alone with all my might.'

"Thus did that purest dove accuse herself of these and many other things . . . and then turning to the priest she said: 'For the sake of Christ Crucified absolve me from all these sins, which I have now confessed before the face of God, and for all the others which I do not remember.' She then again asked for the papal blessing, saying that it had twice been bestowed upon her, first by Pope Gregory and afterwards by Pope Urban; and she said this like one who is ever hungering for the blood of Christ. It was done then, as she wished, and with eyes still fixed on the crucifix she began again to adore it with great devotion, and to say some very deep things, which, because of my sins, I was not deemed worthy to hear, and likewise because I was in such great sorrow, and her breast was so troubled that it was only with difficulty that she could utter the words, and we, who took our turn to stand beside her, heard them as we stood, bending down our ears to her lips and hearing now one word, now two. Thereupon she turned to some of her sons who had not been present earlier and showed them what they ought to do after her death, asking pardon humbly of all for the little care which it seemed to her that she had had for their salvation. Then she said some words to Lucio [a Roman disciple] and to another and last to me and again began to pray.

"Ah, if you had seen with how much humility and reverence she begged her sorrowing mother for her blessing and received it again and again! It was a bitter sweetness for Lapa, and it was touching to see the mother commend herself to her blessed daughter and entreat her to obtain for her the grace of God, that in her sorrow she might not offend against His holy will. During all this Catherine continued praying and as the end drew near she prayed more especially for the Catholic Church, for which she declared that she had given her life. She prayed also for Pope Urban VI, whom she firmly confessed to be the rightful pope, and she asked her sons, if needful, to offer up their lives for this truth. After that she prayed with great fervour for her beloved sons and daughters, whom the Lord had entrusted to her, to love one another, using many of the words spoken by our Saviour when He commended His disciples to His Father, and she besought us so earnestly that it seems that not only our hearts but the very stones must break to hear it. Then at the end she made the sign of the cross and blessed us all and continued praying to the last, saying: 'Thou, Lord, callest me, and I am coming to Thee. I come, not by my merits, but through Thy mercy alone, for which I beseech Thee by virtue of Thy blood!' Then she cried several times: 'Blood, blood!' But at the last, following the example of the Saviour she said: 'Father, into Thy hands I commend my spirit!' and with a countenance shining like an angel's she gently bent her head and yielded up her spirit.

"Her passing was on the Sunday named [April 29th] at the sixth hour [twelve o'clock noon], "but we did not bury her until the Tuesday, at the hour of Compline [i. e. at dusk]. And there was no smell to be perceived, her body remained pure, unharmed, fragrant, and the arms, the neck and the legs could still be bent, as if she were still alive. During those three days her body was visited by the people, who came in great numbers, and those who could touch her thought themselves fortunate. God worked so many wonders at that time, and her grave was visited by the faithful like the graves of the other saints in Rome." [1]

XVII

Raymond of Capua was in Genoa at that time, preparing to go by sea to Pisa and then on to Bologna, where the Dominicans were to hold their annual chapter meeting. Together with other members of the Order, who were also going thither, he had hired a small ship and was now waiting for a fair wind before setting sail. On the morning when Catherine died he had just gone down to the church to say Mass, for the 29th April is the feast of a great Dominican saint, Saint Peter Martyr. After having said his Mass, Raymond returned to his room to pack his valise, and on the way he passed, as usual, a fresco of the Blessed Virgin, and also as usual, he saluted it by stopping for a moment before the picture and saying an *Ave*. Perhaps Raymond prayed more earnestly than usual that morning — he was not a little anxious at the coming voyage and at what he might encounter, especially on the sea between Genoa and Bocca d'Arno: storms, hostile galleys, shipwreck, captivity. Then he heard a voice speaking interiorly, without any exterior sound, and the voice said clearly and distinctly: "Fear not, I am here for you. I am in heaven for you. I will protect you, I will defend you. Be of good courage, fear nothing, I am with you."

Raymond did not at once understand — perhaps it was Our Lady who wanted to comfort him, he thought. Not till later, when he learned that Catherine had at that very instant passed away, did he understand that it was she who from her heaven had wanted to strengthen and encourage her anxious friend, her dear son and spiritual father, "given to me by that sweet Mother Mary."

Raymond survived his *Mamma* nineteen years; he died in Nuremberg on October 5th, 1399. Before him Tommaso della Fonte had already passed away (August 22d, 1390), and young Barduccio Canigiani died earlier still. He became consumptive soon after Catherine's death; Raymond sent him up to Siena for the sake of the air, and he died there as early as 1382 (December 9). Francesco Malavolti obeyed Catherine and became a monk at Mont' Oliveto, but unstable as he continued to be, he changed to another Order later and died in 1415 in the Benedictine abbey of San Miliano, near Sassoferrato. Neri di Landoccio became a hermit, first at the hermitage of San Luca d'Agromaggio near Florence, later at Porta Nuova in Siena; praying, writing, reading Dante and consoling himself in hours of sadness with the radiant promise of everlasting bliss which Catherine had given him when they were in Lucca. He lived till March 12th, 1406, and lies buried in the Misericordia cemetery outside Porta Tufi. Ser Cristofano di Gano, after the death of his wife, gave up his profession as a notary and gave himself and his fortune to Santa Maria della Scala, of which he managed the business affairs. He also engaged in literary activities, wrote his memoirs and a short biography of Giovanni Colombini. Stefano Maconi took the Carthusian habit on March 19th, 1381, in *la Certosa di Pontignano* outside Siena; later he was called as Prior to the new and splendid Certosa built by Gian Galeazzo Visconti near Pavia, and there he died at a great age, on August 7th, 1424. The longest lived of the whole circle was Tommaso Caffarini, who in the Dominican monastery in Venice collected the testimonies of the life of the great Sienese saint which form the basis of the process of canonisation, and wrote his supplement to Raymond's biography, and his abridged edition, with personal modifications here and there, of Raymond's work. This faithful worker for the glory of Catherine did not die till 1434.

And so the disciples went from the death chamber in Via del Papa each his own way out into the world. They grew old, they turned grey, they turned white and leaned towards the grave and towards eternity. The time when they had known Catherine receded more and more into the past — now a year had gone ("last spring at this time . . .") — now two, and five — and ten — and twenty. . . At last there was half a century between now and that Sunday in April when they heard her lips murmur the last *Sangue, sangue*.

But through all the years they could not forget her. Her smile had shone upon their common youth; they saw it still whenever they closed their eyes, saw her *aliquantulum subridens*, as it is said again and again in the books they wrote about her. Her firm, delicate woman's hands had formed their destiny, her finger had pointed out their paths to them, sending one to the Olivetan monastery at Accona in the wild Creta country below

Chiusure and leading another to the solitude among the oak forests of Pontignano, to the little Carthusian house with the three whitewashed cells: oratory, dormitory, laboratory. For Messer Matteo in the house of the Misericordia Brethren, for Ser Cristofano Gano de' Guidini in the hospital of La Scala, bending over the account books or over sick-beds, for Neri dei Pagliaresi in the hermitage of Agromaggio, for Fra Tommaso Caffarini by the canals of Venice, through the dark and narrow *Calle's*, across arched bridges and along *Fondamenta's* — for all of them, everywhere and as long as they lived, Catherine would always be the only one, the unique, whom one meets once in a life time and never afterwards forgets. Therefore, when they wrote to each other, they headed their letters: *nella santa memoria,* "in sacred remembrance of Her." [1]

And more than once it would no doubt happen to them, as it happened to Raymond, standing before the fresco in the cloister in Genoa, that in hours of fear, hours of darkness hours of doubt and hours of sadness in the depths of woe, they would hear the beloved, well-known voice, sisterly sweet and motherly gentle, saying softly: "Fear not, I am with you! *Io son qui per te!*" And we know of at least one of them, of Barduccio,[2] that when he lay dying of consumption in Siena, that he was seen to look up suddenly and begin to smile. "And thus he gave up his spirit, smiling with joy, and the joyful smile remained there, even after his death." "And I," Raymond writes, "think it is quite certain that this happened because at his passing hence he saw Her coming to meet him, whom on earth he had loved with the true love of his heart."

Thus was Dante received by Beatrice at the border between Purgatory and Paradise, and she bends down from her triumphal chariot, saying softly, in the voice of old times: "Look well at me! I *am* Beatrice!" *Guardami ben; ben son, ben son Beatrice!*

EPILOGUE

Raymond of Capua was elected General of the Dominican Order in 1380, at that Chapter in Bologna to which he had feared so much to travel. He made use of this exalted position to fulfil the wish, cherished by many, and not least by himself, of taking, if not Catherine's whole body, then at least her head, back to Siena. When he was in Rome again, in October 1383, he had Catherine's coffin opened, and with the Pope's permission he detached the head and entrusted it to two friars who happened to be going to Siena, one of them being Fra Tommaso della Fonte and the other Fra Ambrogio Sansedoni. The silken bag in which the two Dominicans carried the sacred burden the long way from Rome to the saint's native town, is still preserved in the house of Santa Caterina in Siena.

This was not yet Catherine's triumphal entry, however, into the town which had so often murmured against her. She arrived secretly, no one knew that her head, enclosed in a reliquary of gilded copper, was standing in the sacristy of San Domenico. In the following spring Raymond came to Siena himself, and everything was prepared for the solemn translation of the relic. On April 23d a course of sermons began in San Domenico, and on Sunday, May 1st, it was announced from the pulpit that a procession would be held on the following Thursday. The government of Siena resolved that Catherine's feast should be kept with every solemnity and invited all the bishops, abbots and other prelates within the borders of the state to be present. Among the circle of disciples present were, besides Raymond, Tommaso della Fonte, Bartolommeo de' Dominici, Neri di Landoccio, Caffarini, Messer Matteo and Ser Cristofano; Stefano Maconi came in from his monastery in Pontignano.

The relic was secretly taken out the evening before to San Lazzaro, the leper hospital in Via Romana, that road which had so often seen Catherine going on her errands of charity to the sick, was now also to witness her triumph. Yet once more were the olive trees to wave to her with their branches and whisper their *Benedicta quáe venit*. . .

EPILOGUE

Then the morning of May 5th dawned. . . Flowers and green branches had been strewn in the streets, costly rugs were hanging out of all the windows and fragrant herbs were burning along the road where the procession was to pass. People stood in closely packed ranks from Porta Romana up through what is now Via Ricasoli, to la Croce del Travaglio and along the present Via Cavour under the Arco dei Malavolti down to San Domenico.

There was a great deal to admire, and plenty to rouse enthusiasm. First came two hundred little girls all dressed in white. Then two hundred little boys dressed like pages, in the gayest colours, rich with gold and sparkling with jewels. All the four hundred carried large bouquets of roses and lilies — in memory of the nosegays that Catherine used to tie in her garden.

Then came all the guilds and all the contradas of the town, with banners and flaming torches. And all the confraternities, the white and the black, the red and the grey, with pointed hoods and rustling rosaries and burning candles . . . if the fresh breeze of the May morning had not blown them out. . .

Then the great crucifix, followed by all the hermits of the state of Siena . . . as on Van Eyck's picture of "The Adoration of the Lamb," with long beards and serious faces, barefooted, in garments of camel's hair; they are all maintained by the State, so that, free from earthly cares, they may pray, fast, do penance for us all who are sinners. . . After them come long rows of friars, first and foremost of Dominicans, for Catherine was of their Order, and Franciscans, Olivetans, Benedictines, Augustinians, Carthusians, Camaldulians; they are followed by the priests of the town, newly shaved and wearing their stoles over their white surplices, and there is the Cathedral Chapter, all the Canons, the jovial ones and the ascetics, the ruddy-cheeked and the sallow. . .

The procession grows more and more majestic, for now come all the Abbots, their mitres on their heads and their croziers in their hands. They lean lightly and with dignity upon them as they advance with stately, measured steps. Then come the bishops, wearing mitres still more glittering with jewels, and pectoral crosses sparkling with precious stones, and wearing their large, episcopal ring outside the silken glove. And now, down there, at the turning of the street, you can see the *baldacchino* appearing, the baldacchino beneath which they are carrying Catherine's head. The street is filled with choir boys walking in front of it, all holding candles — all the little golden flames are like a bed of flowers — the censers, flung high, fly up and sink down, fly up and sink down, flinging out clouds of blue fragrance. All the bells are ringing as if in ecstasy, speaking and shouting at each other in their hundreds of little silvery voices. And hark! now the *Campanone* joins in — how it booms and clangs. It is as though someone were hammering at the vault of heaven itself. *Il Campanone* is ringing — and we all begin to weep. . .

For there, there, there is the *baldacchino*, and that which is shining beneath it is the casket, it is *la santa Testa*, it is *la Santa* herself who has come back! It is she — it is Caterina — on your knees! on your knees! Our own bishop walks on the right of the *baldacchino*, and the Dominican on the left is the General of the Order himself; it is Raymond of Capua! Look, he is weeping — and the Bishop is weeping too!

But there, directly behind the *baldacchino*, directly behind those who are carrying the reliquary, foremost among the Mantellate in their white habits and black cloaks, walks a little, thin old woman; she is bent almost double, her wrinkled hands are folded so devoutly, her eyes unswervingly gazing up at the gold and splendour going before her; the thin violet lips are mumbling in prayer; the tears streaming unceasingly from the red-rimmed eyes down the withered cheeks. . .

Why, it's Lapa! Catherine's mother, more than eighty years old! It is she — still living — there she is, walking past, she who gave birth to the saint — blessed Lapa! And we are all on our knees — all weeping, with eyes full of tears we see the baldacchino pass by — and the candles — and the incense and the Bishop — and Raymond — and Lapa — blessed Lapa — *Lapa beata,* Lapa, blessed among women, and blessed the fruit of thy womb, Caterina!

THE SOURCES

The question of the sources of the biography of Saint Catherine of Siena does not offer any complicated problems for solution. The comprehensive material falls naturally into two main groups: her own writings and the stories of her life by her disciples.

A. THE WRITINGS

1. *The Letters.* After the death of Catherine her friends began systematically to collect her letters. Ser Cristofano di Gano Guidini possessed no mean collection; Caffarini had a copy made of it when he was in Siena in 1398 and arranged the letters according to the addressees in two volumes. The first volume comprised 155 letters, all written to ecclesiastics; the second 139, all to layfolk (See Suppl. MS. T. I, 2, Bibl. Comm. Siena f. 182). Another collection was made by Stefano Maconi, Prior of La Certosa di Pontignano near Siena, and to this probably five, perhaps six, of the seven original ones still remaining to us are to be traced. Four of these are to be found in the Municipal Library in Siena in MS. T. III, 3, the fifth likewise in Siena, in the sacristy of the church of the Confraternity of St. Nicholas and St. Lucy. None of these seven letters are written by Catherine: the five Sienese ones are written by Barduccio Canigiani, the Saint's last secretary. In the letter preserved at St. Nicholas and St. Lucy he styles himself *il tuo negligente fratello Barduccio*. The writing of this letter being in all points like that of the letters in the municipal library, there can be no doubt that these letters were also written by Barduccio. These five letters are printed in Tommaseo as Nos. 319, 320, 329, 332 and 365 and are all addressed to Maconi; the letter preserved at St. Nicholas still bears the name of the addressee: *Stefano dicurrado de Maconi Insiena*.

The sixth letter of which we possess the original is to be found in the Church of St. Aloysius in Oxford, and was edited by Robert Fawtier (*Mélanges d'Archéologie et d'Histoire de l'Ecole française de Rome*, t. XXXIV; also under the title: *Catheriniana*, Rome, Imprimerie Cuggiani, 1914). The letter, addressed to Messer Jacomo di Viva, living at La Costarda de' Barbieri at Siena, takes up pages 31–32 of the above-named publication; in a short notice the author remarks that the handwriting "se rapproche très sensiblement de celle de la lettre conservée à la confrèrie de Santa Lucia à Sienne," that of Barduccio Canigiani (*Catheriniana*, p. 6). In the last line there is a remarkable dating: "x Carthusia III Kal. Maji," without any indication of the year, and one wonders from which Carthusian monastery Catherine can have written this letter, as it happens to be that very 29th April, the day on which she died in 1380. Catherine had personal relations and corresponded with several Carthusian monasteries: Maggiano, Belriguardo and Pontignano near Siena, Cervaja near Genoa, Calci near Pisa and the Carthusians on the island of Gorgona. She spent part of her sojourn at Pisa in 1375 near the Carthusians of Calci.

As the letter, however, is written by the hand of Barduccio Canigiani, and Catherine did not make his acquaintance until 1377, this solution of the problem must be abandoned. On and after November 28th, 1378, Catherine was settled in Rome, and the only possible date left to us is April 29th, 1378. On that day Catherine was in Florence, in the house of La Costa di San Giorgio, where she stayed until the 2nd August, and we know absolutely nothing of a stay, however short, near any Carthusian house during that period.

One is therefore tempted to look for another explanation of the mysterious date. The addressee of the letter in question, Messer Jacomo di Viva, who lived in Siena, in La Costarda de Barbieri (i.e., the sloping street by which the Barbary horses enter for the Palio race), had relationships with the Carthusians. We have a letter of Catherine's addressed to a Brother Niccolò di Nanni, an Olivetan monk, and to Dom Pietro Giovanni di Viva, a Carthusian at Maggiano near Siena (where the great friend of Blessed Giovanni Colombini, Dom Pietro Petroni, lived and died). These two correspondents of Catherine's have the same family name, and as both belonged to the Saint's group of friends they must have known each other. It is possible to imagine that the letter in question passed from the possession of Messer Jacomo to that of the Carthusian and that, later, it was given as a pious souvenir to some pilgrim or other who wished to possess a relic of the Saint. No doubt the letter preserved at Santa Lucia came into the possession of that confraternity in the same way. Moreover, this gift would be bestowed on the very day of the anniversary of Catherine's death, April 29th. This reconstructs for us a little scene of devout life in the fourteenth century: a *Caterinato*, whose name is unknown to us, goes out of Siena by the Porta Romana or the Porta Pispini to make his way to the Carthusian monastery of Maggiano (founded in 1313 by Cardinal Riccardo Petroni). He is received by the Fathers and listens devoutly while they tell him about all the holy souls who have lived there and about their pious visitors: a Colombini, a Giovachino Ciani, a Benincasa. And at the end of his visit he receives as a souvenir Catherine's letter to the brother of Dom Pietro di Viva (of whom we know that he was Prior of the monastery in 1380) and the monk inscribes the date for him: *Ex Carthusia III Kal Maj* "from the monastery to which the Saint often came, and on the anniversary of her death" — *nella santa memoria,* as Stefano Maconi, who was also a Carthusian, liked to write.

The seventh letter which we possess in the original handwriting is to be found in the Dominican monastery of San Rocca at Acireale in Sicily. It is dated "a di III di decembre 1379," is written in Barduccio's handwriting and addressed to Neri di Landoccio, who was then staying in Naples, "in Tomasino's house by Santo Alo" (i.e., Eligio). Only the first third of the letter is to be found in Tommaseo's edition (No. 192); the whole letter is edited and examined in *Memorie Dominicane,* Vol. XXIX (1912), pp. 275-278.

Among the chief manuscripts containing more or less complete collections of the Saint's letters, I give first place to the MS. Casanatense B. 92, which contains 47 letters, copied by Barduccio Canigiani MS. XXXVIII, 130 of the Magliabecchiana of Florence and MSS. 56–60 of the Palatina, also of Florence. MS. no. 57 of the Palatina is a copy dating from the fifteenth century from the collection made by Stefano Maconi and contains not only the ten letters published by Tommaseo (No. 148, in Tommaseo 329; 149, in Tomm. 222; 150, in Tomm. 205; 152, in Tomm. 368; 156, in Tomm. 368; 153, in Tomm. 324; 154, in Tomm. 320; 155, in Tomm. 365; 156, in Tomm. 195; 157, in Tomm. 319; 158, in Tomm. 369), but besides these an unpublished letter, marked No. 151. MS. 56 of the Palatina contains many curious details in the rubrics.

These manuscripts, and a great many others, will be utilised by Matilda Fiorilli for the critical edition which she is preparing for the *Scrittori d'Italia* of Laterza (Bari); all those who are devoting themselves to Catherinian studies look forward with impatience to this work.

The first printed edition of the letters (Bologna 1492) comprises only 31 pieces. Then follows the Aldine edition of 1500 with 368 letters, Gigli's (i.e., Vols. II and III of the *Opere di Santa Caterina,* Siena 1713) and the modern edition by Tommaseo (4 vols. Firenze 1860), and, since 1912, issued in a reprint by Piero Misciatelli (*L'Epistolario di Santa Caterina,* Siena 1912 seq.). For his edition Gigli made use of MS. T. III, 3, of the municipal library of Siena, a manuscript which is none other than a volume of the famous collection of the Saint's writings made in Venice before 1412 by one Nicolao Guidiccioni of Lucca who had a great devotion to the Sienese saint. This collection consisted of fourteen volumes and contained the *Dialogue* in Italian and in Latin, five volumes of the Saint's letters, the *Legend* written by Bl. Raymond in Latin and translated into Italian, the *Sermo in reverentiam* of William Flete, the prayers of the Saint, the poetry written in her honour by Anastagio da Montalcino, Neri di Landoccio, Jacopo da Montepulciano and Ser Cristofano di Gano Guidini, and finally, the Process of Venice (see below). All this treasure was carefully kept *in quadam sua capsa recondita,* by the rich merchant of Lucca living in Venice, and the whole collection was *ben ligata et tabulata et de carte edina, et quasi per omnia de eadem et simili ac competenti lictera* (*Depositio* de Tommaso Caffarini in the Process of Venice, Cod. Marcian, f. 19, col. 2–f. 20, col. 1).

After the Process of Venice, for which this collection was to serve as proof, the precious documents were entrusted to the Dominican Order, and Caffarini had the fourteen volumes conveyed to the convent of San Domenico in Siena. (Suppl. de Tantucci, Siena 1765, *avvertimento* to the reader, pp. 9 and 13.) It was there that Gigli could make use of them for his edition of the letters; it was from there that the collection was removed, at the time of the suppression of the convent, to the municipal library of Siena, of which it is at the present day the chief treasure. In the Appendix to his book, *Saint Catherine of Siena* (London 1907), Edmund Gardner has published some letters hitherto unknown and has given better texts to several others (pp. 407-422). Similar publications have been made by M. l'Abbé Bachisio Motzo: *Alcune lettere di S. Caterina da Siena in parte inedite* in Boll. Senese di Storia Patria XVIII (p. 369) and by R. Fawtier: *Catheriniana* (pp. 7-33).

2. *The Dialogue.* "I beg you to have a care of *The Book* and of whatever other writing you may find of mine — you and Brother Bartolommeo [de' Dominici] and Brother Tommaso [Caffarini] and the Master [Giovanni Terzo, of Lecceto] . . . and do with it as seems to you most to the glory of God, together with Messer Tommaso [Buonconti, of Pisa]." Even without this injunction the disciples would assuredly have taken care of *Il Libro,* as it was very simply called, and which was the original

THE SOURCES 405

doctrinal manuscript of the Sienese saint. It was early translated from the original Italian into scholarly Latin; three of her disciples undertook this task: Cristofano di Gano Guidini, Stefano Maconi and Raymond of Capua. As Père Hurtaud has pointed out in his learned introduction to the French translation of the *Dialogue* published by him (Paris 1913), it is probable that Maconi and Ser Cristofano collaborated, so that we are faced with only *two* Latin translations: that of Raymond (printed in Brescia in 1496, in Cologne in 1553, etc.) and that of Maconi-Guidini. The original Italian text has often been printed: in Bologna in 1472; in Naples in 1478; in Venice in 1494; by Gigli in Vol. IV of *Opere di Santa Caterina* in 1727; finally by Matilda Fiorilli in Bari in 1912, in the series *Scrittori d'Italia*. These two modern editions have been made from the Sienese manuscript T. II, 9, written by Stefano Maconi and originating from the Carthusian monastery of Pontignano.*

The Dialogue, like the letters of the Sienese saint, has sometimes had the misfortune to jar upon a too great sensitiveness or shock a modesty too easily offended. The biographers of the Saint and the translators of her works have had to suffer because of this. In the introduction to his French translation of the *Dialogue* the learned Père Hurtaud gives an explanation on this subject in terms on which certain readers would perhaps do well to meditate. Speaking of the picture of the vices of the clergy of the fourteenth century, as painted by the Saint, the Dominican asks himself the question: "Is this picture really one that will shock fastidious minds? Cartier [who published a translation of the Dialogue in 1892] explains this matter in his preface. He pleads the fact that the complete works of Catherine have been approved by the Holy See and have been printed many times in the States of the Church. Can that which was not considered dangerous in Italian become dangerous as soon as it is translated into French? ... The pious Tertiary [Cartier belongs to the Third Order of Saint Dominic] has recoiled from certain particulars, although the description is to be found in all the Italian editions. He has not dared to give them in French and he has had recourse to the Latin text to give them in footnotes. I have not thought it advisable to imitate this reserve, besides, it is not

* The reader is referred, for a complete bibliography, to that compiled by the learned Grottanelli for the *Storia di Santa Caterina da Siena* by Alfonso Capecelatro (Firenze 1863), or to that more confused but very complete one of the Comtesse de Flavigny (*Sainte Catherine de Sienne,* new edition, Paris 1895, pp. 603–658). Shorter references in Gardner (*Saint Catherine of Siena,* London 1907, pp. 423–428).

without some danger. The veil which one tries to throw over vice, without suppressing it and without hiding it completely, only serves to pique a prurient curiosity. I have therefore [Père Hurtaud concludes, and the present writer is in entire agreement with his point of view], simply translated Catherine's thoughts as they occurred to her without leaving the smallest taint upon them, and such as they were imparted to us by her virginal lips." (Op. cit. vol. I, pp. LXXX–LXXXII.*)

3. *Prayers, last words of the Saint*, etc. The prayers and the *ultime parole* of Catherine, such as they were taken down by the disciples who were present during her ecstasies and at her death, are contained in MS. T. II, 7 of the municipal library in Siena, forming part of the large collection of Guidiccioni.

They were printed in the Aldine edition of the *Letters* and in Vol. IV of the *Opere*, edited by Gigli. See also Grottanelli: *Preghiera, ultime parole e transito di S. Caterina, scritti di Barduccio Canigiani* (Turin 1865). A Latin translation of this document has been published by the Bollandists (*A. SS.* April III, pp. 959–961). This document brings us to the second group of the sources:

B. The Biographies

1. *Singularia et mira sanctae Catharinae Senensis.* According to Quétif and Échard (I, 696), this was the title of the first biography of the Saint, the work of her first confessor, Fra Tommaso della Fonte. "Caterina [Caffarini tells us] si per motivo di obbedienza, si per aver sicurezza di non errare, di tutto l'accadutole ne rese consapevole il suo confessore, che in più fogli lasciò registrato quanto di mano in mano succedeva di sopranaturale alla sua di Dio favorita penitente." (Supplemento, P. I, Tr. 2, §5, n. 5.) According to the same author the good Fra Tommaso was "rozzo d'ingegno" to such an extent that he hardly knew how to read or write (ibid. P. III, Tr. VI, §1, n. 1); that is why we see him dictating his notes on Catherine to another friar. His *quaderni* have been utilised by the Saint's official biographer, Blessed Raymond of Capua, who often speaks of them ("Io, per verità,

---

* A work entitled *Dialogus brevis consummatam continens perfectionem* has generally been attributed to Saint Catherine. We do not possess the original Italian text; the existing Italian editions are translations made from a Latin text to be found in the Vatican Library. As Père Hurtaud has well said: "This little work is nowhere mentioned in Catherine's writings, nor in those of her disciples, nor in the depositions in Venice. It has neither the style nor the colour, nor the accent nor the consuming flame of the Letters and the *Dialogue*" (1. c. I, p. LXXIV).

THE SOURCES 407

trovo pieni i quaderni scritti da Fra Tommaso suo confessore, ritrovai negli scritti di Fra Tommaso primo suo confessore." *Leg. maj.* II, vi, 12; II, viii, 4). But it is above all in turning over the leaves of the *Supplementum* of Caffarini that we get some idea of the work of the Saint's good and rough first confessor. This work, in fact, must have been composed, like the *Supplementum* itself, from a series of little notes, one might almost say "jottings," written from day to day. That is why the first place must be given, as a source for the biography of Catherine, not to the Legend of Raymond of Capua, but certainly to

2. The *Supplementum* of Fra Tommaso Nacci Caffarini. "Quoniam tot et tanta de virgine supradicta meas pervenerunt ad manus utpote tam ipsius virginis legenda quam venerandus Magister Raymundus generalis ordinis praedicatorum composuit quam etiam dictae virginis liber quam scribentibus pluribus ipsa in sua volgari et in quodam abstractione constituta dictavit quam etiam libri epistolarum suarum modo prefato et intervenientibus scriptoribus diversis ad omnis utriusque sexus, status et conditionis personas per virginem directas ... ac etiam plures quaterni per primum confessorem dictae virginis de gestis ejusdem virginis transcripti." (MS. T. 12, Bibl. Comm., Siena, f. 4.) Caffarini thus indicates the sources of the large volume which he modestly calls a *supplement* to the official *Legend* of Raymond of Capua, but which is really the biography with the greatest wealth of original features that we possess of the great Sienese saint. This is easily understood, since in this work we constantly meet again with the notes handed over by Tommaso della Fonte ("ut reperi in scripturis primi hujus virginis confessoris" — MS. cit. f. 53), and given by Caffarini such as they are.

Unfortunately we possess as yet no other edition of this important work, and the Italian edition of Ambrogio Tantucci (Siena 1760) is only an abridgment which takes many liberties with the original text. I have therefore felt compelled to have recourse to the Sienese manuscript, dated 1416 (see the date f. 182: "usque in presens, hoc est usque ad annum 1416"), that is to say, written at a time when the author was still living (Caffarini died in 1434). Meanwhile, until an entire publication appears, I have detached from this work a treatise which seems to me to be of special interest, and which explains what those *quaderni* were of good old Fra Tommaso della Fonte. This is the *Tractatus quartus* of the second part; it will be found at the end of the present book.

3. *La Leggenda major* of Raymond of Capua. It was only

natural that the biography of the Saint should be entrusted to him who had been her spiritual director and intimate friend during the last and most important period of her life. Moreover, it was not the first time the learned Dominican exercised his gifts as a hagiographer; during his sojourn at Montepulciano (1363–1366) he had written a life of Blessed Agnes (d. April 20, 1317) which still carries authority, and to his pen is also ascribed a life of Blessed Pope Benedict XI, who died at Perugia in 1304.

Raymond, elected General of the Order of Saint Dominic in 1380, did not accept the charge of writing the life of his *Mamma* until four years after, and did it with reluctance. His health was feeble — he was worn out by the work he had undertaken with a view to the reform of the Dominican Order and he had but very little leisure. Besides this he was a conscientious worker; at the end of each chapter of his biography he scrupulously mentions the sources from which he has drawn: "Tutte le cose che in questo capitolo si contengono, sono state a me riferite da Lapa, sua madre; ed in qualche parte ... ne sono stato informato dalla santa vergine stessa e di una certa Lisa, sua cognata, ch'ancor vive," L. I, c. ii, n. 8. "Le cose che sonosi raccontate in questo capitolo io le intesi da Lapa madre di Caterina e da Lisa moglie d'un suo fratello, e degli altri che allora erano nella sua casa," L. I, c. iv, n. 7. "In quanto ... alla visione di S. Domenico, il confessore di lei, che mi precedette in tempo, ed io l'udimmo da lei medesima," L. I, c. v, n. 5. "Alcune (cose) io vidi e scopersi da me medesimo e particolarmente cio, che appartiene al dono singolare della sua astinenza," L. I, c. vi, no. 11. "Queste cose, che ho scritte la maggior parte ho trovate scritte in diversi luoghi d'Italia ed alcune, ancorchè poche, le ho intese, ricercandole, da persone antiche dell'uno e l'altro sesso, degne di fede, cioé da frati predicatori e dalle sorelle della penitenza di San Domenico," L. I, c. viii, n. 2. "Tutte quelle cose ch'io scrivo, o Caterina stessa me le confessó, o io le ho trovate negli scritti di fr. Tommaso suo primo confessore," L. II, c. iv, n. 16. (I quote these texts from the beautiful Italian translation of Canon Bernardino Pecci, *accademico intronato* in Siena, edited by Girolamo Gigli as the first volume of the *Opere della serafica Santa Caterina da Siena*, Siena, 1707.)

The result of this conscientious procedure was that the work advanced but slowly. On every hand its appearance was impatiently awaited. "Although the Master General is very busy," Caffarini writes in 1391 to Neri Pagliaresi, "I have troubled him continually and every day, offering to help him to the utmost of my powers in finishing the *Legend*. Thanks to this urgency we have begun to correct that which is done of the second part and we have continued, he dictating, I writing. But then, when we were counting on finishing in four or six days, the Master had to go to Pisa, and then to Rome, taking everything with him, so that a considerable delay is to be feared. However, as long as he is in Italy it will be easy to trouble him in many ways, so that he will finish before going away." (*Lettere dei discepoli,* Grottanelli, Bologna 1868, p. 328. See also the letter from Stefano Maconi to Pagliaresi: "Poi acomiatandoci dal maestro Raimondo, *sollicitata prima la santa leggenda,*" ibid., p. 320.) It was in Genoa, in the beginning of February 1391, that this collaboration between Raymond of Capua and Caffarini took place. On June 18th in the following year Raymond writes in Rome to Gabriele Piccolomini: "I inform you that up to the present I have been working with great solicitude at writing the *Legend* of our holy Mother Catherine. By the grace of God the first and second part are finished; numerous and large affairs have prevented me from composing the third, but with the help of God I shall do it as soon as I am free." (Ibid., p. 336.)

It was not until 1395, however, that Raymond finished the third part of his work, of which he left a copy in Venice (at the Dominican convent of SS. Giovanni e Paolo), taking with him the original volume so that copies might be made from it. After the death of Raymond, which occurred on October 5th in Nuremberg, this precious manuscript was brought to Italy by Brother Thomas de Nocera, and unfortunately it is not known what became of it. (See Hyacinthe M. Cormier: *Le B. Raymond de Capoue,* Rome 1902, and *B. Raymundi Capuani Opuscula et litteræ,* Roma 1895.)

In view of the great authority of its author the *Legend* of Raymond was quickly spread abroad everywhere and in general acquired the name of *Leggenda major*. The first printed edition is dated Cologne 1553.

Two Italian versions exist of the original Latin, one made by Neri di Landoccio in collaboration with an unknown *scriptor,* a native of Piacenza (Neri's work goes as far as the fourth chapter of the second part), and another which is entirely the work of the Piacenzan. (See Auvray: *Les deux versions italiennes de la légende de S. Cath. de Sienne,* Paris 1910.) The former of these versions (which is of 1399) was printed in Florence in 1477, the latter in Milan in 1489.

4. *The Process of Venice*. Venice became very early a centre

of what I should call *Catherinianism*. Until 1434 there lived in Venice, at the convent of SS. Giovanni e Paolo, Fra Tommaso di Antonio Nacci Caffarini, all of whose best efforts were devoted to the propaganda of the cult and the teaching of the Sienese saint.

Although the Church had not yet made any pronouncement on Catherine's sanctity, the Dominicans kept the anniversary of her death every year in their church, and Caffarini himself showed, from the pulpit, the writings of the Saint to the faithful, to whom only relics are usually shown. A complaint was lodged against the Dominicans and the Bishop of Castello, to whose diocese Venice belonged, was ordered to institute a process.

The Dominicans took the opportunity of this occasion to prepare the canonical process required for the canonisation of Catherine, and the indefatigable Caffarini was thus able to gather and place before the bishop, Francesco Bembo, assisted by the notary apostolic Francesco Viviani, a whole series of testimonies in favour of the sanctity of the Sienese woman. The process began on May 26th, 1411, and among those who testified we find almost the entire group of the *Caterinati:* Stefano Maconi, Bartolommeo de' Dominici, Francesco Malavolti, William Flete, Neri di Landoccio, Tommaso Petra, Giovanni delle Celle, etc., etc. Unfortunately only a part of this *Processus contestionum super sanctitatem et doctrinam Catharinae de Senis* was edited by Martène and Durand in the sixth volume of their *Amplissima collectio,* Paris 1729, an edition made from an incomplete copy of the Sienese MS. XX, v, 10, of the Casanatense in Rome; later, Lazzareschi has published it from the excellent Codex Marcianus 2977, which is none other than an authentic copy of the original document of the Process, such as it was preserved in the archives of the bishop of Castello. (See Eugenio Lazzareschi: *S. Caterina da Siena in Val d'Orcia,* Firenze 1915, pp. 78–85.)

Two other unpublished testimonies (of Fra Agostino and Fra Baronto, both of Pisa) have been edited by Lazzareschi in the supplement to the work: *S. Caterina da Siena ed i Pisani* by Niccolo Zuchelli and Eugenio Lazzareschi, Firenze 1917, pp. 125–127. A complete edition of the Process, under the charge of the Reverend Father Taurisano, O. P., is in course of preparation.

5. *La Leggenda minore*. Caffarini's efforts for the glorification of Catherine were not exhausted with the *Supplementum* and the Process. In order to make the life and virtues of the Saint known to a larger public he compiled a small biography of

THE SOURCES

her, founded on the *Legend* of Raymond, but with many personal features.

The original Latin was translated by Caffarini himself between 1414 and 1422; Stefano Maconi made another version of it. The Latin text was printed at Cologne in 1553, and, from a manuscript of the National Library in Florence, by R. Fawtier (*La Légende mineure de Ste Cath. de Sienne*, Rome 1913). Maconi's translation is that published by Grottanelli (*Leggenda minore di S. Cat. da Siena*, Bologna 1868).

A later abridgment, undertaken by Caffarini himself, is known as the *Leggenda minima*, edited in the *Sanctuarium* of Mombritius (new edition Paris 1910, I, pp. 297–322). It was likewise at the instances of this faithful and zealous *Caterinato* that Fra Maximino of Salerno in 1417 wrote his *Leggenda valde abbreviata* of the Saint. (See MS. T. I, 2, of the Bibl. Comm. of Siena, where the said legend occupies ff. 193–224.)

6. *Minor sources*. (a) Barduccio Canigiani's letter already mentioned above, of the closing period of Catherine's life and her death, edited by Grottanelli, Torino 1865; by Gigli: *Opere IV*, and in a Latin translation in A. SS. April III, pp. 959–961.

(b) *Epistola Domni Stephani*, i.e., Stefano Maconi's testimony in the Venetian process. Edited in the A. SS. l. c. pp. 961–967 and f. II–VII of the Aldine edition of the Letters of the Saint.

(c) William Flete's writings on Catherine: 1) *Sermo in reverentiam B. Caterine de Senis*, compositus in a-D. 1382; 2) *Narratio fr. Gulielmi de spirituali doctrina oraculo vive vocis beate Katerine habita in anno 1376, die 7 januarii;* 3) *Ep. ejusdem fr. Gulielmi ad Mag. Raimundum de virtutibus B. Katerine*. All these three works have been published, from the Sienese MS. T. II, 7, by Fawtier, who has also published an abridgment made by Maconi of the second one. (See *Catheriniana*, Rome 1914, pp. 86–93.)

(d) *Memoriale di me Cristofano Gano notaio da Siena ... di certe mie cose*. Ser Cristofano's Memoirs, edited by Milanesi in *Arch. stor. ital.* 1843, p. 29 et seq.

(e) *Lettere dei discipoli di S. Caterina*, edited by Grottanelli, Bologna 1868.

(f) The poetry of the disciples in honour of Saint Catherine and above all: 1) *Uno capitolo in rima fatto per Anastagio di Monte Alcino in laude et reverentia di S. Cat. da Siena ... vivendo ancora lei ne la presente vita* (printed e.g. in the edition of 1480 of the Dialogue, f. 213b to f. 216a). 2) *Uno capitolo in rima fatto per Jacobo da Montepulciano in reverentia da la predetta vergine santa Catherina essendo essa gia passata al cielo* (ibid. f. 220b to f. 223a). 3) *Uno capitolo in rima fatto per Raynerio de Pagliaresi da Siena discipulo di santa Catherina* (ibid. f. 216a to 220b). 4) *Laude ad honore de la serafica santa Catherina da Siena composta per Raynerio sopradetto* (ibid., f. 223). See also Grottanelli's editions of the two poems in honour of Catherine by Jacopo del Pecora (Siena 1859), and of a *lauda* attributed to Caffarini (Siena, April 29th, 1863).

REFERENCES AND PARTICULARS

Book I

I. [1] Duccio's Madonna is now in the *Opera del Duomo in Siena;* his house is shown in Via Stalloreggi.

[2] On Feb. 6th, 1107, Sant' Ansano's relics were brought into the town (G. Olmi: *I Senesi d'una volta,* Siena, 1889, pp. 333–341). Porta Sanviene, now Porta Pispini.

[3] G. Pardi: *Della vita e degli scritti di Giov. Colombini,* Siena 1895, p. 28.

[4] The fresco on the wall of San Sebastiano (now *Ricreatorio Pio secondo*) was painted in the year 1700 by Nasini and restored about 1850 by Maffei, but it is now in need of being restored again.

[5] *Leg.* I, ii, 4; *Leg. min.* I, 2, *Supp.* P. 1, Tr. §2.

II. [1] *Leg.* I, ii, 1.

[2] A poem by Nuccio di Piagente printed in F. Tozzi's *Antichi scrittori senesi,* Siena 1913, p. 136.

[3] Busiri-Toti: *La Casa di S. Cat.,* Siena 1880. Toncelli: *La Casa di S. Caterina,* Roma 1909. There was a "frater Rainerius Benlucase" among the friars who, in May 1305, signed their names below the statutes of the hospital of La Scala in Siena. See *Statuti Volgari de la Spedale di Santa Maria Vergine di Siena . . . publicati da Luciano Banchi,* Siena 1864, p. 88.

[4] Grottanelli's edition of *Leg. min.* p. 191.

[5] *Leg.* I, ii. *Leg. min.* I, ii. Raymond says (*A. SS.* April III, p. 861, n. 31): vitam et mores sanctorum patrum . . . nullo tradente hominum . . . sola Spiritus Sancti infusione, dedicit et agnovit." But Raymond did not become acquainted with Catherine until 1374, and we know that Tommaso della Fonte grew up in the home of Catherine's childhood (*Suppl.* P. III, Tr. VII, §1; *Leg.* I, ii, 8).

III. [1] Acts vii, 55–56; ix, 3–5; xxii, 6–8. Swete: *The appearances of our Lord after the Passion,* London 1910, pp. 104–107.

[2] II Cor. xii, 3–4.

[3] *Rev.* VI, 52, IV, 77, Richard Steffen: "Den heliga Birgittas uppenbarelser," Stockholm 1909, p. XXX seq.

[4] Nietzsches Werke, Taschenausgabe, VII, p. XXIV seq. Chr. Claussen: XXIV "En Digterskæbne," Kristiania 1913, p. 178.

[5] Zahn, *Christliche Mystik,* Paderborn 1908, p. 537.

[6] *Leg.* II, ii, 1.

[7] Catherine places these words at the head of her book, *The Dialogue,* as the point of departure of the whole of her mysticism.

[8] *Leg. min.*, I, ii.

[9] *Leg.* I, ii, 7–8. *Leg. min.* I, ii.

[10] I Cor. vii, 34.

[11] *Leg.* I, iii, 1.

[12] *Leg.* I, iii, 5.

³ "mia cognata secondo la carne, ma sorella secondo Christo," *Lettera* 135.
⁴ *Suppl.* P. 2, Tr. 2, §§5, 7, 8. P. 2, Tr. 3, §19.
⁵ *Suppl.* P. II, Tr. 5, §9.
⁶ *Proc.* col. 1314.
⁷ *Proc.* col. 1321.
⁸ *Suppl.* P. I, Tr. 2, §10. *Proc.* col. 1260.
⁹ "Illis utendo verbis qvibus in suis Soliloqvis utitur Augustinus." *Proc.* col. 1259. Cf. *Suppl.* P. 2, Tr. 3, §2 and §4, n. 6.
¹⁰ *Leg.* II, 2.
¹¹ *Suppl.* P. 2, Tr. 3, §3.
¹² Bonafede: *Il Colombino di Giesu,* Roma 1642, p. 319. Caterina Benincasa and Caterina Colombini (d. 1388) did not know each other; the former, on the other hand, knew Matteo Colombini, another second cousin of Giovanni C.

II. ¹ *Dialogo* cap. 7, cap. 64. *Lett.* 8.
² *Statuti volgari de lo spedale di S. M. Vergine di Siena* (1305), ed. Banchi, Siena 1854. Cap. 54: "Che nessuno sia ricevuto per frate dello Spedale . . . s'ello non offera al detto Spedale se e le sue cose." Cap. 52: "con la persona e com tutti li soi beni." In Catherine's time the rectors of the hospital of La Scala were: Mino di Cino Cinughi, from 1340 to 1351; Cione di Mino Montanini 1355 to 1357; Andrea Tori 1357 to 1361; Galgano di Lolo Bargagli 1361 to 1374; Bartolommeo Tucci 1374 to 1383. See Domenico Barducci: *Del governo del ospedale di Siena* (Siena 1895), pp. 53–54. Under the rectorship of Ristoro di Giunta Menghi (1294–1313) the hospital already possessed eighteen important barns, at Grosseto, Montepescali, Montisi, Castelluccio and other localities in the fertile Tuscan Maremma (1. c. p. 17).
³ "Amare el Comune di Siena," "amare, guardare e onorare el Comune di Siena," "a esso Comune servire a suo podere e non frodare . . . del detto Comune per lo detto Spedale" (*Statuti,* cap. 1).
⁴ In the outer wall of the hospital there is a stone with the inscription: *Limosine di grano.* An inscription on another stone informs us that there was room for CCC *gittatelli* (foundling children) *et plus.*
⁵ *Statuti,* cap. 36.
⁶ Bonafede, pp. 33–34.
⁷ *Suppl.* P. 2, Tr. 2, §1. *Leg. min.* II, iii, 5. According to Stefano Maconi this scene in Catherine's life was *figurata in Roma presso al sepolcro di lei.* Raymond makes the incident take place in the *Cappella delle Volte* in San Domenico and a little white stone with a mantle engraved upon it commemorates it. This stone, like the other similar ones in the same place, was placed there by the care of the pious and learned Dominican, Angelo Maria Carapelli, to whom we are indebted for a series of works on Catherine, which up to the present are only to be found in manuscript in the municipal library of Siena (*Corso cronotastico della vita di S. Cat. da Siena; Sommario del Processo di S. Cat.; Sommario di Notizie della vita di S. Cat.*). Padre Carapelli lived in the 17th century. "Better be without a cloak than without charity," *Proc.* col. 1380.
⁸ *Leg.* II, ii, 2–3.
⁹ *Leg.* II, iii, 8.

SUPPLEMENT

[10] *Padre in te sono, in te mi muoio e vivo, se veglio o dormo, se favello o scrivo.*
[11] *Suppl.* P. 2, Tr. 3, §6. *Lett.* 276.
[12] *Leg.* II, 4, 2.

III. [1] *Purgatorio*, XIII, 115–123.
[2] Boccaccio *Vita di Dante* cap. VIII. *Inferno* XXIX, 121–123. *Purg.* XI, 113–114.
[3] "Cantar, danzar a la provenzalesca, con istormenti novi d'Alemagna." Folgore da San Gimignano: *Sonetti*, ed. Neri, Città di Castello 1914, p. 37.
[4] *Cronaca Senese d'Agnolo di Tura*, in Gardner: *The Story of Siena*, London 1909, pp. 25–26.
[5] *Misc. Stor. Senese* V (1898), pp. 175–176: "*Pro statua Fontis Campi. Item quod statua marmorea ad presens in Fonte Campi posita, quam citius potest tollatur exinde, cum inhonestum videatur.*" (The resolution of the Council, passed on Nov. 7th, 1357.)
[6] *Leg. min.* ed. Grottanelli, pp. 209–210.
[7] *Ibid.* 210–214. *Leg.* I, ix, 2. *Proc.* col. 1270.
[8] *Lett.* 10, 18, 20.
[9] *Lett.* 23.
[10] *Proc.* col. 1334.
[11] *Leg.* II, vii, 2–5. *Suppl.* P. 2, Tr. 2, §7, n. 17. *Proc.* col. 1266.

IV. [1] *Lett.* 5, 25, 39, 63, 75 etc.
[2] *Leg.* II, vi, 4.
[3] *Lett.* 74.
[4] *Leg.* II, vi, 1–8. *Suppl.* P. 1, Tr. 2, §§3–4.
[5] *Proc.* coll. 1330–1331. *Leg.* II, vi, 15. *Suppl.* P. II, Tr. 6, §18. See also *Leg. min.* p. 78.
[6] *Leg.* II, vi, 7. *Suppl.* II, Tr. vi, §12.
[7] *Suppl.* P. II, Tr. 6, §6.
[8] *Suppl.* P. I, Tr. 2, §§17–18; Tr. 3, §4; §15; n. 38–39; §16, n. 40.
[9] *Leg.* II, vi, 17–19. *Suppl.* P. II, Tr. 5, §14; Tr. 6, §2, n. 9.
[10] *Leg.* II, vi, 9. *Suppl.* P. II, Tr. 6 §§10–11. *Leg. min.* pp. 75 seq.
[11] *Leg.* II, vi, 20–24. *Proc.* coll. 1332–1333.

V. [1] *Lett.* 113.
[2] *Lett.* 86.
[3] *Dial.* capp. 7, 64, 89.
[4] *Leg.* II, vi, 23 *in fine*.
[5] *Lett.* 147.
[6] *Proc.* col. 1271.
[7] *Suppl.* P. I, Tr. 2, §8 and P. I, Tr. 2, §20. Cf. *Leg.* II, cap. 7, n. 6. *Leg. min.* p. 214 seq., *Proc.* col. 1267. See also *Assempri* capp. 29 and 62, in which the good Fra Filippo recounts similar features. ("D'un uomo che percosse con una daga su'n grosso la figura de la Vergine Maria... D'un uomo che avventò una pietra a la figura de la Vergine Maria.")
[8] *Suppl.* P. II, Tr. 6, §§3–5; §1, n. 4.
[9] *Suppl.* P. II, Tr. 6, §1.
[10] *Suppl.* P. II, Tr. 6, §14.

¹¹ *Leg. min.* p. 216. *Misc. Stor. Sanese*, V (1898), pp. 171-173. *Boll. Senese di Storia Patria*, XVII, fasc. III. According to the article in *Misc. Stor. Sanese*, p. 174, n. 1, the palace of Alessia Saracini would be "il palazzo presso le Loggie di mercanzia, oggi chiamato *il Casone.*" La Porta di Giustizia was built in 1323.
¹² *Leg.* II, vii, nn. 10-13.
¹³ "Lassate predicar i frati pazzi ch'anno troppo bugie e poco vero." Folgore, p. 36.
¹⁴ *Lett.* 64, 112, 28, 191.
¹⁵ *Opusc. S. Francisci*, Quaracchi 1904, p. 78.
¹⁶ *Proc.* coll. 1337-1339.
¹⁷ *Leg.* II, x, 2-5.
¹⁸ *Leg.* II, vii, 14.
¹⁹ *Leg. min.* pp. 95-96 and p. 218.
²⁰ *Suppl.* P. II, Tr. 6, §15.

VI. ¹ *Lett.* 39, 25, 63, etc.
² *Contestatio Francisci Malavoltis*, MS. Casanat. f. 456. *Proc.* col. 1377; coll. 1344-1345; *Leg.* II, v; III, vi, 6.
³ *Lett.* 93, 39.
⁴ *Leg.* II, v, 12.
⁵ *Proc.* coll. 1330, 1315-1316, 1355-1356 where Raymond's account is corrected (*Leg.* II, iv, 9-15).
⁶ *Lett.* 55, 97.
⁷ *Proc.* col. 1271.
⁸ *Proc.* coll. 1347-1351 and 1367. Cf. *Lett.* 225.

VII. ¹ *Dial.* c. 41.
² *Lett.* 41, 144, 153. See in Tommaseo's edition Vol. II, p. 365, note 2. A brother of Giovanna's father-in-law, Niccolò Cinughi, founded La Certosa di Belriguardo near Siena in about 1350.
³ *Lett.* 127.
⁴ *Lett.* 49, 50.
⁵ I John iii, 14.
⁶ Matt. x, 34-36.
⁷ *Leg.* II, viii, 1-4. *Leg. min.* p. 223.
⁸ *Lett.* 1, 6, 117, 240.
⁹ *Suppl.* P. II, Tr. 5, §3; P. III, Tr. 6, §9.
¹⁰ *Suppl.* P. II, Tr. 4, §14; cf. §13, n. 35. P. II, Tr. 6, §2; §14, n. 35.
¹¹ *Lett.* 44.
¹² John xii, 25. Luke ix, 24. Matt. x, 39.
¹³ *Lett.* 99.
¹⁴ *Lett.* 112, 115.
¹⁵ *Lett.* 269.
¹⁶ *Lett.* 281.
¹⁷ *Lett.* 178.
¹⁸ *Suppl.* P. III, Tr. 6, §8.
¹⁹ MS. Casanat. cit. fol. 430-431.
²⁰ "Et ex tunc . . . nihil curavi vel curo quomodo degam in dies, nisi ut possim placere Deo." *Proc.* col. 1364. This is a matter of a vision after Catherine's death, but Tommaso di Petra sees her as if she were bodily alive.
²¹ MS. Casanat. f. 432.

SUPPLEMENT

²² *Lett.* 45.

²³ MS. Casanat. ff. 439–440. *Proc.* col. 1376. *Leg.* III, iv, 3: "un dolce e fervoroso modo di parlare." Her smile, ibid. I, ix, 6; II, xii, 13.

²⁴ *Lett.* 126: "questa povera famigliola della prima dolce Verità." Cf. *Lett.* 80, 105, 52, 150.

²⁵ "Mei dulces filii vocant me." MS. Casanat. f. 467.

²⁶ *Leg.* II, x, 5–7. *Proc.* coll. 1323–1325. *Lett.* 365.

²⁷ MS. Casanat. ff. 466–467.

²⁸ *Ibid.* ff. 453, 455–458, 465. *Leg.* II, vii, 22; III, vi, 23. *Proc.* coll. 1269, 1334, 1346, 1373. *Lett. dei disc.* ed. Grottanelli, pp. 262, 263, 265, 269, 277. Colombini to Monna Pavola Foresi: "dolciata madre mia, mamma dolcie (*Lett.* ed. Bartoli, Lucca 1856, no. 31, no. 32 etc.).

VIII. ¹ Feo Belcari *Vita di Colombini* cap. 33 (*Prose di Feo Belcari*, 1843, I, 96–97).

² MS. Cas. cit. fol. 441–446.

³ Assempri cap. 40.

⁴ Landucci: *Sacra Leccetana Selva*, Roma 1657, p. 106.

⁵ McMahan; *With Shelley in Italy*, London 1907, pp. 154–155.

⁶ "uomo di molto penitenzia, el più del tempo stava nel bosco, poi la sera ritornava al luogo," we are told by Ser Cristofano di Gano Guidini (*Arch. Stor. Ital.* IV, p. 34). Cf. Tommaseo's edition of *Lettere* II, xiii, n. 2.

⁷ Gigli: *Opere di S. Cat.* IV, 376.

⁸ *Lett.* 77, cf. *Lett.* 64.

⁹ *Lett.* 130 in Tommaseo's edition, II, p. 13, n. 2, and also the fuller text published by Gardner (*S. Cath. of Siena*, London 1907, pp. 296–298).

¹⁰ *Assempri* cap. 24. The brother to whom this happened was Fra Giovanni di Guccio Molli.

¹¹ "Siste hic Viator / et has aedes erectas a / beato Io, Incontrio anno 1330 ubi seraphica Catharina Senensis sponsum receptavit Christum." Cf. Landucci, p. 80. Of Blessed Giovanni Incontrio (d. 4th April 1339) *ibid.*, p. 99.

¹² *Suppl.* P. I, Tr. 2, §3. Raymond tells about an excursion to Lecceto on April 25th in *Leg.* II, xii, 6.

IX. ¹ *Lett.* 7.

² G. Mollat: *Les Papes d'Avignon*, Paris 1912, preface.

³ Huck: "Ubertin von Casale und sein Ideenkreis," Freiburg in Breisgau, 1903. Frédégand Callaey: (L'idéalisme franciscain spirituel au XIVe siècle, Louvain & Paris, 1911).

⁴ *Revue d'hist. de l'Eglise de France* I, pp. 557–566.

⁵ *Revel. S. Birg.* VI, 63.

⁶ *Revel.* VI, 96.

⁷ *Revel.* III, 27, IV, 33, 58, 133. Hammerich: *Den hellige Birgitta*, Copenhagen 1863, pp. 147–152.

⁸ Knut B. Westman: *Birgittastudier* (Upsala 1911), pp. 293–295.

⁹ *Revel. S. Birg.* IV, 136.

¹⁰ *Lettere di Colombini*, p. 218.

¹¹ *Revel.* IV, 139–140. Hammerich, p. 192.

¹² Mollat l. c. pp. 123, 129–130, 148–158, 160.

[13] *Lett.* ed. Tommaseo I, p. 181; II, pp. 10 and 349; III, p. 300; IV, p. 344. Cf. I, 79, 80, 83, 96, 163, 181, 224; II, 12, 81, 125, 164, 221, 424, etc.
[14] *Lett.* 318.
[15] "Costei per l'onore di Dio, non curava dispiacere o di piacere." (*Arch. stor. ital.* IV, p. 36).
[16] *Lett.* 239, 185.
[17] *Lett.* 11.
[18] Mark xiv, 71 and 67.
[19] *Lett.* 109.
[20] Muratori: *Scriptores*, vol. XVIII, col. 238.
[21] *Lett.* 24.
[22] *Lett.* 59.
[23] *Lett.* 3.
[24] *Lett.* 28 and 29.
[25] *Lett. dei disc.* ed. Grottanelli, no. 2. The letter is addressed "Devotissime Christi Catelline de Senis dulcissime nostre."
[26] Compare the letter of consolation which Catherine wrote to Monna Mitarella, the anxious wife of Lodovico de Mogliano (*Lett.* 31).

X. [1] In this presentation I deviate from earlier biographers of Saint Catherine, her first meeting with Raymond having always been given as Siena. We know, however, that Catherine was in Florence from May 20th till June 29th, 1374, i.e. five days *after* Saint John's Day, and Gardner, seeing this difficulty, therefore relegates the Mass on June 24th to the previous year (St. Cath. of Siena, p. 123, n. 1). This is scarcely probable. We see that the relations between Raymond and Catherine are very active already in the second half of 1374; they nurse the plague-stricken together, they travel together to Montepulciano — while on the other hand nothing whatever is known about intercourse or association between them during the time from June 24th 1373 to the summer of 1374. The doubts which Raymond entertained about Catherine (*Leg.* I, ix, 6) are also more likely to belong to the very first period of an / acquaintanceship. Finally, I imagine that St. John's Day was remembered because it was the great Florentine feast day, which was celebrated in that city with great solemnity, St. John being the patron saint of Florence, on which occasion Raymond officiated as deacon and Catherine saw him for the first time. (*Suppl.* P. II, Tr. 6, §17. *Proc.* coll. 1380–1381.) It may also have been in remembrance of that day that Catherine liked to call her new confessor her Giovanni, her *Giovanni singolare* (*Leg. Prol. primus*, n. 6. *Lett.* 6). See also *Lett.* 221 (figliuolo dato da quella dolce madre Maria") and *Lett.* 226 ("a voi . . . dato da quella dolce madre Maria").

Since writing the above I have received a confirmation of my view, in a communication sent to me by Padre Innocenzo Taurisano, O.P. In his researches on the history of Florentine Dominican monasteries the learned Dominican has discovered some legal papers which prove that Raymond was in Florence on *August 30th, 1373*. The document in question states: "fra Borgese de Florentia sindaco del convento vende a Bruna quondam Burelli alcuni pezzi di terra, fatte de consensu, presenza e voluntate fr. Dominici de Pantaleonibus de Florentia . . . prioris fratrum capituli et conventus predicti et fratrum dictorum capituli et conventus videlicet fr. Petri Johannis subprioris dicti conventus, fr. Raymundi de Capua" etc. etc. (followed by 28 more names of friars who served as witnesses). It will be noticed that Raymond's name follows immediately after the names of the prior and the sub-prior; his name in this place and under a legal document proves that he was not a guest in the monastery, but a member of the community and therefore resident in Florence and not at Siena (as according to Gardner's supposition he would have been, since we know that he accompanied Catherine on her return journey and remained with her).

[2] Pietro de Vineis. See the genealogical table in *Opuscula B. Raymundi Capuani*, Roma 1895, p. 143. Caffarini (*Suppl.* P. III, Tr. 3, 3) mentions a vision of Saint Catherine in which "it seemed to her that she saw issuing from the bosom of the Infant Jesus a vine bearing ripe grapes. Large dogs approached it in great numbers and ate their fill of them, after which they carried other grapes to the little dogs for food." Père Hyacinthe M. Cormier is of opinion that in this vision there is an allusion to the family name of Raymond (*Le B. Raymond de Capoue*, Rome 1902, p. 95, n. 1).

[3] *Leg.* II, x, 5 and I, ix, 6. *Inferno* I, 32–33.

[4] *Miracoli e transito di S. Caterina*, ed. Grottanelli, cit. Gardner pp. 120–121.

[5] *Purg.* XIII, 106–129. Of Pietro Pettinaro (d. 1289), Olmi: *I Senesi d'una volta*, pp. 109–127.

[6] *Lett.* 119.

[7] Casimir Chledowski: "Siena," I, 70.

[8] Luke iv, 39.

[9] *Leg.* II, viii, 5–16.

[10] *Leg.* II, xi, 1–3.

[11] *Miracoli*, cit. Drane I, 237, *S. Cath. of Siena and Her Friends* (London 1899), I, p. 237.

[12] Biography of Agnes of Montepulciano by Raymond, *A. SS.* ad 20 April.

[13] *Leg.* II, xii, 17–19. *A. SS.* April II, pp. 793–794.

[14] *Lett.* 41.

[15] *Suppl.* P. II, Tr. 6, §15.

[16] *Leg.* I, ix, 6–7.

[17] *Lett.* 61.

XI. [1] *Leg.* II, viii, 17.

[2] *Mem. Dom.* April 1916, pp. 172 seq., July 1916, pp. 379 seq., April 1917, pp. 210–211.

[3] Lazzareschi: *S. Caterina da Siena ed i Pisani* (Firenze 1917), pp. 123–124. *Lett.* 159, addressed to the priest Ranieri. *Proc.* col. 1352–1353. *Mem. Dom.* September 1916, pp. 583–585.

[4] Feo Belcari: *Vita del B. Giovanni Colombini*, cap. 36. *Laudi spirituali del Bianco da Siena*, Lucca 1851, p. 167.

[5] *Lett.* 92 and 127.

[6] *Leg.* II, vi, 10–11.

[7] *Dial.* cap. 78.

Book III

I. [1] Col. i, 24.

[2] *Lett.* 137, 108, 168, 171.

[3] *Lett.* 168.

[4] *Lett.* 28.

[5] *Lett.* 207.

[6] *Opusc. S. Fr.* Quaracchi 1904, p. 78.

[7] *Lett.* 131, to Niccolò Soderini in Florence.

[8] *Leg.* II, x, 20. *Proc.* col. 1304–1307. *Lett.* 134 (to the hermits in Pisa). The monk who was planning suicide *Proc.* coll. 1305–1306. *Proc.* coll. 1305–1306. Cf. Pietro Vigo: *S. Cat. a Gorgona ed a Livorno* in *Voce della Carità*, Siena 1915, pp. 30–32. On Calci see Aristo Manghi: *La Certosa di Pisa;* Pisa 1911.

[9] Ranieri Sardo: *Cronaca Pisana*, ed. Bonaini (*Arch. Stor. ital.* VI, Firenze 1845), p. 186.

[10] *Lett.* 140. *Assempri*, cap. 58. Thureau-Dangin: *San Bernardino da Siena*, Siena 1897, p. 273. G. Temple Leader and G. Marcotti: *Giovanni Acuto* (Firenze 1889), p. 66. On Raymond's work for the Crusade see *Lett.* 136. See also *Mem. Domenic.* 1916, pp. 327–333.

[11] Gherardi: *La guerra dei Fiorentini con papa Gregorio XI* (*Arch. Stor. ital.* 1867–68, vol. V, parte II); Mirot: *La question des blés dans la rupture entre Florence et le Saint-Siège en 1375* (*Mélanges d'arch. et d'hist.*, 1896, pp. 101 seq.).

[12] "In fin che tu non mi farai ben certo di cio che tu m'impromettisti a Lucca." (*Capitolo in rima* by Neri di Landoccio, in the Venetian edition of 1548 of the *Epistole ed orationi di Santa Caterina*, col. 295.)

[13] *Lett.* 164–165. *Suppl.* P. II, Tr. 6, §§7-8. See Eugenio Lazzareschi: *S. Cat. da Siena ed i Lucchesi* (*Mem. Dom.* 1912, pp. 186 seq., 296 seq.).

[14] *Lett.* 139. The "venerable Spaniard," mentioned by Catherine, is the Bishop of Jaen, Alfonso di Vadaterra, who, towards the end of 1374 or in the early months of 1375, had come to see her at Siena, bringing her the "message of indulgence" of the Pontiff. *Lett.* 127 (Tommaseo's edition, II, 315).

[15] Flete: *Sermo in reverentiam* (*Mélanges de . . . l'Ecole franç. de Rome*, XXXIV, 1914, p. 58, p. 80).

[16] *Leg.* II, x, 8–10. *Cronaca di Perugia, detta del Graziani*, in *Arch. Stor. ital.*, ser. I, t. XVI, i, p. 220. The house in which Catherine lived while in Pisa was perhaps the actual *Canonica* of the church of Saint Catherine (dedicated to the patron of the Sienese saint, Saint Catherine of Alexandria).

II. [1] *Lett.* 185. Ep. Gal. II, 11.

[2] *Lett.* 196.

[3] Gherardi, cit. in Gardner, p. 164.

[4] *Lett.* 206.

[5] *Lett.* 209.

[6] *Processus* coll. 1370–1371; *Vita B. Stephani*, auct. Barth. Sen., Siena 1626, I, 4–6.

[7] *Lett.* 207.

[8] Gardner, p. 171 seq.

[9] *Lettere del B. Giovanni delle Celle*, Roma 1845, pp. 27–31. Cf. *Dialogo* c. 129 on the priests who "hanna imparato a fare malie e incantare le dimonia facendosi venire per incanto di demonio, di mezza nocte, quelle creature che miseramente amano."

[10] Biscioni: *Lettere di santi e beati Fiorentini*, Firenze 1736, pp. 57–63.

III. [1] Petrarca, Sonetti CV, CVI (*L'avara Babilonia* and *Fontana di dolore*). Cf. *Ep. sine tit.* 5, 8, 12–15, 17–19. *Rer. sen.*, lib. VII and IX.

[2] L. H. Labaude: *Guide Archéologique du Congrès d'Avignon*, Paris 1910; Mahuet: *Praedicatorum avenionense*, Avignon 1628, p. 76; Girard Requin: *L'ancien couvent des Dominicains d'Avignon*, in *Annales d'Avignon et du Comtat Venaissin*, I, pp. 81 seq. and II, pp. 299 seq.; André Hallays: *Avignon*, Paris 1911; Marcel Chossai: *Les Jésuites à Avignon*, Avignon 1896; P. M. Baumgarten: "Die Papstveste von Avignon" (in "Festschrift an G. v. Hertling," Kempten 1913, pp. 272 seq.).

[3] The cardinal's palace mentioned here later became a Jesuit college and is now a grammar school. It is the building on the Place Saint-Didier, of which the other façades front on the rue de la République, rue Joseph Vernet and rue Laboureur. Some members of Catherine's escort were accommodated "in domo domini Joannis de Regio" (statement by Tommaso Buonconti, quoted by Gigli, *Opere* II, p. 16; III, p. 330. See also *Mem. Dom.* 1916, p. 382). Did Catherine visit Bologna on her journey? It would appear so from tradition. She would naturally have a great desire to visit the tomb of her spiritual father and to pray near his mortal remains. A letter to the Dominicans of "certain convents at Bologna" seems to have been written after a visit to these convents: the Saint speaks in them against "l'adornamento delle cortine, i letti della piuma, i superchi e dissoluti vestimenti" of the religious in question (*Lett.* 215.).

[4] *Proc.* col. 1337. *Leg.* III, vi, 26.

[5] *Lett.* 232. *Proc.* col. 1337.

[6] *Lett.* 230.

[7] Scipio Ammirato: *Storie Fiorentine* XIII, 699.

[8] *Leg.* III, vi, 27.

[9] *Leg.* II, iv, 7. *Proc.* col. 1325.

[10] *Proc.* col. 1374.

[11] *Leg.* II, iv, 7. "Erat cujusdam magni praelati concubina."

[12] *Dial.* cap. 123.

[13] *Ep. Domni Stephani* §§22–24.

[14] *Lett.* 235.

[15] *Lett.* 233.

[16] *Lett.* 234.

[17] *Oratio* I and II in Gigli: *Opere* IV, pp. 337–339.

[18] Gigli, IV, p. XVI: "Laudato Dio, ora e sempre più!"

[19] *Lett.* 239.

[20] Psalm xc (xci), 13.

IV. [1] *Lett.* 240.

[2] *Lett.* 241: "la volontà non è altro che amore; ogni suo affetto e movimento non si muove per altro che per amore."

[3] *Leg.* II, VIII, n. 27.

[4] *Leg.* I, x, 7.

[5] *Purg.* III, 49–56. Lerici, near Spezia, and La Turbie, between Nice and Monaco, indicate the frontiers of Liguria.

[6] *Ep. D. Steph.* §15.

[7] Information given in writing by Dr. Pierre Pouzet and Mademoiselle Jeanne Delcour, at Cannes.

[8] *Opusc. Raim. Cap.* Rome 1895, pp. 25–30. Varazze was the seat of

the bishop of Bethlehem, driven out by the Turks (Cormier: *Raym. de Capoue*, p. 62).

[9] *Ep. D. Steph.* §§12–13.
[10] *Lett.* 247.
[11] *Lett.* 246 and 245.
[12] *Oratio* III (Gigli: *Opere* IV, p. 340). *Suppl.* P. Tr. I, §1.
[13] G. Mollat: *Les Papes d'Avignon*, pp. 127 seq. On Jean Ferdinand d'Hérédia see de Vertot: *Histoire des Chevaliers de Malte*, II, pp. 219–252.
[14] *di Ranieri Sardo*, p. 192. On the journey of Gregory XI see *l'Itinerarium* of Pierre Amely d'Alète (Muratori: *Scriptores* t. III, Milano 1734, P. II, coll. 690–712) and Kirsch: *Die Rückkehr der Paepste Urban V und Gregor XI von Avignon nach Rom*, Paderborn 1898, p. 202.
[15] *Lett.* 252.
[16] *Suppl.* P. II, Tr. I, §§2–3.
[17] *Lettere dei discep.* ed. Grottanelli, nos. 5 and 6.
[18] *Proc.* coll. 1273–1274. Raynaldus *Ann. eccles.* VII, p. 283.
[19] See Letter 219 of Catherine, in which she foresees the event.

V. [1] *Lett.* 209.
[2] *Lettere del b. Giov. delle Celle*, Roma 1845, pp. 81–83.
[3] *Leg.* II, vii, 17–20.
[4] *Leg. min.* ed. Grottanelli, pp. 219–222. It is strange that so late as December 3rd, 1379, Catherine writes in a letter from Rome: "Da Siena ho avuto novelle che eglino hanno avuto licenza di mutare Belcaro." (*Lett.* 192, edited by Motzo from the MS. of Acireale, *Mem. Dom.* 1912, p. 277.) For the history of the convent see G. Camaiori: *Memorie storiche di Belcaro* (*Boll. Senese di Storia Patria*, anno XX, p. 365).
[5] *Pred. volgare di S. Bernardino*, ed. Banchi, Vol. III, Siena 1880, pp. 55–56. Gori: *L'eccidio di Cesena del 1377* (*Arch. stor. ital.* Nuova Serie VIII).
[6] *Lett.* 270.
[7] *Lett.* 260.
[8] *Leg. min.* II, vii.
[9] In the year 1304 a place of execution was set up at Strada Romana on the spot which is to this day called *Corposanto al Pecorile*. Those who were condemned to death were taken by the *Via dei Malcontenti* down to Mercato Vecchio; here they mounted a tumbril and the road now led through *Porta della Giustizia* by *Val di Montone* over to Via Romana. At the hostelry of *la Coroncina* the rosary for the poor sinners was intoned and the last night was spent in the *Albergaccio*, "the bad hostelry." All these places are still to be found.
[10] *Lett.* 273.

VI. [1] *Lett.* 118. Cf. *Lett.* 117 to Lapa and Cecca at Montepulciano.
[2] Verdiani-Bandi: *I Castelli della Val d'Orcia e a la Republica di Siena*, Siena 1906. *Mem. Dom.* 1915, pp. 7–16.
[3] *Lett.* 256 to the brothers Trinci; 264 to Monna Jacopa d'Este; 112 to Bandeca Salimbeni; 114 to Agnolino di Giovanni Salimbeni; 115 to Monna Isa.
[4] "Dolce città, che se fatta de lei tanto aliena" (Giacomo del Pecora, ed. 1540 of *Il Dialogo*, f. 223).
[5] *Lett.* 110.

SUPPLEMENT

[6] Colombini: *Lettere*, ed. Bartoli (Lucca 1856), p. 76. *Proc.* col. 1271. Cf. Gaetano Salvemini: *Un comune rurale nel secolo XIII* (*Rocca di Tentennano*) in *Studi storici* (Firenze 1901).

[7] MS. Casanat. f. 462, ff. 450–452. *Leg.* II, vi, 7–9. *Sprone*, a buttress.

[8] *Leg.* II, ii, 3; III, vi, 24. Catherine's earlier biographers believed that she had invented this expression herself but it can already be found in Giovanni Colombini (*Lettere*, p. 105, p. 219). The name Malatasca for the Devil recalls the Malacoda and Malebranche of Dante (*Inferno*, XXI, 76 and 37).

[9] *Leg.* II, vii, 21. Cod. Marc. f. 131, col. 1 (Lazzareschi, l. c. p. 37, n. 3). Anastagio de Montalcino in the edition of *Il Dialogo* of 1540, ff. 213, b-316.

[10] *Lett.* 223.

[11] *Lett.* 122.

[12] *Lett.* 121.

[13] *Leg.* III, vi, 28. Temple Leader and G. Marcotti: *Giovanni Aguto*, p. 105.

[14] *Leg.* II, xii, 4–6.

[15] Cf. Pietro di Giovanni Ventura at the convent in Montepulciano. Cod. 2977 of Bibl. Marc. of Venice, f. 138, col. I. See Lazzareschi: *S. Cat. in Val d'Orcia*, p. 22, n. 2.

[16] *Suppl.* P. II, Tr. 6, §17. MS. Casanat. ff. 453–455. *Dial.* cap. 79.

[17] *Leg.* II, xii, 10–15. *Leg. min.* ed. Grottanelli p. 142. *Dial.* cap. 142 and cap. 3. *Catheriniana* ed. Fawtier, p. 57 (testimony of William Flete "quod Christus *vel sanctus Petrus* cum illa particula communicavit eam."

[18] *Suppl.* P. I, Tr. I, §10. See also the similar prayer "fatta alla Rocca di Tentennano le 26 octobre 1378" (*Oratio 25*. Is this date authentic? It does not seem to be, as on November 4th of the same year Catherine had not yet left Siena).

[19] *Lett.* 120 and *Lett.* 272. *Lett.* 365: "mandai a chiedere, alla Contessa il libro mio — e non viene."

[20] *Lett.* 272. Père Hurtaud has pointed out, in the introduction to *Le Dialogue de Sainte Cathérine de Sienne* (Paris 1913), I, pp. XXXVII–XLV, that this letter consists of two parts. The main part of the letter (Tommaseo III, 465 seq.) ends (on p. 481) with the words: "Permanente nella santa e dolce dilezione di Dio" and is written in the autumn of 1378. On the other hand, Catherine's account of the mystical manner in which she learned to write, quoted in my text, probably owes its origin to another letter, written in 1377, but now lost. That vanished letter, like no. 272, would be addressed to Raymond shortly after his departure from Tentennano ("subito che fuste partite da me"), and the old collectors only preserved the last part. To throw doubt upon the *miracle itself* — as the learned Dominican does — lacks every justification of critical research. The fragment in question is Catherinian enough, it has even some of that peculiar obscurity characteristic of the most personal letters of the Sienese saint (cf. e.g., no. 273 and the double letter 371–373, in which, incidentally, something has also been dropped out from 371). Besides, how does Hurtaud escape the allusion in that part of the letter regarded by him as genuine? "Lo Spirito Santo m'ha proveduto dentro da me con la clemenzia sua *e di fuori m'ha proveduto di spassarmi con lo scrivere.*" As Catherine had long since had secretaries to whom she was in the habit of dictating, this would not be any new consolation to her. She therefore says, quite

simply, that after Raymond's departure she consoles herself with writing with her own hand, a thing which she did not know how to do before. She does not seem, by the way, ever to have known very well how to do it, as we see that she always employs her secretaries for her correspondence as well as for the *Dialogue*.

[21] *Lett.* 119. According to a description dating from the 18th century there was, on the top of the principal tower (*il mastio*) a terrace from which "si scuopre moltissimo paese e in fine la città di Siena." (Lazzareschi, l. c. p. 53, n. 1.)

[22] *Alcuni miracoli di S. Cat.* (Siena 1862), pp. 17-18.

[23] *Dep. fr. Simonis de Cortona* in the Cod. Marc. f. 147, col. 2, quoted by Lazzareschi, p. 46, n. 2. *Leg.* III, vi, 14.

[24] *Lett. dei disc.* p. 266 seq.

[25] Lazzarino di Pisa in the MS. T. I, i, 3 of the municipal library of Siena, f. 23. *Lett.* 56. Gardner (*S. Cath. of Siena*, pp. 219-221) has pointed out that a letter from Catherine to Brother Simone of Cortona, in the MS. 102 of the library Vittorio Emmanuele, begins with the very words "Carissimo figliuolo *senza nome*," which correspond to the despairing exclamation of the anonymous writer: "El nome mio non ci pongo, perchè io non so come io ò nome." Gently she finishes the letter "allora *voi averete nome*, e io ritrovero il figliuolo." This extraordinary coincidence proves that the anonymous F.S. is really F(rate) S(imone), or *Mone* as Catherine calls him in a letter to Neri (*Lett.* 212).

[26] *Lett.* 226.

[27] Perhaps a connection is to be found between these spiritual defeats and Letter 173 "a un frate che uscì dell' ordine?"

VII. [1] *Lett.* 267.

[2] *Leg.* III, vi, 28.

[3] Gardner places the journey in the spring of 1378. It appears, however, from *Lett.* 278, that Catherine celebrated the feast of St. Lucy (December 13th) away from Siena. St. Catherine's house, Costa S. Giorgio, no. 45, now belongs to the Sisters of the Holy Family; visitors are shown the chapel in which the Saint perhaps prayed. I take this opportunity of expressing my thanks to these Sisters, as well as to Mr. and Mrs. Henry Burton, who occupy part of the house, for their kindness.

[4] *Lett.* 278. For the play on the word *Luce* see *Suppl.* P. I, Tr. 2, §20.

[5] *Lett.* 227 and 277.

[6] *Diario d'Anonimo fiorentino* ed. Gherardi, Firenze 1876, p. 352.

[7] *Lettere dei disc.* p. 260 seq. L. Salembier: *Le grand schisme d'Occident*, Paris 1900.

[8] *Lett.* 295.

[9] *Lett.* 278. *Leg.* III, vi, 34.

[10] *Lett.* 291.

[11] *Lett.* 303: "Mandovi dell'ulivo della pace." See ed. Tommaseo III, p. 120, n. 4.

[12] Gino Capponi: *Il tumulto dei Ciompi*, ed. Tortoli, Firenze 1858.

[13] *Leg.* III, vi, 35, and the letter, hitherto unknown, published by Gardner, *Saint Catherine*, pp. 413-416.

VIII. [1] *Suppl.* P. II, Tr. 6, n. 48. Cf. *Lett.* 214: "Oh disavventurata me! io credo essere quella miserabile che son cagione di tanti mali, per la molta ingratitudine e altri difetti che io ho commessi contra il mio creatore. Oimè, oimè!" *Lett.* 216: "Io miserabile, cagione d'ogni male!" See also *Lett.* 267, 270, 271, 272 etc. San Rocco a Pilli is situated ten kilometres from Siena.

[2] *Lett.* 304.

[3] *Suppl.* P. 1, Tr. 1, §3, Pardi: *Vita e scritti di Giov. Colombini*, Siena 1895, p. 47, n. 2.

[4] *Cath.* ed. Fawtier, p. 59: "Solebat contare in vita sua: ego sum sponsa Dei in virginitate facta," p. 74: "jam beata potest merito cantate laudam suam."

[5] I give the places which I have used in Tommaseo's edition with volume and page number: *sposa del breviario*, I, 6; the soul a garden I, 82, IV, 27, a vine IV, 175; IV, 178; IV, 183 and 228; the lamp of the heart I, 86; II, 90–91; flowers in rotten water I, 90; the flies and the boiling pan II, 320; III, 17; (the same image is used later by Blessed Camilla Battista Varani, *Opere spirituali*, Camerino 1894, p. 168. On this saint see Dina Puliti: *Un asceta del rinascimento*, Firenze 1915); the soul is a fortified city, I, 111; II, 39 and 52; a city abandoned to fire III, 254; IV, 139 and 224; the roasted lamb, I, 140; I, 234; II, 147; II, 343; the cell of Christ's wound I, 165; the staff of the Cross I, 264; Christ a knight II, 18; II, 50; II, 239; III, 385; the manuscript written on lambskin II, 44; "I am fire" II, 46; the *bottega* of the blood of Christ II, 70; II, 138; IV, 6; the ship with fire and blood III, 347; the bath in the Blood II, 93 and 99; the leaf in the wind, II, 237, 257; IV, 212; the dog I, 83; II, 252; IV, 224, 231; the chariot of fire of humanity II, 285; the ring of circumcision III, 247 and 417; the initials IV, 145, 202, 217; Jesus a flower which bears fruit on the Cross II, 376; *chiovi chiavi* II, 435; the body of Christ a cask of wine II, 136; fire in straw IV, 82; the teeth of patience IV, 89; stars seen from the well IV, 322; wood in the fire II, 416, *Dialogo* ed. Fiorilli p. 179. Anna Fumagalli (*Santa Caterina da Siena e Dante* in *Boll. Sen. di Storia Patria,* XIX) and Matilda Fiorilli (*Rassegna nazionale*, sett. 1913) have wanted to derive the last-mentioned image from *Inferno* XIII, 40.

"Men of wind," see *Lett.* 256; *ablattatus*, *Lettere dei Disc.* p. 253, cf. p. 257.

Quotations from the Gospels inter alia *Lett.* I, 55, 140, 150, 197, 261; II, 21, 42, 57, 177, 278, 360, 412, 439, 447, 454; III, 13, 14; IV, 189. From St. Paul inter alia I, 21, 22, 53, 63, 142; II, 43, 44, 104, 130, 171, 179, 194, 434, 449, 472; III, 265 (Paul a vessel full of fire); III, 156 (Paul sees himself reflected in the eye of God). — "Not to put one's hand to the plough" I, 170, 193, 213, 219; II, 57, 101, 120, 154, 443, 455; III, 22. "Let the dead bury their dead" II, 77. — St. Thomas Aquinas (*Summa* P. III, q. 55, art. 4, cf. 2^a 2^{ae} q. IV, a. 7,) cf. *Dialogo* cap. 55. — "quello pezo del Dante," *Lett. dei disc.* p. 292.

[6] *Lett.* 113. "cras, cras," *Lett.* II, 125. Perhaps she has obtained this image from St. Augustine who uses it somewhere ("vocem quidem occultae inspirationis audiunt, sed vitam non corrigunt dicentes *cras, cras* . . . cum voce corvina." Sermo 82, c. II, n. 14); "bend one's head," II, 475. The rusty key, *Dialogo* p. 370.

[7] *Lett.* 299 (Vol. IV, p. 102). Leopardi, *I canti*, Milano 1907, p. 228.

[8] "traendovi dalla bruttura e dalla tenebrosa vita fetida, piena di puzza e vituperio," Lett. 75 (II, 69; cf. I, 112, 123; II, 34, 331, 439 etc.).

[9] *Lett.* 101; *Lett.* 113.

¹⁰ *Lett.* 62.
¹¹ *Lett.* 87.
¹² *Lett.* 117 and 123. On self-will see inter alia I, 29 seq.; I, 103, 144, 173, 179, 184, 204, 217, 235, 248; II, 56, 93, 149, 173, 176, 220, 244, 292; Love of God I, 126; II, 59 seq., 125, 129, 342, 423, 439; III, 23. The knife I, 10, 12, 14, 67, 83, 112, 130, 153, 253; II, 9, 59, 96, 110, 433, 465; III, 26. Love of one's neighbour I, 25, 31, 62, 72, 154, 194; II, 9, 12, 22, 128, 132, 134, 157, 246, 389, 412, 448. Deo servire regnare est II, 146, 239. "correte il palio" II, 11. The strength of the Blood II, 301. The fire II, 224, 351; IV, 226. "I am fire" II, 46–47, become one with the fire II, 224; be hammered in the fire II, 438. *Pazzo d'amore* II, 46 and *Dial.* cap. 153 and cap. 167. "Tanto ci manca di lui quando ci riserviamo di noi," II, 182.

IX. ¹ *Arch. stor. it.* IV, 1843, p. 43, n. 50, cf. p. 47. *Lett. dei Disc.* pp. and 310 ("romitoro di Gromagio." This hermitage was founded by Leonardo di Niccolò Frescobaldi and was situated on the right bank of the Arno, near the mouth of the Ombrone Pistoiese).

² *Arch. stor. it.* IV, p. 37.

³ *Dialogo*, ed. Fiorilli p. 413.

⁴ *Le Dialogue*, Paris 1913, XXXV–LI. On the other hand Matilda Fiorilli, *Rassegna nazionale,* Dec. 1914. The date given, October 13th, is not stated in the chief manuscript (T II 9 Bibl. Comm. Siena).

⁵ "Lo detto arcangelo anco si apparbe in visione a Galgano e dixeli: sequitami. Allora Galgano con esmisurata allegrezza et gaudio levandosi ... et con grandissima devotione le pedate e le vestigie sue seguitava insino ad un fiume, sopra el quale era un ponte il quale (era) molto longo, et sença grandissima fadiga non si poteva passare. Sotto lo qual ponte, siccome la visione li mostrava, si era uno mulino lo quale continuamente si rotava et si volleva, lo quale significava le cose terrene, le quale sono in perpetua fluxione et movimento, et sença neuna stabilità, et in tutto labili et transitorie. Et passando oltre pervenne in un bellissimo dilettevole prato" etc. (MS C. VI, 8 Bibl. Comm. Siena. Stated to me by Signorina Lina Tamburini in Siena on St. Galgano. Cf. Olmi: *I Senesi d'una volta* pp. 298–305; Rondoni: *Leggende di Siena*).

⁶ *Catheriniana* ed. Fawtier pp. 92–93.

⁷ *Lett.* 272. On other parallels between the letters and *Dialogo* see I, 151; II, 65; II, 274 (the three steps); II, 405; III, 147, 217, 267 (cf. *Dial.* c. 6); III, 85 (cf. *Dial.* c. 75).

⁸ *Dial.* c. 52. *Lett.* 154: "siccome voi sapete che si contiene nello *Trattato delle Lagrime*" (i.e., *Dialogo* capp. 88–98). In the *Dialogue* itself Catherine alludes to a *Treatise on the Resurrection* which forms part of it ("si come di sopra nel tractato della resurreczione ti contiai," cap. 62). Such expressions seem to support my assertion that the *Dialogue* was, in a great measure, a compilation, which has, incidentally, been clearly stated in the Explicit of the work: "Qui finisce el libro facto *e compilato*." The letter to Raymond, no. 272, makes us understand what these first attempts were, these rough drafts, so to speak, another of which has been preserved for us in letter no. 120 to Monna Rabe Tolomei, in which Catherine explains in the same way her doctrine of the three steps (Tommaseo II, pp. 274–275). These two letters were written at La Rocca di Tentennano, and it was also there that Catherine asked Maconi to go and take her

SUPPLEMENT

book ("Mandai chiedere alla contessa el libro mio, e ollo aspettato parecchi di, e non viene. E però se tu vai là, di che'l mandi subito" etc. *Lett.* 365. I quote from the original manuscript, preserved in the church of St. Nicholas and St. Lucy in Siena).

This hypothesis would have the advantage of reconciling two affirmations which have seemed contradictory to the latest French translator of the *Dialogo:* that of Raymond, who says that the whole work was dictated, and that of Caffarini who would have it that the Saint wrote some pieces with her own hand. (See the preface by Père Hurtaud, pp. XXVII–XXXIII.) That which Catherine wrote at La Rocca di Tentennano can be found in the *Dialogue*, introduced into it under the influence of ecstasy and forming part of a supernaturally inspired whole.

[9] *Dial.* c. 167. Matilda Fiorilli gives (l.c.) the following schematic presentation of how Catherine imagines the way of salvation ("the bridge" and its three "steps"):

THE BRIDGE (*Dialogo*, ed. Fiorilli, pp. 43–44, 55–57).

First step: *The feet:* imperfect love, slavish fear (p. 106, p. 402);
  Feeling is lifted up from the earth (5. 50, p. 157);
  The soul sets itself free from sin (p. 50, p. 151);
  serves God for wages (p. 106);
  weeps with the weeping of fear (p. 169–171, p. 175).
Second step: *The wound in the side* (p. 50; p. 401);
  perfect love, friendship with God (p. 106);
  the soul conceives love of virtue (p. 50, p. 151, p. 187);
  weeps the tears of love, though yet imperfect (p. 170–171, p. 176, p. 187–188).
Third step: *The mouth* (p. 50):
  filial love (p. 106);
  self-love is dead (p. 146);
  love of God and one's neighbour (p. 141, p. 149–50, p. 174, p. 190).
  This love is again divided into two degrees, a lower:
  love of friends (p. 112),
    gives birth to virtues in one's neighbour (pp. 144–146),
    bears trials with patience (p. 172),
    has the tears of perfect love (p. 170);
  and a higher, a highest:
    filial love (p. 115–116) which
    rejoices in suffering (p. 150, p. 162)
    and knows ecstasy, knows the tears of rapture (p. 154, p. 166, p. 174; p. 170, p. 172).

X. [1] *Lett.* 316.
[2] *Lett.* 292 after Gardner's text (*S. Cath. of Siena* pp. 416 seq.).
[3] *Lett.* 305.
[4] Salembier: *Schisme*, pp. 71–78.
[5] *Lett.* 293.
[6] *Lett.* 310.
[7] *Lett.* 312, 313, 317.
[8] *Lett.* 306.
[9] *Leg.* III, i.
[10] *Lett.* 287, 294, 296.

¹¹ *Lett.* 319.
¹² *Lett. dei disc.* XIII (ed. Grottanelli, p. 282).
¹³ *Lett. dei disc.* p. 272.
¹⁴ *Leg. min.* ed. Grottanelli, p. 132 seq. *Lett.* 325, *Lett.* 336, *Proc.* col. 1268 and coll. 1274. See also *Lett. dei disc.* p. 289: "Venneci frate Petruccio, e ieri si parti con quelle grazie che voleva." Cf. *Lett.* 325, *Lett.* 336 and *Processus* col. 1268 and coll. 1273-1274. In *Lett. dei disc.* p. 287 Simone da Cortona reminds Neri of a letter of indulgence for "domina Donata uxor olim Neri de Citille." "Mandovi per frate Jacomo Manni . . . el privilegio con la bolla papale," Catherine writes on May 8th, 1379, to Bartolo Usimbardi and Francesco di Pippino in Florence (Gardner: *Appendix* p. 418). See also Fawtier, *Catheriniana*, pp. 16-17.

XI. ¹ *Lett. dei disc.* 16. *Lett. di S. Cat.* 335, 345, 352, 353, 354, 356, 360, 361. On female slaves in the houses of wealthy Christians see Bongi: "Le schiave orientali in Italia" (Nuova Ant. II, 1866, 215-246); Zanelli: "Le schiave orientali a Firenze nei secoli XIV & XV" (Firenze 1885); *Misc. stor. sanese* II, 1894, 102-106 and 120-124.
² *Leg.* III, i, 6.
³ *Lett.* 333.
⁴ *Lett.* 306.
⁵ *Lett.* 322-335. Matth. xxiv, 11-18. *Spasimato, Oratio* 23.
⁶ *Catheriniana* ed. Fawtier, p. 55.
⁷ *Lett.* 328. On the letters of William Flete see Raynaldi *Ann. Eccl.* ad 1378, n. 51. Perhaps it is this letter of which Maconi is speaking when writing to Neri on June 22nd, 1379: "questa altra lettere con quella copia di quella che aud al Re d'Inghilterra" (*Lett. dei disc.* p. 281).
⁸ *Lett.* 346.

XII. ¹ *Oratio* V.
² MS Casanat, XX, V, 10, f. 460-461. *Processus*, col. 1272.
³ *Lett.* nos. 347 to 350.
⁴ *Lett. dei disc.* nos. 11 and 12.
⁵ *Lett.* 320, 332, 321. *Dial.* cap. 140 with the first line of cap. 132.
⁶ *Oratio* VIII. Owing to an error the prayer is dated *martedi adi 22 di febbraio*. The correct date can be seen from *Oratio* 9, where the date is given as *lunedi adi primo di marzo*.
⁷ *Orationes* IX-XIV.
⁸ *Lett.* 347-350. *Lett.* 344 in Gardner, p. 320.
⁹ *Lett.* 344. See Fr. Bliemetzrieder: "Raimund von Capua u. Caterina von Siena zu Beginn des grossen abendl. Schisma" ("Hist. Jahrbuch," 1909, 231-273).
¹⁰ *Mem. Dom.* 1912, p. 277. "nui amo tolta una casa presso a Santo Biagio fra Campo di Fiori e Santo Eustachio" (letter of December 3rd 1379, to Neri di Landoccio).

XIII. ¹ On Gallerani see Olmi l. c., p. 174 seq. The present house of the Misericordia Brethren in the Via San Martino dates from 1391. Cf. *Arch. stor. ital.* IV (1843) I, p. 35, n. 22.
² *Lett. dei disc.* pp. 282-283.
³ *Lett.* 311.
⁴ *Lett.* 321.
⁵ *Lett. dei disc.* no. 13, the text slightly abridged and rearranged. From

1362 to 1396 Francesco del Tonghio and his son Giacomo carved the magnificent choir stalls in the cathedral of Siena.

[6] *Lett.* 339.
[7] *Lett.* 337.
[8] *Lett.* 338.
[9] *Lett.* 362.
[10] *Lett.* 357.
[11] *Lett.* 358 and 363.
[12] *Lett.* 365.

XIV. [1] *Oratio* 24.
[2] *Leg. min.* III, 2.
[3] *Leg.* III, ii, 2.
[4] *Oratio* 22.
[5] *Catheriniana* p. 72.
[6] "questa tua navicella conduttrice," "oramai conduci essa navicella." *Oratio* 19.
[7] *Leg. min.* III, 2.
[8] *Leg.* III, ii, 5. *Leg. min.* p. 156, III, 2. *Proc.* coll. 1299–1300. William Flete in MS. T. II, 7 in Bibl. Comm. in Siena, fol. 17.
[9] *Lettera di Ser Barduccio di Pier Canigiani* (Gigli: *Opere* I, p. 482).
[10] *Lett.* 370.
[11] *Oratio* XXVI.
[12] *Lettera di Barduccio*, 3.
[13] *Oratio* XVII, dated 14th February.
[14] *Oratio* XVIII, di martedì 15 febbrajo in Roma. If this date is correct, the prayer in question would be from the preceding year, when February 15th happened to be a Tuesday.
[15] In Tommaseo's edition the letter is divided into two parts. The first half is numbered 373, the second 371. And, as Grottanelli has already observed (*Leg. min.* p. 243), the second half has erroneously been provided with the address "to Urban VI." Both letters only form one, addressed to Raymond of Capua; it is probable, however, that Catherine wrote it in two sittings, that is, on February 15th and 16th.

XV. [1] *Leg. min.* III, 2.
[2] *Lett. di Barduccio* 4, ibid. §2; "Madre di mille e mille anime."
[3] *Lett.* 152.
[4] Matt. xi, 18–19.
[5] *Suppl.* P. III, Tr. 2, §§1–11. *Sermone che fece la Santa a suoi discepoli* in Gigli: *Opere* IV, 381–383. *Leg.* III, iv, 1–5. *Leg. min.* III, 4.
[6] Gigli IV, 383. According to Grottanelli (*Leg. min.* p. 243) this testament was written already on February 27th. Maconi was present on this occasion for he quotes (*Ep. Domni Stephani* §7) almost verbatim a passage from Catherine's parting exhortation (cf. Gigli I, 465 at head of column with IV, 382, col. 2 at foot). Gardner is wrong in placing (p. 349) Stephano's arrival *after* the visit of Bartolommeo de' Dominici (March 24th–25th); Catherine was then no longer able to speak so long or to give such detailed advice and directions.
[7] *Lett.* 365. See, however, the restricting remark about not scandalising the parents (IV, p. 449).
[8] *Ep. Domni Steph.* §8.

⁹ *Processus* MS T I 3 Bibl. Comm. in Siena, f. 144.
¹⁰ *Proc.* coll. 1358–1361. *Leg. min.* pp. 161–162, p. 245.

XVI. ¹ Gigli: *Opere* I, 484–489. The death chamber was moved later to the Dominican church of Santa Maria sopra Minerva. Only the ceiling of the room remained in the house in Via del Papa, now 44, Via Santa Chiara, where it is still shown in the room now transformed into a chapel. The house belongs to the Roman *Congregazione di Carità*. Catherine's first dwelling in Rome was pulled down in the sixteenth century, when the Piazza San Pietro came into existence.

XVII. ¹ *Leg.* III, iv, 9. "nella santa memoria," *Lettere dei disc.* n. 21, n. 33. Neri di Landoccio, ibid. no. 27, 31, 35, 36, 44.
² Death of Barduccio, *Leg.* III, i, 11. *Purgatorio* XXX, 73.

Epilogue. The description given here has been built up on Fra Tommaso Angiolini's *Breve Relazione del modo come fu portata da Roma a Siena la sacra testa di S. Caterina* (ed. Carapelli, Siena 1683). Cf. also Marelli: *La S. Testa di S. Caterina* (Siena 1904).

CAFFARINI

It was not Siena, where Catherine had lived, not Rome, where she died, that after her passing became the centre of her remembrance. This honour fell to distant Venice, in which she had never set foot, but it was here that one of her disciples lived until 1434. He was among the earliest and had perhaps known her best. This was Tommaso di Antonio Nacci Caffarini, like Catherine a native of Siena, and of the same age as herself. She had sent him flower greetings when he was still a young Dominican in the monastery in Siena, and after her death he went to S. Giovanni e Paolo in Venice, the church of the Black Friars in the square in which the bronze statue of Colleoni was to be reared up a hundred years later. Rio dei Mendicanti gurgles along the walls of the monastery and in the quiet of the night the lonely monk might imagine that he was still hearing Fontebranda murmur in the valley below. And then in remembering Caterina his pen would glide over the parchment, as he carefully printed letter after letter in her honour.

In 1395 he saw for the last time Catherine's other great biographer, he who had come into her life later, the labourer who had come into the vineyard at the eleventh hour, Raymond of Capua. As in the Gospel their wages were the same; both have a place in the fresco painting and keep watch on either side of the chapel in Siena, where the head of the saint is preserved. Caffarini, though, might justly say of himself that he had borne the burden of the day and the heats — that long day which did not end until — when he was over eighty years old — he closed his eyes — the last pair of eyes which had beheld Caterina Benincasa on this earth. . .

Three works remain to us from the hands of the gifted and enthusiastic *Caterinato: Leggenda minore,* written first in Latin, then in Italian, in both languages a selection from Raymond's work, with additions by Caffarini himself — then the *Supplementum,* the large collection of anecdotes and small incidents about Catherine, which stands in the same relation to Raymond's biography as Thomas of Celano's *Vita secunda* of Francis of Assisi to his first Life — and finally the *Process of Canonisation* of 1411–1413. This process was initiated by Fra Tommaso and it was he who had it collected and published.

All the time the work went on unweariedly in SS. Giovanni e Paolo of multiplying Catherinian literature by copying and distributing it at home and abroad. So great was the reverence of the old Dominican for the writings of and about Catherine that once, on the day of the commemoration of the saint, he showed them to the people from the ambona, where otherwise only relics are shown (*Processus,* Cod. Marciano coll. 19-12. cit. *Mem. Dom.* Series II, vol. XIV, p. 303). In the year 1413 he sent, by one of the saint's disciples from Lucca, fourteen Catherinian volumes to the Dominican monastery in Siena, among them being the *Dialogue,* five volumes of letters, Raymond's biography in Latin and Italian, etc.

Both Caffarini's chief works (*Supplementum* and *Processus*) are unpublished. An edition of the latter, however, is being prepared by P. Innocenzo Taurisano, O.P. In regard to the *Supplementum* those who have not access to the manuscripts must still be content with P. Ambrogio Tantucci's adaptation. Meanwhile three sections are not contained in this reproduction, viz.: Part II, Tract IV; Part II, Track VII; Part III, Tract IV. The first of the two last-named sections deals with Catherine's stigmata (MS. T. I, 2 in Bibl. Comm. in Siena, fol. 56–112) and is a long-drawn discussion on the authenticity of these stigmata, of the same kind as Lombardelli's work; the fourth section of Part III is a similar explanation of the conformity between Catherine's death and the death of Christ, in the same style as the Franciscan *Conformitates* of Bartolommeo da Pisa. (In the above-named manuscript this section takes up pp. 153 to 167.)

Only Part II, Tract IV is of real historical interest. It gives a number of small incidents, all of greater or lesser value, and the reading of this chapter gives one an impression of what Fra Tommaso's notes have been, the whole section having been taken from his *quaderni,* his diaries, to use a modern expression. I therefore give a reprint, from the above-named Sienese manuscript (of the fourteenth century) of the tract in question — in the hope that the whole *Supplementum* may soon find its editor.

QUARTUS TRACTATUS de quibusdam ut supra per me recollectis specialem mentionem facientibus de impetratione certarum gratiarum tam corporalium quam spiritualium per virginem tam pro se quam pro aliis obtentarum, etiam vitae corporalis. Et de certis specialibus gratiis a quibusdam personis a virgine modo imperativo reportatis. Necnon et de efficacia suae attractivae conditionis. Et distinguitur iste tractatus in XXV articulis ad diversa capitula 2^{ae} partis (sc. *Legendae majoris*) aptabilibus.

Quantum ad primum. Quadam vice virgo perdiderat unum annulum in qvo erat salvatoris imago et non poterat reperire qua de causa dolebat

SUPPLEMENT 435

qvia non erat suus. Cum autem orasset ad dominum statim illum reperit in manibus suis.

Item 2°. Quoniam virgo volebat loqui vel confiteri, semper in principio ipsa tacebat. Et cum confessor ab ea peteret quod faceret cum sic tacebat, respondit quod rogabat sponsum suum dominum Jesum Christum ut loqueretur ea quae sunt ad gloriam et laudem Dei. Et sic erat quod ipsa erat attendens in locutionibus et nunquam loquebatur de factis aliorum, primo semper de deo et de virtutibus.

Item 3°. Aliquando in tanto se reperiebat fervore quod non solum non curabat de comestione sua vel potatione seu dormitione nec sentiebat frigus sive calorem, sed etiam multum rogabat Deum ut daret sibi istam gratiam ut semper hic cruciaretur pro amore suo. Et ita erat quod semper delectabatur cum aliquid recipiebat adversum.

Item 4°. Cum multum aliquando a demonibus infestata fuisset, in tantum ut sibi aliquando dicerent: Miserrima, non poteris de manibus nostris evadere, tunc ipsa prosternebat se in oratione, dicens: Domine Jesu, adjuva me quoniam sponsa tua sum, et semper in te speravi. Et statim recesserunt cum magna confusione, et ipsa remansit cum magna consolatione et dulcedine cum sponso suo Jesu Christo. Et ita multoties contingebat.

Item 5°. Cum semel multas pateretur tentationes, in tantum quod quasi deficiebat, portavit lagenam aqvae per totam domum, et erat magnum frigus. Sudans tunc propter anxietatem laboris, tandem prosternens se in oratione, liberata est et habuit magnam consolationem de deo suo. Nec possent faciliter enarrari, quae et quanta passa sit seu portaverit pro sponso suo. Nec unquam potuit separari ab amore suo quem ipsa semper habebat in corde, quo ipsa semper ardebat, et nunquam consumebatur, sed semper augmentabatur ejus fervor.

Item 6°. Cum semel stetisset in oratione per magnum spatium, in tantum quod volens surgere, quasi attracta non posset, genibus deficientibus. Timens ne mater sua turbaretur, oravit ad dominum quod sibi provideret. Et ecce venit super eam lux una quae circumdedit eam et tetigit genua sua, et statim liberata est.

Item 7°. Aliquando petivit virgo in oratione sua a domino quod nunquam in oratione sive in orando tediaretur. Et obtinuit. Et ideo in illa semper delectabatur.

Item 8°. Quodam semel petivit a deo, qualiter aliquando anima devota videtur sibi esse derelicta ab eo ipso et divinis consolationibus privata. Quam dominus exaudiens et sibi satisfacere volens dixit: Ego facio sicut in passione Christi. Nam Christus videbatur tunc totus derelictus, cum tamen divinitas esset secum. Item aliquando ego sic facio in animabus michi devotis quod derelinquo eas, quamvis semper cum eis sim. Et hoc facio ut exercitent se et conserventur in humilitate, videantqve qualiter sine me nihil possunt facere.

Item 9°. Cum semel rogavit eam confessor suus quod deum oraret pro peccatis suis, et ipsa respondit sibi quod libenter. Contigit autem, ut ipso existente in cella absque alio exercitio recepit unam contritionem cum multis lacrimis et spirituali dulcedine. Postea contigit quod audiret a virgine, quomodo tali die rogaverit pro eo, et reperit qualiter in illa hora in qua virgo oraverat, dictam gratiam receperat. Et confessori dixit multoties, quod quidquid ipsa volebat, a deo recipiebat.

Item 10°. Cum semel virgo rogabat Deum in ecclesia pro quodam germano suo, sperans quod faceret sibi gratiam, imo erat certa, ut diceret deo: Ego non recedam hinc, donec tu michi facias gratiam pro eo. Et statim cum fiducia magna surrexit et venit ad domum suam et invenit praefatum in camera plorantem peccata sua, et postea confessus est et communicavit, de quo virgo recepit admirabilem consolationem, et regratiata est Deo de tanta gratia.

Item 11°. Cum quidam frater Bartholomeus de Senis, qui fuit secundus virginis confessor, se reperiret quondam semel cum primo supradicto confessore cum virgine, et ipsi virgini referret qualiter erat totus accidia plenus et caput esset sibi grave et fumositatibus plenum, illa sibi compatiens manus suas extendit ad dicti caput et dixit: Ego nolo quod hic sit amplius aliquid! et levans oculos ad coelum dixit, ipso fratre audiente: Domine, ego nolo, quod amplius remaneat aliquid, et quasi cum manu pretendit, se tunc facere signum crucis. Et statim taliter se sensit totum mente et corpore expeditum, ac si nunquam scivisset ac probasset, quid esset accidia aut capitis dolor.

Item 12°. Cum semel cognata virginis esset in partu et in maxima pena, voluit cognata quod virgo staret cum ea, quia sperabat in ea et voluit etiam, quod personae venirent sicut est consuetudo. Et virgo stabat ibi corporaliter sed mentaliter erat in coelo, ubi semper conversabatur, et petebat gratiam pro ea. Et videbatur sibi stare personaliter coram Deo, et quod Dominus daret sibi gratiam quam ipsa petebat. Et statim peperit unum filium masculum quasi cum nulla pena, qui postea fuit religiosus et diem salutis clausit extremum.

Item 13°. Cum semel virgo tenuisset ad baptismum filium unius pauperculae mulieris propter amorem Christi, accidit quod ipsa mulier perdidit lac nec poterat ipsum nutrire. Et nesciens quid facere deberet, recommendavit se virgini, ut virgo dominum precaretur, quatenus sibi providere deberet in tali nativitate. At virgo misericordia et caritate commota dixit, quod libenter. Et ponens se in oratione cum multis lacrimis dominum precata est, ut praefatae nativitati dignaretur providere, misericordia sua. Et statim facta oratione dominus, sua misericordia tantam lactis habundantiam contulit mulieri praefatae, quod nutrivit filium suum ad votum. Et ita exaudiebat dominus orationes suas.

Item 14°. Cum semel supradicta cognata virginis venisset ad partum et parare coepisset, rogavit praefatam Christi ancillam, ut secum staret, tenebatqve eam, ne ab ipsa discederet, quasi prophetans, nesciens quid diceret, esse virginem tunc eam sibi necessariam. Nam multum in ea confidebat quia cognoscebat eam et conversabatur cum ea. Ipsa tamen ex praefata devotione, tum quasi previdens quod futurum erat, acquievit eidem. Cum ergo pareret, praesentibus pluribus dominabus peperit, sic ut medium exiret tantum. Et sic cum non posset egredi puer, in periculo mortis se videns, praefata domina Lysa, virginis cognata, cum puero quem parere non poterat, eidem famulae Christi se, devotione qua potuit, recommendavit. Ipsa virgo, periculum videns et ab aliis se secedens, aliquantulum levavit mentem et oculos ad coelum et cum lacrimis dixit: Rogo te, Deus meus, ut eruas istam a periculo isto. Ista rogo et hoc volo, ut eam modo liberes. Statimque vidit totam trinitatem assistentem sibi, annuens ipsam fore exauditam. Propter quod oratione completa statim illa peperit, post spatium qvo fere diceretur bis pater noster, cum tamen nulla spes esset apud parentes, quod posset evadere, et ita etiam postmodum dicta Lysa confessa est, quod verum nulla spes erat sibi naturaliter evadendi.

Cum igitur puerum peperisset, nec lac ipsa haberet unde puerum alere posset, iterum virgo de hoc rogavit dominum suum, et statim tantam lactis habuit habundantiam, ut evidenter cognosceret, hoc sibi contigisse miraculose, sicut erat. Unde hoc ipsum domina Lysa per omnia confirmavit, firmiter credens, totum habuisse meritis orationum virginis almae et sponso suo acceptae per omnia.

Item 15°. Quodam semel virgo retulit confessori, quod cum sua genitrix infirmata fuisset ad mortem, tandem mortua est. Quod videns virgo levavit oculos ad coelum et dixit: Domine, hoc non est illud quod promiseras michi, scilicet quod omnes de domo ista salvarentur. Nam ista mater mea mortua est non confessa. Et ideo rogo, ut reddas eam michi, et hoc volo, et nunquam recedam hinc, nisi reddas eam michi. Et post parvum temporis spatium commotum est valde corpus matris ejus, rediitque anima et revixit. Fuerunt autem praesentes praefatae mortis testes quam plures dominae quae omnes ipsam vere mortuam indicaverunt. Addens virgo confessori et dixit, quod quando ipsa, ab ea hoc petente, narrabat, nunquam se tantum sicut nunc humiliabat et plus suam recognoscebat miseriam.

Item 16°. Cum semel virgo esset in villa, accidit quod venit magna pluvia cum grandinibus et erat tempestas magna. Quod videns se posuit in oratione, et statim recessit de vineis et de locis illis, nec aliquid in partibus illis dampni fecit. Cui miraculo ejus genitrix fuit praesens.

Item 17°. Cum quaedam de Senis ordinis de poenitentia beati Dominici dicta soror Francischa Marci habens infirmitatem quamdam quam mulieres habere aliquando consueverant, et habens devotionem ad virginem, in tantum quod se eidem subjecerat atqve commiserat, accessit ad eam, dicens sibi infirmitatem suam. Virgo autem in ipsam respiciens dixit: Nolo quod cogites amplius de ista infirmitate et sibi mandavit quod plus non haberet eam. Et ita factum est. Et plus: quod tempore quo occurrere sibi solebat dicta infirmitas, occurrebat sibi gaudium et consolatio spiritualis. Et sic quamplures utriusque sexus et status liberavit virgo per istum modum.

Item 18°. Cum semel primus confessor virginis multum pateretur in capite, in tantum quod non poterat oculos levare, idipsum virgo cognoscens dixit eidem: Quid habetis vos? Et ille: Sic. Tunc illa cepit caput suum. Et statim sensit se plenarie liberatum, prout etiam ipsemet de se refert in scriptis suis.

Item 19°. Cum quaedam appellata Gemma soror de poenitentia beati Dominici de Senis magnam devotionem haberet ad virginem in tantum quod eidem se in cunnctis subjiceret, contigit semel ipsam apud virginem querulari, qualiter ipsa non faciebat nisi dormire, et maxime cum vellet orare et aliquid facere secundum deum. Cui virgo: Soror mea, tu deciperis, et ideo facias tibi vim et de cetero vigiles et invenies consolationes dei etc. Tunc dicta soror cepit vigilare, et in nocte sequenti sibi contigit in oculo sinistro quaedam infirmitas, et erat totus rubeus et inflatus et quasi videre de illo non poterat. Et dixit virgini: Ecce quod ego propter verba tua sum de oculo infirmata, sicut vides. Cui virgo: Accipe de cicerbita et ponas super oculum. Quo audito soror habuit de illa, sed habens majorem fidem ad virginem quam ad virtutem herbe voluit, quod virgo ipsam tangeret. Quod virgo advertens accepit et postea reddidit sibi dicens: Ponas super oculum. Posuit, et statim facta positione plenariam sanitatem recepit.

Item 20°. Habuit dicta soror referre virginis confessori, quoniam quandocumque habebat aliquam temptationem vel tribulationem vel cogitationes malas vel tedium, statim quod respiciebat in eam liberabatur ab omnibus supradictis.

Item 21°. Cum quodam semel dicta soror erat multum attediata et afflicta et non inveniebat requiem neque pacem mentis, propter quod accessit ad domum virginis et non potuit sibi loqui quia erat clausa in cella sua in abstractione mentis, et sic non erat in statu quod sibi aperire valeret. Unde ipsa ex hoc retrocessit et rediit ad domum suam. Et tantum habuit gaudium et dulcedinem de domino, quantum unquam alias habuerit vel habuisset. Alio autem die rediens ad virginem dixit ei: Qualiter heri michi non aperuisti, quando veni? Et ipsa dixit: Non cures, quia rogavi pro te. Et invenit, qualiter in illa hora fuit, quod gaudium supradictum recepit.

Item 22°. Quaedam domina narravit dicto confessori, quod quandocumque respiciebat virginem, ex devotione plorabat et similiter consolabatur et devotionem singularem sentiebat.

Item 23°. Consimiliter dicto confessori narravit, quod cum cogitabat de virgine, non erat ita tristis quin statim sentiret se totam consolatam et letam et cum precipua devotione mentis.

Item 24°. Erat totaliter attractiva, ita qualiter de omni sexu statu et conditione personas immutabat in bonum et attrahebat ad Deum prout patuit per effectum.

Item 25°. Cum quaedam socia virginis conquesta pluries fuisset cum confessore et cum virgine, qualiter multum dormiebat, semel virgini dixit: Ego non facio nisi dormire. Roges deum quod ego non tantum dormiam. Cui virgo respondit, dicens: Ego mando tibi quod non dormias tantum. Et cum reciperet illud verbum quasi sibi dictum, adeo mirabiliter secutum est quod ipsa ex tunc dormire non poterat, etiam cum vellet et conaretur, cum ante sompno resistere non valeret. Et etiam recepit multas alias gratias a virgine, unde postea faciebat de corpore suo quicquid volebat, propter quod ex tunc singulariter commisit se virgini, dicens: Facias quicquid vis de me, nec volo reddere rationem de me. Quicquid enim dices michi, faciam. Et exinde quando videbat eam tremebat ex reverentia quam habebat ad ipsam. Quia etiam aliquando dicebat sibi cogitationes suas, quas habebat in corde.

INDEX

Abati, Bocca degli, 84.
Agatha, St., 12, 55.
Agazzari, Fra Filippo, 21, 146, 151.
Agnes, St., 12, 55, 108.
Agnes of Montepulciano, St., 178, 184, 187, 263, 408.
Albizzi, Florentine party of the, 206.
Albizzi, Pietro degli, 192.
Albornoz, Spanish cardinal legate, 162.
Alessia, Monna. *See* Saracini, Alessia.
Alexander VI, Pope, 170.
Alphonso of Jaën. *See* Vadaterra.
Altoviti, Stoldo di Messer Bindo, 281.
Amadeo III, Genevan count, 326.
d'Amely, Pierre, 249.
Anagni, popes resident in, 155.
Anastagio of Montalcino, 266.
d'Andrea, Agnolo, 258.
Angela of Foligno, St., 157, 276, 296.
Angelico, Fra, 111.
Angiolieri, Cecco degli, 85.
Anjou, Duke of, 232-3, 324, 353, 367.
Anjou, house of, 162.
Ansano, St., 3-5, 313.
Antella, Alessandro dell', 217, 229.
Aquinas, Thomas of. *See* Thomas.
d'Aquino, Countess Johanna, 334.
Aragon, house of, 162.
Arbia, river, 84.
Arezzo, 156.
Arosocchi, Nigi di Doccio, 140, 171.
Arzocchi, Biringhieri degli, 171.
Assisi, 155. *See also* Francis of Assisi, St.
Augustine, St., 35, 36, 70, 300.
Augustinians, 145, 146-7, 171.
Avignon, 52, 155 *et seq.*, 225-37.

Babylonian exile of Church, 155 *et seq. See also* Avignon.
Balbani, Monna Mellina, 209.
Balbiano, Alberigo da, 343, 353.
Bandino de Balzetti da Siena, Fra, 147-8.
Barbadori, Donato, 211, 217, 218.
Bartoli, Domenico, 77.
Bartolommea, Monna, 209.
Bartolommeo, hermit, 204.

Basil, St., 314.
Beaufort, Pierre Roger, 161.
Belcari, Leo, 192.
Belcaro, castle of, 254-5, 329.
Bellanti, Andria di Naddino de', 104-7, 112.
Bellanti, Pietro, 221, 345.
Bembo, Francesco, bishop of Castello, 410.
Benedict XI, Pope, 156, 408.
Benedict XIII, antipope, 171.
Benevent, battle of, 84.
Bénézet, St., 226.
Benincasa, Agnes, 9.
Benincasa, Anna, 30.
Benincasa, Bartolommeo, 9, 90, 179, 181.
Benincasa, Bonaventura, [wife of Niccolò di Giovanni Tegliacci], 3, 9, 11, 21-2, 30.
Benincasa, Catherine. *See* Catherine of Siena, St.
Benincasa, Giacomo, 9, 10-11, 20, 24, 79, 91.
Benincasa, Giovanna, 9.
Benincasa, Lapa (di Piagenti di Puccio): 9, 82, 261, 328, 400; character and temperament, 10-11, 16, 19-20, 140; wishes Catherine to marry, 21 *et seq.*; conflict with Catherine, 28, 29; family reverses, 90; becomes Catherine's disciple, 131-2; restored to life by Catherine, 131-2; accompanies Catherine to Pisa, 191-2; letter from Catherine, 238-9; joins Catherine in Rome, 330.
Benincasa, Lisa, [sister of St. Catherine], death of, 9, 181.
Benincasa, Lisa (née Colombini). *See* Colombini, Lisa.
Benincasa, Maddalena, 9.
Benincasa, Niccola, 9, 12.
Benincasa, Stefano, 1, 3, 8, 9, 90, 97, 179, 181.
Bernard of Clairvaux, St., 300, 314.
Bernardine of Siena, St., 255.
Biogi, Cristofano, 146.
Birgitta of Sweden, St., 14 *et seq.*, 158 *et seq.*, 161, 162, 163, 194, 331, 369.

SAINT CATHERINE OF SIENA

Black Death, 87.
Boccaccio, 310.
Bologna, 217.
Bonaventura, St., 314.
Boniface VIII, Pope, 156.
Bonsignori, Girolomo, 150.
Branca, Cardinal Niccolò di, 227.
Brentano, Clement, 189.
Brossano, Cardinal, 285, 325, 334.
Bruna, Monna, 261, 264.
Budes, Silvestre, 334, 353.
Buonconti brothers, 224, 236, 379, 404.

Caffarini, Tommaso d'Antonio Nacci, quoted, 17, 27, 34, 43, 55, 58, 60, 66, 70, 78, 80, 101, 104, 105, 106, 110, 115, 116, 128, 133, 187, 210, 237, 258, 271, 272, 292, 295, 332, 369, 387; in Pisa, 191; in Lucca, 209; correspondence with Catherine, 298, 338; life and letters of Catherine, 394, 401, 404, 406-7; in Venice, 397; *Supplementum*, 407, 434; initiated Catherine's process of beatification, 410-11, 433; note on, 433-8.
Calci, Carthusian monastery in, 204-5, 206.
Camerino, Rodolfo Varano di, 280.
Camporeggi hospital, 78, 80.
Canigiani, Barduccio, 223, 283, 287, 311, 323, 328, 364, 368, 369, 370, 376, 380, 381, 390-4, 395, 401 *et seq.*
Canigiani, Piero, 281.
Canigiani, Ristoro, 223.
Canischi party, 87 *et seq.*
Cappella delle Volte, 33, 37, 54, 94, 108, 110, 140. See also San Domenico, Church of.
Capo, Giovanna di, 70, 264, 328, 332.
Carpellini, editor of Aggazari's work, 150.
Carraciolo, Cardinal Niccolò, 369.
Carraciolo, Monna Lariella, 334.
Carthusians, 171, 204-5, 226, 402-3.
Casale, fortress of, 89.
Cascina, Niccolò da. See Pisano, Niccolò.
Casini, Francesco, 232.
Castel Sant' Angelo, 353, 361, 370.
Castel Vecchio, 4.
Castelloni, Michele, 229.

Catella, Monna, 334.
Catherine of Alexandria, St., 19.
Catherine of Siena, St., childhood, 3 *et seq.;* early visions, 6-8, 13-20; parentage, 9 *et seq.;* influence of Tommaso della Fonte, 12-13; refusal to marry, 21-5; mortifications, 26-9; desire to become Dominican, 28 *et seq.;* joins Mantellate, 30, 33; visions, 30-2, 33-4, 43 *et seq.*, 55, 71, 96, 98-9, 107; fundamental views, 34 *et seq.;* ecstasies and temptations, 37-40; independence of ecclesiastics, 52-3; learns to read, 54-5; intuitive powers, 54; mystical betrothal, 58-61; begins active life, 65 *et seq.;* gift of second sight, 67-8; disciples, 70-1, 127 *et seq.;* charity and nursing, 78-9, 80-3; letters, 81, 90-1, 117, 128 *et seq.*, 133-5; family reverses, 90; death of father, 91; spiritual growth, 93; fasting, 96, 117-18, 193-4; her stigmatization, 100-1, 194-5; mystical death, 101-2, 104; conversions by, 111-26, 135-9; first appeal to papal legate, 153-5, 162, 163, 166-8; beginning of political activity, 155 *et seq.;* compared with Birgitta of Sweden, 163; political message, 165 *et seq.;* and abbot of Marmoutier, 168-71; urges reform of clergy, 171-4, 200; plan for Crusade, 175-6; and Raymond of Capua, 178-9, 184, 187-90; work during plague in Siena, 181-3; visit to Pisa, 191 *et seq.;* her fasting, 193-4; love of Church, 199 *et seq.;* attitude toward Pope, 201-2; appeal to Sir John Hawkwood, 207-8; in Lucca, 208-10; return to Pisa, 210; letters to Pope Gregory XI, 213-16, 218-19, 251, 256; mediates between Florence and Holy See, 220-2; sojourn in Florence, 222-4; in Avignon, 224-37; receives Gregory XI in Genoa, 245-6; in Rome, 256; and Sienese prisoners, 257-60; and Blessed Sacrament, 268 *et seq.;* her writings, 271-2; attempted murder of, 274-5; letters to Raymond, 276-9; mediates between Pope and Florence, 290-1; last visit to Florence, 281-91; first letter to Pope Urban VI, 289-90; letter to Ludovica di Gra-

INDEX

nello, 293-4; her poetic gift, 295 *et seq.;* familiarity with Scripture and writings of Fathers, 298 *et seq.;* writes *The Dialogue,* 310 *et seq.;* last journey to Rome, 323-33; audience with Pope Urban VI, 330; and mission to Naples, 330-1; life in Rome, 332 *et seq.,* 342, 351-2; mode of letter writing, 342-3; last illness and death, 371 *et seq.;* spiritual testament, 384-7; translation of relic to Siena, 398-400; writings of, 401-6; biographers, 406 *et seq.*

Cavacobuoj, Andreasso, 362.
Cecca, Monna. *See* Gori, Francesca.
Ceccano, Annibale, 227.
Cecia, Monna, 334.
Cerretani, 89.
Cesena, storming of, 255-6.
Ceve, Giocomo di, 336.
Charles IV, Emperor, 87-8, 161.
Charles V, king of France, 233, 324, 353, 355, 356.
Charles of Durazzo, 363, 365.
Cinughi, Nello, 127.
Ciolo, Ser Antonio di, 133.
Città di Castello, revolt against papal rule, 212.
Clareno, Angelo, 157.
Clement IV, Pope, 155.
Clement V, Pope, 156-7, 227.
Clement VI, Pope, 158-9.
Clement VII, antipope, 320, 324-6, 345, 353, 355, 361.
Colomba, Monna, 209.
Colombini, Lisa, [sister-in-law of Catherine], 9, 11, 67, 70, 101, 127, 181, 191, 224, 261, 263, 264, 392.
Colombini, St. Giovanni, 9, 65, 71, 78, 87, 132, 146, 161, 192, 266, 310, 328, 329, 396.
Cononica, la, 11, 292.
Conrad of Offeda, 157.
Contrada dell' Oca, 6.
Corsini, Cardinal, 249, 285, 325, 334.
Cristofano, Dom, 334.
Crusade, 175-6, 194, 203-6, 219, 230, 247, 337.

Dahiella, Sister, 323, 330.
Dante, 35, 84, 85, 180, 209, 241 note, 300.

Davino, Gabriele di. *See* Piccolomini.
Dentice, Monna Catarina, 334.
Dialogue, The, 15, 50, 73, 195-6, 221, 230, 270, 272-3, 294, 310 *et seq.,* 379, 404-6.
Difensori of Siena, 88, 89, 258, 266.
Dini, Giovanni, 286.
Dominici, Bartolommeo de', 53, 68, 69, 96, 101, 114, 116, 119, 122-6, 128, 140-1, 178, 181, 182, 191, 209, 220, 224, 239, 249, 261, 263, 265, 269, 328, 334, 379, 389, 398, 404, 410.
Dominic, St., 12, 44, 56, 107, 352.
Dominicans, 10, 12-13, 23-4, 27, 41-2, 54, 69, 91, 107-8, 119, 145, 178, 186, 214, 255.
Donato, Neri di, 171.
Duccio, Cheli di, 9.
Duccio di Buoninsegna, 3.

El Bianco da Siena, 192-4.
Eligio, Abbé Lisolo, 334, 365.
Elizabeth of Poland, Queen, 205.
Emmerich, Catherine, 189.
d'Estaing, Pierre, 155, 162, 166-8, 230, 249.
Euphrosyne, St., 13, 23.
d'Euse, Jacques, 156.

Fawtier, Robert, 401, 404, 411.
Fazi, Matteo di Cenni, 132, 181, 183.
Felice of Massa, Fra, 218.
Ferro, Paola del, 381.
Flete, William, English Augustinian monk in Lecceto, 50, 53, 132, 148-52, 211, 223-4, 249, 253, 255, 282, 295, 315, 338-9, 370, 410, 411.
Florence: 52, 84 *et seq.,* 178, 211-12; Florentine-Milanese League, 208, 216; revolt against papal power, 217 *et seq.;* excommunicated by Gregory XI, 217-18; mediation with Holy See, 220-2; envoys to Pope in Avignon, 229-30; refusal of peace with papal power, 236; success against papal troops, 245; war continued, 280; Catherine's mediation and last visit to, 281 *et seq.;* civil war in, 286; peace with Urban VI, 290; labour uprising in, 291.
Fondi, Count of, 331.
Fonte Gaja, 85.

Fonte, Palmiero di Nese della, 9, 12 22.
Fonte, Tommaso della, 9, 12, 44, 52-3, 56, 68, 69, 70, 93, 94-5, 97, 100, 101, 105, 106, 108, 114, 117, 122, 139, 140, 145, 178, 186, 188-9, 191, 210, 247, 263, 264, 265, 269, 282, 379, 393, 398, 400, 406-7.
Fontebranda, 3, 6, 7, 9, 10, 11.
Foresi, Monna Pavola di Ser Gino, 71-2, 133, 144, 323.
Forteguerri, 89.
Forti, revolt against papal rule, 212.
Francis of Assisi, St., 24-5, 26, 27, 82, 113-14, 121, 147, 148, 175, 202, 214, 241, 295, 371.
Franciscans, 122-6, 156 *et seq.*, 171, 186.
Friars Minor. *See* Franciscans.
Friars Preachers. *See* Dominicans.

Gabriele of Volterra, Fra, 145 *et seq.*
Gaddi, Taddeo, 300.
Gaëtani, Cardinal Annibale, 159.
Galgani, Gemma, 121.
Galgano, St., 313.
Gallerani, Andrea, 360.
Gambacorti, Andrea, 286.
Gambacorti, Piero, 192, 211, 213.
Gano, Cristofano di. *See* Guidini.
Gano, Giovanni di, 266.
Gardner, E. G., biographer of Catherine, 276, 404.
Ghelli, Niccolò di Bindo, 139.
Gherardo da Borgo San Donnino, Franciscan, 156.
Ghetto, Caterina di. *See* Scetto, Caterina di.
Ghezzo, Giovanni di, 11.
Ghibellines, 84, 286.
Giovanni delle Celle, Dom. 223-4, 252-3, 338, 410.
Giovanni Terzo, [Tantucci], Fra, 145, 146, 148, 191, 218, 226, 232, 239, 249, 328, 379, 390, 404.
Gorgona, island of, 205.
Gori, Francesca, 70, 127, 145, 190, 191, 224, 261, 263, 265, 281, 328.
Got, Bertrand de, 156.
Granello, Ludovica di, 293.
Grange, Jean de la, French cardinal, 285.
Grasselli, party of the, 87.
Grazia, Bonaguinta di, 300.

Great Schism, 324 *et seq.*
Gregory X, Pope, 155.
Gregory XI, Pope, 161, 162, 166, 168, 171, 175-6, 179, 194, 205, 391; and Florentine revolt, 216-17; Catherine's letters to, 213-16, 218-19, 251, 256; receives Catherine in Avignon, 228-37; leaves Avignon, 244-5; visits Catherine in Genoa, 245-6; entry into Rome, 249; disagreement with Catherine, 278-80; difficulties with Florentines, 280; asks Catherine's mediation, 281; death, 283.
Gregory of Rimini, Brother, 269.
Gregory the Great, St., 300, 352.
Grisac, Guillaume Grimoard de (Pope Urban V), 161.
Grosseto, fortress of, 89.
Grottanelli, collection of letters of Catherine's disciples, 275.
Gubbio, revolt against papal rule, 212.
Guelfacci, Tommaso di, 140, 145, 146.
Guelphs, 84, 281, 286.
Guide to a Spiritual Life, dictated by St. Catherine to William Flete, 149.
Guidini, Cristofano di Gano, 140, 149, 165-6, 281, 287, 288, 343, 388, 394, 397, 398, 401, 404, 405, 411.
Gutalebraccia, Giovanni, 192.

Hawkwood, Sir John, 206-8, 217, 255, 267-8, 280, 362, 368.
Hello, Ernest, quoted, 299.
Henry II of Castile, 324.
d'Hérédia, Jean Ferdinand, Grand Master of the Knights of St. John, 245.
Hohenstaufen, family of, 84.
Honorius III, Pope, 155.
Honorius IV, Pope, 156.
Hurtaud, Père, 311, 405.

Ignatius of Loyola, 35.
Innocent III, Pope, 155.
Innocent IV, Pope, 155.
Innocent VI, Pope, 158, 159, 226.
Interminelli, Alderigo, 345.

Jacopo, hermit, 204.
Jacopo da Varazze, 242.
James, St., the apostle, 43.
Jerome, St., 300.
Joachim of Santa Fiora, 156, 158.

INDEX

Joanna of Naples, 203, 249, 280, 324, 326, 331, 334, 343, 353, 354, 361, 365-7.
John XXI, Pope, 156.
John XXII, Pope, 156, 158.
John Gualbertus, St., 289.
John of La Verna, Brother, 314.
John of Parma, deposed general of the Franciscans, 157.
John the Evangelist, St., 43.

Karin of Vadstena, daughter of St. Birgitta, 163, 331.

Lacordaire, quoted, 57.
Lando, Francesco di, 132.
Lando, Michele di, 291.
Landoccio, Neri di. *See* Pagliaresi, Neri di Landoccio dei.
Lapa, Monna. *See* Benincasa, Lapa.
Lapo, Buonaccorso di, 222, 223, 234, 236.
Lardo, Lucio di, 362.
La Scala, hospital of, 5, 73 *et seq.*, 80, 90, 183.
Lazarus, St., 12.
Lazzarino of Pisa, Fra, 122-6, 276.
Lecceto, 146-52.
Leonardo da Vinci, 86.
Leopardi, quoted, 303-4.
Liberato da Loro, Franciscan, 157.
Lippa, Monna, 209.
Lippo, Tommaso di Neri di, 252-3.
Lolo, Galgano di, 183.
Lorenzetti, Ambrogio, 86, 151, 364.
Lucalberti, Spinello, 206.
Lucca, republic of, 208-10; joins Florentine league, 216.
Lucy, St., 12, 55, 105, 108, 281-2.
Ludwig, king of Hungary and Poland, 324, 365, 367.
Luna, Pedro de, 171, 284, 324-5, 356.
Lyons, city of, 155.
Lysias, Roman governor of Siena, 4.

Maco, Sano di, 140, 247, 290, 329.
Maconi, Sienese family, 86, 239.
Maconi, Stefano, 118, 140, 220-2, 224, 226, 232, 239, 241, 242-4, 247-9, 272, 274, 281, 283, 311, 327, 328, 330, 338, 342, 343, 344, 345, 360-3, 365, 368, 387, 388-9, 396, 398, 401, 403, 405, 409, 410, 411.
Malatesta de' Malatesta, 88, 89.
Malavolti, Francesco, 117-18, 135-9, 141-2, 145-6, 263, 264, 265, 266, 269, 274, 342, 363, 387, 395-6, 410.
Malavolti, Sienese family, 86, 89, 190.
Malestroit, Jean de, 334.
Manetti, Giovanna, 127.
Mantellate, 9, 24, 29-30, 33, 37, 54, 70, 78, 107, 110, 209, 283, 388. *See also* Dominicans.
Margaret, St., 55.
Margarita of Cortona, 157.
Marmoutier, Abbot of, 161-2, 168, 169-71, 211.
Martin IV, Pope, 156.
Martino, Simone di, 86.
Mary Magdalene, St., 12, 14, 43, 44, 46-7, 55, 96.
Massa, castle of, 88, 89.
Matteo, Brother. *See* Tolomei, Matteo.
Matteo di Giovanni, artist, 110.
Medici, Salvestro di, 286.
Mellina, Monna. *See* Balbini, Mellina.
Michael of Cesena, Franciscan general, 157.
Mini, Niccolò de', 145, 146.
Misciatelli, Piero, 404.
Misericordia Confraternity of Siena, 360.
Moligno, Ludovico da, 176.
Montaigu, Gilles Ayecelin de, 230.
Montalcino, Anastagio di Ser Guido di, poet, 184, 187, 404, 411.
Montalcino, fortress of, 89.
Mont' Amiata, 65, 275, 277 note, 292, 330.
Monteaperti, battle of, 84.
Monte Cetona, 330.
Montefiascone, 155.
Montepulciano, 178, 183-4, 263, 264.
Montjoie, Louis de, 353.
Mont' Oliveto, 65.
Montucci, Bartolomeo, 33, 101, **110**.
Motte, Cardinal Gaillard de la, **227.**

Naddi, Francesco di, 113.
Naddo, Fra Giorgio di, 140.
Naples, 162, 330.
Negri, Paolo di, 150.
Neri di Landoccio dei Pagliaresi. *See* Pagliaresi.

Neri, Paolo di, 111.
Niccolò, Father. *See* Pisano, Niccolò.
Nicholas IV, Pope, 156.
Nietzsche, 15-16, 311.
"Nine, The," 85, 87-8, 90.
Nizza, Fra Antonio da, 149-50, 339.
Noëllet, Guillaume de, 176, 206.
Nogaret, Guillaume de, 200.

Olivi, Pietro Giovanni, 156, 158.
Oristano, Mariano, 203.
Orsini, Cardinal, 285, 325, 334, 365.
Orvieto, 155.
Orvieto, Francesco da, 291.
Osimo, Niccolò da, 213.
Otto of Brunswick, 366, 367.

Pagliaresi, Neri di Landoccio dei, 132-3, 134, 136, 141-5, 174, 184, 209, 220, 222, 226, 242, 247-8, 263, 264, 274, 275, 277, 281, 287, 300, 310, 311, 328, 330, 334, 335, 342, 343, 360, 363, 388, 396, 397, 398, 403, 404, 408, 409, 410.
Palazzo Buonconti, 191-2.
Papal States, composition of, 162.
Paul, St., the apostle, 43, 55, 299-300, 314.
Pavola, Monna. *See* Foresi.
Pazzi, Giovanna, 184, 186.
Pazzi, Jacopo, 84.
Pecora, Giacomo del, 184, 263.
Pedro IV of Aragon, 324.
Pentella, Madonna, 334.
Peretti, Lonzio, 158.
Perugia, 155, 212, 216, 363.
Peruzzi, Simone, 206.
Peter Martyr, St., 12, 108.
Peter of Aragon, 236.
Petra, Tommaso, 233, 234, 383, 384, 387, 410.
Petrarch, 159, 161, 225.
Petribondi, Caterina, 390-4.
Pettinaro, Pier, 157, 180.
Piagente, Nuccio di, 9-10.
Piccolomini, Gabriele, 263, 328, 409.
Piccolomini, Sienese family, 86, 87, 89, 135, 145.
Pietro, Salvi di, 267.
Pietro da Milano, Dom, 338.
Pietroni, Pietro, 310.
Pippino, Agnese di, 223.

Pippino, Francesco di, 223, 289, 323.
Pisa, city of, 191, 206-7, 210, 216, 247.
Pisano, Niccolò, 70, 187, 188.
Pius II, bull canonizing Catherine, 53.
Porta San Viene, 4.
Prato, uprising in, 208.
Prignano, Bartolommeo. *See* Urban VI, Pope.
du Puy, Gérard, 168.

Radicofani, 330.
Raymond of Capua, quoted, 10, 11, 13, 27, 28, 33, 43, 50, 51, 53, 65, 67, 82, 90, 91, 99, 100-1, 104, 115, 118, 121, 131, 183, 190, 192, 194-5, 212, 218, 239-40, 263, 264, 265, 266, 369, 388; appointed Catherine's spiritual director, 178-9; and plague in Siena, 181-2; journeys to Montepulciano, 183-4; won to Catherine's cause, 187-90; accompanies Catherine to Pisa, 191-2; sent to Avignon by Catherine, 218-19; in Avignon, 226, 228; papal bull of appointment as confessor of Catherine, 249; on mission to Rome, 267-8, 273; prior of monastery of Santa Maria sopra Minerva, 273; Catherine's letters to, 276-7, 278-9, 327-8; and Pope Gregory XI, 281; Catherine's prayer for, 319; reunion with Catherine in Rome, 330; disapproves mission of Catherine to Naples, 331; sent by Pope to France, 335; last parting with Catherine, 335-6; attempted mission to France, 355-9; vicar of province of Genoa, 358; last communication from Catherine, 374 *et seq.;* General of Dominican Order, 389; career after Catherine's death, 389, 398; biographer of Catherine, 396, 404, 407-9.
Reformatori, 88, 90.
Ricasoli, Angelo, 222.
Ricci, Florentine party of, 206.
Richard II, king of England, 324, 373.
Rieti, 155.
Robert of Geneva, 334, 353.
Rocca di Tentennano, 264, 266, 267.
Rocca d'Orcia, 277.
Roman See, 155, 208, 217-22, 224-30.
Roquetaillade, Jean de, 158.
Ruf, St., 225.

INDEX

Sacchetti, Giannozzo, 283.
Saint Sebastian, monastery of Gésuati, 5.
Saint-Tropez, 240.
Salimbeni, Andrea di Niccolò, 176, 177.
Salimbeni, Giovanni di, 262.
Salimbeni, warlike Sienese family, 86, 87, 88, 89, 90, 112-13, 168, 180, 261-2, 263, 264, 265.
Salle, Bernard de la, 334, 353.
Salvani, Provenzano, 84, 87.
Salvatico, Monna Bartolommea. *See* Bartolommea, Monna.
San Domenico, Sienese church of, 6, 10, 33, 36, 37, 41, 56, 94, 96, 105, 109, 116, 179, 249, 250, 398, 399.
San Lazzaro, leper hospital in Siena, 78, 82, 83.
San Leonardo al Lago, monastery of, 148.
San Mamiliano, Sienese church of, 83.
Sano di Pietro, artist, 83, 110.
Sansedoni, Fra Ambrogio, 398.
Sant' Angelo, Cardinal of. *See* Noëllet, Guillaume de.
Sant' Antimo, 266.
Santa Bonda, 71, 83, 292, 295, 329.
Santa Fiore, 65.
Santa Maria degli Angeli, Sienese church of, 83.
Santa Maria in Bethleëmme, 83.
Santi, Fra, hermit of Teramo, 140, 181, 182, 310, 322, 328.
Saracini, Alessia, 54, 70, 97-8, 101, 111-13, 116, 127-30, 145, 183, 184, 186, 191, 224, 261, 263, 264, 265, 273, 281, 283, 328, 388, 391.
Saracini, Francesco, 112-14.
Saracini, Niccolò, 114.
Saracini, Sapia, 84, 180.
Saracini, Sienese family, 86, 87, 89.
Sarzana, meeting of, 283.
Savini, Nonni di Ser Vanni, 113, 253-4.
Scala, Beatrice della, 174, 175-6.
Scetto, Caterina di, 70, 101, 130, 281.
Scotti, Sienese family, 86, 242 *et seq.*
Serafini, Dom Bartolommeo, 205, 338.
Shelly, Percy B., 148.
Sicily, ruled by Aragon and Anjou, 162.
Siena, plague in, 52, 181; carnival, 58-9; descriptions of city, 65, 86, 180, 185-6, 255, 309-10; hospitals, 73 *et seq.*, 346; victory over Florence, 84; civil war in, 84 *et seq.*; government, 85; visit of Charles IV and papal legate, 88-9; uprising of woolspinners, 112; war on Holy See, 211-12; suspicious of Catherine, 266-7; quarrel with Pope Gregory XI, 280.
Siena, Giovanni da, 101.
Simone of Cortona, Fra, 276.
Smeduccio, Bartolommeo di, 203, 280.
Soderini, Niccolò, 90, 179, 216, 217, 222, 280, 281, 287.
Spedaluccio, Caterina della, 70, 264.
Stephen, St., 14.
Strozzi, Monna Laudomia, 222.
Strozzi, Pazzino, 229.
Suso, Henry, 16, 27, 35, 296, 302, 314.

Talamone, fortress of, 89.
Tancredi di Mossa, Felice de', 150.
Tantucci, Giovanni. *See* Giovanni Terzo, Augustinian brother.
Tebaldeschi, Cardinal, 249, 284, 325.
Tecca, 82-3, 328.
Tegliacci, Niccolò di, 9.
Thomas of Aquinas, 12, 35, 108, 300.
Todi, revolt against papal rule, 212.
Toldo, Niccolò di, 258, 329.
Tolomei, Bernardo, 360.
Tolomei, family, 84, 86, 87, 89, 115, 221, 327.
Tolomei, Giacomo di Sozzino, bishop, 345, 365.
Tolomei, Jacomo, 114-15.
Tolomei, Matteo, 145, 262, 263, 362-3, 397, 398.
Tommaso della Fonte. *See* Fonte, della.
Tondi, Simone di Giacomo, 29.
Torre del Mangia, 65, 86, 89.
Trelawney's *Memoirs*, quoted, 148.
Trinci, Bandeca, 262-3.
Trinci, Corrado, 262.
Trinci, Isa, 262, 263.
Trinci, Paolo, 262.
Turenne, Elys de, 230.
Tuscan republics, 162.
"Twelve, The," 85-8, 89, 90, 112-13.

Ubertino of Casale, Franciscan, 156, 157-8.
Ucello, Paolo, 207.
Ugurghieri, Neri di Guccio degli, 139.

Ungaro, Lando di Francesco, 330.
Urban IV, Pope, 155.
Urban V, Pope, 161, 162.
Urban VI, Pope, 232, 283-6, 289-90, 324 *et seq.*, 330, 334-7, 339, 343, 353, 354, 355, 361-2, 365, 367, 372-3, 392.
Urbino, revolt against papal rule, 212.
Usimbardi, Bartolo, 223.
Usimbardi, Orsa, 223.

Vadaterra of Jaën, Alphonso, bishop, 161, 194, 211, 213.
Vallepiatta, 5.
Vanni, Andrea di, 140, 365, 405.
Vanni, Nanni di Ser. *See* Savini.
Vanni, Noccio di, 177.
Vannino, Bartolo di, 9.
Vareggio, Jacopo, 12, 242.

Velletri, Fra Pietro da, 212.
Ventura, Matteino di, 89.
Ventura, Pietro di Giovanni, 264, 267, 274, 362, 401.
Vico, Francesco Moricotti di, archbishop, 211.
Vincenti, Francesco, 78.
Vigne, delle, family of, 10-11, 178.
Vigne, Luigi delle, 249.
Visconti, Bernabò, 162, 168, 174, 176, 206, 208.
Visconti, Galeazzo, 174.
Viterbo, 155, 156, 212.
Viva, Jacomo di, 401, 402.
Viva, Don Pietro di, 328.
Volterra, bishop of, 291.
Voulte, Guillaume de la, 336.

Wenceslaus, German emperor, 324.

www.ingramcontent.com/pod-product-compliance
Lightning Source LLC
Chambersburg PA
CBHW052049290426
44111CB00011B/1669